Analysis and Design of Information Systems

Third Edition

Arthur M. Langer

Analysis and Design of Information Systems

Third Edition

 Springer

Arthur M. Langer, EdD
Fu Foundation School of Engineering & Applied Science
School of Continuing Education
Graduate School of Education
Columbia University
New York, NY 10027
USA

British Library Cataloguing in Publication Data
A catalogue record for this book is available from the British Library

Library of Congress Control Number: 2007928317

ISBN 978-1-84628-654-4   e-ISBN 978-1-84628-655-1

Printed on acid-free paper

9 8 7 6 5 4 3 2 1

Springer Science+Business Media
springer.com

Preface

Throughout the last 40 years the impact and importance of information technology (IT) continues to transform the world. Indeed, we are very much at the beginning stages of what I believe will be known as the technology revolution—a revolution that will change every aspect of business and life in general. While technology, both hardware and software, continues to evolve, the one remaining constant is the challenge of understanding what the users of applications really need, what they think they want, and what they will want as their uses of systems mature.

Still, the process of mastering the analysis and design phase of the Software Development Life Cycle (SDLC) continues to perplex the most sophisticated IT organizations and software development companies. And to make matters even more complex, the IT industry has transitioned to a heavily outsourced model of software development, making the requirements of what is necessary even more important because of the risks of having applications developed abroad that do not meet user expectations.

Perhaps the most significant development in applications has been the Internet, with all the corresponding pieces: branding, Web development, and interactive user interfaces have established many more substantial challenges to how applications evolve. The most critical change, however, is the participation of a more sophisticated and unknown user: the *consumer*. The consumer is a most unusual individual: he/she does not participate as part of an internal organization, or external client, rather a transactional force that comes in and out of the application with an enormous amount of uncertainty and constant change in behaviors and needs. Furthermore, this "consumer" represents a broad population, of culture, age, gender, and ethnicity differences.

With the significant challenges described above, it is imperative that we expand analysis and design to provide developers from inside and outside the business to clearly understand what is needed. Furthermore, applications need to change more often, so that object-based design is no longer an alternative, rather a necessity to allow organizations to continually evolve and mature their abilities to serve their clientele. This book then focuses on providing direction on the many alternatives to dealing with all types of systems, from large legacy applications to on-line transactional systems that interface with a myriad of internal and external systems.

Many of these failures of systems developed have occurred because they have not been built on strong foundations. In particular, there is a lack of understanding of the engineering processes through which applications must be built. This book seeks to remedy this problem by focusing on the applied aspects of analysis to create systems that meet the needs of their users, consumers, and businesses. The analyst/designer encounters many obstacles on the road to designing applications. Many of these obstacles have nothing to do with technical challenges at all—they are problems that come from outside the realm of IT: politics, budget and time constraints, and marketing pressures. All of these can challenge the structured approach to analysis and design. This book addresses these obstacles and recommends ways to overcome them. I have always warned my students by telling them: "Follow the Yellow Brick Road." That is, start out on the right path and you will end up in the place you want to be—in spite of all the obstacles you may encounter on the way. I hope this book shows many IT professionals that the analyst/designer is the most important component of the SDLC.

This new edition aims to enhance the set of techniques and tools that the analyst/designer requires for success. It also addresses some of the "softer" but critical other skills such as creativity and the ability to understand the market needs of the business. Furthermore, the successful analyst/designer must be able to understand consumer needs; ensure integration with legacy systems; provide user interface requirements; establish standards, security, and network architecture; and finally to provide the necessary project management to ensure implementation.

New to the Third Edition

This third edition provides more examples and case studies; however, it contains two major upgrades from its predecessor: first, responding to feedback, I have framed the modeling tools within an SDLC framework so that readers can have a step-by-step understanding of when and how to use each of the modeling tools of analysis. To accomplish this, I provide a popular SDLC approach called "the Barker Method" which was developed by Richard Barker from Oracle Corporation. Second, the scope of analysis and design has been expanded to include more specific information on Logic Data Modeling, specifically referential integrity, naming conventions, logical-to-physical design steps, XML, data values, and denormalization. I have also added new chapters on Web interface tools, security and change control and data warehouse system design.

The Aim of This Book

The risks involved in performing analysis are significant: Those projects that involve reengineering activities have a failure rate over 70 percent. With the expansion of the Internet as a vehicle for electronic commerce, the stakes are even higher than before, and identifying the sources of failure can be invaluable. In general, failures can be attributed to two kinds of risks: those associated with the process of change and those relating to the technology itself. I am confident that the success rate can be dramatically improved if we focus less on the methodology and more on the ability of the analyst to perform the work. This book is therefore meant as a "practitioner's guide" to doing analysis through every facet of developing software solutions.

The book defines the word "analyst" to include any individual involved in establishing the requirements and design of a system. For this reason, the book includes subjects like joint application development (JAD) and prototyping, which may not always be performed by analysts but which nevertheless fall within the confines of the definition.

My enthusiasm for writing this book was supported by many of my students who found that existing books on analysis are:

- *very theoretical.* Although they explain the methodologies, they do not provide enough examples of their actual application.
- *too procedural.* They do not deal with the "human" aspects of developing requirements and thus do not provide a complete understanding of how to be successful. After all, the whole point of analysis is to service human enterprises, not just to create systems for their own sake. The human side of analysis is as important as the technical side.
- *lacking simple but effective case examples.* The examples do not demonstrate the concepts effectively or are too complex for practice study.
- *too one-sided in their views.* It is important to establish all available methodologies, even those that conflict with each other. Putting opinions into perspective and leaving many of the ultimate decisions to the practitioner is a significant part of the analyst's education.

The Intended Audience for This Book

This book assumes a reasonable understanding of computer concepts and terminology. The material is presented to be used in a first-level analysis course or university program. In addition, it can be used by practicing information systems professionals or executives who are managing information technology and need an in-depth understanding of the principles of the analysis and design process, particularly as it relates to Web-based development. Furthermore, many programmers who are also performing analysis may find this book a way of developing a useful approach to structured and object methodologies.

Acknowledgments

I want to thank my colleague Melanie Caffrey for her contributions to the Third Edition, namely, her expertise in both the System Development Life Cycle and the Barker Model was extremely valuable. Ms. Caffrey also contributed her exercises and case study used in our courses at Columbia University.

I also want to thank the students in the Service Learning in the Community Environment (SLICE) at Columbia University's Fu Foundation School of Engineering and Applied Science (SEAS) for their feedback on the Second Edition. This Third Edition will continue to be used to train underserved inner-city adults in the hopes of building their careers as tomorrow's analysts and designers. Many thanks to Dr. Jack McGourty, the Associate Dean of Undergraduate Students, for allowing us to implement the program at SEAS.

New City, New York, USA   Arthur M. Langer
September 2007

Contents

1
Introduction

What Is, Is

Over Forty years of developing requirements for systems have taught us that the only successful approach to analysis is to accept what exists in the user's environment, however far from ideal those conditions may be, and work within those limitations. It may be very tempting to use analysis time to try to refocus how the user does business. Yet efforts to re-design or reengineer, unless specifically requested by the user, will typically be a waste. Although your assessment may be correct and your suggestions potentially useful, being correct is less important in this situation than being wise and understanding the ability of your users to successfully implement and utilize what they need. Analysts tend to ignore this simple wisdom, much to their own distress and that of their clients.

Looking at a typical example of an analysis situation will help to illustrate this point. Let us assume that an enterprise needs a relational database model to gather information about a subject area of the business. There are 200 offices that will need to connect into a nationally provided service. Users disagree on the mission of the applications and cannot determine what reports or query information they want. Some offices are automated, but they do not have the same software and hardware. There is little expertise in the user community to determine the data requirements and file layouts (identifying elements in each file). Management has requested that the analyst establish a specification which identifies the requirements of the system as well as the necessary hardware and software.

Faced with so unwieldy a task, many analysts will adopt the following approach in an attempt to impose order on a disorderly situation:

1. Force users to define all requirements. Since they are unable to do so, this insistence will probably result in their guessing or providing incomplete information.
2. Determine the hardware and software configuration, despite having inaccurate or incomplete requirements.
3. Ignore the political environment.
4. Establish a project plan that everyone knows will fail, but push ahead with it anyway.

It should be clear that this approach is the wrong one, on a number of different counts. Yet such an approach is all too typical for analysts confronted with a less-than-ideal working-environment. Happily, there is a better approach for all concerned, one that recognizes and responds to the conditions actually present at the users' site. In this case it is evident that the users are not positioned to provide the requirements for a system, largely because they do not fully understand their own needs and because they do not agree on what those needs are. What the analyst must understand in such a situation is that because of this lack of knowledge and organization, user needs will tend to change during the process of product analysis and design. Such changes are to be expected; they are simply part of the life cycle for this particular implementation. To ignore the situation and try to implement a system is to invite failure. Put simply then, what is, is. The task of the analyst is to work with what is rather than trying to change it or— even worse—simply denying it. Once you as an analyst understand that reality, you understand that your solution must accommodate what will inevitably occur.

Here is a more sensible approach to the situation described above:

1. Focus on designing a model that can provide the users with the capability they want. Create a project plan that assumes that the database will be incomplete during phase I because of the users' inability to define the correct information. The process will therefore be iterative and thus will be finalized during the later parts of the development life cycle.

2. Do not try to identify hardware before it is clear what the usage requirements are, such as peak-time processing, number of users, and so on. It will be more beneficial to establish the operating system or architectural environment that you want to support, pending the results of the analysis.

3. Utilize a software system or CASE tool that will allow users to generate new scenarios such that they can see how these scenarios relate to the entire system.

4. Set up a pilot program. This will require that certain offices agree to be test sites for the early versions of the software. The function of the pilot is to provide feedback on the effectiveness and shortfalls of the product. It is important to state clearly the objectives of the pilot and the format of the feedback in order to ensure the success of the exercise.

5. Formulate a plan that depicts a schedule for getting the entire enterprise implemented and live on the new system. Be sensitive to the politics of the situation, and use a realistic approach that will not require a cultural change in order to implement software in the existing environment.

The essence of this approach is to develop a strategy that fits the reality of the environment rather than force the environment to change. Throughout this book, we will explore this simple but crucial concept. No two system development projects are identical, and the more familiar the analyst is with the environment, the more successful the project will be. This book will also argue against the conventional wisdom that suggests using an approach based on only a single methodology (e.g., Yourdon, Martin, Booch, etc.). The mixing of methodologies allows the analyst a wider range of tools. Hands-on experience shows that this kind of mixing of methodologies can be done quite successfully and that it is appropriate in a large number of analysis situations.

Just What Is a Complex Project?

Most analysts, project team members and users worry about the complexity of their projects. Their requirements seem entirely unique to them, and therefore a very special approach seems to be required. How many times have you heard: "the tools and approaches used elsewhere just won't work in this environment"?

The truth, however, is very different: the only truly complex projects are those that people make so! It is important for the analyst to recognize that the procedures utilized, regardless of the size of the project, should remain fundamentally the same. As we have discussed above, the analyst's approach to the implementation of each project should be tailored individually; however, the procedures for this implementation should remain constant. Very often the organization of interviews, the utilization of techniques such as Joint Application Development (or JAD), discussed later in this chapter) or the simple addition of more analysts to the project can solve what appear to be insurmountable problems.

In fact, most of the myriad problems that arise in product development can be traced to two fundamental issues:

1. People are trying to solve the wrong problem, i.e., the identified problem is not really what is wrong.
2. The solution to the real problem is often much simpler than it first appears to be.

Because we have failed to recognize these issues, the industry's frustration with developing appropriate software solutions has been chronic, and this situation has not really improved over the last twenty-five years! The question is why?

To put it bluntly, analysts often fail to do their jobs properly! We tend to put together plans and schedules that are doomed from the start to fail, an issue treated in more detail later. The ultimate goal of the analyst must take into account the reality of the environment in which the work is occurring. Remember, work within the environment. Let users decide what degree of change is appropriate for their own operation; do not take it upon yourself to demand that they change.

For example, how many times have you seen a Gantt Chart[1] for a project schedule that resembles Figure 1.1 below?

---

[1] A Gantt Chart is a tool that depicts progress of tasks against time. It was developed by Henry L. Gantt in 1917.

Activity		March	April	May	June	July	August	Sept	Oct
Feasibility		□							
Analysis			□						
Design				□					
Development					□				
Quality Assurance							□		
Implementation									□

Figure 1.1 Sample Gantt Chart.

It looks nice, but in reality the plan it depicts could never happen. Focus in particular on the intersection of Development and Quality Assurance (QA) activities. The plan shows that once Development is finished, the materials are forwarded to QA for testing. The sequence assumes, however, that QA will never find an error and that therefore the materials will never be returned to Development! Any analyst knows that this scenario is very unlikely to occur. Such poor planning results in deficient allocation of resources to the project. Should the development schedule be met, programming resources most probably will be allocated to other projects. Thus, if QA finds errors (which they undoubtedly will), reallocating these programming resources becomes difficult and problematic. And remember: programmers do not like returning to an "old" program to do maintenance or error fixing.

Figure 1.2 reflects a more realistic view of the life cycle of the project:

The difference in approach is striking. The question is, as sensible as this plan appears to be, why don't we always do it this way? Quite frankly, this plan does not look as nice—as neat and tidy—as the previous plan. But of course simply denying the pain of reality—the inevitable inconveniences and delays—does not make that reality go away. In defense of the previous configuration,

Activity		March	April	May	June	July	August	Sept	Oct
Feasibility		□	□						
Analysis			□	□		□			
Design				□	□		□		
Development				□		□	□		
Quality Assurance						□		□	
Implementation									□

Figure 1.2 Modified Gantt chart reflecting realistic project activity behavior.

some developers might suggest that the iterations of efforts between testing and fixing the software are assumed to be included in the QA time. Maybe, but don't count on it! Just look at the second schedule and you will see how the results of this proper allocation added to the delivery time of the project. It is clear that the original plan was simply incorrect.

There is absolutely no reason that a schedule should not reflect the reality of what will most probably occur. The results are clear: Realistic planning provides a more reliable schedule. Among the many benefits of such a schedule are the confidence and respect gained by both the users and the development staff. There is nothing like producing a schedule that reflects what everyone is confident will occur.

At this point, experienced analysts are no doubt wondering what happens when management dictates how much time we have and shows no flexibility about running behind schedule. This problem is unfortunately not uncommon, and typically fits into one of three scenarios:

1. Management is ignorant of the analysis and construction of systems and simply has no idea how much time is required to complete the project. In this case the analyst will need to develop a convincing presentation for management about how systems are designed and developed. The presentation should be carefully documented to refer to the industry statistics for similar projects in similar companies. This kind of documentation adds much credibility to the discussion. You can also consider having an independent source, such as a respected consulting firm, support your position.

2. Management has little confidence in Development. They feel that picking a date and sticking to it is the best method of getting the project finished. Yes, this is the bully technique! It usually results from bad experiences, probably from looking at those unrealistic Gantt Charts. In this situation, the analyst must take steps to gain the management's confidence. Using the suggestions above would be a good start. In addition, you will need to research and to understand the history of what your predecessors did to encourage this type of distrusting and dictatorial attitude from management, and you will need to find a tactful way to address those issues.

3. Unfortunately, bad management does exist. If you cannot win any concessions or understanding from management, you may have reached what is known as the "no-win scenario." Management is simply unwilling to allot adequate time for the completion of the project and to be persuaded otherwise. When this situation exists in the workplace, the advice is straightforward: You can leave, or you can find some way to deal with this constraint. In either case, be aware that under the no-win scenario there is little hope that the project will result in the development of quality software. This perspective is not cynical, but

instead realistic: some projects are doomed to fail before they begin. What is important is that the analyst recognize as early in the life cycle as possible that the project cannot be successful.

The Tiers of Software Development

The lifecycle of software development continues to evolve, particularly with the advent of the object paradigm (discussed in Chapter 11). The lifecycle of development inevitably affects the way analysis and design are accomplished. Indeed, it seems only natural that the rapid changes in software methodologies would be accompanied by parallel development in analysis and design. Unfortunately, such is not the case, and the advances in software development continue to overshadow the importance of analysis and design.

As the software industry focuses on electronic commerce (e-commerce) through robust Web-based development, it becomes vitally important for the analyst to use the appropriate sequence of tiers to arrive at requirements. Developers cannot expect good results from taking shortcuts, tempting as it may be to do so. The recommended sequence of tiers is outlined below.

User Interface

Regardless of the type of software applications being developed, systems cannot be effectively designed without an appropriate user interface. The user interface tier acts as the foundation for the project: Without a solid foundation at this level, the project is at risk of collapsing at some point during development. Despite its importance, the user-interface tier is often overlooked: Many software projects today move too quickly into development without the effort having been spent to determine what is really needed from the user community. Successful analysts are aware of the critical importance of the user interface phase of any project. Chapter 3 focuses on methods of formulating user interfaces that can significantly improve software development.

Tools

Software systems require that analysts have the appropriate tools to do their job. Furthermore, an even more significant challenge is understanding which of the many available tools to use at any given point. Software development tools are often designed for specialized use rather than for general application, and using the wrong tool can potentially cause significant damage. Finally, the sequence of use for each specialized tool is also critical to success. Indeed, the order of operation, as well as the relationship among specialized analysis tools, must be mastered to ensure success. Chapters 4 and 5 focus on which tools are needed to accomplish which tasks. The chapters also outline the advantages and disadvantages of each tool.

Productivity Through Automation

Having the appropriate tools and knowing how and when to use them is only part of the formula for success. Analysts must also be productive—and productivity can be accomplished only through the use of automation. Automation is implemented using integrated computer aided software engineering (CASE) products. These products provide the analyst with an automated and integrated toolbox of features that are centralized through a core data dictionary and repository.

Object Orientation

Successful projects employ the concepts of object orientation (OO). Whether or not software systems are OO compliant, analyzing systems using the object method builds better systems that are more cohesive, reusable, and maintainable (see Chapter 11). More cohesive code is "tighter" code, and is more easily fixed and maintained. It is also the foundation of the reusable components that can be incorporated into other applications later. Without the OO construct, systems tend to have pieces that are recoded and hard to maintain. With the advent of the enterprise solutions and e-commerce transactions that will be vital to business strategies, building object-based systems has become more a requirement than an option. However, as this book will show, businesses and organizations cannot just jump into OO, but rather they must create the foundations first through the previous tiers of development. Put another way, it is more important to understand the concepts of OO during analysis and design than it is to have the OO scheme actually programmed. This idea is discussed further in Chapter 11.

Client/Server

Today's software is still governed by client/server processes. While client/server has become more widespread, it has not necessarily become better understood. As with the OO paradigm, client/server software development is often confused with network hardware strategy. While client/server hardware topology is an important issue in itself, it has little to do with the process of deciding how software modules should interact across the network and where such modules should be placed. Such decisions will be driven by issues that arise during the process of analysis. Client/server software processing, in its true implementation, involves the interaction of objects and defining the way in which they will communicate with each other. Thus, analysts must first be versed in the laws governing OO if they are to pursue the client/server model. Incidentally, almost all Web-based applications that use JAVA, Active-X and other controls are designed essentially under the guidelines of interaction objects in a client/server environment.

Internet/Intranet

The advent of Web-based technology, sometimes known as Internet/Intranet processing, has led the industry to the use of a new breed of software applications. This new breed requires more robust processing and involves careful design and placement of pictures that provide users with a true "cafeteria" style of operation. These new applications bring new challenges to analysts and designers. Increasingly, it is not programmers who are designing the interface; rather, analysts themselves are beginning to work with commercial advertisers and marketing departments to create a "look and feel" that will be critical to the survival of many businesses. E-commerce, a result of the Internet/Intranet boom, represents another level of analysis. I believe that in the future, e-commerce will exert the strongest shaping influence on the analyst's profession–a profession destined to become tomorrow's integrators of systems development. Indeed, programming tools will continue to become easier to develop and more abundant in precoded forms. There will, undoubtedly, be less distribution of development teams, that is, companies will find more and more outsourced solutions to fill their needs. Notwithstanding the "automation" of code, the need for integrators who can communicate with executives and with line management and operations personnel will ultimately be the most significant forces in the development of strategic-based systems over the Internet.

Internet/Intranet processing requires that analysts have mastered the client/server paradigm. Indeed, many professionals have dubbed Internet development as "client/server grown up." While this may or may not be the best definition of Internet/Intranet development, it is another statement that supports the tier concept, the concept that underlies the approach of this book.

•   •   •

This introduction is focused on presenting the steps necessary to success as a professional analyst. I call each of these steps tiers because of their building block nature and their dependencies on each other. I believe, therefore, that to learn to become an effective analyst, one must master the specifics within each of these tiers and must pass critical information to the next level. Rather than look at analysis sequentially, I would present the steps as levels as depicted in Figure 1.3.

The table graphically shows how each tier must be dependent on the other. There is a profound message in this diagram that suggests that no tier can be

Tier	Analyst Application
6	Internet/Intranet—Web-based transaction processing, media, and graphics
5	Client/server—breaking down objects to their client and server applications
4	Object orientation—selection of objects and classes
3	CASE—automation and productivity of tier 2
2	Structured Tools—DFD, PFD, ERD, STD, process specification, data repository
1	User Interface—interviewing skills, JAD, RAD

Figure 1.3 Tiers of analysis and software application development.

developed or exist without the previous one. To ensure success on a project, everyone involved in the design and development of application software must fully understand the interdependent nature of these tiers. Analysts must be able to convey to their colleagues that to do Internet/Intranet development, organizations must first have excellent user interfaces, mastery of a structured toolset, a vehicle for automation so that the process will be productive, an understanding of the concept of objects, and a way to deploy these objects in a client/server environment. It all sounds so simple, and in many ways it is. The question answered by this new edition is *how?*

Problems and Exercises

1. Professionals often refer to software projects as being very complex. Explain why this complexity might be overstated and misunderstood.
2. What is a Gantt chart? How are Gantt charts used and why is it important that they be realistic estimates of how the project will proceed?
3. Explain what is meant by "tiers of software development."
4. The user interface represents the first critical step to obtaining the proper needs of users. Provide five examples of different user positions that might be critical to interview.
5. Discuss the importance of using the appropriate analysis tool when interviewing users and building specifications.
6. How is productivity obtained in analysis? What tool is best used?
7. Explain why object orientation is beneficial to software developers.
8. What is the use of client/server with respect to software development?
9. Why is Internet/Intranet processing so important to today's Web development?

2
System Development Life Cycle (SDLC)

System Development Life Cycle—Steps in Analysis and Design

The purpose of this chapter is to build on the Tiers of Software Development and to provide a framework for the life cycle of most software development projects. This is important prior to explaining the details of the user interface and analysis tools that are needed to bring software to fruition. Another way of viewing this chapter then is to get a sense of how the tiers of development actually interface with each other and what specific events and tools are used to successfully complete each step. This chapter consists of two sections: the first explains the notion that software goes through three basic phases or cycles, that is, Development, Testing, and Production. The second section provides an example using a seven-stage method called "The Barker Method," which represents one approach to defining the details of each of the three cycles.

No matter which methodology might be used when designing a system including its related database, the key elements involved in the methodology usually include, at a minimum, business process reengineering and the life cycle for design and implementation. Business process reengineering (BPR), simply defined, is the process used for either reworking an existing application or database to make improvements, or to account for new business requirements. BPR will be discussed in more detail in Chapter 13. The life cycle of the database includes all steps (and environments) necessary to assist in the database's design and final implementation and its integration with application programs. Irrespective of which design methodology is used, analysts/designers will find that system development projects will usually include the following generic steps:

1. Determine the need for a system to assist a business process
2. Define that system's goals
3. Gather business requirements
4. Convert business requirements to system requirements
5. Design the database and accompanying applications
6. Build, test, and implement the database and applications

This *traditional method* is the most commonly used design approach and includes at least three primary phases:

1. Requirements analysis
2. Data modeling
3. Normalization

During the first phase, requirements analysis, the development and design team conduct interviews in order to capture all the business needs as related to the proposed system. The data modeling phase consists of the creation of the logical data model that will later be used to define the physical data model, or database structures. After the database has been modeled and designed, the normalization phase is implemented to help eliminate or reduce as much as possible any redundant data. All of the specifics of how this is accomplished will be detailed in the tools of analysis chapters. Below is a more specific description of what activities are included in the Development, Testing, and Production cycles of the SDLC.

Development

The Development life cycle includes four overall components. Using this perspective, "development" would consist of all the necessary steps to accomplish the creation of the application. This includes feasibility, analysis, design, and the actual coding. Feasibility represents the tasks necessary to determine whether the software project makes business sense. Most organizations would integrate the process of Return-On-Investment (ROI) during this step. ROI consists of the financial steps that determine mathematically whether the project will provide the necessary monetary returns to the business. Focusing solely on monetary returns can be a serious pitfall, since there are many benefits that can be realized via non-monetary returns (Langer, 2005). Feasibility often contains what is known as a high-level forecast or budget. The "high" would represent the "worst case" scenario on cost and the "low," the best case or lowest cost. The hope of course is that the actual cost and timetable would fall somewhere in between the high and the low. But feasibility goes beyond just the budget; it also represents whether the business feels that the project is attainable within a specific timetable as well. So, feasibility is a statement of both financial and business objectives, and an overall belief that the cost is worth the payback.

Analysis is the ultimate step of creating the detailed logical requirements, or as I will define in Chapter 4, the architecture of the applications and database. As we will see in this book, there are numerous analysis tools that are used along each phase of analysis. Ultimately, the analyst creates a requirements document that outlines all of the needs for the coders to work from, without going back to the users directly for clarification. Analysis, as an architectural responsibility is very much based on a mathematical progression of predictable steps. These steps are quite iterative in nature, which requires practitioners to understand the gradual nature of completion of this vital step in Development. Another aspect of the mathematics of analysis is decomposition. Decomposition as we will see establishes the creation of the smaller components that make up the whole. It is like the bones, blood, and muscles of the human body that ultimately make up what we physically see in a person. Once a system is decomposed, the analyst can be confident that the "parts" that comprise the whole are identified and can be reused throughout the system as necessary. These decomposed parts are called "objects" and comprise the study and application of object-oriented analysis and design. Thus, the basis of working with users ultimately leads to the creation of parts known as objects that act as interchangeable components that can be used whenever needed. One should think of objects like interchangeable parts of a car. They sometimes are called "standard" parts that can be reused in multiple models. The benefits are obvious. Such is the same objective with software: the more reusable the more efficient and cost effective.

Design is far less logical than analysis but a far more creative step. Design is the phase that requires the physical decisions about the system, from what programming language to use, which vendor database to select (Oracle, Sybase, DB2 for example), to how screens and reports will be identified. The design phase can also include decisions about hardware and network communications or the *topology*. Unlike analysis, design requires less of a mathematical and engineering focus, to one that actually serves the user view. The design process is perhaps the most iterative, which could require multiple sessions with users using a trial and error approach until the correct user interface and product selection has been completed. Design often requires "experts" in database design, screen architecture experts as well as those professionals who understand the performance needs of network servers, and other hardware components required by the system.

Coding represents another architectural as well as mathematical approach. However, I would suggest that mathematics is not the most accurate description of a coding structure, rather it is about understanding how logic operates. This component of mathematics is known as "Boolean" Algebra, or the mathematics of logic. Boolean algebra is the basis of how software communicates with the real machine. Software is the physical abstraction that allows us to talk with the hardware machine. Coding then is the best way to actually develop the structure of the program. Much has been written about coding styles and formats. The best known is called "structured" programming. Structured programming was originally developed so that programmers would create code that would be cohesive, that is, would be self-reliant. Self-reliance in coding means that the program is self-contained because all of the logic relating to its tasks is within the program. The opposite of cohesion is coupling. Coupling is the logic of programs that are reliant on each other, meaning that a change to one program necessitates a change in another program. Coupling is viewed as being dangerous from a maintenance and quality perspective simply because changes cause problems in other reliant or "coupled" systems. More details on the practice of cohesion and coupling are covered in Chapter 11. The relationship to coding to analysis can be critical given that the decision on what code will comprise a module may be determined during analysis as opposed to coding.

Testing

Testing can have a number of components. The first form of testing is called program debugging. Debugging is the process of a programmer ensuring that his/her code in a program executes as designed. Debugging, therefore, should be carried out by the programmer, as opposed to a separate quality assurance group. However, it is important to recognize that debugging does not ensure that the program is performing as required by end users, rather only confirms that the code executes and does not abort during program execution. What does this mean? Simply that a programmer should never pass a program to quality assurance that does not execute, at least showing that it does perform under all conditions. Once again, this process does not ensure that the results produced by the program are correct or meets the original requirements set forth by users.

Once a program has been "debugged" it should then be sent through the quality assurance process. Today, most large organizations recognize that quality assurance needs to be performed by non-programming individuals. As a result, organizations create separate quality assurance organizations that do nothing but test the correctness and accuracy of programs. Quality assurance organizations typically accomplish this by designing what is known as Acceptance Test Planning. Acceptance Test Plans are designed from the original requirements, which allow quality assurance personnel to develop assurance testing based on the users' original requirements as opposed to what might have been interpreted. For this reason Acceptance Test Planning is typically implemented during the analysis and design phases of the life cycle but executed during the Testing phase. Acceptance Test Planning also includes system type testing activities such as stress and load checking (ensuring that the application can handle larger demands or users) or integration testing (whether the application communicates and operates appropriately with other programs in the system), as well as compatibility testing, such as ensuring that applications operate on types of browsers or computer systems. Testing, by its very nature is an iterative process that can often create "loops" of redesign and programming. It is important to recognize that acceptance testing has two distinct components: first, the design of the test plans, and second, the execution of those acceptance plans.

Production

Production is synonymous with the "going-live" phases. Ultimately, Production must ensure the successful execution of all aspects of a system's performance. During Production, there is the need to establish how problems will be serviced, what support staff will be available and when and how inquiries will be responded to and scheduled for fixing. This component of Production may initiate new Development and Testing cycles because of redesign needs (or misinterpreted user needs). This means that the original requirements were not properly translated into system realities.

On the other hand, Production as a Life Cycle includes other complex issues:

1. Backup, recovery, and archival
2. Change control
3. Performance fine-tuning and statistics
4. Audit and new requirements

Backup, Recovery, and Archiving

Operational backup should be defined during the Development phases; however, there are inevitably backup requirements that need to be modified during Production. This occurs because the time it takes to complete data backup is difficult to predict. The speed at which data can be placed on another media is not an exact science and is based on the complexity of how data is selected and the method of placement to another location and/or media. The speed also heavily relies on factors such as disk input/output speed, network throughput (speed of communication network), database backup algorithms, and the actual intervals between backup cycles. Why does this matter? It matters because backups require systems to be "off-line" until they complete, meaning that the system is in effect not operational. Thus, the longer the backup process, the longer the system is off-line. A most popular example of the potential backup dilemma is overnight processes that must complete by the beginning of the next morning. If the process of backup will take longer than the allowed time, then analysts/designers need to determine a way that can condense the time-line. The alternatives might typically include limiting the actual data used to back up, or multiple devices to increase throughput, etc.

Recovery, on the other hand, is more about testing the quality of the backed up data, and determining whether the data stored can be recovered in the operational system. So, the first aspect is to see whether the necessary data needed to bring the system "back" can be accomplished. One hopes that recovery will never be necessary, but the most glaring exposure on quality assurance is to not really know whether the data we think we have, can actually be restored back to operational forms. For example, it is one thing to back up a complex database; it is another to restore that data so that the key fields and indexes are working appropriately after restoration. The only assurance for this is to actually perform a restore in a simulation. Simulations take analysis and design talent and need to be conducted on some intervals that ensure that backup data integrity is preserved.

Restoration and backup become even more comprehensive when portions are what is called "archived." Archived data is data that is deemed no longer necessary in the "live" system, but data that may be required under some circumstances. So, data that is determined to be ready for archival, needs to be backed up in such a way that it can be restored, not to the live system, but rather a special system that will allow for the data to be queried and accessed as if it was live. The most relevant example that I can provide here, is accounting data from past periods that is no longer needed in the operations system, but may need to be accessed for audit purposes. In this example it might be necessary to restore a prior year's accounting data to a special system that simulates a prior year in question, but that has no effect on the current system.

The Barker Case Method

Now that we have covered the essential tools that can be used to do analysis and design, it is worthwhile to look at a strategy or CASE method. One of the most popular approaches is known as the Barker Seven Phase Case method. The seven phases provides a step-by-step approach to where an analyst/designer uses the tools we have discussed. The phases are as follows: Strategy, Analysis, Design, Build, Documentation, Transition, and Production. The sections below provide an in-depth description of each of these phases.

Strategy

Strategy tends to include two major components: basic process and data flow models that can be used to confirm an understanding of the business objectives, processes, and needs. The deliverables Barker calls a "Strategy Document," which can be correlated to what I have previously defined as a business specification. However, unlike just a pure business specification, the Strategy Document also includes an estimated budget, delivery schedule, project personnel, and any constraints and development standards that are required. Therefore, the Strategy Document contains all of the high-level issues and allows management to understand the objectives, timeframe, and budget limits of the project. It also is consistent with decomposition and sets the path to develop a more detailed specification. Below is an example of the Barker Strategy Document components:

Barker Document	Related Langer Tool and Approach
Business objectives, priorities, constraints, and critical success factors. This is essentially a section that outlines the user's expectations and the basis for successful completion.	The User Interface, Business Specifications Format
Strategy Entity Relational Diagram. This is a high-level diagram that shows the relationship among entities without detailed attribute information. The strategy ERD provides an overall map of how the data will be related across various systems.	Logic Data Modeling
Functional Hierarchy. This shows how the various functions of the business relate to each other in a functional way.	Process-Based Tools, specifically Process Flow Diagrams

System Boundaries. This provides the limits of the project, that is, where the system begins and where it ends or meets with other systems.

Process-Based Tools, specifically Data Flow Diagrams, and State Transition Diagrams

Possible Architecture Issues. This part addresses what hardware or network design issues may need to be considered to deliver the solution. This could include new hardware needs such as performance upgrades, more disk space, or printers, etc

Network Analysis

Phased Development Plan. This section typically includes a Gantt chart depicting the project plan showing each deliverable.

Project Complexity

Personal Resource Statement and Organizational Needs. This part focuses on the effects of the project on the organization and roles and responsibilities of staff.

Business Process and Reengineering

Delivering the Strategy Document

Barker's method provides a number of detailed steps to complete the Strategy Phase:

Project Administration and Management. This is defined as an ongoing process that occurs throughout the project. It can be related to a form of project management including reporting, control, quality assurance and various administrative tasks. The deliverable is typically in the form of progress reports, plans, and minutes of project meetings.

Scope the Study and Agree on Terms of Reference. This step is the first phase to agreeing on the actual objectives, constraints, and deliverables. It also includes the estimated number of interviews and how they will be completed (individual, JAD, for example), as well as specific staff assignments.

Plan for Strategy Study. This is a detailed plan for identifying specific staff resources and schedules for meetings.

Results of Briefings, Interviews, and Other Information Gatherings. This step engages a number of outcomes, including a functional hierarchy (Object Diagram) and rough Entity Relational Diagram. It becomes the first high-level modeling depicting the form of the architecture of the system.

Model the Business. This step includes a more detailed model of the business flows including process flows, data flows, and a more functional ERD. It also includes a glossary of terms and business units that are involved with the system flow.

Preparation and Feedback Sessions and Completion of the Business Model. These are actually two steps: the initial planning for the feedback sessions, and the actual feedback sessions themselves. The first step requires preparation for outstanding issues to be resolved from strategy sessions and to determine how the feedback sessions will be conducted with key users and stakeholders. The feedback sessions usually result in changes to the models and a movement to the more detailed analysis phase of the project.

Recommended System Architecture. This task summarizes the finding of the strategy and recommends a system architecture based on the assumptions and directions from stakeholders. This includes available technologies, interfaces with existing systems, and alternative platforms that can be used.

Analysis

Analysis expands the Strategy Stage into details that ensure business consistency and accuracy. The Barker analysis stage is designed to capture all of the business processes that need to be incorporated into the project. Barker divides Analysis into two components: Information Gathering and Requirements Analysis.

Information Gathering: includes the building of more detailed ERD called an Analysis ERD (equivalent to what I called a logical model), process and data flows, a requirements document, and an analysis evaluation. This step also includes an analysis of the existing legacy systems. Much of the information gathering is accomplished via interviews with users. As discussed in the next chapter this is accomplished by understanding the user interface and determining whether to do individual and/or group analysis techniques.

Requirements Analysis: Once the information gathering is complete a detailed requirements analysis or specification documents must be produced. It contains the relevant tools as outlined in my analysis document, namely, the detailed PFDs, DFDs, ERDs and Process Specifications. In the Barker approach the requirements document may also include audit and control needs, backup and recovery procedures, and first-level database sizing (space needs).

Design

The Design Stage consists of the incorporation of physical appearances and other requirements that are specific to actual products, for example, coding and naming conventions. The typical design needs are screen layouts, navigation tools (menus, buttons, etc.) and help systems. The Design Stage must also ultimately achieve the agreed upon performance or service levels.

The ERD will be transformed to a physical database design. Detail specifications will be translated into program modules, and manual procedures to operate the system should be documented. In terms of screens, reports, and "bridges" that connect modules, various prototype designs can be incorporated to show users how the navigation and physical "look and feel" will occur during the user interface.

As previously discussed, Design is not a step that occurs without iteration. The Design Stage often iterates with analysis, where questions and suggestions from designers can raise issues about alternatives not considered during the analysis stage. The iterative cycle is best depicted by Barker's diagram as shown in Figure 2.1.

What is critical about this design method is its interactive yet interdependence with non-application components such as network design, audit and control, backup and recovery design, data conversion, and system test planning.

Build Stage

The Barker Build Stage is defined as the coding and testing of programs. Much of this stage depends on the technical environment and the attributes of the programming environment, that is, Web, mainframe, mid-range, etc. The Build Stage involves the typical planning, design of the program structure,

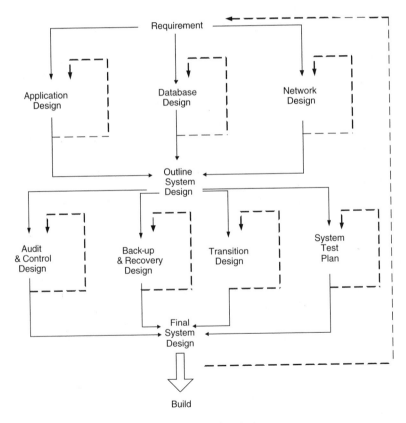

Figure 2.1 Barker's iterative design process.

actual coding, program methodology (top-down, structured coding, etc.), version control, testing approaches, and test releases.

The most convoluted component of the Build Stage is what represents program debugging versus what represents testing. Testing can also be done by programmers, but it is typically segregated into a separate function and group called Quality Assurance. Debugging can be defined as a programmer's ability to ensure that his/her code executes, that is, does not fail during execution. Quality Assurance, on the other hand, tests the ability and accuracy of the program to perform as required. In other words, does the program, although executing, produce the intended results? Current trends separate QA departments and have programmers focus on coding. Much of the QA objective is to establish Acceptance Test Plans as I outline in Chapter 12 and this concept is more aligned with the Barker Build Stage.

User Documentation

This Stage in the Barker approach creates user manuals and operations documentation. Barker (1992) defines this as "sufficient to support the system testing task in the concurrent build stage, and documentation must be completed before acceptance testing in the transition stage" (p. 7–1).

The Barker User Documentation Stage is very consistent with my definition: significant parts of documentation must be accomplished during the strategy and analysis stages, when the principal aspects of the system architecture are agreed upon with users and stakeholders. The format of user and operations documentation is always debatable. What is most important is its content as opposed to its format. Barker's method suggests that documenters design this Stage with the user or "reader" in mind. Thus, understanding how such users and readers think and operate the system within their domains is likely to be a key approach to providing the most attractive format of the document.

The user documentation should contain a full-reference manual for every type of user. Tutorials and on-line help text are always an important component in today's Web-based systems. Another aspect of user documentation is to include information on error messages, cross-reference to related issues, as well as helpful hints. The operations documentation needs to cover day-to-day and periodic operations procedures. The operations guide includes execution procedures, backup and various maintenance processes that are necessary to sustain the system.

Transaction Stage

Barker describes the Transition Stage as a pre-live process that ensures that acceptance testing is completed, hardware and software installation is done, and critical reviews or "walkthroughs" have been finished. Another aspect of the

Transition Stage is to understand data conversion and its effects on whether the system is ready to go into production.

Since the original publication of Barker's work, users today are much more experienced with the Transition Stage—simply because they have experienced it more often. As such, much of the resistance and ignorance to the importance of acceptance testing and validation do not occur at the frequency that they used to. Still, the transition process is complex. The steps necessary to go live in any new system requires an important integration with users and existing legacy applications.

Production

The Production Stage can be seen as synonymous with "go live." It is the smooth running of the new system and all of its integrated components including manual and legacy interfaces. During this Stage, IT operations and support personnel should be responsible for providing the necessary service levels to users as well as bug fixing for programmers. Thus, the development staff acts as a backup to the production issues that occur.

3
The User Interface

Establishing User Interfaces

The success factors in analysis start with the established interfaces from day one. What does this mean? You must start the process by meeting with the right people in the organization. In the best projects, the process is as follows:

1. *Executive interface*: There needs to be an executive-level supporter of the project. Without such a supporter, you risk not being able to keep the project on schedule. Most important, you need a supporter for the political issues that you may need to handle during the project (discussed in detail later). The executive supporter, sometimes known as a *sponsor* (JAD reference), should provide a preliminary schedule advising the organization of what is expected and the objectives of the project. The executive supporter should attach a letter to the preliminary schedule and send it to the project team members. The letter must put the importance of the project into perspective. Therefore, it is strongly recommended that you draft this letter yourself or at least have influence over its content, since doing so can ensure that the message is delivered appropriately. The executive supporter should also establish regular reviews with the analyst and the user community to ensure that objectives are being met.
2. *Department head or line manager interface*: If appropriate, the department head should provide guidance about which individuals should represent the department needs. If several people are involved, the analyst should consider a JAD-like approach. Depending on the size of the organization, the department head might also establish review sessions to ensure compliance.
3. *Functional user interface*: Perhaps the most important people are the ones who can provide the step-by-step needs of the system. Figure 3.1 shows a typical organization interface structure.

Forming an Interview Approach

Your primary mission as an analyst or systems designer is to extract the physical requirements of the users and convert each to its logical equivalent (see Chapter 4 for a full discussion of the concept of the logical equivalent). The most critical

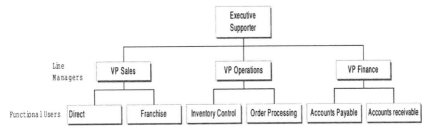

Figure 3.1 Established interface layers.

step in this mission is the actual interview, in which you must establish a rapport with the user(s) that will facilitate your obtaining the information you need. Your approach will dramatically change based on the level and category of the individual being interviewed. Therefore, prior to meeting with any user, it is critical to understand the culture of the company, its past experiences with automation, and most important its organizational structure.

The following five-step procedure will help guide you more smoothly through the interview process.

Step 1: Get The Organization Chart

Few things are more useful in understanding the chain of command and areas of responsibility than the organization chart. Depending on the size of the enterprise and the scope of the project, the organization chart should start at the executive supporter level and work down to the operational users.

Step 2: Understand Everyone's Role in the Organization Chart

If there are any individuals not involved in the project who should be, given their position in the organization, first ask why and then make a notation for yourself that they are not to be included. Management may assume an individual or role should not be included and may often overlook their importance. Do not be afraid to ask why a person is not deemed necessary for the analysis of the system, and determine if you are satisfied with the reasons for their exclusion. Remember, you can still control and change the approach at this point, and management will probably respect you for doing so.

Step 3: Assume the Situation Is Political

Be sure you understand the personalities with which you will have to deal. In almost any implementation, politics among people becomes part of the process. To ignore its existence—and the constraints it is likely to impose—is to invite failure. The question is how to obtain information about internal politics. The best approach is to start as high up in the organization as possible, typically at the executive supporter level. You might be surprised at the amount of information they have. Of course, you should not explicitly ask about the politics but rather phrase your question as follows: "Can you give me some perspective on potential department and personnel conflicts that may occur during the interview cycle and that I should be aware of?" You may not always get the answer you need, but if you keep asking the question during every interview, you will discover a great deal about the way the organization functions. And remember, only people make projects complex!

Step 4: Obtain Information About User Skill Sets

Starting an interview without knowledge of the user's technical skills puts the analyst at a huge disadvantage. Having this information will allow you to formulate a plan of questions and to determine the best approach to the interview. If the user has no knowledge, the questions should be tailored to include a minimum of technical content. The following guidelines for preparing for interviews reflect a common sense approach, yet it is amazing how many analysts fail even to consider such strategies!

1. Gather information before the session to allow the user—as well as yourself—to be prepared and to give you both a much clearer understanding of what will be covered during the interview.
2. Develop a questionnaire. Technical questions should be phrased differently depending on the level of knowledge the user possesses.
3. Determine whether the interview will provide enough input to obtain the necessary information. This is not always the case; however, it happens more often than you might think. Understanding user capabilities before the interview may not only change the scope of the meeting but also suggest who, in addition to the user, should attend the interview.

Step 5: Arrange for a Pre-Meeting with the User

A pre-meeting may not always be possible. In any case it must be a short meeting, perhaps half an hour. The session should be designed to be high-level and provide a general idea of what will be covered during the actual interview. But more important, it will allow you to get a snapshot of the user. You might say you are obtaining a "comfort level" (or "discomfort level") for that user, and such meetings can provide you with an idea of what to expect and how to finalize your approach. What do you look for? Here is some direction.

1. The pre-meeting should give you enough feedback to place or confirm the user's technical level.

2. Look at everything in the user's office or his or her environment. Is it sloppy? Is it tidy and organized? The state of the user's environment will often be consistent with the way he or she provides information. The insight you gain from observing the environment should give you guidance about the types of questions to ask this individual.

3. Look for signs of attitude. The user's level of interest should be evident. Does he or she view the upcoming session as a waste of time, or is he or she excited about the meeting?

The information gleaned in the pre-meeting can provide you with helpful hints about what to expect from the interview and from the user in general.

Dealing with Political Factions

The importance of internal politics at the user's site should never be underestimated. Perhaps the most common question raised by both professionals and student analysts is how to provide quality analysis when office politics get in the way. Here are some guidelines.

1. First, assess whether you are in the no-win scenario. Many of us hate to admit that the no-win scenario does indeed exist in many environments, but you should be on the lookout for the signs. If your manager will not support you, if the company is underpaying you, if the users hate you, if there are no automated tools to do the analysis, and if upper management doesn't care, then you are in a difficult position. If you cannot change the situation, you must inform management that the results of your analysis will be significantly impaired by the lack of support and tools to complete the project properly. The techniques offered in this book assume that all parties are interested in providing the best solution possible, not in providing a system that is barely adequate.

2. On the other hand, do not be too quick to assume that you are in the no-win scenario. Most politically hampered projects need some strategy to get them on course, and most problems can be overcome if you know how to approach them. Here is a typical example of such a problem and some ideas you can apply to solve it.

Problem

The users who currently operate the system won't talk to me. They are afraid either that the new system might replace them or that their jobs will significantly change. In short, they fear change.

Recommended Solution

Most operational users are managed by a supervisor or "in-charge." Sometimes, even a line manager can be directly responsible for production workers. In any event, you must determine who is responsible and meet with that person. The purpose of the meeting is to gain their support. This support is significant, since you might find that the supervisor was once in operations and will be able to understand the problems you may encounter. If the meeting is successful, the supervisor may be able to offer a strategy. This strategy can vary from a general meeting with the users, to individual discipline, to escalation to upper management. Whatever you do, do not allow such a situation to continue and do not accept abuse; to do so will ultimately reflect on you and your abilities.

Obviously, if the supervisor is also a problem, then you have no choice but to go to upper management. However, this option is not a desirable one from the analyst's viewpoint. Upper management's reaction may not be helpful, and it could be damaging. For example, they might be indifferent to your problem and instruct you to deal with it yourself, or they might simply send the supervisor a letter. In some cases you may be fortunate and the supervisor's responsibilities regarding the system will be given to another manager. Consider, though, how unpleasant the consequences may be if you appeal to upper management and get no support: You may be left working with an already unhelpful supervisor who has been made even more so by your complaint. It is important to remember that once you go to upper management, the line has been drawn. Supervisors typically are responsible for the day-to-day operation. They usually know more about the entire operation than anyone else, and therefore you are well advised to find a way to get them on your side. A supportive supervisor can be invaluable in helping you overcome problems, as long as you are not shy about suggesting ways to get the users comfortable.

Categories and Levels of Users

Establishing user interfaces represents the vehicle to formulate much of the interview approach. It is necessary, however, to go further into the characteristics of the people particularly with respect to the *category* and *level* they have within the organization. Figure 3.1 established the three general categories, called executive, department head or line manager, and functional. It is important to explore their characteristics. In order that we better understand each category, I have always asked the following question: *What would be their interest in the success of the project, that is, what would make them happy with the new system?* Let's apply this question for each user category.

1. *Executive users:* Individuals at this layer are most interested in the concept of return on investment (ROI). ROI basically focuses on whether an investment will provide a financial return that makes the effort worthwhile to the organization. While there are many comprehensive formulas that are often applied to the study of ROI, our context pertains to the short- and long-term benefits of investing in building new software. There are generally five reasons why executives agree

to fund software development. They are listed in order of significance to the investor.

a. *Monetary return*: Simply put, this means that the software will generate dollar revenue. An example might be the Internet software that supports on-line ordering systems such as Amazon has for book shipments. Their system not only provides the functionality to handle shipments, but provides a Web interface that can be directly associated with revenues provided by book orders through the Internet.

b. *Increased productivity*: Many software systems are unable to demonstrate direct monetary benefits. However, many of them are developed to increase productivity. This means that the system will allow organizations to actually produce and deliver more. Thus, the system allows the organization to derive higher revenues through increased productivity of its resources.

c. *Reducing costs*: Software projects are approved so that organizations can reduce their existing overhead costs. This typically relates to the replacement of manual activities with computer ones. While reducing costs appears to be similar in nature to increasing productivity, they are often implemented for different reasons. Increased productivity usually relates to organizations that are growing and are looking for ways to improve output because of very high demand. Reducing costs, on the other hand, can represent a defensive measure, where an organization is seeking to find ways to cut costs because of a shrinking market.

d. *Competition*: Software systems are created because the competition has done so. Therefore, producing software for competitive reasons is a defensive measure against someone else who has demonstrated its value. An example of this is in the banking sector. Citibank was one of the first banks to introduce automated teller machines (ATM). Other banks soon followed because of the success that Citibank had with proliferating ATMs throughout New York State. This does not imply, however, that competitive systems are always defense mechanisms. Indeed, many commercial Web sites are being introduced based simply on market forecasts for their potential to increase business.

e. *For the sake of technology*: While not the most popular reason, some organizations will invest in new systems because they think that it is time to do so or they are concerned that their technology is getting old. This way of supporting new systems development is rare, as it suggests the spending of money without a clear understanding of its benefits.

Therefore, the executive category of users is one that is interested in the value of the investment. These users have a global view of needs as opposed to the details. In fact, they may know little of how things are really done. The value of the executive interface is to provide the scope and objectives of the project against the perceived value they intend to get from the software. Another popular phrase for this is the *domain* of the system. Domain often refers to *boundaries*. Ultimately, what makes them happy is a system that delivers what was promised or the expected ROI.

2. *Department head or line manager users*: These users represent two main areas of user input. First, they are responsible for the day-to-day productivity of their respective departments. Thus, they understand the importance of meeting the objectives of the organization as set forth by the executives. Indeed, they often report to the executives. On the other hand, department heads and line managers are responsible to their staff. They must deal with the functional users and prescribe ways to improve both their output and their job satisfaction. These users perhaps provide what I call *the best bang for the buck,* a phrase that usually means for the time invested, you get the most payback. One can see that the department heads and line managers are responsible for most of what happens every day in an organization. Another phrase that can be used to describe them is your *most valuable players (MVPs)*. However, beware: MVPs are the hardest to find and get for the interviews. What makes department heads and line managers happy is the most complex. They want a system that produces the output that they are expected to provide and they need a system that keeps their staff happy and productive.

3. *Functional users*: Also known as the users in the trenches, these people essentially do the operational activities. While they know a lot about their processes, they usually care little about the productivity and expected ROI. I often see these users as people who want little pain, and just want to work the hours they need to. Thus, fancy systems are of little interest to them unless they provide no pain—and no pain to these users means having a system that makes their job easier.

The next area to understand about users is their level. By level, I mean their understanding of computers. There are three levels of users:

1. *Knowledgeable*: The determination of knowledge can be tricky and is certainly based on someone's opinion. I define knowledge in reference to experience. An experienced user can be defined as a person who "has been through it before." A user who has been through the development of a new system can therefore be defined as "knowledgeable" within this context.

2. *Amateur*: The definition of an amateur is based not so much on experience, but rather on the type of experience the user has. Amateurs can be thought of as hobbyists who enjoy working with computers at

home, but have no professional experience in developing software in an organization. In this perspective, I believe that the meaning of amateur is globally defined as one who does not get paid for the work they perform.

3. *Novice*: These users have no experience with computers. While there are fewer such users than there were ten years ago, they still exist. A better way of perceiving a novice user is to consider my definition of knowledgeable. In this context, a novice user is one who has never been part of the implementation of a new system in a professional environment.

Perhaps the most problematic of the above levels is the amateur. I have found that users who are knowledgeable provide benefit to projects. They in many ways act as a checkpoint for the analyst in that they can ask good questions and particularly remember historical problems that actually can help the development process. Novice users add little value and also add few problems. They tend to do what you ask of them. Amateurs, on the other hand, tend to know enough to be dangerous. They also tend to have such a profound interest in the topic that they often go off on tangents about the technology instead of concentrating on the particulars of the project.

What is most important is the mapping of these categories and levels. An analyst might interview a knowledgeable executive, or a novice functional user. Each permutation can affect the way interviews are conducted. For example, an interview with a group of amateurs would focus the analyst on ensuring that the agenda is very specific. Otherwise, discussions could easily get off track. Therefore, the understanding about user levels and categories can only assist in the development of effective interview approaches.

Joint Application Development (JAD)

JAD is a process that was originally developed for designing computer-based systems. JAD centers on a three-to five-day workshop that brings together business area people (users) and IS (Information Systems) professionals. Under the direction of a facilitator, these people define anything from high-level strategic plans to detailed system specifications. The products of the workshop can include definitions of business processes, prototypes, data models, and so on.

Simply put, JAD is a method for holding group sessions with users, instead of individual sessions. You may have no choice but to use JAD when there are simply too many users to interview. JAD is also an excellent tool for use in highly political situations where obtaining consensus among users is difficult. JAD significantly differs from standard analysis in that it requires an up-front commitment from the user community. Specifically, the users must ultimately run the sessions themselves and make commitments to provide the requirements of the system. Finally, if prototypes are used, JAD is an excellent means of applying rapid application development (RAD). Both prototyping and RAD will be discussed in greater detail later.

The most important part of implementing JAD is the management of the process and the determination of the appropriate individuals to be involved. The standard roles used in JAD are as follows:

- *executive sponsor*: This individual effectively plays the same role as the executive supporter introduced earlier in this chapter. This person is typically at the vice-president level and ultimately has the responsibility for the business area. The ideal person for this role is someone to whom users will have to report if they plan to miss a session and who can reprimand them if they do. This thinking may seem harsh or cynical, but the risk is high that users may find more important things to do when the sessions begin. Such absenteeism can entirely undermine the process, and IS should not be called upon to police users.

- *facilitator*: In the best situations, the facilitator should not come from either the user community or IS, but rather from an independent area or consulting firm. This arrangement allows the session to be independent. That is, the facilitator of the JAD must be impartial and have overall responsibility for controlling the flow of the sessions. In the ideal scenario, the facilitator should report to the executive sponsor.

- *scribe*: This person is designated to record minutes and decisions and in many cases actually produces the models using a computer-aided software engineering (CASE) tool (see Chapter 7). A good scribe has knowledge of the business area, good analytical skills, and knowledge of CASE software. For these reasons, scribes often come from IS.

- *IS representatives*: IS personnel should be in the meetings not to provide requirements but rather to answer questions about the existing hardware and software. This information can be critical when discussing physical constraints of the existing systems and what data are currently available.

- *participant*: These are the users who have been selected to represent their respective areas. They attend the JAD sessions and are expected to come prepared to voice their opinions about what the system must do to accommodate the needs of their business unit. Participants are thus part of the "agree-to-agree" process and are empowered to vote on the actual specifications incorporated into the final software specification.

- *session leader*: This user is a participant who has been selected to lead the discussion on a particular subject. Such users must be prepared to provide specific topic issues so that the participants can openly discuss their opinions about what the session leader presents. The session leader may be asked to lead the discussion in a particular direction, or in some instances may have some preliminary work and may advocate a position on what the system should do. In these instances, the session leader may come to the meeting to ask for ratification from his/her peers.

- *observer*: These are users who attend the session to observe what is occurring, or in some cases to answer specific questions that may arise during the course of discussion. Observers are not empowered to talk unless they are asked. IS personnel, executives, and other interested parties typically attend JAD sessions to understand the process and learn from it. A special role exists when an observer serves as a "tiebreaker." In this capacity, the observer can be called upon, either by the facilitator or the session leader, to make a final judgment on a deadlocked issue. While this role is effective in getting decisions made, it can damage the democratic process under which JAD sessions are suppose to operate.

Below is an example of an 11-phase implementation outline for a JAD session with approximately 60 users in 10 different business areas.

Phase I: Define JAD Project Goals

The purpose of these sessions will be to meet with senior management and other key organization people in order to:

- get a clear understanding of the history of the project;
- finalize the scope and time frame requirements of the existing plan;
- understand the current organization and whether political or other constraints exist;
- jointly determine the number and size of the JAD sessions to be held;
- determine the best role of Information Systems in the JAD;
- define which key users and other managers should be interviewed individually prior to the JAD.

Produce a management guide after Phase I. Its purpose will be to define management's purpose, scope and objectives of the project. That is, it communicates management's direction and commitment. The management guide will be approved and issued by upper management to the participating users and information system personnel.

Phase II: Meet with Key Users and Managers

Estimate that you may need to interview about 20 people from key organizations prior to the JAD. These key users and managers should typically represent three levels of the organization. The purpose of these meetings will be to:

- get familiar with the existing systems;
- validate the number of sessions and specific participants needed;
- assess the technical expertise of the participating users;
- determine what specific information can be gathered by the users prior to the JAD sessions;

- gather previous analysis and design materials and documents that may exist and explain user requirements;
- discuss types of agendas and length of sessions;
- focus on specific requirements of certain users.

Schedule interviews to last about 60 to 90 minutes and prepare an agenda that will put the purpose and scope of the interview into perspective.

Phase III: Meet with Information Systems

Get a technical overview of the existing analysis performed and state of all working documents. Gather information on:

- project history;
- potential problems envisioned in implementing the new system;
- proposed hardware to support the new system (if relevant);
- IS representatives to participate in the JAD sessions;
- models and information that can be used in the JAD sessions.

Phase IV: Prepare JAD Approach

Prepare a complete JAD program that will outline recommendations for the number and types of sessions to be held. The JAD approach will also consider the modeling tools to be used and the methods for getting user sign-off. You should focus on the following specific issues:

- the number and type of preparation sessions necessary to get users familiar with the modeling terminology;
- what business processes have already been previously modeled and can be reviewed during the sessions. This is done to avoid discussing processes that users feel have already been defined from previous analysis sessions;
- the number and types of sessions along with specific users in attendance at each session;
- a Work Document of the proposed agendas for each type of session;
- overview of materials to be used such as overheads, flip charts and room requirements;
- proposed format of the user sign-off documents.

You should meet with upper management to review the proposed approach for implementation.

Phase V: Finalize JAD Organization Structure

Assign JAD Facilitators to specific sessions along with information systems support personnel (scribes, etc.). Determine the number of JAD facilitators required. You may need one JAD project leader to take overall responsibility for the entire engagement. A detailed timeline of specific deliverables and reviews should be produced for the entire project, including reports to upper management on the JAD session progress.

Phase VI: Hold Overview Training Sessions

Depending on the results of Phase IV, hold any necessary sessions to get users familiar with the methods that will be used during the JAD. This is typically a one-day course on analysis and includes an overview of modeling lingo and tools such as:

- business area analysis,
- process flow diagrams (data flows),
- entity relational diagrams and normalized data modeling,
- process specifications,
- activity matrices,
- state transition diagrams,
- decomposition models,
- object-oriented techniques,
- prototyping.

Phase VII: Hold JAD Workshop Sessions

Prior to these sessions, participants will be asked to come prepared with certain information they will need to assist in the process. This information may typically include sample forms and reports that they use or need. The workshop sessions will be held with a set time frame and an agenda of items typically including:

- *examine assumptions*: These will be reviewed with the users and opened for discussion. An assumption will either:

  - stay as it is,
  - be revised,
  - become an *open issue* (if consensus cannot be reached).

- *design business processes*: Review the collection of activities relating to the business and the system.
- *define data requirements*: Data are defined to support the business process. Data models are used, developed, and reviewed as necessary.

- *design screens*: The screens will typically use a series of menus or other branching techniques to define how users need to access the various functions. This is usually accomplished by identifying main menu and submenu selections.
- *design reports*: Report names are collected and completed with detailed report descriptions. These normally include

  - report name,
  - description,
  - frequency,
  - number of copies,
  - distribution list,
  - selection criteria,
  - sort criteria,
  - data elements.

- *identify open issues*: These issues are added throughout the sessions. Open issues are those that are not resolved after a period of discussion. These are kept on a separate chart.

Throughout the above processes, the scribe will be tracking minutes of the meeting as well as the open issues and new diagramming requirements.

Phase VIII: Resolve Open Issues

Prior to subsequent sessions, all open issues must be resolved, either by smaller work groups or if necessary by upper management. In any event, it is critical that this is managed by both the facilitator and upper management prior to moving to the next level sessions.

Phase IX: Prepare Materials for Workshop Review Sessions

The facilitator should produce a sign-off level document for review. Process and data models and process specifications will be reviewed and finalized. These sessions can also include prototype screens and reports.

Phase X: Hold Sign-Off Workshops

These workshops will be designed to review the results of the initial JAD sessions. The process and data models will be reviewed. If prototypes are used, the sessions will utilize screen walkthroughs as a method of gaining user acceptance. The exact number of review sessions will depend on the complexity of the system as well as the number of screens and reports to be prototyped.

During these sessions, user acceptance test plans may also be discussed and outlined for eventual submission to the responsible QA organization. This will typically involve a discussion of the minimum acceptance testing to be validated against the product and the mechanism for testing in the field.

Phase XI: Finalize Specification Document

After review sessions are completed, the Facilitator will prepare the final document to be submitted for approval and eventual implementation. If prototypes are used, the screens and reports can be moved into the software development (construction) phase. There should also be post-JAD reviews with the development teams to clarify information supplied in the final system specification document.

JAD is introduced and discussed in this chapter because of its generic inclusion in the user-interface phase of analysis. However, it should be noted that the above outline can be integrated with many of the subjects contained in later chapters of this text. The analyst may, therefore, wish to review this outline again after completing the book in order to determine how the other concepts of analysis can be used in a JAD session.

Problems and Exercises

1. Why is it so critical for the analyst to understand the "culture" of the organization?
2. Management support is a key component of the success of any project. Sometimes management may unfairly dictate the terms and deadlines of projects. Provide examples of different possible management opinions and how analysts can prepare effective responses to them.
3. What are the benefits of obtaining an Organization Chart prior to conducting interviews with users?
4. How does politics affect the role of the analyst and his/her approach to the information-gathering function of the interviews?
5. Why does understanding user skills provide the analyst with an advantage during interviews?
6. Explain how meeting a user in their office or place of work can assist the analyst in developing a better approach prior to the interview.
7. What is the purpose of JAD sessions? How do they compare to individual interviewing? Discuss the advantages and disadvantages of JAD.
8. Define each of the roles necessary for effective JAD sessions.
9. What is the purpose of a Management Guide?
10. Develop a proforma JAD outline for a project of 20 users in 3 business locations.

11. Name and explain what is meant by user categories.
12. How do user levels assist the analyst when preparing for user interviews?

Mini-Project

You have been assigned by your boss to interview Mr. Smith. Mr. Smith runs a department within Human Resources that essentially provides two tasks: (1) assigning employee identification numbers to new employees, and (2) sending applications for individual insurance to the firm's insurance provider.

The following is a list of processes that were learned about Mr. Smith's department procedures. It is dated January 1, 2005:

- The hiring department sends a copy of the hire letter to the department to notify them about a new hire.
- New employees must report to the department on their first day. The employee must bring the original hire letter.
- New employees are validated and asked to fill out a new hire employee form. The form contains the necessary information needed by the department.
- After the form is filled out, employees receive an identification card. Every identification card has a unique ID number.
- The insurance form information (on the new employee) is sent to the insurance company.
- The insurance company must accept all applications.
- The insurance company has 30, 60, or 90 days to respond to an application. The number of days depends on the employee's level.
- The department will follow up on late acceptance verifications.

Insurance confirmations are returned to the department, but the actual insurance package is sent to the individual.

All information on the employee collected by the department is filed in an employee folder.

Mr. Smith has been running this operation manually for over 25 years.

Assignment

Prepare 15 questions that you would ask Mr. Smith during the interview.

4
Overview of Analysis Tools

The Concept of the Logical Equivalent

The primary mission of an analyst or systems designer is to extract the physical requirements of the users and convert them to software. All software can trace its roots to a physical act or a physical requirement. A physical act can be defined as something that occurs in the interaction of people, that is, people create the root requirements of most systems, especially those in business. For example, when Mary tells us that she receives invoices from vendors and pays them thirty days later, she is explaining her physical activities during the process of receiving and paying invoices. When the analyst creates a technical specification which represents Mary's physical requirements, the specification is designed to allow for the translation of her physical needs into an automated environment. We know that software must operate within the confines of a computer, and such systems must function on the basis of logic. The logical solution does not always treat the process using the same procedures employed in the physical world. In other words, the software system implemented to provide the functions which Mary does physically will probably work differently and more efficiently than Mary herself. Software, therefore, can be thought of as a logical equivalent of the physical world. This abstraction, which I call the concept of the *logical equivalent* (LE), is a process that analysts must use to create effective requirements of the needs of a system. The LE can be compared to a schematic of a plan or a diagram of how a technical device works.

Your success in creating a concise and accurate schematic of the software that needs to be developed by a programmer will be directly proportional to how well you master the concept of the Logical Equivalent. Very often requirements are developed by analysts using various methods that do not always contain a basis for consistency, reconciliation and maintenance. There is usually far too much prose used as opposed to specific diagramming standards that are employed by engineers. After all, we are engineering a system through the development of software applications. The most critical step in obtaining the LE is the understanding of the process of Functional Decomposition. Functional Decomposition is the process for finding the most basic parts of a system, like defining all the parts of a car so that it can be built. It would be possible not from looking at a picture of the car, but rather at a schematic of all the functionally decomposed parts. Developing and engineering software is no different.

Below is an example of an analogous process using functional decomposition, with its application to the LE:

In obtaining the physical information from the user, there are a number of modeling tools that can be used. Each tool provides a specific function to derive the LE. The word "derive" has special meaning here. It relates to the process of Long Division, or the process or formula we apply when dividing one number by another. Consider the following example:

```
                256      remainder 4    } Result or Answer
    5  |       1284                     } Problem to Solve
                10
              _____
                284
                 25     } Formula applied to produce result or answer
                 34
                 30
              _____
                  4
```

The above example shows the formula that is applied to a division problem. We call this formula long division. It provides the answer, and if we change any portion of the problem, we simply re-apply the formula and generate a new result. Most important, once we have obtained the answer, the value of the formula steps is only one of documentation. That is, if someone questioned the validity of the result, we could show them the formula to prove that the answer was correct (based on the input).

Now let us apply long division to obtaining the LE via functional decomposition. The following is a result of an interview with Joe, a bookkeeper, about his physical procedure for handling bounced checks.

> Joe the bookkeeper receives bounced checks from the bank. He fills out a Balance Correction Form and forwards it to the Correction Department so that the outstanding balance can be corrected. Joe sends a bounced check letter to the customer requesting a replacement check plus a $15.00 penalty (this is now included as part of the outstanding balance). Bounced checks are never re-deposited.

The appropriate modeling tool to use in this situation is a Data Flow Diagram (DFD). A DFD is a tool that shows how data enters and leaves a particular process. The process we are looking at with Joe is the handling of the bounced check. A DFD has four possible components:

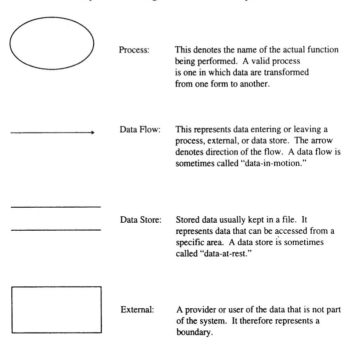

Process: This denotes the name of the actual function
            being performed. A valid process
            is one in which data are transformed
            from one form to another.

Data Flow: This represents data entering or leaving a
            process, external, or data store. The arrow
            denotes direction of the flow. A data flow is
            sometimes called "data-in-motion."

Data Store: Stored data usually kept in a file. It
            represents data that can be accessed from a
            specific area. A data store is sometimes
            called "data-at-rest."

External: A provider or user of the data that is not part
            of the system. It therefore represents a
            boundary.

Now let us draw the LE of Joe's procedure using DFD tools:

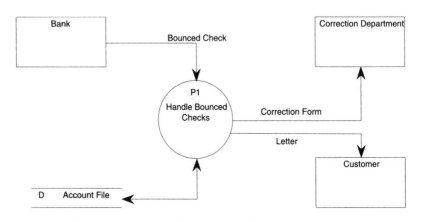

Figure 4.1 Data flow diagram for handling bounced checks.

The above DFD in Figure 4.1 shows that bounced checks arrive from the bank, the Account Master file is updated, the Correction Department is informed and Customers receive a letter. The Bank, Correction Department and Customers are considered "outside" the system and are therefore represented logically as

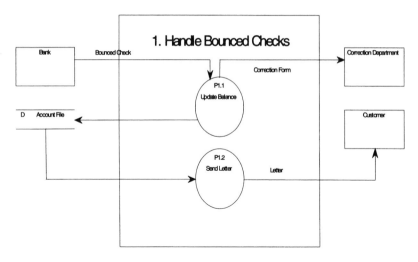

Figure 4.2 Level 2 data flow diagram for handling bounced checks.

Externals. This diagram is considered to be at the first level or "Level 1" of functional decomposition. You will find that all modeling tools employ a method to functionally decompose. DFDs use a method called "Leveling."

The question is whether we have reached the most basic parts of this process or should we level further. Many analysts suggest that a fully decomposed DFD should have only one data flow input and one data flow output. Our diagram currently has many inputs and outputs and therefore it can be leveled further. The result of functionally decomposing to the second level (Level 2) is as shown in Figure 4.2.

Notice that the functional decomposition shows us that Process 1: Handling Bounced Checks is really made up of two sub-processes called 1.1 Update Balance and 1.2 Send Letter. The box surrounding the two processes within the Externals reflects them as components of the previous or parent level. The double sided arrow in Level 1 is now broken down to two separate arrows going in different directions because it is used to connect Processes 1.1 and 1.2. The new level is more functionally decomposed and a better representation of the LE.

Once again we must ask ourselves whether Level 2 can be further decomposed. The answer is yes. Process 1.1 has two outputs to one input. On the other hand, Process 1.2 has one input and one output and is therefore complete. Process 1.2 is said to be at the Functional Primitive, a DFD that cannot be decomposed further. Therefore, only 1.1 will be decomposed.

Let us decompose 1.1 in Figure 4.3 as follows:

Process 1.1 is now broken down into two sub processes: 1.1.1 Update Account Master and 1.1.2 Inform Correction Department. Process 1.1.2 is a Functional Primitive since it has one input and one output. Process 1.1.1 is also considered a Functional Primitive because the "Bounced Check Packet" flow is between the

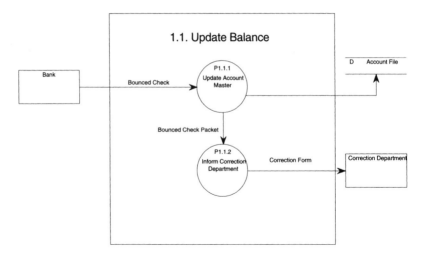

Figure 4.3 Level 3 data flow diagram for handling bounced checks.

two processes and is used to show connectivity only. Functional decomposition is at Level-3 and is now complete.

The result of functional decomposition is the following DFD in Figure 4.4:

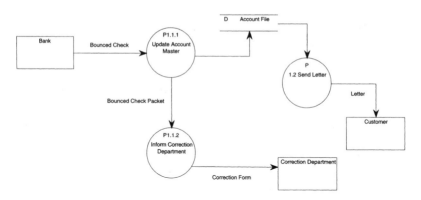

Figure 4.4 Functionally decomposed level-3 data flow diagram for handling bounced checks.

As in long division, only the complete result, represented above, is used as the answer. The preceding steps are formulas that we use to get to the lowest, simplest representation of the logical equivalent. Levels 1, 2 and 3 are used only for documentation of how the final DFD was determined.

The logical equivalent is an excellent method that allows analysts and systems designers to organize information obtained from users and to systematically derive the most fundamental representation of their process. It also alleviates unnecessary pressure to immediately understand the detailed flows and provides documentation of how the final schematic was developed.

Tools of Structured Analysis

Now that we have established the importance and goals of the logical equivalent, we can turn to a discussion of the methods available to assist the analyst. These methods serve as the tools to create the best models in any given situation, and thus the most exact logical equivalent. The tools of the analyst are something like those of a surgeon, who uses only the most appropriate instruments during an operation. It is important to understand that the surgeon is sometimes faced with choices about which surgical instruments to use; particularly with new procedures, there is sometimes disagreement among surgeons about which instruments are the most effective. The choice of tools for analysis and data processing is no different; indeed, it can vary more and be more confusing. The medical profession, like many others, is governed by its own ruling bodies. The American Medical Association and the American College of Physicians and Surgeons, as well as state and federal regulators, represent a source of standards for surgeons. Such a controlling body does not exist in the data processing industry, nor does it appear likely that one will arise in the near future. Thus, the industry has tried to standardize among its own leaders. The result of such efforts has usually been that the most dominant companies and organizations create standards to which others are forced to comply. For example, Microsoft has established itself as an industry leader by virtue of its software domination. Here, Might is Right!

Since there are no real formal standards in the industry, the analysis tools discussed here will be presented on the basis of both their advantages and their shortcomings. It is important then to recognize that no analysis tool (or methodology for that matter) can do the entire job, nor is any perfect at what it does. To determine the appropriate tool, analysts must fully understand the environment, the technical expertise of users and the time constraints imposed on the project. By "environment" we mean the existing system and technology, computer operations, and the logistics—both technically and geographically—of the new system. The treatment of the user interface should remain consistent with the guidelines discussed in Chapter 3.

The problem of time constraints is perhaps the most critical of all. The tools you would ideally like to apply to a project may not fit the time frame allotted. What happens, then, if there is not enough time? The analyst is now faced with selecting a second-choice tool that undoubtedly will not be as effective as the first one would have been. There is also the question of how tools are implemented, that is, can a hybrid of a tool be used when time constraints prevent full implementation of the desired tool?

Making Changes and Modifications

Within the subject of analysis tools is the component of maintenance modeling, or how to apply modeling tools when making changes or enhancements to an existing product. Maintenance modeling falls into two categories:

1. *Pre-Modeled*: where the existing system already has models that can be used to effect the new changes to the software.
2. *Legacy System*: where the existing system has never been modeled; any new modeling will therefore be incorporating analysis tools for the first time.

Pre-Modeled

Simply put, a Pre-Modeled product is already in a structured format. A structured format is one that employs a specific format and methodology such as the data flow diagram.

The most challenging aspects of changing Pre-Modeled tools are:

1. keeping them consistent with their prior versions, and
2. implementing a version control system that provides an audit-trail of the analysis changes and how they differ from the previous versions. Many professionals in the industry call this Version Control; however, care should be taken in specifying whether the version control is used for the maintenance of analysis tools. Unfortunately, Version Control can be used in other contexts, most notably in the tracking of program versions and software documentation. For these cases, special products exist in the market which provide special automated "version control" features. We are not concerned here with these products but rather with the procedures and processes that allow us to incorporate changes without losing the prior analysis documentation. This kind of procedure can be considered consistent with the long division example in which each time the values change, we simply re-apply the formula (methodology) to calculate the new answer. Analysis version control must therefore have the ability to take the modifications made to the software and integrate them with all the existing models as necessary.

Being Consistent

It is difficult to change modeling methods and/or CASE tools in the middle of the life cycle of a software product. One of our main objectives then is to try avoid doing so. How? Of course, the simple answer is to select the right tools and CASE software the first time. However, we all make mistakes, and more importantly, there are new developments in systems architecture that may make a new CASE product attractive. You would be wise to foresee this possibility and prepare for inconsistent tools implementation. The best offense here is to:

- ensure that your CASE product has the ability to transport models through an ASCII file or cut/paste method. Many have interfaces via an "export" function. Here, at least, the analyst can possibly convert the diagrams and data elements to another product.

- keep a set of diagrams and elements that can be used to establish a link going forward, that is, a set of manual information that can be reinput to another tool. This may be accomplished by simply having printed documentation of the diagrams; however, experience has shown that it is difficult to keep such information up to date. Therefore, the analyst should ensure that there is a procedure for printing the most current diagrams and data elements.

Should the organization decide to use different tools, e.g., process-dependency diagrams instead of data flow diagrams, or a different methodology such as crows'-foot method in Entity Relational Diagramming, then the analyst must implement a certain amount of reengineering. This means mapping the new modeling tools to the existing ones to ensure consistency and accuracy. This is no easy task, and it is strongly suggested that you document the diagrams so you can reconcile them.

Version Control

This book is not intended to focus on the generic aspects of version control; however, structured methods must have an audit trail. When a new process is changed, a directory should be created for the previous version. The directory name typically consists of the version and date such as: xyz1.21295, where xyz is the name of the product or program, 1.2 the version and 1295 the version date. In this way previous versions can be easily re-created or viewed. Of course, saving a complete set of each version may not be feasible or may be too expensive (in terms of disk space, etc.). In these situations, it is advisable to back up the previous version in such a manner as to allow for easy restoration. In any case, a process must exist, and it is crucial that there be a procedure to do backups periodically.

Legacy Systems

Legacy systems usually reside on mainframe computers and were developed using 3GL[2] software applications, the most typical being COBOL. Unfortunately, few of these systems were developed using structured tools. Without question, these are the systems most commonly undergoing change today in many organizations. All software is comprised of two fundamental components: processes and data. Processes are the actual logic and algorithms required by the system. Data, on the other hand, represent the information that the processes store and use. The question for the analyst is how to obtain the equivalent processes and

---

[2] 3GL stands for "Third Generation Language." These programming languages belong to a family of design that typically uses compilers to transform a higher-level language into assembly code for the target computer.

data from the legacy system. Short of considering a complete rewrite, there are two basic approaches: the *data approach* and the *process approach.*

The Data Approach

Conversion of legacy systems for purposes of structured changes requires the modeling of the existing programs to allow for the use of analysis tools. The first step in this endeavor is the modeling of the existing files and their related data structures. Many 3GL applications may not exist in a relational or other database format. In either case, it is necessary to collect all of the data elements that exist in the system. To accomplish this, the analyst will typically need a conversion program that will collect the elements and import them into a CASE tool. If the data are stored in a relational or database system, this can be handled through many CASE products via a process known as reverse engineering. Here, the CASE product will allow the analyst to select the incoming database, and the product will then automatically import the data elements. It is important to note that these reverse-engineering features require that the incoming database is SQL (Structured Query Language) compatible. Should the incoming data file be of a non-database format (i.e., a flat file[3]), then a conversion program will need to be used. Once again, most CASE tools will have features that will list the required input data format.

Figure 4.5 is a sample of the reengineering capabilities of the System Architect product by Popkin Software and Systems.

Once the data has been loaded into the CASE product, the various data models can be constructed. This process will be discussed further in Chapter 8.

Although we have shown above a tool for loading the data, the question still remains: How do we find all the data elements? Using COBOL as an example, one could take the following steps:

1. Identify all of the File Description (FD) tables in the COBOL application programs. Should they exist in an external software product like Librarian, the analyst can import the tables from that source. Otherwise the actual file tables will need to be extracted and converted from the COBOL application program source. This procedure is not difficult; it is simply another step that typically requires conversion utilities.

2. Scan all Working Storage Sections (see Figure 4.6) for data elements that are not defined in the File Description Section. This occurs very often when COBOL programmers do not define the actual elements until they are read into a Working Storage Section of the program. This situation, of course, requires further research, but it can be detected by scanning the code.

---

[3] A file consisting of records of a single record type, in which there is no embedded structure information governing relationships between records. Microsoft Press, *Computer Dictionary*, 2nd ed., p. 169.

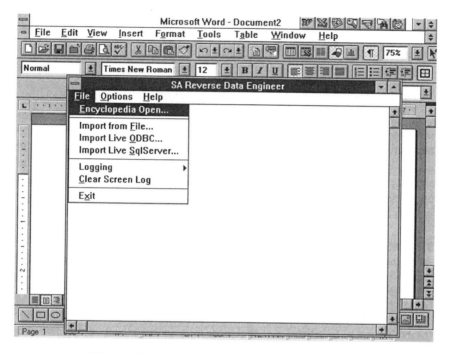

Figure 4.5 Reverse engineering using System Architect.

3. Look for other data elements that have been defined in Working Storage that should be stored as permanent data. Although this can be a difficult task, the worst case scenario would involve the storing of redundant data. Redundant data is discussed further in Chapter 5.

4. Once the candidate elements have been discovered, ensure that appropriate descriptions are added. This process allows the Analyst to actually start defining elements so that decisions can be made during logic data modeling (Chapter 6).

```
WORKING-STORAGE SECTION.
01 PAYROLL-RECORD.
   05      NAME.
           10      INITIAL-1                    PIC X.
           10      LAST-NAME                    PIC X(20).
   05      DATE-OF-HIRE.
           10      MONTH-OF-HIRE   PIC 99.
           10      DAY-OF-HIRE     PIC 99.
           10      YEAR-OF-HIRE    PIC 99.
   05      PAY-NUMBER              PIC 9(6).
```

Figure 4.6 Working Storage Section of a COBOL program.

The Process Approach

The most effective way to model existing programs is the most direct way, that is, the old-fashioned way: start reading and analyzing the code. Although this approach may seem very crude, it is actually tremendously effective and productive. Almost all programming languages contain enough structure to allow for identification of input and output of files and reports. By identifying the data and reports, the analyst can establish a good data flow diagram as shown in Figure 4.7.

The above example shows two File Description (FD) tables defined in a COBOL program. The first table defines the input file layout of a payroll record, and the second is the layout of the output payroll report. This is translated into a DFD as shown in Figure 4.8.

In addition, depending on the program language, many input and output data and reports must be defined in the application code in specific sections of the program. Such is true in COBOL and many other 3GL products. Furthermore,

```
DATA DIVISION.
FILE SECTION.
FD        PAYROLL-FILE
  LABEL RECORDS ARE OMITTED.
01        PAYROLL-RECORD.
  05        I-PAYROLL-NUMBER                    PIC X(5).
  05        I-NAME                              PIC X(20).
  05        I-HOURS-WORKED                      PIC 99V9.
  05        FILLER                              PIC XXX.
  05        I-PAYRATE                           PIC 99V999.
  05        I-DEPENDENTS                        PIC 99.
  05        FILLER                              PIC X(20).


FD        REPORT-FILE
  LABEL RECORDS ARE OMITTED.
01        REPORT-RECORD.
  05        O-PAYROLL-NUMBER                    PIC X(5).
  05        FILLER                              PIC XX.
  05        O-NAME                              PIC X(20).
  05        FILLER                              PIC XX.
  05        O-HOURS-WORKED                      PIC 99.9.
  05        FILLER                              PIC XX.
  05        O-PAYRATE                           PIC 99.999.
  05        FILLER                              PIC XX.
  05        O-DEPENDENTS                        PIC 99.
  05        FILLER                              PIC XX.
  05        O-GROSS-PAY                         PIC 999.99.
  05        FILLER                              PIC XX.
  05        O-TAX                               PIC 999.99.
  05        FILLER                              PIC XX.
  05        O-NET-PAY                           PIC 999.99.
```

Figure 4.7 Input data and report layouts of a COBOL program.

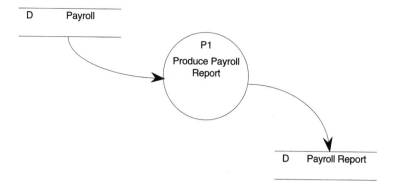

Figure 4.8 Translated COBOL file descriptions into a data flow diagram.

many 4GL products force input and output verbs to be used when databases are manipulated. This is very relevant to any products that use embedded SQL to do input and output. The main point here is that you can produce various utility programs ("quick & dirty," as they call them) to enhance the accuracy and speed of identifying an existing program's input and output processing.

Once the flows in the data flow diagram are complete, the next step is to define the actual program logic, or what is typically called the *process specifications* (discussed later in this chapter). Once again there is no shortcut to save your going through the code program by program. There are some third-party software tools on the market that can provide assistance, but these tend to be very programming-language specific. Although the manual method may seem overwhelming, it can be accomplished successfully and will often provide great long-term benefits. Many companies will bring in part-time college interns and other clerical assistance to get this done. It should be noted that a CASE tool is almost always required to provide a place to document logic. This is especially important if the CASE tool will be used to generate actual program code.

Specification Formats

An ongoing challenge for many IS and software firms is determining what a good specification is. Many books written about analysis tools tend to avoid answering this question directly. When addressing the quality of a process specification, we must ultimately accept the inevitable prognosis that we can no longer be exclusively graphical. Although Yourdon and DeMarco[4] argue that structured

---

[4] Ed Yourdon, *Modern Structured Analysis*, Yourdon Press, and Tom DeMarco, *Structured Analysis and System Specification*, Yourdon Press, focus on the importance of using graphic diagrams wherever possible.

High-Level, Nontechnical Users	Technically Literate Users	Very Technical Users or MIS Personnel
Business specification in prose	Business specification in prose	No need for separate business specification
Do not show programming specification	Show and review programming specification	Incorporate business specification with programming specification

Figure 4.9 Types of process specifications based on user computer literacy.

Client: XYZ Corporation	Date: 9/5/99
Application: Operations Database	Supersedes:
Subject: Contact Management	Author: A. Langer
Process: Overview - Business Spec	Page: 1 of 2

Overview

The contact management process will allow users to add, modify or delete specific contacts. Contacts will be linked to various tables including Company. A contact refers to a person who is related to XYZ for business reasons. It can be a client, a vendor, a consultant, a person involved in a negotiation, etc.

Contact General Information:

The database must allow for the centralization of all the contacts handled by all the departments in XYZ.
The database and screens will be focused on the following information component groupings:

Basic Information
This is the minimum data requirement and includes such elements as Name, Title, Organization, Phone, Fax, Address, Country, etc.

Contact Profile Information
Further qualification and related elements. Relations include:

- department
- type of client
- nature of client (primary, technical)
- interest of prospect
- importance of client
- memberships (FTUG)
- FT employee

This is a business specification that reflects the overall requirements in prose format. Its focus is to provide the user who is not technical with a document that he or she can authorize. This business specification should then point to the detailed programming logic that is shown in Fig. 3.11.

Figure 4.10 Sample Business Specification.

tools need to be graphical, the essence of a specification is in its ability to define the algorithms of the application program itself. It is therefore impossible to avoid writing a form of pseudocode. Pseudocode is essentially a generic representation of how the real code must execute. Ultimately, the analyst must be capable of developing clear and technically correct algorithms. The methods and styles of process specifications are outlined on the following pages. The level of technical complexity of these specifications varies based on a number of issues:

1. the technical competence of the analyst. Ultimately, the analyst must have the ability to write algorithms to be most effective.

2. the complexity of the specification itself. The size and scope of specifications will vary, and as a result so will the organization of the requirements.

3. the type of the specifications required. There are really two levels of specifications: business and programming. The business specification is very prose-oriented and is targeted for review by a non-technical user. Its main purpose is to gain confirmation from the user community prior to investment in the more specific and technical programming

Client: XYZ Company	Date: 9/15/99
Application: Contact Management	Supersedes: 9/5/99
Subject: Program Specification Detail	Author: A. Langer
Spec-ID FTCM01 - Add/Modify Screen Processing	Page: 1 of 1

Process Flow Description:

The user will input information in the top form. At a minimum, at least the Last Name or Contact ID will be entered. The system must check a Security indicator prior to allowing a user to modify a Contact. The Security will be by Department or Everyone. Therefore, if the Modify button is selected and the user is restricted by a different department, Display:

" Access Denied, not eligible to modify, Department Restriction"

If Security authorized, the Add/Modify Button will activate the following business rules:

    If Contact-ID (cntid) not blank
      Find match and replace entered data into record
      If no match display "Invalid Contact-ID" and refresh cursor

  If Contact-ID (cntid) Blank and Last-Name (cntlname) Blank then
    Display " Contact-ID or Last-Name must be entered"
    Place Cursor at Contact-ID (cntid) entry.

> This area actually states the algorithm required by the program. It is in a format called Pseudocode" meaning "false code." This type of logic resembles Cobol format. (see Chapter 4)

If Contact-ID (cntid) Blank and Last-Name (cntlname) + First-Name (cntfname) is Duplicate
Display Window to show matches so that user can determine if contact already in system
If user selects the Add Anyway button
    assume new contact with same name and assign new Contact-ID (cntid)
  else
      upon selection bring in existing data and close window.
Else
  Create new record with all new information fields and assign Contact-ID (cntid)

If Company button activated
  Prompt user for Company-ID (cmpcd) and/or Company-Name (cmpna)
  If duplicate
    link foreign-key pointer to matched company
  else
    add Company-Name (cntcmpna) to Contact Table only
    Display "You must use Company Screen to Link, Company Master File Not Updated"

Figure 4.11 Sample Programming Specification.

specification. The programming specification, on the other hand, needs to contain the technical definition of the algorithms and is targeted for technical designers and programmers.

4. the competence of the programming staff as well as the confidence that the analyst has in that staff. The size and capabilities of the programming resources will usually be directly proportional to the emphasis that the analyst will need to place on the specifics and quality needed for a process specification.

Although the alternative techniques for developing a Process Specification are further discussed in Chapters 5 and 14, the chart below should put into perspective the approach to deciding the best format and style of communication. It is important to understand that overlooking the process specification and its significance to the success of the project can have catastrophic effects on the entire development effort. Figure 4.9 reflects the type of specification suggested based on the technical skills of the users:

Figures 4.10 and 4.11 are sample business and programming specifications, respectively, that depict the flow from a user specification to the detailed program logic.

Problems and Exercises

1. Describe the concept of the logical equivalent as it relates to defining the requirements of a system.
2. What is the purpose of functional decomposition? How is the leveling of a DFD consistent with this concept?
3. How does Long Division depict the procedures of decomposition ? Explain.
4. What is a legacy system ?
5. Processes and data represent the two components of any software application. Explain the alternative approaches to obtaining process and data information from a legacy system.
6. What is reverse engineering? How can it be used to build a new system?
7. Why is analysis version control important?
8. Explain the procedures for developing a DFD from an existing program.
9. What is the purpose of a process specification? Explain.
10. Outline the differences between a business specification and a programming specification. What is their relationship, if any?

5
Process-Based Tools

Data Flow Diagrams

Chapter 4 discussed the concept of the logical equivalent, justifying and defining it by showing a functional decomposition example using data flow diagrams (DFD). In this section, we will expand upon the capabilities of the DFD by explaining its purpose, advantages and disadvantages (described later as the Good, the Bad and the Ugly) and most important: how to draw and use it.

Purpose

Yourdon's original concept of the DFD was that it was a way to represent a process graphically. A process can be defined as a vehicle that changes or transforms data. The DFD therefore becomes a method of showing users strictly from a logical perspective how data travels through their function and is transformed. The DFD should be used in lieu of a descriptive prose representation of a user's process. Indeed, many analysts are familiar with the frustrations of the meeting where users attend to provide feedback on a specification prepared in prose. These specifications are often long descriptions of the processes. We ask users to review it, but most will not have had the chance to do so before the meeting, and those who have, may not recollect all the issues. The result? Users and analysts are not in a position to properly address the needs of the system, and the meeting is less productive than planned. This typically leads to more meetings and delays. More important, the analyst has never provided an environment in which the user can be walked through the processes. Conventional wisdom says that people remember 100% of what they see, but only 50% of what they read. The graphical representation of the DFD can provide users with an easily understood view of the system.[5]

The DFD also establishes the boundary of a process. This is accomplished with two symbols: the terminator (external) and the data store. As we will see, both represent data that originate or end at a particular point.

---

[5] Ed Yourdon, *Modern Structured Analysis*, pp. 134–35.

The DFD also serves as the first step toward the design of the system blueprint. What do we mean by a *blueprint*? Let us consider the steps taken to build a house. The first step is to contact a professional who knows how to do design. We call this individual an *architect*. The architect is responsible for listening to the homebuilder and drawing a conceptual view of the house that the homebuilder wants. The result is typically two drawings. The first is a prototype drawing of the house, representing how the house will appear to the homebuilder. The second is the blueprint, which represents the engineering requirements. Although the homebuilder may look at the blueprint, it is meant primarily for the builder or contractor who will actually construct the house. What has the architect accomplished? The homebuilder has a view of the house to verify the design, and the builder has the specifications for construction.

Let us now translate this process to that of designing software. In this scenario, the analyst is the architect and the user is the homebuyer. The meeting between the architect and the homebuyer translates into the requirements session, which will render two types of output: a business requirements outline and prototype of the way the system will function, and a schematic represented by modeling tools for programmers. The former represents the picture of the house and the latter the blueprint for the builder. Designing and building systems, then, is no different conceptually from building a house. The DFD is one of the first—if not *the* first—tools that the analyst will use for drawing graphical representations of the user's requirements. It is typically used very early in the design process when the user requirements are not clearly and logically defined.

Figures 5.1 and 5.2 show the similarities between the functions of an architect and those of an analyst.

Designing the House

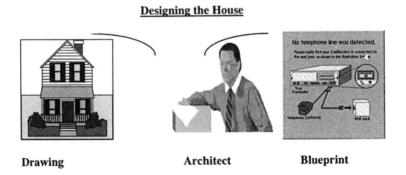

Drawing   Architect   Blueprint

Figure 5.1 The interfaces required to design and build a house.

Designing the System

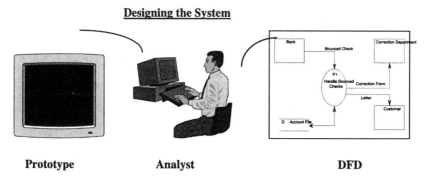

| Prototype | Analyst | DFD |

Figure 5.2 The interfaces required to design and build a system.

How do we begin to construct the DFD for a given process? The following five steps serve as a guideline:

1. Draw a bubble to represent the process you are about to define.
2. Ask yourself what thing(s) initiate the process: what is coming in? You will find it advantageous to be consistent in where you show process inputs. Try to model them to the left of the process. You will later be able to immediately define your process inputs when looking back at your DFD, especially when using them for system enhancements.
3. Determine the process outputs, or what things are coming out, and model them to the right of the process as best you can.
4. Establish all files, forms or other components that the process needs to complete its transformation. These are usually data stores that are utilized during processing. Model these items either above or below the process
5. Name and number the process by its result. For example, if a process produces invoices, label it "Create Invoices." If the process accomplishes more than one event, label it by using the "and" conjunction. This method will allow you to determine whether the process is a functional primitive. Ultimately, the name of the process should be one that most closely associates the DFD with what the user does. Therefore, name it what the user calls it! The number of the process simply allows the analyst to identify it to the system and most important to establish the link to its children levels during functional decomposition.

Let us now apply this procedure to the example below:

> Vendors send Mary invoices for payment. Mary stamps on the invoice the date received and matches the invoice with the original purchase order request. Invoices are placed in the Accounts Payable folder. Invoices that exceed thirty days are paid by check in two-week intervals.

Step 1: Draw the bubble (Figure 5.3)

Figure 5.3 A process bubble.

Step 2: Determine the inputs

In this example we are receiving an invoice from a Vendor. The Vendor is considered a Terminator since it is a boundary of the input and the user cannot control when and how the invoice will arrive. The invoice itself is represented as a data flow coming from the Vendor terminator into the process as shown in Figure 5.4:

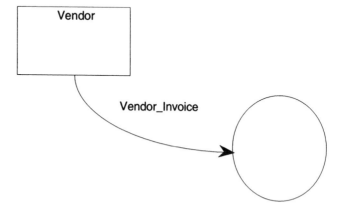

Figure 5.4 Terminator sending invoice to the process.

Step 3: Determine the outputs of the process

In this case the result of the process is that the Vendor receives a check for payment as shown in Figure 5.5:

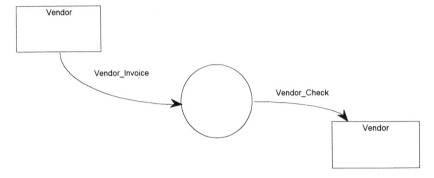

Figure 5.5 DFD with output of check sent to vendor.

Step 4: Determine the "processing" items required to complete the process

In this example, the user needs to:

- match the invoice to the original purchase order;
- create a new account payable for the invoice in a file; and
- eventually retrieve the invoice from the Accounts Payable file for payment.

Note that in Figure 5.6 the Purchase Order file is accessed for input (or retrieval) and therefore is modeled with the arrow coming into the process. The Accounts Payable file, on the other hand, shows a two-sided arrow because entries are created (inserted) and retrieved (read). In addition, arrows to and from data stores may or may not contain data flow names. For reasons that will be explained later in the chapter, the inclusion of such names is not recommended.

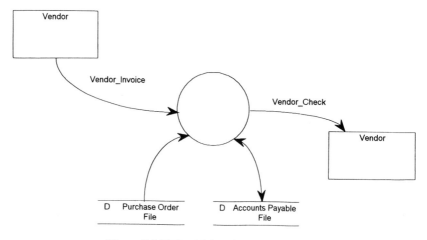

Figure 5.6 DFD with interfacing data stores.

Step 5: Name and number the process based on its output or its user definition.

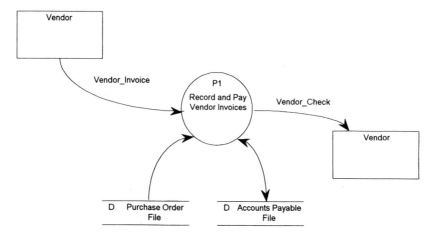

Figure 5.7 Final named DFD.

The process in Figure 5.7 is now a complete DFD that describes the event of the user. You may notice that the procedures for stamping the invoice with the receipt date and the specifics of retrieving purchase orders and accounts payable information are not explained. These other components will be defined using other modeling tools. Once again, the DFD reflects only data flow and boundary information of a process.

The DFD in Figure 5.7 can be leveled further to its functional primitive. The conjunction in the name of the process can sometimes help analysts to discover that there is actually more than one process within the event they are modeling. Based on the procedure outlined in Chapter 4, the event really consists of two processes: Recording Vendor Invoices and Paying Vendor Invoices. Therefore, P1 can be leveled as shown in Figure 5.8.

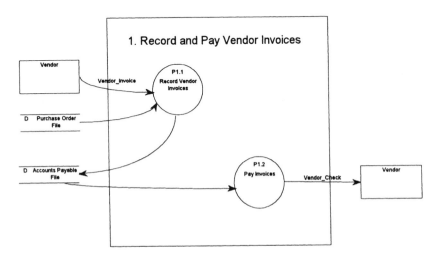

Figure 5.8 Leveled DFD for Record and Pay Invoices process.

Advantages of the DFD

Many opponents of the DFD argue that this procedure takes too long. You must ask yourself: What's the alternative? The DFD offers the analyst several distinct advantages. Most fundamentally, it depicts flow and boundary. The essence of knowing boundary is first to understand the extent of the process prior to beginning to define something that may not be complete or accurate. The concept is typically known as *top-down*, but the effort can also be conceived as step-by-step. The analyst must first understand the boundary and flows prior to doing anything else. The steps following this will procedurally gather more detailed information until the specification is complete.

Another important aspect of the DFD is that it represents a graphical display of the process and is therefore a usable document that can be shown to both users and programmers, serving the former as a process verification and the latter as the schematic (blueprint) of the system from a technical perspective. It can be used in JAD sessions and as part of the business specification documentation. Most important, it can be used for maintaining and enhancing a process.

Disadvantages of the DFD

The biggest drawback of the DFD is that it simply takes a long time to create: so long that the analyst may not receive support from management to complete it. This can be especially true when there is a lot of leveling to be performed. Therefore, many firms shy away from the DFD on the basis that it is not practical. The other disadvantage of the DFD is that it does not model time-dependent behavior well, that is, the DFD is based on very finite processes that typically have a very definable start and finish. This, of course, is not true of all processes, especially those that are event driven. *Event-driven systems* will be treated more thoroughly when we discuss State Transition Diagrams later in this chapter.

The best solution to the time-consuming leveling dilemma is to avoid it as much as possible. That is, you should avoid starting at too high a summary level and try to get to the functional primitive as soon as you can. If in our example, for instance, the analyst had initially seen that the DFD had two processes instead of one, then the parent process could have been eliminated altogether. This would have resulted in an initial functional primitive DFD at Level 1. The only way to achieve this efficiency on a consistent basis is through practice. Practice will eventually result in the development of your own analysis style or approach. The one-in, one-out principle of the logical equivalent is an excellent way of setting up each process. Using this method, every event description that satisfies one-in, one-out will become a separate functional primitive process. Using this procedure virtually eliminates leveling. Sometimes users will request to see a summary-level DFD. In these cases the functional primitives can be easily combined or "leveled-up."

Process Flow Diagrams

While the data flow diagram provides the analyst with the LE of a process, it does not depict the sequential steps of the process, which can be an important piece of information in analyzing the completeness of a system. Understanding the sequence of steps is especially important in situations where the information gathered from users is suspect or possibly inaccurate. A process flow diagram (PFD) can reveal processes and steps that may have been missed, because it requires users to go through each phase of their system as it occurs in its actual sequence. Having users go through their process step by step can help them remember details that they might otherwise have overlooked. Therefore, using process flows provides another tool that can test the completeness of the interview and LE.

Because of this advantage of the PFD, many methodologies, such as the James Martin technique,[6] suggest that analysts should always use PFDs instead of DFDs. However, it is my opinion that these two models not only can coexist but may actually complement each other. This section will focus on how a process model is implemented and balanced against a DFD.

What Is a PFD?

PFDs were derived originally from flowcharts. Flowcharts, however, while they are still valuable for certain diagramming tasks, are too clumsy and detailed to be an effective and structured modeling tool. The PFD represents a more streamlined and flexible version of a flowchart. Like a DFD, the PFD suggested here contains processes, externals, and data flows. However, PFDs focus on how externals, flows, and processes occur in relation to sequence and time, while DFDs focus only on the net inputs and outputs of flows and the disposition of data at rest.

The diagram on the following page is an example of a process flow.

---

[6] The James Martin technique is a methodology that replaces data flow with process flows as its vehicle to depict events as opposed to Yourdon's method of data flow diagrams.

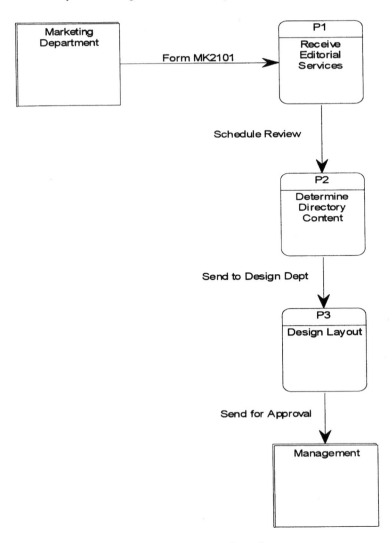

Figure 5.9 Sample process flow diagram.

The above figure shows how a PFD depicts flows from one task to another. As with a DFD, externals are shown by a rectangle. Flows are labeled and represent information in transition. Unlike DFDs, process flows do not necessarily require labeling of the flow arrows, and the processes themselves reflect descriptively what the step in the system is attempting to accomplish, as opposed to necessarily defining an algorithm.

Perhaps the most significant difference between a DFD and a process flow is in its integration as a structured tool within the data repository. For example, a labeled data flow from a DFD must create an entry into the data dictionary or repository. Flow arrows from PFDs do not. Furthermore, a functional primitive data flow points to a process specification; no such requirement exists in a process flow. Figure 5.10 represents a DFD depiction of the same process shown in Figure 5.9 above.

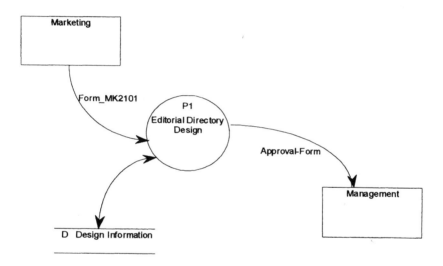

Figure 5.10 PFD in DFD format.

Note that the PFD and the DFD share the same boundaries of externals (i.e., Marketing and Management). The DFD flows, however, must be defined in the data dictionary or repository and therefore contain integrated formulas. The other notable difference lies in the interface of the data store "Design Information," which will eventually be defined as an entity and decomposed using logic data modeling techniques.

What are the relative benefits of using a PFD and a DFD? The answer lies in the correspondence between the process rectangle and the DFD process bubble. Process rectangles actually represent sequential steps within the DFD. They can be compared to an IF statement in pseudocode or a simple statement to produce a report or write information to a file. The PFD, in a sense, can provide a visual depiction of how the process specification needs to be detailed. One functional primitive DFD can thus be related to many process rectangles.

Based on the above analysis, therefore, a PFD can be justified as a tool in support of validating process specifications from within a DFD. In addition, the PFD might reveal a missing link in logic that could result in the creation of a new DFD. Based on this argument, the process flow can be balanced against a DFD and its functional primitives. Finally, the PFD has the potential to provide a graphic display of certain levels of logic code. The corresponding PFD for the DFD shown in Figure 5.8 is illustrated in Figure 5.11.

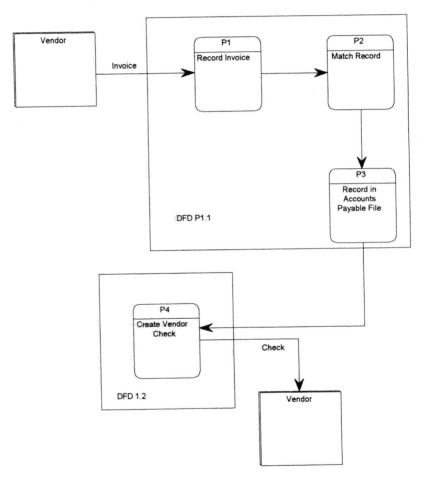

Figure 5.11 PFD and DFD cross-referenced.

Sequence of Implementation

If both a DFD and a PFD are to be created, which should be done first? While the decision can be left to the preference of the analyst, it is often sensible to start with the DFD. A DFD can be created very efficiently, and it is useful to be able to compare the DFD children against the sequential flow of the PFD. Creating the DFD first also supports the concept of decomposition, since the PFD will inevitably relate to the process specification of a functional primitive DFD. While this approach seems to be easier in most cases, there is also justification for creating a PFD first, especially if an overview flow diagram provides a means of scoping the boundaries of an engineering process.

Data Dictionary

The data dictionary (DD) is quite simply a dictionary that defines data. We have seen that the data flow diagram represents a picture of how information flows to and from a process. As we pick up data elements during the modeling design, we effectively "throw" them into the data dictionary. Remember, all systems are comprised of two components: Data and Processes. The DD represents the data portion.

There is a generic format followed by analysts, called DD notation. The conventional notations are listed below:

=	Equivalence
+	Concatenation
[ ]	Either/Or Boundary
/	Either/Or separator
( )	Optional
{ }	Iterations of
**	Comment

Equivalence (=):

The notion of equivalence does not express mathematical equality but rather indicates that the values on the right side of the equal sign represent all the possible components of the element on the left.

Concatenation (+):

This should not be confused with or compared to "plus"; it is rather the joining of two or more components. For example: Last_Name + First_Name means that these two data elements are being pieced together sequentially.

Either/Or with Option Separator ([/]):

Means "one of the following" and therefore represents a finite list of possible values. An example would include the definition of Country = [USA/Canada/United Kingdom/etc.].

Optional ():

The value is not required in the definition. A very common example is middle initial: Name = Last_Name + First_Name + (Middle_Init).

Iterations of { }:

The value between the separators occurs a specific or infinite number of times. Examples include:

1{ X }5	The element "X" occurs from one to five times
1{ X }	The element "X" occurs from one to infinity
3{ X }3	The element "X" must occur three times.

Comments (**)

Comments are used to describe the element or point the definition to the appropriate process specification should the data element not be definable in the DD. We will explain this case later in this section.

Now that we have defined the components of the DD, it is important to expand on its interface with other modeling tools, especially the DFD. If we recall the example used earlier to describe drawing a DFD, the input data flow was labeled "Vendor_Invoice" (see Figure 5.4). The first DD rule to establish is that all labeled data flow names must be defined in the DD. Therefore, the DFD interfaces with the DD by establishing data element definitions from its labeled flows. To define Vendor_Invoice, we look at the physical invoices and ascertain from the user the information the system requires. It might typically be defined as follows:

Vendor_Invoice = Vendor_Invoice + Invoice_Number + Vendor_Invoice_Date+
        Vendor_Invoice_Name + Vendor_Invoice_Address_Line_1 +
        Vendor_Invoice_Address_Line_2 +
        Vendor_Invoice_Address_Line_3 + Vendor_State + Vendor_City +
        Vendor_Zip_Code + Vendor_Salesperson + PO_Number +
        Vendor_Date_Shipped + Vendor_Shipped_Via +
        Vendor_Required_Date + Vendor_Terms + 1 {Item-Quantity +
        Item_Description + Item_Unit_Price + Item_Amount} + Subtotal
        Sales_Tax + Shipping/Handling + Invoice_Total_Due

The above example illustrates what a vendor invoice would usually contain and what is needed to be captured by the system. Note that Vendor_Invoice is made up of component data elements that in turn need to be defined in the DD. In addition, there is a repeating group of elements { Item-Quantity + Item_Description + Item_Unit_Price + Item_Amount } that represents each line item that is a component of the total invoice. Since there is no limit to the number of items that could make up one invoice, the upper limit of the iterations clause is left blank and therefore represents infinity. Figure 4.12 is a sample of how the physical invoice would appear.

It should be noted that many of the DD names have a qualifier of "Vendor" before the field name. This is done to ensure uniqueness in the DD as well as to document where the data element emanated from the DFD. To ensure that all data elements have been captured into the DD, we again apply functional decomposition, only this time we are searching for the functional primitive of the DD entry. We will call this functionally decomposed data element an Elementary Data Element. An Elementary Data Element is therefore an element that cannot be broken down any further. Let us functionally decompose Vendor_Invoice by looking to the right of the definition and picking up the data elements that have not already been defined in the DD. These elements are:

Vendor_Invoice_Number	=	1 { Numeric } 5
Vendor_Invoice_Date	=	8 { Numeric }8
Vendor_Invoice_Name	=	1 { Alphanumeric } 35
Vendor_Invoice_Address_Line_1	=	1 { Alphanumeric } 25
Vendor_Invoice_Address_Line_1	=	1 { Alphanumeric } 25
Vendor_Invoice_Address_Line_1	=	1 { Alphanumeric } 25
Vendor_State	=	** All States in USA, Self Defining
Vendor_City	=	1 { Alphanumeric } 30
Vendor_Zip	=	5 { Numeric } 5 + (4 {Numeric} 4)
Vendor_Salesperson	=	1 { Alphanumeric } 20
PO_Number	=	4 { Alphanumeric } 4
Vendor_Date_Shipped	=	8 { Numeric } 8
Vendor_Shipped_Via	=	1 { Alphanumeric } 10
Vendor_Required_Date	=	8 { Numeric } 8
Vendor_Terms	=	1 { Numeric } 3
Item_Quantity	=	1 { Numeric } 3
Item_Description	=	1 { Alphanumeric } 30
Item_Unit_Price	=	** Dollars Self-Defining
Item_Amount	=	** See Process Spec xxx
Subtotal	=	** See Process Spec yyy
Sales_Tax	=	1 { Numeric } 3 ** Assumed Percentage
Shipping/Handling	=	** Dollars Self-Defining
Invoice_Total_Due	=	** See Process Spec zzz

The following rules and notations apply:

1. A *self-defining definition* is allowed if the data definition is obvious to the firm or if it is defined in some general documentation (e.g., Standards

and Reference Manual). In the case of Vendor_State, an alternative would be: Vendor_State = [AL/NY/NJ/CA. . ., etc.] for each state value.

2. Data elements that are derived as a result of a calculation cannot be defined in the DD but rather point to a process specification where they can be properly identified. This also provides consistency in that all calculations and algorithms can be found in the Process Specification section.

3. Typically values such as Numeric, Alphanumeric, and Alphabetic do not require further breakdown unless the firm allows for special characters. In that case, having the exact values defined is appropriate.

4. An *iteration definition*, where the minimum and maximum limit are the same (e.g., 8 { Numeric } 8), means that the data element is fixed (that is, must be 8 characters in length).

The significance of this example is that the DD itself, through a form of functional decomposition, creates new entries into the DD while finding the elementary data element. A good rule to follow is that any data element used in defining another data element must also be defined in the DD. The DD serves as the center for storing these entries and will eventually provide the data necessary to produce the stored data model. This model will be produced using logic data modeling (discussed in Chapter 6).

Precision Products
1456 Emerson St
Parsippany, NJ 07055-1254

INVOICE NO: 12345
DATE: February 25, 1997

To:

A. Langer & Assoc., Inc.
20 Waterview Blvd
Third Floor
Parsippany, NJ 07054

SALESPERSON	P.O. NUMBER	DATE SHIPPED	SHIPPED VIA	REQUIRED DATE	TERMS
John Smith	AC34	9/15/95	UPS	10/5/95	30 days

QUANTITY	DESCRIPTION	UNIT PRICE	AMOUNT
4	Towels	$ 10.00	$ 40.00
3	Shirts	$ 25.00	$ 75.00
			$ 0.00
			$ 0.00
			$ 0.00
			$ 0.00
			$ 0.00
		SUBTOTAL	$ 115.00
		SALES TAX	$ 0.00
		SHIPPING & HANDLING	$ 4.50
		TOTAL DUE	$ 119.50

Figure 5.12 Sample invoice form.

SQL Data Types

Relational database products define data elements using a construct called structured query language (SQL). SQL was originally created by IBM as a standard programming language to query databases. SQL quickly became the de facto standard in the computer industry, and while the generic data types used above are useful in understanding the pure definition of data elements, database analysts use SQL data types to define data elements. The principal SQL data types are as follows:

Alphanumeric or Character Data Elements

These elements can be defined in two ways: (1) as a fixed-length string; or (2) as a variable-length string. The word "string" means that there is a succession of alphanumeric values that are concatenated to form a value. For example, the string "LANGER" is really equivalent to five iterations of different alphanumeric characters that are connected, or concatenated, together. A fixed-length alphanumeric data type is denoted by CHAR(n), where n is the size, or qualifier, of the element. Fixed length means that the size of the data element must always be n. This correlates to the generic definition of n { alphanumeric } n, which states that the lower and upper limits of the iteration are the same. For example, if the data element INVOICE was defined as a fixed-length string of seven characters, its SQL definition is defined as CHAR(7).

Variable alphanumeric fields, on the other hand, relate to strings that can vary in size within a predefined string limit. This means that the size of the string can fall anywhere between one character and its maximum size. The SQL data type definition of a variable-length field is VARCHAR2 (n),[7] where n represents the maximum length of the string. If the data element "LAST_NAME" was defined as having up to 35 characters, its SQL data definition would be VARCHAR2(35). This SQL data definition is equivalent to 1{alphanumeric}35.

Numbers or Numeric Data Elements

These elements can be defined in various ways. Let's first look at the representation of a whole number in SQL. Whole numbers are known mathematically as integers. SQL supports integers using the INTEGER(n) format, where n is the number of digits in the whole number. However, as is so often available with SQL definitions, there is an alternative way of specifying an integer using the NUMBER clause. Thus NUMBER(n) will also store a whole number value up to n positions in length. The equivalent representation using the generic format is n\{number\}n.

Real numbers, or those that contain decimal positions, cannot be defined using the INTEGER clause but can be defined using NUMBER. For example, a number that contains up to 5 whole numbers and 2 decimal places would be defined as NUMBER(7,2). Note that the first digit represents the total size of the field, that is, 5 whole digits plus 2 decimal positions, which equals 7 positions in total. The number "2" after the comma represents the number of decimal places after the integer portion of the number. The second position preceding the comma represents the number of places from the total digits that are assumed to be decimal positions. The word assumption is important here in that it means that

---

[7] There is an SQL data definition called VARCHAR, but most database products use the revised definition of VARCHAR2.

an actual decimal point (.) is not stored in the data type. An alternative notation is NUMERIC. NUMERIC, as opposed to NUMBER, can be used only to define real numbers. However, it uses the same format as the NUMBER datatype to define a real number: NUMERIC (7,2). Depicting real numbers using the generic format is possible but tricky. The generic specification would be (1{number}5) + 2{number}2. Note that the first part of the definition, the whole number portion, is defined within optional brackets. This is done to allow for the situation where the number has only a decimal value, such as ".25."

Special Data Types

SQL offers special notation that makes it easy to depict specialized data definitions, like date and time. Below are just some examples of the common special notation used:

DATE: denotes a valid date by assigning a 4-digit year. This kind of notation is compliant with year-2000 standards. The validity of the value is handled internally by SQL.

TIME: denotes a valid time using the format *hh/mm/ssss*, where *hh* is two digits of the hour; *mm* is two digits of the minute, and *ssss* are four digits of the second. This format can vary by SQL product.

TIMESTAMP: denotes the concatenation of the Date and the Time SQL clauses. The combination of the two values provides a unique specification of the exact time, day, and year that something has occured.

FLOAT: denotes the storage of a value as a floating point number. The format is usually FLOAT (*n*), where *n* represents the size in digits.

The data element list below shows the definitions from Figure 5.12 in both the generic and SQL formats:

Data Element	Generic Format	SQL Format
Vendor_Invoice_Number	1 { Numeric} 5	Number (5)
Vendor_Invoice_Date	8 { Numeric }8	Date
Vendor_Invoice_Name	1 { Alphanumeric } 35	Varchar2 (35)
Vendor_Invoice_Address_Line_1	1 { Alphanumeric } 25	Varchar2 (25)
Vendor_Invoice_Address_Line_2	1 { Alphanumeric } 25	Varchar2 (25)
Vendor_Invoice_Address_Line_3	1 { Alphanumeric } 25	Varchar2 (25)
Vendor_State	** All States in USA, Self Defining	Char (2)[8]
Vendor_City	1 { Alphanumeric } 30	Varchar2 (30)
Vendor_Zip	5 { Numeric } 5 + (4 {Numeric} 4)	Varchar2 (9)[9]
Vendor_Salesperson	1 { Alphanumeric } 20	Varchar2 (20)
PO_Number	4 { Alphanumeric } 4	Char (4)
Vendor_Date_Shipped	8 { Numeric } 8	Date
Vendor_Shipped_Via	1 { Alphanumeric } 10	Varchar2 (10)
Vendor_Required_Date	8 { Numeric } 8	Date
Vendor_Terms	1 { Numeric } 3	Number (3)
Item_Quantity	1 { Numeric } 5	Number (5)
Item_Description	1 { Alphanumeric } 30	Varchar2 (30)

Process Specifications

Many analysts define a *process specification* as everything else about the process not already included in the other modeling tools. Indeed, it must contain the remaining information that normally consists of business rules

---

[8] The contents of the data element would be enforced by using a database constraint. A database constraint is provided by the database product and is used to enforce the contents of a particular data element or attribute.

[9] The contents of a nine-digit ZIP code can be handled in SQL by adding a constraint as explained in Footnote 8, or by breaking the element into two separate parts, or as two data elements.

and application logic. DeMarco suggested that every functional primitive DFD point to a "Minispec" which would contain that process's application logic.[8] We will follow this rule and expand on the importance of writing good application logic. There are, of course, different styles, and few textbooks that explain the importance to the analyst of understanding how these need to be developed and presented. Like other modeling tools, each process specification style has its good, bad and ugly. In Chapter 3, we briefly described reasons for developing good specifications and the challenges that can confront the analyst. In a later chapter, the art of designing and writing both business and technical specifications will be discussed in detail; here we are concerned simply with the acceptable formats that may be used for this purpose.

Pseudocode

The most detailed and regimented process specification is *pseudocode* or structured English. Its format requires the analysts to have a solid understanding of how to write algorithms. The format is very "COBOL-like" and was initially designed as a way of writing functional COBOL programming specifications. The rules governing pseudocode are as follows:

- use the Do While with an Enddo to show iteration;
- use If-Then-Else to show conditions and ensure each If has an End-If;
- be specific about initializing variables and other detail processing requirements.

Pseudocode is designed to give the analyst tremendous control over the design of the code. Take the following example:

> There is a requirement to calculate a 5 % bonus for employees who work on the 1st shift and a 10 % bonus for workers on the 2nd or 3rd shift. Management is interested in a report listing the number of employees who receive a 10 % bonus. The process also produces the bonus checks.

The pseudocode would be

```
Initialize 10 % counter = 0
Open Employee Master File
Do While more records
        If Shift = "1" then
                Bonus = Gross_Pay *.05
Else
        If Shift = "2" or "3" then
```

---

[8] Tom DeMarco, *Structured Analysis and System Specification*, Yourdon Press, pp. 85–86.

```
                        Bonus = Gross_Pay *.10
                        Add 1 to Counter
          Else
                        Error Condition
      Endif
          Endif
Enddo
Print Report of 10 % Bonus Employees
Print Bonus Checks
End
```

The above algorithm gives the analyst great control over how the program should be designed. For example, note that the pseudocode requires that the programmer have an error condition should a situation occur where a record does not contain a 1st, 2nd or 3rd shift employee. This might occur should there be a new shift which was not communicated to the information systems department. Many programmers might have omitted the last "If" check as follows:

```
Initialize 10 % counter = 0
Open Employee Master File
Do While more records
      If Shift = "1" then
                  Bonus = Gross_Pay *.05
      Else
                  Bonus = Gross_Pay *.10
                  Add 1 to Counter
      Endif
Enddo
Print Report of 10 % Bonus Employees
Print Bonus Checks
End
```

The above algorithm simply assumes that if the employee is not on the 1st shift then they must be either a 2nd or 3rd shift employee. Without this being specified by the analyst, the programmer may have omitted this critical logic which could have resulted in a 4th shift worker receiving a 10 % bonus! As mentioned earlier, each style of process specification has its advantages and disadvantages, in other words, the good, the bad, and the ugly.

The Good

The analyst who uses this approach has practically written the program, and thus the programmer will have very little to do with regards to figuring out the logic design.

The Bad

The algorithm is very detailed and could take a long time for the analyst to develop. Many professionals raise an interesting point: do we need analysts to be writing process specifications to this level of detail? In addition, many programmers may be insulted and feel that an analyst does not possess the skill set to design such logic.

The Ugly

The analyst spends the time, the programmers are not supportive, and the logic is incorrect. The result here will be the "*I told you so*" remarks from programmers, and hostilities may grow over time.

Case

Case[9] is another method of communicating application logic. Although the technique does not require as much technical format as pseudocode, it still requires the analyst to provide a detailed structure to the algorithm. Using the same example as in the pseudocode discussion, we can see the differences in format:

```
Case 1st Shift
        Bonus = Gross_Pay * .05
Case 2nd or 3rd Shift
        Bonus = Gross_Pay * .10
        Add 1 to 10 % Bonus Employees
Case Neither 1st, 2nd or 3rd Shift
        Error Routine
EndCase
Print Report of 10 % Bonus Employees
Print Bonus Checks
End
```

The above format provides control, as it still allows the analyst to specify the need for error checking; however, the exact format and order of the logic are more in the hands of the programmer. Let's now see the good, the bad, and the ugly of this approach.

The Good

The analyst has provided a detailed description of the algorithm without having to know the format of logic in programming. Because of this advantage, Case takes less time than pseudocode.

The Bad

Although this may be difficult to imagine, the analyst may miss some of the possible conditions in the algorithm, such as forgetting a shift! This happens because the analyst is just listing conditions as opposed to writing a specification. Without formulating the logic as we did in pseudocode, the likelihood of forgetting or overlooking a condition check is increased.

---

[9] The Case method should not be confused with CASE (computer-aided software engineering) products, software used to automate and implement modeling tools and data repositories.

The Ugly

Case logic can be designed without concern for the sequence of the logic, that is, the actual progression of the logic as opposed to just the possibilities. Thus the logic can become more confusing because it lacks actual progressive structure. As stated previously, the possibility of missing a condition is greater because the analyst is not actually following the progression of the testing of each condition. There is thus a higher risk of the specification being incomplete.

Pre-Post Conditions

Pre-post is based on the belief that analysts should not be responsible for the details of the logic, but rather for the overall highlights of what is needed. Therefore, the pre-post method lacks detail and expects that the programmers will provide the necessary details when developing the application software. The method has two components: Pre-Conditions and Post-Conditions. Pre-conditions represent things that are assumed true or that must exist for the algorithm to work. For example, a pre-condition might specify that the user must input the value of the variable X. On the other hand, the post-condition must define the required outputs as well as the relationships between calculated output values and their mathematical components. Suppose the algorithm calculated an output value called Total_Amount. The post-condition would state that Total_Amount is produced by multiplying Quantity times Price. Below is the pre-post equivalent of the Bonus algorithm:

Pre-Condition 1:
>   Access Employee Master file and where 1st shift = "1"

Post-Condition 1:
>   Bonus is set to Gross_Pay * .05.
>   Produce Bonus check.

Pre-Condition 2:
>   Access Employee Master file and where 2nd shift = "2" or
>   3rd shift ="3"

Post-Condition 2:
>   Bonus is set to Gross_Pay * .10
>   Add 1 to 10 % Bonus count.
>   Produce Bonus check and Report of all employees who receive
>   10 % bonuses.

Pre-Condition 3:
>   Employee records does not contain a shift code equal
>   to "1", "2", or "3"

Post-Condition 3:
>   Error Message for employees without shifts = "1", "2", or "3"

As we can see, this specification does not show how the actual algorithm should be designed or written. It requires the programmer or development team to find these details and implement the appropriate logic to represent them. Therefore, the analyst has no real input into the way the application will be designed or the way it functions.

The Good

The analyst need not have technical knowledge to write an algorithm and need not spend an inordinate amount of time to develop what is deemed a programming responsibility. Therefore, less technically oriented analysts can be involved in specification development.

The Bad

There is no control over the design of the logic, and thus the potential for misunderstandings and errors is much greater. The analyst and the project are much more dependent on the talent of the development staff.

The Ugly

Perhaps we misunderstand the specification. Since the format of pre–post conditions is less specific, there is more room for ambiguity.

Matrix

A *matrix* or *table approach* shows the application logic in tabular form. Each row reflects a result of a condition, with each column representing the components of the condition to be tested. The best way to explain a matrix specification is to show an example (see Figure 5.13).

Bonus Percent	Shift to be tested
5 % Bonus	1st Shift
10% Bonus	2nd Shift
10% Bonus	3rd Shift

Figure 5.13 Sample matrix specification.

Although this is a simple example that uses the same algorithm as the other specification styles, it does show how a matrix can describe the requirements of an application without the use of sentences and pseudocode.

The Good

The analyst can use a matrix to show complex conditions in a tabular format. Many programmers prefer the tabular format because it is organized, easy to read, and often easy to maintain. Very often the matrix resembles the array and table formats used by many programming languages.

The Bad

It is difficult, if not impossible, to show a complete specification in matrices. The example in Figure 5.13 supports this, in that the remaining logic of the bonus application is not shown. Therefore, the analyst must incorporate one of the other specification styles to complete the specification.

The Ugly

Matrices are used to describe complex condition levels, where there are many "If" conditions to be tested. These complex conditions often require much more detailed analysis than shown in a matrix. The problem occurs when the analyst, feeling the matrix may suffice, does not provide enough detail. The result: the programmer may misunderstand conditions during development.

Conclusion

The same question must be asked again: what is a good specification? We will continue to explore this question. In this chapter we have examined the logic alternatives. Which logic method is best? It depends! We have seen from the examples that each method has its advantages and shortcomings. The best approach is to be able to use them all and to select the most appropriate one for the task at hand. To do this effectively means clearly recognizing both where each style provides a benefit for the part of the system you are working with, and who will be doing the development work. The table in Figure 5.14 attempts to put the advantages and shortcomings into perspective.

Pseudocode	Case	Pre–Post	Matrix
Complex and detailed algorithms that need significant clarification.	The application logic is detailed, but it is not necessary to develop the complete flow of the process.	Tremendous level of confidence in development staff to get the necessary application logic detail.	Large number of conditions ("If'statements) with an emphasis on lots of conditions before the answer is reached (i.e., complex "If' statements).
The analyst is also having difficulty with defining the logic.	There is more confidence in the programming staff.	The application logic is very simple and does not need further clarification.	No need for error-checking condition.
Should be used when the analyst is very concerned about the aptitude of the programming staff.	The analyst wants to define all error-handling conditions but not to design them.	Few conditions ("If' statements).	Little application logic that needs to be further explained.
The analyst is very sensitive to error handling.	There are a reasonable number of "If' statements.	No need for or limited error-handling requirements.	

Figure 5.14 Process specification comparisons.

State Transition Diagrams

State transition diagrams (STD) were designed to model events that are time-dependent in behavior. Another definition of the STD is that it models the application alternatives for event-driven activities. An event-driven activity is any activity that depends directly on the behavior of a pre-condition that makes that event either possible or attractive. Before going any further, let's use an example to explain this definition further:

> Mary leaves her office to go home for the day. Mary lives 20 minutes' walking distance from the office. When departing from the office building, she realizes that it is raining very hard. Typically, Mary would walk home; however, due to the rain, she needs to make a decision at that moment about how she will go home. Therefore, an event has occurred during the application of Mary walking home which may change her decision and thus change the execution of this application.

As shown above, we have defined an event that, depending on the conditions during its execution, may have different results. To complete the example, we must examine or define what Mary's alternatives for getting home.

The matrix in Figure 5.15 shows us the alternative activities that Mary can choose. Two of them require a certain amount of money. All of the alternatives have positive and negative potentials that cannot be determined until executed; therefore, the decision to go with an alternative may depend on a calculation of probability. We sometimes call this a calculated risk or our "gut" feeling. Is it not true that Mary will not know whether she will be able to find a taxi until she tries? However, if Mary sees a lot of traffic in the street and not many taxis, she may determine that it is not such a good idea to take a taxi.

Alternative	Pre-Condition	Positive Result	Negative Result
1. Walk Home	None	Mary gets home and does not spend money	Mary gets very wet
2. Take Subway train	Must have $1.50 for Subway	Mary gets home without getting too wet.	Mary spends money and must be careful for her safety when going into the Sub-way
3. Take a Taxi	Must have $15.00 for the Taxi ride	Mary gets home faster and without getting wet.	It's expensive and it may be difficult to find a Taxi. There could also be a lot of traffic, resulting in delays.

Figure 5.15 Mary's event alternatives.

Much of the duplication of the scenario above falls into the study of Artificial Intelligence (AI) software. Therefore, AI modeling may require the use of STDs. The word "state" in STD means that an event must be in a given pre-condition before we can consider moving to another condition. In our example, Mary is in a state called "Going Home From the Office." Walking, taking a train or taking a taxi are alternative ways of getting home. Once Mary is home she has entered into a new state called "Home." We can now derive that walking, taking a train or taking a taxi are conditions that can effect a change in state, in this example leaving the office and getting home. Figure 5.16 shows the STD for going home.

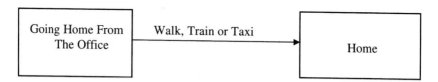

Figure 5.16 State transition diagram for going home.

This STD simply reflects that two states exist and that there is a condition that causes the application to move to the "Home" state. When using STDs, the analyst should:

1.   identify all states that exist in the system (in other words, all possible permutations of events must be defined),

2. ensure that there is at least one condition to enter every state,
3. ensure that there is at least one condition to leave every state.

The reasons for using STD differ greatly from those for a DFD. A DFD should be used when modeling finite, sequential processes that have a definitive beginning and end. We saw this situation in the previous examples in this chapter. The STD, on the other hand, is needed when the system effectively never ends, that is, when it simply moves from one state to another. Therefore, the question is never whether we are at the beginning or end of the process, but rather the current state of the system. Another example, one similar to that used by Yourdon in *Modern Structured Analysis*, is the Bank Teller state diagram shown in Figure 5.17.

Although you may assume that "Enter Valid Card" is the start state, an experienced analyst would know better. At any time, the automated teller is in a particular state of operation (unless it has abnormally terminated). The "Enter Valid Card" state is in the "sleep" state. It will remain in this mode until someone creates the condition to cause a change, which is actually to input a valid card. Notice that every state can be reached and every state can be left. This rule establishes perhaps the most significant difference between the DFD and STD. Therefore, a DFD should be used for finite processes, and an STD should be used when there is ongoing processing, moving from one status to another.

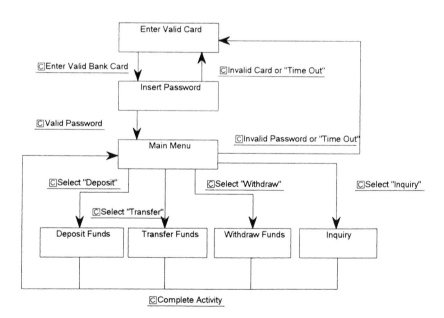

Figure 5.17 Bank Teller state transition diagram.

Let us now show a more complex example which emphasizes how the STD can uncover conditions that are not obvious or were never experienced by the user. Take the matrix of states for a thermostat shown in Figure 5.18.

Current State	Condition to cause a change in State	New State
Furnace Off	Temperature drops below 60 degrees	Furnace On
Furnace On	Temperature exceeds 70 degrees	Furnace Off
Air On	Temperature drops below 65 degrees	Air Off
Air Off	Temperature exceeds 75 degrees	Air On

Figure 5.18 Thermostat states.

Figure 5.19 depicts the STD for the above states and conditions.

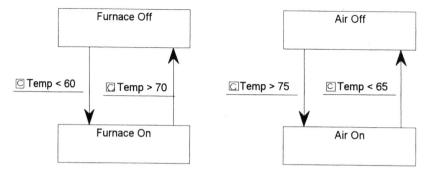

Figure 5.19 State transition diagram based on the user-defined states.

Upon review, we notice that there are really two systems and that they do not interface with each other. Why? Suppose, for example, that the temperature went above 70 and that the system therefore went into the Furnace Off state, but that the temperature nevertheless continued to increase unexpectedly. Users expect that whenever the Furnace Off state is reached, it must be winter. In the event of a winter heat wave, everyone would get very hot. We have therefore discovered that we must have a condition to put the air on even if a heat wave had never occurred before in winter. The same situation exists for the Air Off where we expect the temperature to rise instead of falling. We will thus add two new conditions (see Figure 5.20).

Current State	Condition to cause a change in State	New State
Furnace Off	Temperature exceeds 75 degrees	Air On
Air Off	Temperature drops below 65 degrees	Furnace On

Figure 5.20 Additional possible states of the thermostat.

The STD is then modified to show how the Furnace and Air subsystems interface (see Figure 5.21).

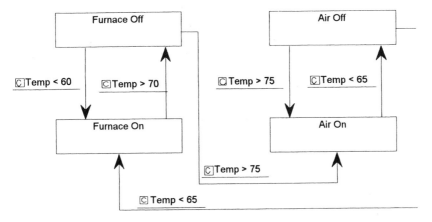

Figure 5.21 Modified state transition diagram based on modified events.

Using STDs to discover missing processes (that would otherwise be omitted or added later) is very important. This advantage is why STDs are considered very effective in Artificial Intelligence and Object Oriented analysis, where the analyst is constantly modeling event-driven, never ending processes. We will see further application of STDs in Chapter 11: Object-Oriented Techniques.

Entity Relational Diagrams

The model that depicts the relationships among the stored data is known as an *entity relational diagram* (ERD). The ERD is the most widely used of all modeling tools and is really the only method to reflect the system's stored data.

An *entity* in database design is an object of interest about which data can be collected. In a retail database application, customers, products, and suppliers might be entities. An entity can subsume a number of attributes: product attributes might be color, size, and price; customer attributes might include name, address, and credit rating.[10]

The first step to understanding an entity is to establish its roots. Since DFDs have been used to model the processes, their data stores (which may represent data files) will act as the initial entities prior to implementing logic data modeling. Logic data modeling and its interface with the DFD will be

---

[10] Microsoft Press, *Computer Dictionary*, 2nd ed, p. 149.

discussed in Chapter 6, thus the scope of this section will be limited to the attributes and functions of the ERD itself.

It is believed, for purposes of data modeling, that an entity can be simply defined as a logical file which will reflect the data elements or fields that are components of each occurrence or record in the entity. The ERD, therefore, shows how multiple entities will interact with each other. We call this interaction the "relationship." In most instances, a relationship between two or more entities can exist only if they have at least one common data element among them. Sometimes we must force a relationship by placing a common data element between entities, just so they can communicate with each other. An ERD typically shows each entity and its connections as shown in Figure 5.22:

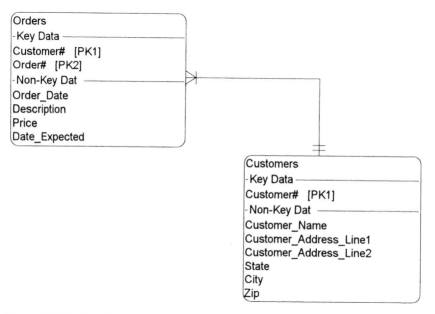

Figure 5.22 Entity relational diagram showing the relationship between the Orders and Customers entities.

The above example shows two entities: Orders and Customers. They have a relationship because both entities contain a common data element called Customer#. Customer# is depicted as "Key Data" in the Customers entity because it must be unique for every occurrence of a customer record. It is notated as "PK1" because it is defined as a Primary Key, meaning that Customer# uniquely identifies a particular customer. In Orders, we see that Customer# is a primary key but it is concatenated with Order#. By *concatenation* we mean that the two elements are combined to form a primary key. Nevertheless, Customer# still has its separate identity. The line that joins the entities is known as the relationship identifier. It is modeled using the "Crow's Foot" method, meaning that the many relationship is shown as a crow's foot, depicted in Figure 5.22 going to the Order entity. The double vertical lines near the Customer entity signify "One and only One." What does this really mean? The proper relationship is stated:

"One and only one customer can have one to many orders."

It means that customers must have placed at least one order, but can also have placed more than one. "One and only One" really indicates that when a Customer is found in the Order entity, the Customer must also exist in the Customer entity. In addition, although a Customer may exist multiple times in the Order entity, it can exist in the Customer master entity only once. This relationship is also know as the association between entities and effectively identifies the common data elements and the constraints associated with their relationship. This kind of relationship between entities can be difficult to grasp, especially without benefit of a practical application. Chapter 6 will provide a step-by-step approach to developing an ERD using the process of logical data modeling.

Problems and Exercises

1. What is a functional primitive?
2. What are the advantages and disadvantages of a data flow diagram? What is meant by "leveling up"?
3. What is a PFD? Describe its relationship to a DFD.
4. What is the purpose of the data dictionary?
5. Define each of the following data dictionary notation symbols: =, +, [], /, (), { }, **
6. What is an elementary data element? How does it compare with a functional primitive?
7. Define the functions of a process specification. How does the process specification interface with the DFD and the DD?
8. Compare the advantages and disadvantages of each of the following process specification formats:

   - Pseudocode
   - Case
   - Pre–Post Condition
   - Matrix

9. What is an event-driven system? How does the Program Manager in Windows applications represent the behavior of an event driven system?
10. When using an STD, what three basic things must be defined?
11. What is an Entity? How does it relate to a Data Store of a DFD?
12. Explain the concept of an Entity Relational Diagram.
13. What establishes a relationship between two entities?
14. Define the term "association."

Mini-Project #1

An application is required that will calculate employee bonuses as follows:

1. There are three (3) working shifts. The bonuses are based on shift:

    - 1st Shift: 5 % bonus
    - 2nd Shift: 10 % bonus
    - 3rd Shift: 10 % bonus

2. The bonus is calculated by multiplying the percentage by the annual gross pay of the employee.
3. The employee records are resident on the employee master file, which resides on a hard disk.
4. Bonus checks are produced for all employees.
5. There is a report produced that lists the number of employees who received a 10 % bonus.

Assignment

Draw the PFD.

Mini-Project #2

You have been asked to automate the Accounts Payable process. During your interviews with users you identify four major events as follows:

I. Purchase Order Flow

1. The Marketing Department sends a purchase order (P.O.) form for books to the Accounts Payable System (APS).
2. APS assigns a P.O. # and sends the P.O.-White copy to the Vendor and files the P.O.-Pink copy in a file cabinet in P.O.#.sequence.

II. Invoice Receipt

1. A vendor sends an invoice for payment for books purchased by APS.
2. APS sends invoice to Marketing Department for authorization.
3. Marketing either returns invoice to APS approved or back to the vendor if not
4. authorized.
5. If the invoice is returned to APS it is matched up against the original P.O.-Pink. The PO and vendor invoice are then combined into a packet and prepared for the voucher process.

III. Voucher Initiation

1. APS receives the packet for vouchering. It begins this process by assigning a voucher number.
2. The Chief Accountant must approve vouchers > $5,000.
3. APS prepares another packet from the approved vouchers. This packet includes the P.O.-Pink, authorized invoice and approved voucher..

IV. Check Preparation

1. Typist receives the approved voucher packet and retrieves a numbered blank
2. check to pay the vendor.
3. Typist types a two-part check (blue,green) using data from the approved voucher and enters invoice number on the check stub.
4. APS files the approved packet with the Check-green in the permanent paid file.
5. The check is either picked up or mailed directly to the vendor.

Assignment

1. Provide the DFDs for the four events. Each event should be shown as a single DFD on a separate piece of paper.
2. Level each event to its functional primitives.
3. Develop the Process Specifications for each functional primitive DFD.
4. Create a PFD.

Mini-Project #3

Based on the mini-project from Chapter 3, the following information was obtained from Mr. Smith during the actual interview:

1. The hiring department forwards a copy of a new hire's employment letter.
2. The copy of the hire letter is manually placed in a pending file, which has a date folder for every day of the month. Therefore, Mr. Smith's department puts the letter in the folder for the actual day the new employee is supposed to report for work.
3. When the employee shows up, he/she must have the original hire letter.
4. The original and copy are matched. If there is no letter in the file, the hiring department is contacted for a copy.
5. The new employee is given a "New Employee Application" form. The form has two sides. The first side requires information about the individual; the second side requests insurance-related information.

6. The employee is given an employee ID card and is sent to work.
7. The application form and letter are filed in the employee master cabinet.
8. A copy of side two of the application form is forwarded to the insurance company. The copy of the form is filed in an insurance pending file, using the same concept for follow-up as the new-hire pending file system.
9. The insurance company sends a confirmation of coverage to the department. At that time, the pending file copy is destroyed.
10. Based on the employee level, insurance applications are followed up with a call to the insurance company.

Assignment

Based on the above facts, create the DFDs that depict the system. Level the DFDs until they are at a functional primitive level.

Mini-Project #4

The following is the information obtained during an interview with the ABC Agency:

People or potential renters call the ABC Agency and ask them if apartments are available for rent. All callers have their information recorded and stored in an information folder. The agency examines the file and determines whether their database has any potential matches on the properties requested. People also call the agency to inform them that they have an apartment for rent. Fifteen days before rent is due, the agency sends invoices to renters. Sixty days before the lease is up, the agency sends a notice for renewal to the renter.

Assignment

1. Draw the DFDs.
2. Level DFDs to functional primitive.
3. Provide process specifications for each functional primitive DFD. Use at least three different process specification "styles."

6
Logic Data Modeling Tools

Logic data modeling is a set of procedures that examines an entity to ensure that its component attributes (data elements) should reside in that entity, rather than being stored in another or new entity. Therefore, LDM focuses solely on the stored data model. The LDM process is somewhat controversial and subject to various opinions; however, listed below are the common steps used by many professionals in the industry:

1. identify major entities
2. select primary and alternate keys
3. determine key business rules
4. apply normalization to 3rd normal form
5. combine user views
6. integrate with existing models (legacy interfaces)
7. determine domains and triggering operations
8. de-normalize carefully

Normalization Defined

Perhaps the most important aspect of logical data modeling is Normalization. Normalization, at a high level, is generally defined as the elimination of redundancies from an entity. Although this is an accurate definition, it does not fully convey the true impact of what normalization is trying to accomplish, and more important, what it means not to apply it to your model.

We can see from the above list that normalization is only one step in the LDM process, albeit the most critical. I have found, however, that there is an advantage to understanding normalization first, before trying to understand the entire LDM process.

Before we explain this any further it is necessary to define the three forms of normalization.[11] These forms are known as 1st normal form, 2nd normal form

---

[11] Although there are 5 published normal forms, most industry leaders have accepted that normal forms 4 and 5 are difficult to implement and typically unnecessary. Therefore, this book omits forms 4 and 5.

and 3rd normal form. Normal form is typically abbreviated "NF." Each normal form should be dependent on the completion of the previous form, therefore, normalization should be applied in order. Below are the rules that satisfy each normal form:

1st NF: No repeating elements or repeating groups
2nd NF: No partial dependencies on a concatenated key
3rd NF: No dependencies on non-key attributes

Normalization Approaches

If DFDs have been completed, all data stores that represent data files become the initial major entities or the first step in the LDM. Therefore, if process models are done first, the selection of major entities is easier. If process models are not used then the analyst must hope that a legacy system exists from which the data can be converted and then tested for compliance with normalization. If no legacy system exists, you will need to examine forms and try to determine what constitutes an entity.[12] The following example assumes that a DFD exists and shows that the process creates a data store called "Orders." This data store represents the storage of all orders sent by customers for the various items that the company sells. Figure 6.1 is a sample of a customer order and the data elements that exist on the form.

We begin this normalization example assuming that steps 1, 2 and 3 of the LDM are complete (Identifying Major Entities, Selecting the Primary and Alternate Keys, and Identifying Key Business Rules, respectively). Our major entity is the data store "Orders" and its Primary Key is "Order#." There are no Alternate Keys (a concept discussed later). The first aspect to point out is that the data store from the DFD becomes an entity in the LDM process (see Figure 6.2).

To show how normalization works, Figure 6.3 depicts the Orders entity with its primary key Order# inside the box. The non-keyed attributes (data elements are often called *attributes* of an entity when performing LDM) are shown as dependent cells. These cells or attributes basically belong to or "depend on" the entity and do not affect the outcome of the normalization process. However, a dependent attribute may become a key attribute as a result of normalization. We will see this in the example shown in Figure 6.3.

The form shows that a repeating body of elements exists in the area of items ordered. That is, many items can be associated with a single order. We call this a repeating group, and it is shown within the box in Figure 6.3. Looking at this entity, we must first ask ourselves: are we in 1st NF? The answer is clearly *no*

---

[12] There are several techniques that analysts have used, but they are beyond the scope of this book.

Precision Products
1456 Emerson St
Parsippany, NJ 07055-1254

ORDER

ORDER NO: 12345
DATE: March 4, 1997

To:

A. Langer & Assoc., Inc.
20 Waterview Blvd
Third Floor
Parsippany, NJ 07054

P.O. NUMBER	DATE SHIPPED	SHIPPED VIA	REQUIRED DATE	TERMS
AC34	9/15/95	UPS	10/5/95	30 days

QUANTITY	ITEM ID	ITEM NAME	UNIT PRICE	AMOUNT
4	31	Towels	$ 10.00	$ 40.00
3	27	Shirts	$ 25.00	$ 75.00
				$ 0.00
				$ 0.00
				$ 0.00
				$ 0.00
				$ 0.00
		SUBTOTAL		$ 115.00
		SALES TAX		$ 0.00
		SHIPPING & HANDLING		$ 4.50
		TOTAL DUE		$ 119.50

Figure 6.1 Sample customer order form.

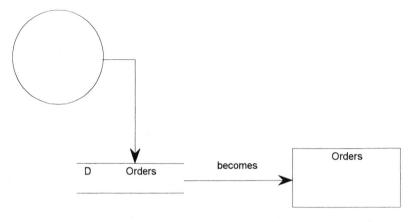

Figure 6.2 This diagram shows the transition of a data store into an entity.

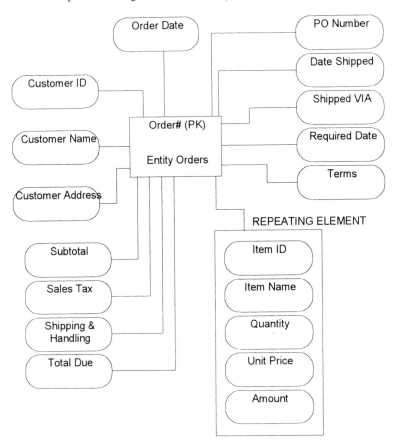

Figure 6.3 The Orders entity and its associated attributes.

because of the existence of a repeating element or group. By showing the box surrounding the repeating body, we are, in effect, exposing the fact that there is a primary key being treated as a non-key attribute. In other words, there really is another entity embedded within the Orders entity. *Whenever a normal form is violated, the solution is to create a new entity.* If it is a 1st NF failure, the new entity will always have a concatenated primary key composed of the primary key from the original entity joined with a new key from the repeating group. This new key must be the attribute in the group that controls the others. All other attributes will be removed from the original entity and become part of the new one, as shown in Figure 6.4.

Figure 6.4 now shows a new entity: Order Items which has a concatenated primary key composed of the Order# from the original entity and the Item ID which is the identifier of each item that is contained within an order. Note that all the non-key (dependent) attributes now become part of the new entity. First NF now allows the system to store as many items associated with an order as

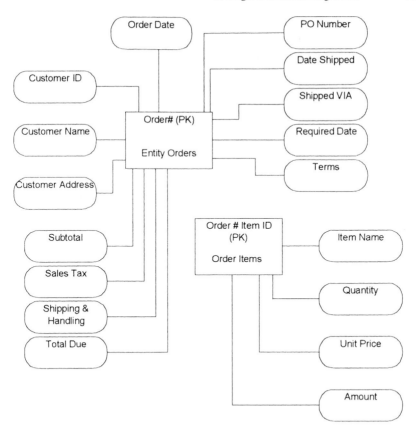

Figure 6.4 This diagram shows the entities in 1st NF.

required. The original file would have required an artificial occurrence to be included in each record. This would result in (1) order records that waste space because the order had fewer items than the maximum, and (2) the need to create a new order if the number of items exceeds the maximum allotted per order in the file.

Our entities are now said to be in 1st NF. Don't rejoice yet—we must now check 2nd NF. Second NF applies only to entities that have concatenated primary keys. Therefore, any entity that is in 1st NF and does *not* have a concatenated primary key must be in 2nd NF, simply by definition. As a result, the Orders entity must be in 2nd NF. The issue becomes the Order Items entity. To check for 2nd NF compliance, the analyst needs to ensure that every non-key attribute is totally dependent on all parts of the concatenated primary key. When we run this test on Item Name, we see that it depends only on the Item ID and has no dependency on Order#. It is, therefore, considered a 2nd NF violation. Once again, a new entity must be created. The primary key of this new entity will always be the key attribute for which elements had a partial dependency. In this case, it is Item ID. All non-key attributes dependent only on Item ID will become part of the new entity, which we will call "Items." Note that non-key attributes "Quantity" and "Amount" stay with the Order Items entity because they are dependent on both the order and item keys. To be clearer, the quantity of an item ordered will be different for each order (or the same by coincidence). The result now is three entities as shown in Figure 6.5.

We are now in 2nd NF. Once again, don't rejoice too early—we must test for 3rd NF. Third NF tests the relationship between non-key attributes to determine if one is dependent on another, that is, if a non-key attribute is dependent on another non-key attribute. If this occurs, then the controlling non-key attribute is really a primary key and should be part of a new entity. If we look at the Order

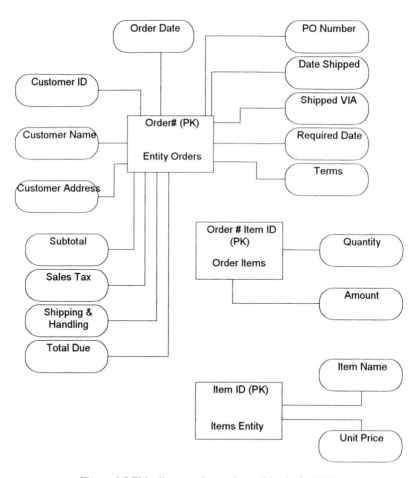

Figure 6.5 This diagram shows the entities in 2nd NF.

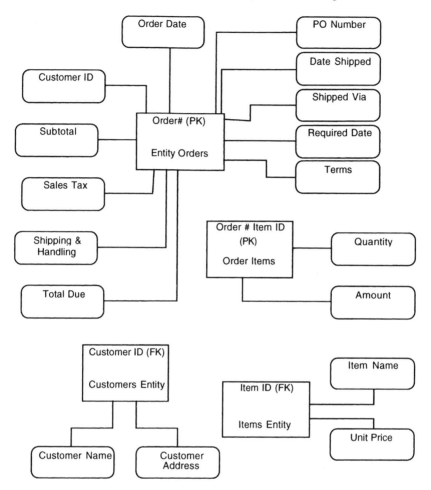

Figure 6.6 This diagram shows the entities in the first phase of 3rd NF.

entity, we will find that both Customer Name and Customer Address[13] are really dependent on the non-key attribute Customer ID. Therefore, it fails 3rd NF, and a new entity is formed with the controlling attribute, now a key. The new entity is Customers (see Figure 6.6).

Note that the Customer ID also remains as a non-key attribute in Orders. All 3rd NF failures require this to happen. The non-key attribute Customer ID is called a *foreign key* and enables the Customer entity and Order entity to have a relationship.

---

[13] Customer Address would normally be comprised of more components, namely more than one address line, city, state, and zip, but it has been left out of this example for the sake of simplicity.

We may ask ourselves if we have now reached 3rd normal form. The answer is still no! Although not intuitively obvious, there are still non-key attributes that are dependent on non-key attributes. These are, however, slightly different from the Customer ID case. For example, if you look at the Order Items entity, there is a non-key attribute called Amount. Amount represents the total of each item included in an order. Amount is a calculation, namely Quantity * Unit Price. Attributes that are calculations are said to be dependent and are known as a *derived* value. One can see that Amount is indirectly dependent on Quantity in the entity Order Items. When non-key attributes are deemed derived and thus redundant because their values can be calculated at any time, they are removed from the entity.[14] The same problem also exists in the entity Orders. Subtotal and Total Due are also derived and therefore must be removed from the logical model. Our 3rd NF LDM is now modified as shown in Figure 6.7.

At this point we believe that 3rd NF has been reached and we should now produce the Entity Relational Diagram (ERD), which will show the relationships (connections) of one entity with others. The ERD is fairly simple to draw, and the analyst should start by putting each entity into the accepted ERD format (see Figure 6.8).

The ERD in Figure 6.8 depicts the relationships of all the entities. Let's see what it tells the analyst:

- The Order entity has a "one and only one to one to many" relationship with the Order Items entity. That is, there must be at least one item associated with an Order, or the order cannot exist.
- The Items entity has a "one and only one to zero to many" relationship with the Order Items entity. The difference between this relationship and the one established with Orders, is that here an Item does not have to be associated with any order. This would be the case for a new item that has not yet been ordered by any customer.
- The Order Items entity has a primary key that is comprised of the concatenation of order# and item_id, which are the primary keys of Order and Items, respectively. The Order Item entity is said to be an "associative" entity, in that it exists as the result of a many-to-many relationship between Order and Items. Specifically, one or many orders could be associated with one or many items. A many-to-many relationship not only violates normalization, but creates significant problems in efficient SQL[15] coding. Therefore, associative entities are

---

[14] Although derived attributes are removed from the logical model during normalization, they may be put back into the entity in the physical model. The physical model is the entity in actual database format. These attributes are put back due to performance problems in physical database products. We call this *de-normalization*, which will be discussed later in the chapter.

[15] SQL stands for Structured Query Language. SQL is the standard query language used in relational database products. SQL was invented by IBM in the early 1980s.

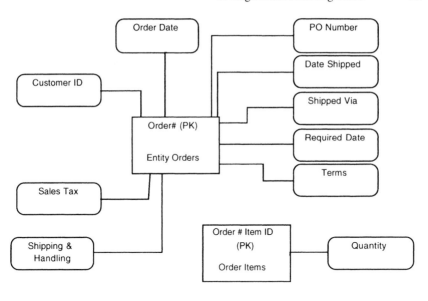

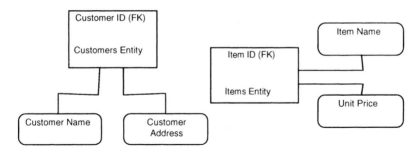

Figure 6.7 This diagram shows the entities in the second phase of 3rd NF.

created to avoid these relationships. First NF failures often result in associative entities. It should also be noted that the primary keys of Order Items are shown with an "(FK)" symbol. This model, which was developed using Popkin's System Architect CASE tools, shows all primary keys that originate in a foreign entity with a "(FK)" notation. Although this is not an industry standard, software products vary in their depiction of derived primary keys.

- Customers has a "one and only one to zero-to-many" relationship with the Order entity. Note that a Customer may not have ever made an order. In addition, this model shows customer_id in the Order entity as a non-key attribute pointing to the primary key of Customers. This is the standard definition of a foreign key pointer.

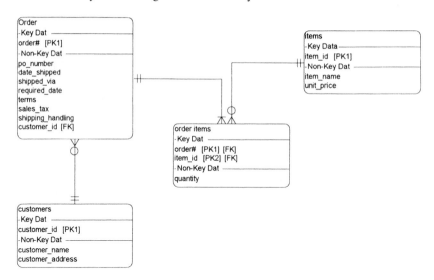

Figure 6.8 The entities in ERD model.

What Normalization Does Not Do

Although we have reached 3rd NF and completed the ERD, there is a problem. The problem is serious and exists in the case of a change in Unit Price. Should the Unit Price change, there is no way to calculate the historical costs of previous order items. Remember that we eliminated Amount because it was a derived element. This poses an interesting problem in that it appears that normalization has a serious flaw—or does it ? Before making this evaluation, let's first determine the solution to this problem. Does replacing Amount in the Item entity solve the problem? Although we could "back into" the old price by dividing the Amount by Quantity, it would not represent a true solution to the problem. Looking closer, we will ultimately determine that the real problem is a missing attribute: Order Item Unit Price or the price at the time of the order. Order Item Unit Price is dependent on both the Order and the Item and is therefore wholly dependent on the entity Order Items. It becomes a non-key attribute of that entity, which means our ERD must be modified. It is important to note that Order Item Unit Price is not a derived element. It is only related to Unit Price from the Item entity at the time of the order[16]; thereafter they are separate elements. Because of this phenomenon, the analyst has actually discovered a new data element during normalization. To be consistent with the rules, this new data element must be added to the ERD and the Data Dictionary (see Figure 6.9).

---

[16] The Order Item Unit Price would retrieve the Unit Price during data entry of the order and would therefore be controlled via the application program that governs the entry of orders.

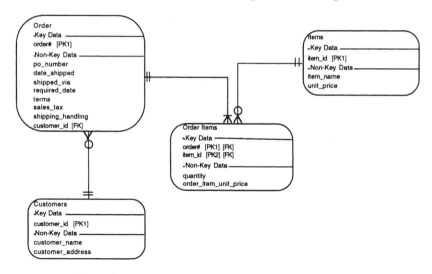

Figure 6.9 ERD with the addition of order_item_unit_price.

The question now is: what does all this mean? To put the above problem and solution into perspective is actually quite simple: normalization will not work completely unless all attributes are included during the process. While normalization itself will not uncover missing elements, the good news is that the normalization process and the ensuing ERD did uncover the problem! If the analyst stands to learn anything from this example, it is that normalization does not ensure that the model is complete nor is it a panacea for the art of data modeling. It is simply another tool that the analyst can use to reach the logical equivalent, albeit a very important one.

The Supertype/Subtype Model

A troublesome database issue occurs in the LDM when there are records within an entity that can take on different characteristics or have many "types" of data elements. By "type" we mean that a portion of the data elements in a specific record can vary depending on the characteristic or identification of the record within that entity. Another way of describing this issue is that a portion of the elements contained within a given record can be different from other records of the same entity depending on the *type* of row it represents, or as it is defined as a "subtype" of the record. A subtype, therefore, is the portion of the record that deviates from the standard or "supertype" part of the record. The "supertype" portion is always the same among all the records in the entity. In other words, the "supertype" represents the global part of the attributes in an entity. A diagram of this phenomenon can best explain this concept in Figure 6.10:

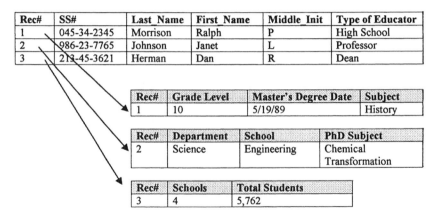

Rec#	SS#	Last_Name	First_Name	Middle_Init	Type of Educator
1	045-34-2345	Morrison	Ralph	P	High School
2	986-23-7765	Johnson	Janet	L	Professor
3	213-45-3621	Herman	Dan	R	Dean

Rec#	Grade Level	Master's Degree Date	Subject
1	10	5/19/89	History

Rec#	Department	School	PhD Subject
2	Science	Engineering	Chemical Transformation

Rec#	Schools	Total Students
3	4	5,762

Figure 6.10 Supertype/subtype relationship.

The significant difference between a subtype and just a type identifier (using a foreign key) is the existence of at least one nonkey attribute that follows just that subtype part of the record. Thus, the main reason to design a supertype/subtype database is the existence of multiple permutations of different elements that exist in just certain types of records. Keeping all the permutations of elements within a record format can be problematic. First, it can waste storage, especially if each subtype has a significant number of unique elements. Second, it can create massive performance issues, particularly as it relates to the querying of data. Using the above example, we show two potential ways to store the data. The first (Figure 6.11) represents a simple solution with all the permutations existing in the record. The "type" of record is identified using a foreign key pointer to an entity called "Educator Type."

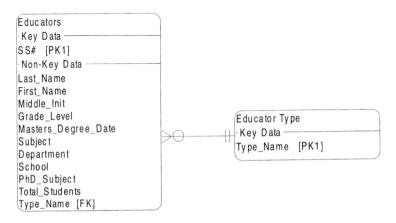

Figure 6.11 Educator ERD using one entity with foreign key identifier.

This solution, while having only one main entity, wastes space because all elements are not used in any one "type" of record. The user must be aware of the meanings of the type identifier and remember which elements exist for each type of educator. This method of logic data modeling violates the concepts of normalization, and entrusts the integrity of values of elements in an entity to either an application program's control, or to the memory of the user. None of these choices are particularly dependable or have proven to be a reliable method of data dependency.

On the other hand, Figure 6.12 provides a different solution using the supertype/subtype construct.

This construct depicts each type of educator as a separate entity, linked via a special notation in the relational model, known as the supertype/subtype relation. The relationship is mutually exclusive, meaning that any global supertype can have only one of the three subtypes for any one supertype occurrence. Thus, the relationship between any row of a supertype must be one-to-one with a subtype. The supertype/subtype model creates a separate subtype entity to carry only its related elements that are unique to its subtype.

There are two major benefits to this alternative structure. First, the construct saves storage, in that only elements that exist in a subtype are stored in each entity. Second, the subtype information can be directly addressed without first accessing its supertype. This is because each permutation subtype entity contains the same primary key as the parent. Having this capability is significant because a user can automatically obtain the unique information from any subtype without having to search the entire database, as would be the case with one entity holding all the elements (as in Figure 6.11). The benefits from this construct are particularly advantageous when the number of rows among the subtypes varies significantly. Suppose, for example, there are 5 million educators in the database.

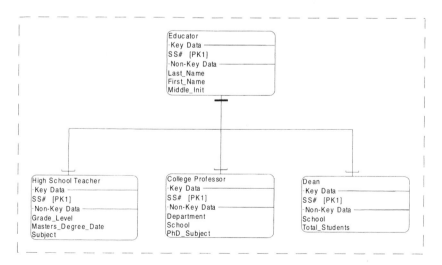

Figure 6.12 Supertype/subtype entity construct.

The Educator database would therefore contain 5 million rows. Four million of the educators are high-school teachers, and as such, the High School subtype entity has 4 million records. Nine hundred thousand educators are professors and the remaining 100,000 educators are deans. Therefore, the Professor database and Dean database have 900,000 and 100,000 records, respectively. In the supertype/subtype configuration applications could access the sample of each type without searching through every record. This improves not only performance, but also access speed, in that each entity is separate and would not interfere with access to the other.

The supertype/subtype construct is not limited to mutual exclusivity; it can support multiple subtype permutations. For example, suppose an educator could be a high-school teacher, college professor, and a dean at the same time, or any combination from among the three types. The model would be modified to show separate one-to-one relationships as opposed to the "T" relationship depicted in Figure 6.13.

Supertype/subtypes can cascade, that is, can continue to occur within the subtypes. Take the following example in Figure 6.14.

The above example reflects how subtypes can continue to cascade. Notice that the same primary key continues to link the one-to-one relationships of the entities. In addition, Figure 6.14 also exposes another interesting aspect of the supertype/subtype model relating to a subtype that has no non-key attributes. Such is the case with the subtype entity *Adjunct Prof*. In this situation, the empty entity serves only to identify the existence of the subtype, but has no other distinct elements that are attributed to its occurrence. The use of *Adjunct Prof*, therefore, was created only because the other two subtypes (*Tenured Prof* and *Contract Prof*) had unique elements and were used as subtypes. This example serves only to show that the supertype/subtype model is not perfectly balanced, and often has components that are necessary due to other factors that benefited the model.

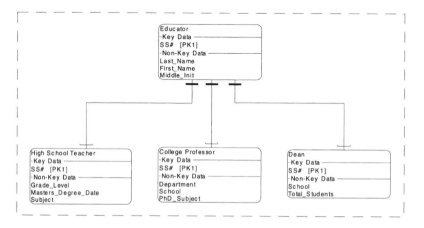

Figure 6.13 Supertype/subtype model without mutual exclusivity.

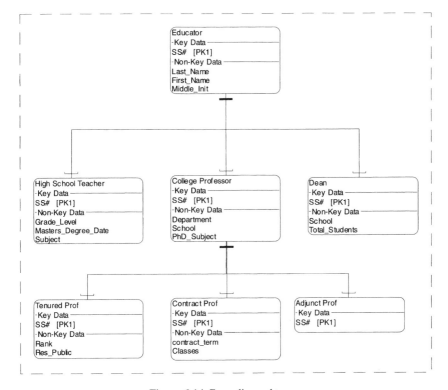

Figure 6.14 Cascading subtypes.

Cascading subtypes do not need to be of the same relationship. In other words, the subtype educator could have been exclusive to a cascade that is mutually exclusive as follows in Figure 6.15.

Note that the example shows the subtype identifier Professor Types is a validation entity in 3rd normal form (see Figure 6.16).

Supertypes and subtypes must also be normalized following the same rules that govern any entity decomposition. For example, the subtype Educator Types contains elements that are not fully normalized. For example, Grade_Level and Subject in the subtype entity High School Teacher can be validated using a look-up table. Department, School, and PhD_Subject can also be validated. The resulting fully normalized ERD is shown below in Figure 6.17.

Combining User Views

Normalization has concentrated our analysis on the challenges of moving and placing attributes in the correct entity. In each of the normalization examples, a violation of an NF has always resulted in the creation of a new entity. However, experienced analysts must deal with combining user views. In many aspects

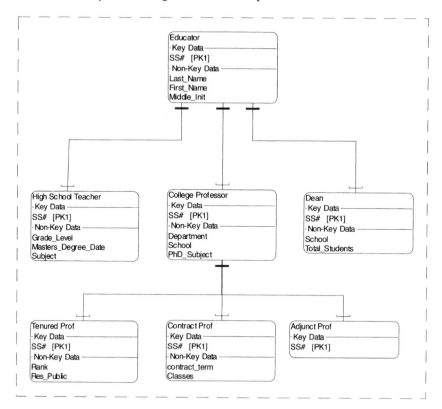

Figure 6.15 Cascading subtypes with alternating exclusivities.

this has the opposite result of normalization in that entities will most likely be combined. Combining or joining entities typically occurs when users have separate views of the same data. A better way to comprehend this concept is to remember the lesson of the logical equivalent. Although this lesson focused on processes, we can try to redirect its point to the stored data model. First we must ask, can data elements that have been physically defined differently really be logically the same (or equivalent)? The answer is yes, and it occurs regularly during the analysis process. Let us now use an example to help illustrate this idea:

> The Analyst met with Charles on the 15th floor. During the interview, a data store called Clients was created. The Clients data store was made up of the following data elements shown in Figure 6.18.

After the meeting, the Analyst then went to the 19th floor and visited with Mary of another department. During this interview a data store called Customers was created with the data elements listed in Figure 6.19.

In reality, these two entities are both part of the same object. Whether the entity name is Client or Customer, these entities must be combined. The difficulty

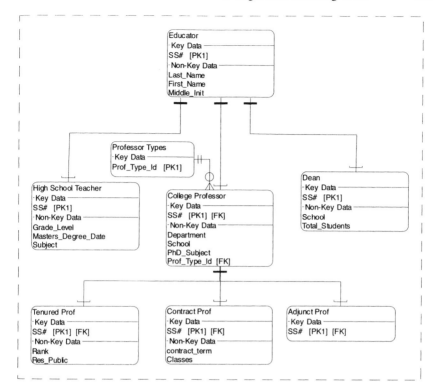

Figure 6.16 Supertype/subtype with subtype identifier element.

here is the combining of the identical elements versus those that need to be added to complete the full view of the entity. Charles and Mary, unbeknownst to each other, had similar but different views of the same thing. Their names for the objects were also different. By applying the concept of the logical equivalent, we determined that only one entity should remain (see Figure 6.20).

Finding that two or more entities are really identifying the same object may be difficult, especially when their names are not as similar as the ones used in the above example. It is therefore even more important that the analyst ensure the logical meaning of entities and their component elements. Note that we chose to call the combined entity "Customers" and added to it the unique elements not already stored. However, combining these user views raises a new and ugly issue: Why Customer, not Client? Charles and his staff may not care about the internal name of the entity, but may find the name Customer used in screens and reports to be unacceptable. What do we do? The answer is to provide what is called an Alias entry into the Data Dictionary. This will allow both names to point to the same element and allow each to be used in different screen programs and reports. The use of an Alias is not new, as it has existed as a feature in many programming languages such as COBOL for years. Its usefulness continues, and both Charles and Mary should remain happy. (But don't tell

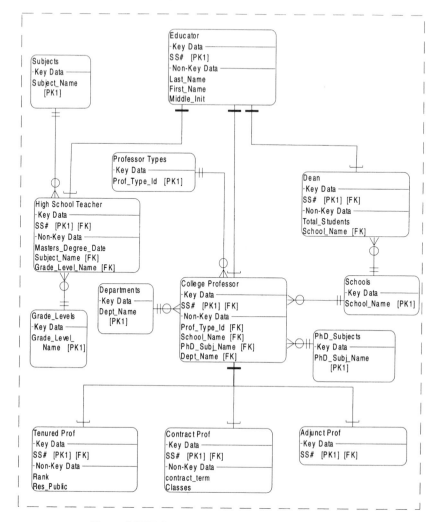

Figure 6.17 Fully normalized supertype/subtype ERD.

```
Clients
- Key Data ───────────────
Client_Id  [PK1]
- Non-Key Data ───────────
Client_Name
Client_Address
Client_Age
Client_Quality_Indicator
```

Figure 6.18 The data store for Clients.

```
Customers
-Key Data───────────────────
Customer_Id  [PK1]
-Non-Key Data───────────────
Customer_Name
Customer_Address
Customer_Buyer_Indicator
Customer_Credit_Rating
```

Figure 6.19 The data store for Customers.

```
Customers
-Key Data ──────────────────
Customer_Id  [PK1]
-Non-Key Data───────────────
Customer_Name
Customer_Address
Customer_Buyer_Indicator
Customer_Credit_Rating
Customer_Age
Customer_Quality_Indicator
```

Figure 6.20 The combined data store for Clients and Customers.

Charles that the internal name is Customer!) Combining user views will always boost performance of the database, as it reduces the number of entities and the related links to make the connection.

Integration with Existing Models: Linking Databases

We have discussed the challenges of dealing with Legacy Systems. Most firms are approaching the replacement of legacy systems by phasing business area components into completely re-developed systems. As each business area is completed, there needs to be a "Legacy Link" with data files that connect business area components. This strategy allows a gradual porting of the entire system. The problem with the "Legacy Link" is that the normalized databases must interface and in many cases be dependent upon non-normalized files. This effectively upsets the integrity of the new component and may permanently damage the stored data in the new model. The linking of legacy applications is only one example of this problem. Often, subsidiary companies or locations must depend on data being controlled by less dependable master files. Therefore, linking databases may force analysts to rethink how to preserve integrity while still maintaining the physical link to other corporate data components. Let us use the following example to show how this problem arises:

The Analyst is designing a subsystem that utilizes the company's employee master file. The subsystem needs this information to allocate employees to projects. Project information is never purged, and therefore the employee project file will contain employees who may no longer be active. Unfortunately, the company master deletes all terminated employees. The employee master must be used in order to ensure that new employees are picked up. The subsystem cannot modify any information on the company master. The ERD in Figure 6.21 depicts these relationships:

Note that the Employee Project entity has a one or zero relationship with the Employee Master entity. This simply means that there could be an employee that exists in the Employee Project entity that does not exist in the Employee Master. Not only does this violate normalization rules, it has a serious integrity problem. For example, if we wanted to print a report about the project and each participating employee, all employees who do not exist in the Employee Master will print blanks, since there is no corresponding name information in the master file. Is there an alternative that could provide integrity and normalization? The answer is yes. The subsystem needs to access the Company employee master and merge the file with an Employee Master subsystem version. The merge conversion would compare the two files and update or add new information and employees. It would not, however, delete terminated employees. Although this is an extra step, it maintains integrity, normalization, and most of all, the requirement not to modify the original Employee Master. The ERD would be modified as shown in Figure 6.22.

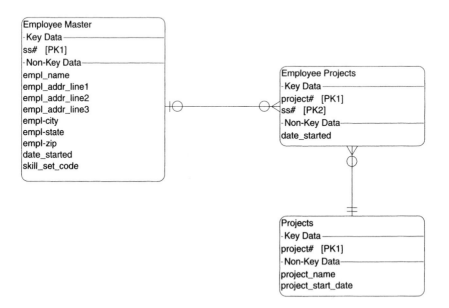

Figure 6.21 ERD showing an association between Employees and Projects.

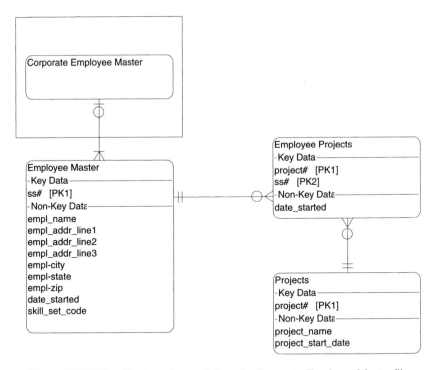

Figure 6.22 ERD reflecting a legacy link to the Corporate Employee Master file.

The Corporate Employee Master and its relation to Employee Master is shown only for informational purposes. The Corporate Employee Master in effect becomes more of an application requirement rather than a permanent part of the ERD. It is important to understand that this solution may require the analyst to produce a list of existing projects in which terminated employees are needed. The first conversion from the Corporate Employee Master will not contain these terminated employees, and they will therefore have to be added directly to the subsystem Employee Master.

Referential Integrity

Referential integrity is a feature provided by most databases. The idea behind referential integrity is that it prevents users of the database from corrupting or providing inconsistent data into a table. Normalization, as discussed before, is the vehicle that ensures referential integrity in a database because it stops records from being entered into one table that is not linked to another one (assuming the two tables should be linked by a common data element). Referential integrity is implemented through the use of a foreign key.

So, by the above definition, a 3rd normal form logical model if implemented in the physical database, would establish referential integrity in the product. Everything would seem to be very simple then; however, the reality is that 3rd normal form physical databases are difficult to achieve. By achieve, I mean 100%, for what is almost integrity? While this book provides all of the steps to accomplish 3rd normal form, there are a number of issues that block us from ever reaching the magical 100% compliance:

1. Third normal form databases can have performance degradation in a physical implementation. The foreign keys are indexes, and indexes become incrementally slower as they become larger—so large systems tend to run into significant performance problems that necessitate violating the foreign key implementation of referential integrity.
2. Most applications today have not been created from scratch—they are legacy migrations from existing systems. As such, there tend to be a number of applications that contain the database rules within the application code. To change these applications can be a daunting if not overwhelming recoding effort that is likely not to receive either the money or the time requisite to complete such an overhaul effort. This results in new applications replicating the coding that exists and the database is left unprotected, especially when users write their own queries.
3. There is little compatibility of foreign key restraints across proprietary database products. The definition languages and uses of SQL (structured query language) vary among database vendors, and as a result maintaining 3rd normal form across multiple products is very challenging—particularly with respect to having the necessary in-house talent to understand all of the "flavors" of SQL. Furthermore, application vendors, that is, companies that produce products that work with databases, are careful not to be allegiant to any specific database vendor, because their clients have their own preference. As a result, these vendors want to make it as easy as possible for their applications to operate with the database that their client uses. Implementing referential integrity at the database level in these cases would create a maintenance nightmare for these application vendors. The result: most vendors and companies have tended to shy away from putting foreign key controls and restraints in their product because of portability issues.

Database Naming Conventions

How should analysts and designers determine the name of a physical table, field names, and keys in the database? It is important to avoid redundant names such as "Description" which might define a description attribute in a number of different physical databases. For example, tables can often have a "name" field, like the company name, or the contact name, etc. Each of these attributes in turn needs a descriptive field that explains more about the name. So analysts often create a field called "description" in each separate table, but this habit has serious consequences from a data dictionary perspective. Each "description" attribute when entered into the DD creates a replication of the same name—so it creates a confusing situation. Although many CASE products automatically prefix the name with the name of the table, e.g., "Customer.Description" it is important for the analyst/designer to control this with appropriate naming conventions that all engineers of systems can understand and follow. Thus, there are a number of guidelines for providing names—names that assist developers as well as users (particularly those who use SQL) to understand the meanings of various field names in the database.

For the purpose of this book, I will use the most popular Oracle naming conventions as an example of widespread and "standard" database naming conventions.

1. Table Names
   Table names should be plural, should not contain spaces, separated by _underscores, and limited to 23 characters. If a table name contains multiple words, only the last word should be plural:

   > Customers
   > Customer_Applications
   > Customer_Application_Functions

2. Field Names
   Fields should have a unique name in the database (as opposed to duplicate names in separate tables which is often allowed in most vendor database products). The Oracle field naming conventions are for fields to lead with two or three character contractions of the table name:

   > Customer_Options would have a field called CO_Vendor_name.
   > Patient_Names would have a field called PN_Patient_Addresses.
   > Vendors would have a field called VE_Telephone_Numbers.

   Cases can occur where two or more tables have the same prefix. This can best be avoided by first being careful in the way the analyst names a table, thus avoiding the dilemma. However, in very large tables, let's say one might consider concatenating another letter—so instead of Customer_Options as CO, the analyst can add another character: COP.

3. Primary Key Fields
   Primary key fields should be identified by appending "_pk." For example:

   > Customers would have a primary key field called CU_Customer_Id_pk.
   > Vendors would have a primary key field called VE_Vendor_Id_pk.

When a primary key is used as a foreign key in another table, it should be referred to as "_fk," omitting "_pk" as follows:

Invoices might have a foreign key called IN_Customer_Id_fk.

In the case on concatenation of fields, forming a primary key, pk should be replaced by "_ck" as follows:

Customer_Id_ck
Customer_Id_Locations_ck

View Naming Conventions

A view is a subset picture of a database table or physical database. During the design stage it is important to determine the number of subset views that may be required. Views can typically be associated with a screen program that is either updating or viewing data. The use of a view is essentially a design decision that has impact or performance. By creating subset views, less data and only data that is relevant from the larger table is stored. The view can best be seen in Figure 6.23.

The downside of a view is that it replicates physical data, and as such, requires more manipulation to ensure data integrity. Thus, if a view is used for update, then the changing of data must be re-applied to the superset table as follows:

Update Quantity in Item 3 to 3000 requires two updates

Note that a recalculation to Total of 90000 is also required in both tables.

Therefore, one can take the position that views are best used when referential integrity is not necessary—as it would not be when just retrieving data for viewing only. For this reason, views can be very effective in data warehousing operations (see Figure 6.24).

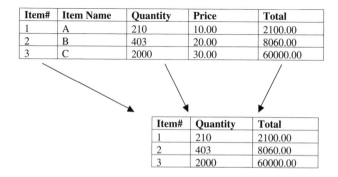

Item#	Item Name	Quantity	Price	Total
1	A	210	10.00	2100.00
2	B	403	20.00	8060.00
3	C	2000	30.00	60000.00

Item#	Quantity	Total
1	210	2100.00
2	403	8060.00
3	2000	60000.00

Figure 6.23 Subset view.

Item#	Item Name	Quantity	Price	Total
1	A	210	10.00	2100.00
2	B	403	20.00	8060.00
3	C	3000	30.00	60000.00

Item#	Quantity	Total
1	210	2100.00
2	403	8060.00
3	3000	60000.00

Update Quantity

Figure 6.24 Recalculation of view fields.

Indexing in Views

Once the logical database is designed by identifying the primary, secondary, and foreign keys in the logic data model, indexing can be used in the Design Stage to incorporate specific query activity in the physical database. Separate indexes allow for sorting without moving the physical data records as shown in Figure 6.25:

Physical indexes are produced either in the primary key (see 1st normal form failure primary key propagation) or as a foreign key (see 3rd normal form failure). The primary key indexes have certain naming conventions that are important for the analyst/designer using the format "idx_<TableName>_pk." For example.

Items Table

ItemID	Name	Price
H	Rulers	2.00
G	Tape	.75
C	Pencils	1.25
B	Erasers	1.00

Index -- Sort Ascending

ItemID
B
C
G
H

Figure 6.25 Table indexing.

>   PATIENTS would have a primary key index called
>   "idx_patients_pk."

If the primary key is a series of concatenations, each sequential concatenation would be named as follows:

>   idx_patients_01
>   idx_patients_02 and so forth.

Foreign keys are typically called "constraints" and are represented as follows:

>   PATIENTS would have a foreign key called "fk_patients", where
>   "patients" is the name of the Table or TableName.

There are also some other conventions that apply to non-key attributes, particularly those that carry a Boolean or Yes/No value. These non-key attributes usually end in "_yn". For example:

>   acceptance_status_yn is an attribute that contains either a "yes"
>   value or "no" value.

Field Length and Character Conventions

There are also maximum length naming conventions that are published and vary by database vendor. Figure 6.26 contains recommended maximum length names for databases created using IBM (DB2 database), Microsoft (SQLServer database), and Oracle (Gulutzan and Pelzer, 1999).

The comprising length from the above table appears to be 30, so I recommend that analysts use this number as their maximum assignment of any database names.

Allowable Characters in a Name

What are the acceptable characters that can be used to comprise a name field? Once again, the recommendations and limitations vary by database vendor as depicted in Figure 6.27 (Note: I have added MY_SQL, which is a popular open source database product):

In general, it is acceptable that the first characters of an attribute name can be a letter and that subsequent characters may contain digits or "_" (an underscore). $, #, @, while allowed, may not be compatible across all database products.

	IBM	Microsoft	Oracle
Attribute (Column)	30	128	30
Constraint (Foreign Key)	18	128	30
Table	128	128	30

Figure 6.26 Maximum length naming conventions.

	IBM	Microsoft	Oracle	My_SQL
First Character	Letter, $,#,@	Letter, $,#,@	Letter	Letter
Later Characters	Letter, digit, _, $,#,@	Letter, digit, _, #,@	Letter, digit, _, #,@	Letter, digit
Case Sensitivity	No	Maybe	No	No

Figure 6.27 Acceptable characters in field names.

Delimited Identifiers

Delimiters are used as a way to define the beginning and end of a field name. They are, in effect, the character that is allowed to act as the field that designates the beginning and end of such a field name. Delimiters are extremely useful when a named field includes spaces. The most popular delimiters are "". For example:

Create table "art langer"

The above delimiter "" defines that the space between "t" and "l" is part of the table name. Figure 6.28 shows the requirements by database vendor:

Null Values

There are often many questions raised about what Null is. What does it mean to have a null attribute? Perhaps the first thing to discuss is what Null is not! Null is not a value, zero, or spaces. The definition of Null is "does not exist." That is, a value is not provided or the value is unknown. Unfortunately, null is often misused by database professionals. Perhaps a good example of appropriate use of null is the field "Employee_Termination_Date." This field would be defined as a date value. However, if an employee was currently employed, he/she would not have an "Employee_Termination_Date." Therefore, the field will "not exist" for active employees. This requires the data definition of "Employee_Termination_Date" to allow for a null assignment since any date

	IBM	Microsoft	Oracle	My_SQL
Delimiting Character	""	" or [ ]	""	""
First Character	Anything	Anything	Anything	Anything
Later Characters	Anything	Anything	Anything	Anything
Case Sensitivity	Yes	Maybe	Yes	Yes

Figure 6.28 Allowed character delimiters by database vendor.

value would be fictitious and actually create an integrity problem (by assigning a date that would likely be out of range or bogus).

Nulls should never be used as a key-field identifier, either in a primary, secondary, or foreign key. This would also suggest that "Employee_Termination_Date" should never be used as a key-field identifier. Popular database products allow for the specification of a column to not permit null assignment. This feature obviously helps maintain data integrity by ensuring that an attribute in a row will always contain data. From a physical application perspective, this means that a user would be required to enter a value for a specified field in an entry screen.

Another complication of using null is the results that can be rendered when they are involved in complex database queries. While most advanced database products handle queries on nulls, the Boolean results from these queries can vary and result in unexpected output and aggregations. The details of how this occurs are beyond the scope of this book, but I suggest care when using them for database reporting needs.

Denormalization

Because of referential requirements, many databases need to be *denormalized*. At the beginning of this chapter, I identified that denormalization was the eighth and final step in the LDM. Denormalization is a reality, but a process that needs to be carefully measured in the exposure it creates for integrity—they just go hand-in-hand together.

Analysts/designers who consider denormalizing should weigh the value between time vs. space trade-offs. Normalized databases are not designed to minimize access time, and as a result they do not perform particularly efficiently when using tables to perform simple tasks like printing reports. This is especially true when such reports need data from multiple tables that are connected by normalized links like foreign keys. For example, if a report analyzing Order Items was required by a user, the normalized database would have the following tables linked in Figure 6.29:

Figure 6.29 Normalized view of order table.

Thus, the report would need to access both tables for each search—causing degradation in access times. Alternatively, a denormalized version would only have one table as shown in Figure 6.30:

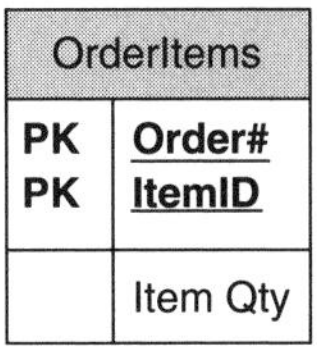

OrderItems	
PK **PK**	**Order#** **ItemID**
	Item Qty

Figure 6.30 Denormalized view.

This table concatenates Order with Item and eliminates the link. While this denormalized architecture has great advantages in the identified application, it can also have the opposite advantage if the report just needed to list each Order number. This technique is often called *combining tables*. In this case, the application would need to read every record and contain logic that would print the next Order Number that did not match the prior one. So as one can see by this example, electing denormalization is very tricky indeed. An alternative approach would be to create a data warehouse which maintains the integrity, but produces table structures for reporting only applications. This is covered more in-depth in Chapter 13, Business Process Re-Engineering.

So while time may be enhanced via denormalization, space may suffer. Given that denormalization creates replication of data, there are more records stored and therefore more space required. While normalized databases need significant storage during data manipulations, that is, producing a report, this space need is temporary, meaning that the space is released after the program completes. With denormalized databases, the storage is permanent because the data is stored in a more "report-ready" mode. Because storage is much cheaper today than in the past, many database analysts are not concerned with data storage and tend to ignore the consequences in the design stage. Those consequences usually relate to longer backup and restore times, and the need for multiple disk arrays to handle massive databases that span multiple physical hardware devices. Multiple device addressing will inevitably also cause time degradation, so as you can see excessive space requirements may ultimately negate what analysts/designers are attempting to originally improve.

Analysts and designers must ultimately ask themselves what denormalization can do for them. Below are some key questions that should be asked before considering using denormalization:

- Are their alternative ways to achieve better performance than denor-malizing tables?
- Will denormalization get the database to the objective performance level?
- What reliability and data quality exposure will occur from the denor-malization and are those exposures acceptable and understood by all stakeholders?

The answers to the above questions may provide important guidance to what the analysts should recommend in their functional analysis and design of the database. Given that performance is a key driver to denormalization decisions, the following indicators may also provide useful guidelines for making effective decisions (Mullins, 2006):

1. A number of queries and reports heavily rely on data from more than one database.
2. Multiple repeating groups (e.g., ORDER—ITEMS as shown above) exist and there are many queries and reports that need to show them together.
3. Many calculations are needed across multiple tables before a query can be completed (that is, the query must first do the calculation before a report can be produced).
4. Multiple access to specific tables is required by many different users for different operations.
5. Large concatenated keys become so large that foreign key connections become lengthy.

Logic to Physical Databases

This chapter thus far has covered the analytics and complexities of designing a logical database schema. Features of the logical model have been:

1. Entities and relationships.
2. Definitions of attributes within entities.
3. The assignment of primary and secondary keys.
4. Foreign key definition in 3rd NF.
5. Normalization.
6. Supertype/Subtype relationships.

At the above level, analysts do the best they can to describe data generally, that is, without regard to how the database will "physically" be implemented. There is a need, however, to specify the logic model in terms of its physical implementation. By physical we mean the actual real database that the schema will be implemented in—so once the analysts know the physical database (this "knowing" will vary, but is often known early in the analysis process), then they need to provide a "physical" data model which should include:

1. Specification of all logical tables and columns to their actual database specification.
2. Identified actual foreign key names and link conventions.
3. Denormalization needs based on physical database constraints or limitations which cause the ERD to become very different than originally constructed.

Therefore, the analysts need to specify how the LDM will be transformed into an actual database schema. This transformation, as with all analytics, must provide an audit trail as to how the analyst made the decisions. This audit trail requires the following four steps:

1. Convert the logical entities into actual database tables.
2. Convert logical relationships into actual product-based foreign-key links often called "constraints."
3. Convert attributes into physical columns.
4. Modify the physical data model the formats required by the database product.

Notwithstanding the possibility of differences between the logical and physical database, the further the analysts drifts from the LDM, the increased risks of integrity exposures. Perhaps the most important statements about this dilemma have been published in March 2002 by Fabian Pascal. Pascal published what he called the "first five quotes" as follows:

1. "The more you drift away from any physical implementation, the more performance is going to suffer... The choice is between best logical structure or best physical structure, or a compromise."

   This is pure falsehood. The performance of a database is based on many things, including how the data is stored, access paths, and hardware configuration to name a few—yet many believe the above statement.

2. "Ironically, there is really no difference between a document and a database – In both cases, you have to abstract information and a certain amount of metadata that helps the system understand the meaning and uses of that extracted information... XML could put an end to that by breaking down the traditional barriers between document and database processing. Interactive Web applications have characteristics of both... Running an auction on a Web site is a massive database challenge... But it's also a massive document processing challenge, because you have to offer all the descriptions of all the products and so on."

   Once again, there is no logic to this statement. A database is much different than a document and has more complex architecture and logic in the way it is designed. Overgeneralization about database relationships with Web-enabled infrastructure can be very misleading.

3. "I am designing a database system but I am a little unsure about normalization–could anyone tell me if the information is in third normal form? If it isn't could anyone suggest where I've gone wrong?"

   Normalization is a mathematical process of functional decomposition. One cannot just look at the tables, but needs to understand the definition of dependencies as I have outlined earlier in this chapter. The only way is to apply the formula.

4. "I am having difficulty creating a table with one of the columns in a composite primary key being NULL[able]. Example: table ABC with columns in the PK ' A' NOT NULL, ' B' NOT NULL, and ' C' NULL. Logically, I have a valid business reason for wanting to implement a table with at least one column of the compound PK being nullable."

   By definition you should never have a Null key—it simply makes no sense.

5. "In creating a database, normalization is the process of organizing it into tables in such a way that the results of using the database are always unambiguous and as intended. Normalization may have the effect of duplicating data within the database and often results in the creation of additional tables. (While normalization tends to increase the duplication of data, it does not introduce redundancy, which is unnecessary duplication.) Normalization is usually a refinement process after the initial exercise of identifying the data objects that should be in the database, identifying the relationships and defining the tables required and the columns within each table."

   Nothing could be further from the truth. Normalization does not propagate redundancy, but rather removes it. All links are accomplished through pointers or indexes which provide the referential integrity needed in complex database architectures.

In summary, the most important aspect of the physical model has everything to do with the actual database product and the hardware being used, as opposed to false generalizations of things that must be changed from the logical model. There is also confusion about the term "conceptual model." The conceptual model is a view of the data from a business perspective or view. This model is designed so that the user community can understand how the database is being constructed and can comment on its accuracy, especially with regard to relations of entities. However, the conceptual model is not an architecture that can be implemented. For example, the conceptual model allows many-to-many relationships to be depicted because it is not an engineering model—so that showing these types of relationships helps users understand and agree to the way the entities relate to each other. Thus the logical model is formed from the conceptual design but employs the rules of information science. The physical model is then transformed based on the vendor requirements for implementation and hardware features where the database will ultimately reside and the way indexes and keys are actually constructed by the product itself.

Data Types Usage and Conventions

There are a number of alphanumeric data types to use when defining an attribute or column in a table. Varchar2, which was used earlier in this chapter, is the preferred alphanumeric data type for alphanumeric fields. The main benefit of Varchar2 over Char is that Char will store blanks in characters not being used—therefore actually using more storage. For example, Name is defined as 30 varying length characters, thus meaning that its value could be from 1 to 30 characters in length. If this field is defined as Varchar2 and a value of 20 characters is stored, then only 20 characters of space will be used. On the other hand, if the same field was defined as Char 30, then the same example would require 30 characters; 20 of actual data definition, and 10 of blanks to fill the definition field.

However, the use of Char is important when logical comparisons are made between fields where trailing blanks are not considered as part of the comparison (this is an American National Standard Institute (ANSI) requirement. In these cases using Char is more efficient because the comparisons are accomplished on the same size fields. A comparison is commonly used in sorting data for example. If trailing blanks are considered in the comparison, then the Char definition is not viable. Figure 6.31 shows a comparison of ANSI standards with Oracle.

Business Rules

The growth of the relational model has created a mechanism for storing certain application logic at the database level. Business rules are application logic that enforces the integrity of the business, that is, that maintains the rules as set forth by the users. Such rules could include: If Last_Name is entered, the First_Name must also be entered. This "rule" simply means that a valid name must contain both the first and last name of the individual being entered into the database. These business rules were traditionally part of the application program code. This meant that every program that would need to

ANSI Standard	Oracle Data Type
Character And Char	Char
Character Varying And Char Varying	Varchar2
Numeric, Decimal, Dec, Integer, Int And Smallint	Number
Float, Real, Double Precision	Float

Figure 6.31 ANSI/Oracle data types compared.
(Source: Ben Shepherd, 2003)

enforce a rule would need to encapsulate the same logic within each application program. What followed historically was a maintenance nightmare which required programmers to remember where the logic had been used, especially when changes to the code were required. In addition, there was always the issue of re-coding the same logic without error, so it meant greater testing time. Although there were and are techniques for storing common code in global libraries for applications to incorporate into the code, the procedures tended to be archaic and awkward to support. The establishment of SQL as a robust and end-user query tool also posed a new problem. Business rules coded in applications can enforce them only if the program is executed. Because SQL allows users to create and execute query sessions, they can easily avoid an applications enforcement of a business rule. This therefore created a serious integrity problem in the implementation of database products. Although the tendency in the industry has been to separate data from applications, we will see here that the industry is moving back towards combining data and applications again. It is important not to view this as a return to the old way, but rather as a more intelligent and structured way to combine data with its permanent logic. The word permanent is crucial: certain logic is really an inherent part of the relationship that elements have with other elements. Having business rules stored as part of the data, then, allows anyone to use the information without violating the permanent relationship rules as set forth by the business. It means that SQL users can query all they want or even create and modify data without losing the controls necessary to support integrity.

Business rules are implemented at the database level via stored procedures. Stored procedures are implemented by each database manufacturer, and although they are similar, they are not the same as business rules. Therefore, moving stored procedures from one database to another is not trivial. Why do we care? Networks are being built around the concept of client/server computing and may often require communication among many different database vendor systems. If business rules are to be implemented at the database level, the compatibility and transportability of such code becomes a challenge. This issue will be discussed in greater detail throughout the later chapters of this book.

Business-rule implementations fall into three categories: keys, domains, and triggers. Key business rules are concerned with the behavior of a primary key in an entity. They include the rules that can affect the insertion, deletion, and updating of primary and foreign keys. For example, if an order is deleted, all order items must also be deleted automatically. Many people call this feature *referential integrity*. Domains represent the constraints related to an attribute's range of values. If an attribute (key or non-key) can have a range of values from 1 to 10, we say that range is the domain value of the attribute. This is, of course, very important information to be included and enforced at the database level through a stored procedure. The third and most powerful business rule is triggers.

Triggering Operations

Triggers are defined as stored procedures that, when activated, "trigger" one or a set of other procedures to be executed. Triggers usually act on other entities, although in many databases such as Oracle, triggers are becoming powerful programming tools to provide significant capabilities at the database level. In many ways they represent their own programming languages and allow embedded SQL code to be used in the stored procedure. Stored procedures resemble BAT files in DOS and are actually implemented as an option in many RDBMS packages. Below is an example of an Oracle 8 trigger:

```
/* Within B.D. only users who are president or director may mark */
/* company as confidential.      */

if user_type not in ('P', 'D') then
 :new.cmpConfidential := 'N';
end if;

end if;

/* Ensure user has right to make a company executive private.      */
if exec_com = 'N' then
 :new.cmpexec_private := 'N';
end if;
```

This trigger is designed to allow a company's information to be marked as confidential only by the President. This means that the president of the company can enter information that only he or she can see. The second part of the trigger is set to allow certain executives to mark their contacts with companies as private. Here we see two sets of application logic that will execute via Oracle triggers. In addition, it will be enforced by the database regardless of how the information is accessed.

Too much power can be a problem, however, and it can cause difficulties with triggers. Why? Because triggers can initiate activity among database files, designers must be careful that they do not cause significant performance problems. For example, let's say a trigger is written which accesses 15 database files. If this trigger is initiated during a critical processing time in the firm, major problems with productivity could result. Once again, the good and the bad!

The subject of business rules is broad but very specific to the actual product implementation style. Since analysts should remain focused on the logical model, it is important for them to define the necessary key business rules, domains and triggers required by the system. It should not be their responsibility to implement them for a specific Relational Database Management Software (RDBMS) product.

Problems and Exercises

1. What is logic data modeling trying to accomplish?
2. Define Normalization. What are the three normal forms?
3. What does normalization *not* do?
4. What is meant by the term "derived" data element?
5. Describe the concept of combining user views. What are the political ramifications of doing this in many organizations?
6. What are legacy links? Describe how they can be used to enforce data integrity.
7. Name and define the three types of business rules.
8. Why are stored procedures in some ways a contradiction to the rule that data and processes need to be separated?
9. What are the disadvantages of database triggers?
10. What is meant by denormalization? Is this a responsibility of the analyst?
11. Define a supertype/subtype. When should this entity construct by used?

Mini-Project #1

The Physician Master File from a DFD contains the following data elements:

Data Element	Description
Social Security #	Primary Key
Physician ID	Alternate Key
Last_Name	Last Name
First_Name	First Name
Mid_Init	Middle Initial
Hospital_Resident_ID	Hospital Identification
Hospital_Resident_Name	Name of Hospital
Hospital_Addr_Line1	Hospital Address
Hospital_Addr_Line2	Hospital Address
Hospital_Addr_Line3	Hospital Address
Hospital_State	Hospital's State
Hospital_City	Hospital's City
Hospital_Zip	Hospital's Zip Code
Specialty_Type	The Physician's specialty
Specialty_Name	Description of specialty
Specialty_College	College where received degree
Specialty_Degree	Degree Name
Date_Graduated	Graduation Date For Specialty
DOB	

Physician's Date of Birth	
Year_First_Practiced	First year in practice
Year's_Pract_Exp	Practice Experience Years
Annual_Earnings	Annual Income

Assumptions

1. A physician can be associated with many hospitals, but must be associated with at least one.
2. A physician can have many specialties, or have no specialty.

Assignment

Normalize to 3rd normal form.

Mini-Project #2

1. Check the appropriate column that best identifies the use of each named item as to whether it describes an element or whether it is an element.

Item Examples:	Used to Describe	May be Described
Blue	X	
Temperature of a plain in Spain		X

20 Degrees celsius		
Color		
The White House		
1600 Pennsylvania Avenue		
Continental drift		
1.5 inches		
Hourly wage		
$80		
Difficulty of this exercise		
5th Grade school level		
Ed Sullivan		
Duration of study		
45 days		
Appointment date		
01/01/2004		
Physical location of a university campus		
Odds of winning the publishers clearinghouse sweepstakes		
1/100,000 of 1 percent (or 0.00001% or one in ten million)		

2.   For the following list of named entity types, provide a natural and unique identifier that provides significant information. Where no natural unique indentifier exists, create a new one and describe it

Example: Checking Account	*Bank ID + Check Account Number*
Hospital Patient	
Your Residence	
Box of Cereal	
Bottle of Vintage Wine	
Carton of Milk	
The Wall Street Journal	
Textbook	
Beach Boys Music CD	
Pair of Nike Sneakers	
Rolex Wristwatch	
Airline Flight to London	

Exercise provided by Greg Vimont.

Mini-Project #3

Crow's-Foot Exercise

1.   (a)   What is the total number of possible pairings of crow's-foot indicators? _____
How many mirror image pairs exist in these possible combinations (like matching bookends)? _____
(b)   How many unique pairs exist? _____ And if you didn't count the reversed version of each unique pairing, how many are there? _____

Hint: Use this table diagram of crow's-foot indicators to plot all of the possible instances.

	O|	||	O<	|<
|O	|O — O|			
||				
>O				
>|				

2.   Draw the crow's-foot cardinality for the following situation:

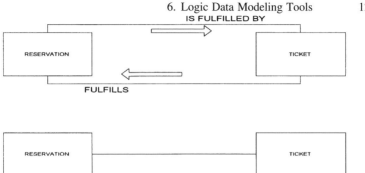

A1 Travel takes reservations from clients and provides them with travel arrangements on common carriers throughout the world. For some reservations, tickets are never issued. Reservations can be made and tickets can be issued for them at a later time. Sometimes, when reservations are made one or more tickets are issued simultaneously. A ticket may fulfill only a single reservation. Tickets, once issued, are never reissued to fulfill anything other than the original reservation.

(3)   Draw the crow's-foot cardinality for the following situation:

The Party Palace is a catering facility that hosts many types of social engagements. One type of event is the dinner party. Guests and their respective dates are normally issued seating cards with table assignments. Every guest will have a seating assignment. Not every guest will have a date. Dates may not be unaccompanied, and they must accompany only one guest.

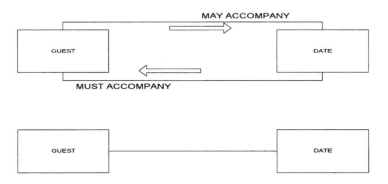

4.   Based on the following business case, draw an entity relation diagram. You need only to name the entities; no keys or attributes are required.

   (a)   In the operation of its business, *Top-Flight Limo Service* records information about drivers who chauffeur the company's patrons. Drivers must own and drive their own cars. A driver may own more than one vehicle. *Top-Flight*

Limo tracks driver traffic citations during the time of their employment with the company. Drivers begin employment with a clean slate.

(b)   In the ERD that you have created, what is the functional significance of "optional" vs. "required" as it is applied to business rules in implementing a database and populating it with data?

Exercise provided by Greg Vimont.

7
Web User Interface Tools

Introduction

In this chapter I will focus on Web page creative design and the Graphical User Interface (GUI), another crucial part of the analysis and design of systems. Furthermore, this chapter will define the important components of designing Web sites—Web sites that represent the vision and brand of their organization. Web design has conventionally been considered an artistic process, outside the traditional analysis and design process. Yet, Web design needs to have a place in the development cycle; the key is to integrate it into the life cycle without destroying its creative process.

Web designers face significant challenges. Powell (2000) pointed out that many Web sites create visual effects that do nothing more than replicate paper brochures. While these designs rely on sophisticated software, ultimately they do little to establish the brand and identity needed by successful ecommerce systems. Furthermore, attractive design is not necessarily functionally effective; to be successful, Web designs must be technically sound. On the other end of the spectrum are Web sites that are too focused on technology and pay little attention to the user experience. The features and functions of these sites tend to be sound, but confusing and complicated to the user. These sites may become so "dressed up" that each function becomes a design in itself. This is sometimes known as "brochureware."

Unlike in more traditional analysis and design projects, users of Web systems may not even be users, rather consumers—users who the analysts may not even know! Therefore, the job of the analysts and designer is to translate what users may want without really speaking to them. Thus, viable Web sites must be useful to their users. Usefulness can be defined as a combination of utility and usability (Grudin, 1992). Utility describes the site's functionality, which ideally meets the user's needs. Usability describes the user's ability to manipulate the site's features in order to accomplish a specific goal.

Components of Web Design

The major question of Web analysis and design projects is "who" will be using the system and what features and functions will provide the best experience for the user. There are four major parts to Web design:

1. *Content*: the features that will persuade users on the site.
2. *Technology*: ways to implement the functions of the Web site.
3. *Visuals*: form of the site and its navigation.
4. *Purpose*: economic ramifications for the site's implementation.

Figure 7.1 is a graphical depiction of the four components in the form of a pyramid (Powell, 2000). In this picture, content provides the bricks to build the pyramid; the foundation consists of the visuals and technology (form and function, respectively), and the economics the critical factor or purpose of creating the pyramid. It is important to note that the economics of Web development are beyond the scope of this book. This chapter will focus on two of

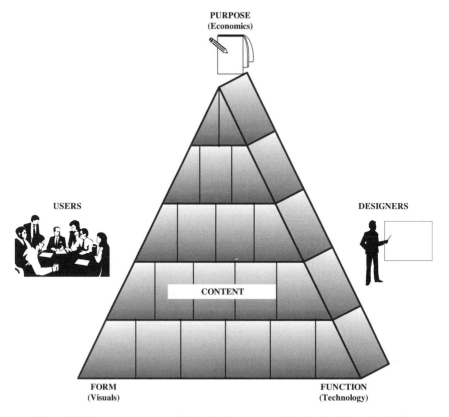

Figure 7.1 The components of Web design source: Web design (Powell, 2000).

the four components: Content and Visuals. These two components include the requirements that Web analysts and designers must have in order to create the features, functions, and interfaces of effective Web-oriented systems.

Content

Content is a very complex issue. While content is at the core of the message to be communicated, it must be carefully designed to accommodate the limitations of user preferences—preferences that become more variable and unknown outside the controlled internal user base of more traditional analysis projects.

Branding

The first challenge of good content Web design is strategic brand building. Brand building or "branding" is an important part of how an organization shapes the image it projects to a large audience in cyberspace. A business' brand can be seen as a set of promises to its customers: for example, Federal Express' "The World on Time." A brand is also a set of expectations. Successful brands connect to users on an emotional level; Burger King's "Have It Your Way" campaign, for example, seeks to establish emotional connections with their customers. The brand is the cumulative effect of all the interactions a user has with the business; it represents a company's personality. Why is branding so important for ecommerce? The answer lies in its ability to reach wide varieties of markets across the Internet. Strong branding is even more important when Internet-based transactions replace personal transactions. What does branding have to do with the analysis and design of ecommerce systems? The answer lies with its contribution to making the ecommerce process attractive to its users. Users may include internal constituents who use the system every day and can receive a strong company brand image from the site. Understanding these external users represents a challenge—so the branding exercise becomes a significant part of the Web design process. A well-designed brand on the Web leaves a lasting impression on users, especially customers and consumers. Great Web brands have a consistent look and feel, and a high level of design integrity.

Figures 7.2 and 7.3 are examples of an old look and new branding approach, respectively, created by Thirteen WNET New York. Thirteen is a public television station that changed their logo to enhance their image to their viewers.

Figure 7.2 Old brand logo.

thirteen
WNET NEW YORK

Figure 7.3 New brand logo.

The updated logo gave the Thirteen brand a more contemporary, younger, energetic, and modern feel, while at the same time, upholding the core values of the company and its products. The red three-dimensional sphere dotting the "i" was conceived as an activation point, reminiscent of the Big Apple, and one that could be used to click to the Web site.

Web branding, however, does not require a firm to re-brand itself or change its image. The Thirteen example serves merely to illustrate that brand elements can exist at many different levels within a firm. Organization Web sites can have a powerful brand, which may or may not be identical to the company's core brand. The branding of the site in relation to the company's brand must be considered during the design process, and ecommerce analysts and designers need to be part of this process. How do brands affect a Web site? Thirteen is again used as an example, but this time looking at its Web site as shown in Figure 7.4.

Notice that the new logo is visible, but the brand/identity is also used effectively on the site. This is accomplished by using link names such as "explore thirteen," "join thirteen," etc. Thus, in this case, the brand is complemented within the Web site scheme of navigation. This is what we mean by Web site branding.

The Web Branding Process

Too many organizations associate Web branding narrowly with marketing. According to Susan Baston (Vice-President and Creative Director at the New York-based Interactive Bureau) "branding is more the foundation on which to build every experience the customer has with the company." This foundation includes the existing legacy applications or "brick and mortar" parts of the business. Earlier, I stated that ecommerce encompasses *all* of the components of the system. Branding can be broken down to its sub-components as well. Effective branding for a customer, for instance, may not be the same for internal constituents. It is necessary to operationalize these concepts into a clear, coherent process for analysts/designers to follow.

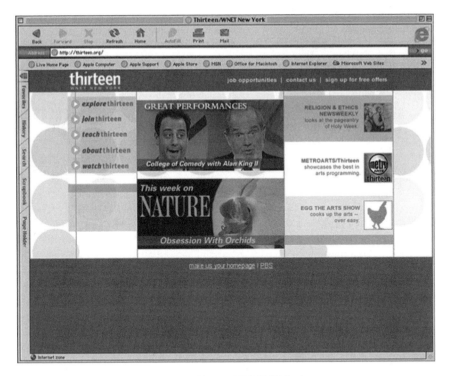

Figure 7.4 Thirteen WNET Web site.

The User Interface

The first component of the branding process concerns the users. In each interview, certainly in a JAD, ecommerce analysts are encouraged to invite the creative staff to participate, so that they can learn what is important to the user community. Creative staffs may also want to hold their own sessions, but such meetings should be incorporated into the entire project plan and should be attended by analysts. For customers and consumers, market information may be required along with focus group sessions; these sessions must also be integrated with the overall analysis and design process. In sum, the creative work relating to branding really represents the first aspect of Web design, and it must be treated as part of the analysis and design process. In essence, the creative outputs from the user interfaces should be clear graphic branding concepts that:

1. Define the user marketplace.
2. Define what users want to do on the site.
3. Establish the way the Web will provide a method for users to use the firm's products and services.
4. Create some excitement and message for the experience.

In order to address branding during the interview analysis phase, it is important to ask users what their objectives are for using the ecommerce system. Part of the discussion should focus on the degree to which the user base is concerned with branding versus feature function. Obviously the more "external" the user, the more important branding and image will be in the design of the site. However, internal branding is also important because it makes employees more knowledgeable about the company's image, its mission, and how it wants to be seen by its customers. This all becomes part of the Web site design solution.

User Profile Strategy

A user profile strategy is a plan for registering users and collecting information from them that can make their Web experience more personalized (Smith, 2000). Typically this step might be considered part of design and development, but it is arguably more a component of branding because it allows users to define their personal relationship with the company. Care needs to be taken in this evaluation. For example, if your users are leery about supplying personal information, it really means that they are not seeking a personal relationship with the brand. This would not be the case, though, for a business such as Thirteen WNET, which projects its brand and identity to users who may wish to become members. So the "membership branding" is critical to the success of the ecommerce system. Figure 7.5 is an example of the "membership brand" Web page of Thirteen WNET in Figure 7.4.

Decisions about how brand should affect design should be made during focus groups with external consumers. Therefore, analysts and creative designers need to work together to understand ecommerce Web branding strategies. Profile strategy is another technique that aids the evolution of Web site branding design. Profiles can continually collect information about your user community and can be used to ascertain changes in preference, level of computer sophistication, and the array of preferences and capabilities of the user interfaces that were presented in Chapter 3. Furthermore, profiling substantiates the need to adopt the spiral life cycle, as the process of tracking user brand preferences using profiles is a constantly evolving process. Given the complexity and sophistication of implementing user profiles, it is wise to start with a simple strategy and build on it. It is easier to go from a simple profile strategy than to undo a complex one that completely misses the mark.

Content Preference

Content and branding seek to make users feel that they see themselves on your Web site. That is, users should feel that they are in the setting that they prefer in interfacing with your business. How can you accomplish this, and how can you deal with users who have alternative preferences? The answer to the first

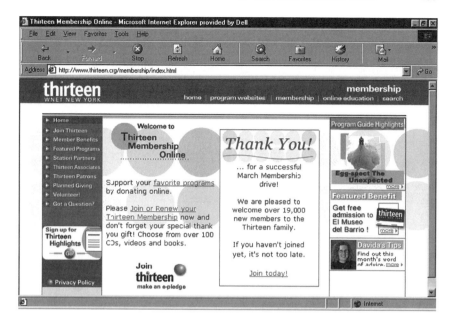

Figure 7.5 Thirteen WNET membership brand Web site.

question is to treat branding as part of the analysis phase of the user interface. Customer preferences must drive the design decisions made by creative branding professionals. All too often, the brand process is segregated from the application, and the result is a disjointed Web site design. The second question raises another issue: Should a brand attempt to be all things to all users? I believe not, and as a result, it is suggested that your brand be tailored to your most important user base. If the user base is not dominated by any single preference design, then analysts might consider having multiple home pages. This concept was discussed earlier and raises the challenge of maintaining multiple content sites. Another alternative is to pick a type of site that many users can accept, that is, a "middle-of-the-road" style that will alienate no one. Figure 7.6 shows Citibank's home page, designed in an attempt to facilitate many different ecommerce user preferences.

Still another approach is to allow users to modify the site by choosing from a select group of design preferences. Figure 7.7 shows Egomedia's Web site that allows users to customize the site, offering options to change shapes, desktop features, and music.

Web Site Personalization

Personalization is another way to build a brand on the ecommerce system. The goal of personalization is to allow users to feel that they have a special

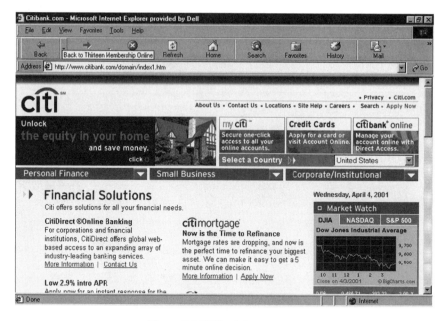

Figure 7.6 Citibank home page.

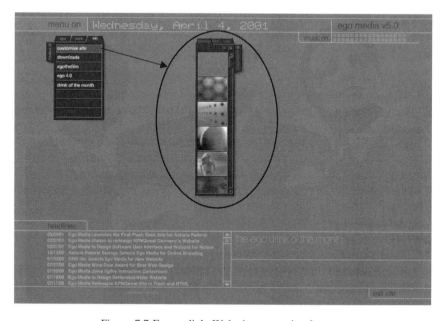

Figure 7.7 Egomedia's Web site customize feature.

relationship with the business. Personalization adds brand equity because the user feels "valued." An example of personalization is Amazon.com (Figure 7.8).

On Amazon's personalized ecommerce site, returning buyers are greeted by name. The site saves a lot of information about the user, such as credit card numbers, shipping address, and prior book preferences. The personalization enables the user's site to cater to their specific preferences and creates a one-to-one relationship between the company and user. This one-on-one can be created through a greeting message and through suggestions to the user that fit their prior shopping preferences. It also allows the company to "speak" to users in their language, e.g., as college kids, as adults, etc. Gender also plays a role in attracting users and branding the Web experience. Once again, analysts should be capturing this information as part of their user requirements documentation, that is, it should appear as a requirement of the system in both the business specifications and technical specifications.

Furthermore, content "language" is another important issue in designing Web brand. Content language is a type of "writing style." Writing styles can create comfort for users or insult them. The latter can occur when user content assumes that the customer knows little about the product, or does not recognize users as returning customers. The process of creating good content requires that skilled copywriters and editors be involved in the analysis and design process. The solution is either to have such personnel attend the interviews (a difficult and time-consuming process) or to have analysts provide writers with information

Figure 7.8 Amazon.com screen personalization.

about the style of the content that should be used. In many projects, there is little planning of the written content, and as a result first drafts need to be significantly modified. This type of "hit and miss" approach to site content is another reason that Web projects are frequently over budget.

Customer Service

Customer service has always been an important way to develop brand identity. Words associated with customer service are "quality" and "caring"—words that convey an important message to users. Notwithstanding the personalization of the ecommerce system, it is important for ecommerce businesses to convey the same quality and caring to users as brick and mortar companies traditionally do. Quality characteristics can be conveyed over the Web by having a dedicated section about how products are made and why they should be considered high quality. Caring can be accomplished by providing customer testimonials and by sending customers messages that (1) thank them for their order; (2) advise them of when they can expect to receive their order; and (3) keep them posted on the status of their order. The easiest way to provide these services is to replicate the procedures in the current business. Unfortunately, this kind of caring is not always easy to transfer from brick-and-mortar situations to ecommerce Web sites. In retail stores, for example, good customer service is often provided by individuals who are especially dedicated to their work. Therefore, it is advisable that reliable ways to provide good customer support be explored during the analysis phase. Some common branding-related customer service options are listed below:

- Offer more services for purchasers of higher-margin products.
- Provide on-line support for the most valued customers.
- Provide exclusive hot-lines.
- Offer discounts for customer lifetime value, volume orders, and frequent purchasers.
- Adjust shipping prices according to volume and frequency of purchase.
- Create a special sale area on the site.
- Offer advance-purchase opportunities on new products for existing customers

    Source: *e-Loyalty* (Smith, 2000)

All of the above options create special relationships between the company and their customers. These customers become part of a "preferred" group, which is treated differently because of their loyalty to the company. The loyalty is an identity then presented to the users as a reminder of how important they are to the company.

This section provided a perspective of how Web branding integrates with the process of analysis and design. In a number of cases I stated that the ecommerce analyst should provide or participate with creative personnel during the user interview process. The purpose was to attempt to capture as much about the creative brand vision that users have, as well as the technical feature functions that they need. In order to provide creative staff with this information, it is necessary for analysts to integrate into the business and technical specification sections that are devoted to assisting the creative development of the system. Figure 7.9 summarizes the information that has been discussed above into a sample questionnaire and checklist that can be used during the interview cycles.

Client:	Date: 2/28/07
Application: Web Branding	Supersedes: 12/28//06

Process:
     Information Questionnaire
	Author:
	     A. Langer
	          Page _____ of _____

Type of User: Internal _____   Customer: _____   Consumer: _____

User Market: (Briefly Describe)

Expected Length of User Longevity: _____

Number of Users in the Market: _____

Briefly Describe Why Users will use this Web Site:

What Functions do Users need on this Web Site:

What Products and Services do you Plan to Offer:

Figure 7.9 *(Continued)*

Application:
Web Branding

Page _____ of _____

What Messages, Logos, and Other Information do you want Users to Experience?:

How often does the Design and Content need to Change?

Daily: _____
Weekly: _____
Monthly: _____
Quarterly: _____
Other: _____

Profile Strategy: Define Information that you plan to obtain from your users

Address: _____
Age: _____
Gender: _____
Computer Experience: _____
Connectivity: _____

Preferences: Describe the intended audience a   nd the overall goals that you want your users to experience:

Preference Type: Focused: _____   Multiple: _____   General: _____

Personalization Options:

Color: _____
Music: _____
Graphics: _____
Other: _____

Figure 7.9 *(Continued)*

Application: Web Branding	Page _____ of _____

Customer Service:

Order Confirmation Message: _____
Messaging: _____
Message Attachment: _____
Selective E-Mail: _____
Order Status: _____

Special Service Offers:

Service Types: _____
Basis of Eligibility: _____

Description:

Figure 7.9 Web branding input questionnaire.

Text

What is the role of ecommerce analysts and designers in the creation of text content? Certainly their responsibilities lie outside the actual content itself. Many ecommerce books confuse the issue of who is to create the text content. To clarify this issue is to simply go back to the core definition of analysis and design, which is essentially to create logical equivalents for development. Therefore, ecommerce analysts/designers need to understand how users want the text arranged, categorized, and formatted. There are also architectural issues of how content needs to be maintained. This section sets forth the key components to provide Web developers with what they need to complete the site.

Text Layout

Layout refers to the placement and arrangement of text on the page. This includes text justification (left, center, etc.), columns, and text frames. Layout also has to do with formatting text—e.g., bolding, type size, type color, etc.—to highlight important information. Such methods of text contrast work to direct users' interest to the focal point of the page. For example, the center and top part of a page are usually the best places to get a user's attention. Consideration of the focal point also involves repetition—of key design elements and patterns of text. Repetition is important to consider, because users seek to become comfortable with any

Web site they use. Consistent layout and formatting can help users begin to feel "at home" on a site.

Text Categorization

Text categorization relates to placement of text. Categorization also focuses on the grouping of text to enable users to find it. Text can be grouped by categories like location, gender, date, time, etc. Such grouping allows users to find relevant information quickly, such as in searching for movie theatres in a specific location. Included in text categorization is the use of search criteria, which allows users to see views of data based on some dynamic sorting of text. One method to determine the proper groups and categorizations is the storyboarding concept. In storyboarding, slides are developed to represent the text that needs to appear on a specific Web page. Having each slide in a particular order allows analysts, designers, and users to get a better understanding of how the text needs to be viewed and what options need to be available. Storyboarding, which was also utilized in prototyping, can be used during design to determine text placement in relation to graphics. The prototype storyboards that were used in Chapter 3 lack the combination of real text and real graphics, so this step during Web design is really the basis of finalizing the Web page prototypes.

Text Formatting

The formatting of text focuses more on presentation than the other two components. Formatting refers to the methods of screen presentation usually through the use of menus, maps, and frames.

Menus can be defined as single-column lists or multiple-column lists; they can even be designed as tables. Functionally, menus can be used for two purposes: (1) to display information in a hierarchical format or (2) as way of linking to other sites from the current Web page. Combinations of the two are also often used, as shown in Figure 7.10: *www.fathom.com*. This example shows how a menu of member schools appears when the user places the mouse pointer by the words "Member Institutions." The user can then click on items in the list to go to the sites of the member institution.

While menus are easy to develop, they sometimes can be boring to a user. An alternative format is a map that combines a graphic with text. This is accomplished by placing a cursor over an image. The cursor will eventually display the name of description in text, which also contains a hyperlink to another Web location. These hyperlink areas are called *hot regions* (Conger and Mason, 1998). Figure 7.11 is an example of how a map is used in the Web site *www.cluetrain.com*. When the user places the mouse pointer on the book, it displays text that tells the user more about the graphic and allows the user to hyperlink to another Web page.

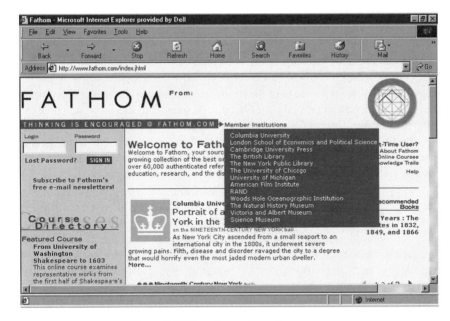

Figure 7.10 Text formatting using menus.

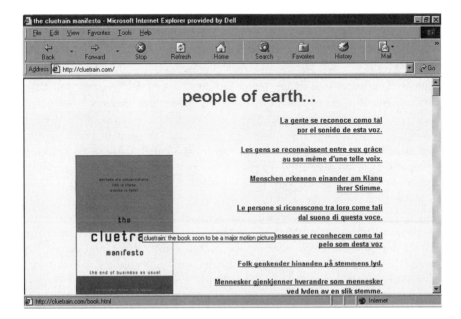

Figure 7.11 Text formatting using maps.

The problem with maps is that they tend to become very large and can take time to load on the Web page. Because of this dilemma, many Web designers also provide a text-only version of the site, which can add to the complexity of design and incur more development time.

Frames are a way to segregate Web page text into separate windows that can behave independently. These sub-areas allow certain parts of the Web site to remain visible while the user moves to another screen. Frames are similar to headers or sidebars in printed text. Figure 7.12 shows the site *www.alanger.com*. The first example shows a screen with a standard header screen and a body section for "Programs at Columbia," which is one of the options in the header menu. The second screen shows the same header frame, with a different body section for "The Firm."

A key benefit of frames is that they can accommodate multiple types of media including graphics and text. They are also easy to display in different browsers and compatible with lower versions of HTML. Another benefit of frames is that they can be used as reusable components. So once the frame has been designed, it can be encapsulated within many screens and even within ecommerce systems. Developers need only to employ an engineering tool or program that allows frames to be updated when changes are made. The disadvantages of frames are that they tend to be small, and they have limited space on each screen. Sometimes the display of a frame on one Web page may need to be different on another, so formatting frames can be a problem.

Content Templates

I mentioned briefly above that frames can be devised in the form of reusable objects and that there are systems that automate the updating of changes in content. The actual unit of the frame's storage is called a Content Template. Content templates are objects of text and/or graphics that are stored as separate files, and reused by a Web site. Using content templates reduces the need to reprogram information and graphics that are repeated throughout a Web system. The benefit also relates to maintenance programming; instead of changing multiple sites, Web developers simply "link" content templates to frames within a Web page. Each time the Web page is loaded, the most current version of the template is loaded. The benefits in maintenance savings must of course outweigh the overhead considerations, which affect the load time and storage requirements for the site. The other obstacle in template development recalls the challenge of creating object-oriented systems: the overall effort, scope, and complexity of designing reusable systems. While it sounds easy, it requires the necessary cooperation of skills to develop, especially for ecommerce systems, which have an enormous reach throughout the organization. Finally, an important benefit of content templates relates to good publishing practices; they allow the appropriate personnel to participate in the creation and updating of content, from logos,

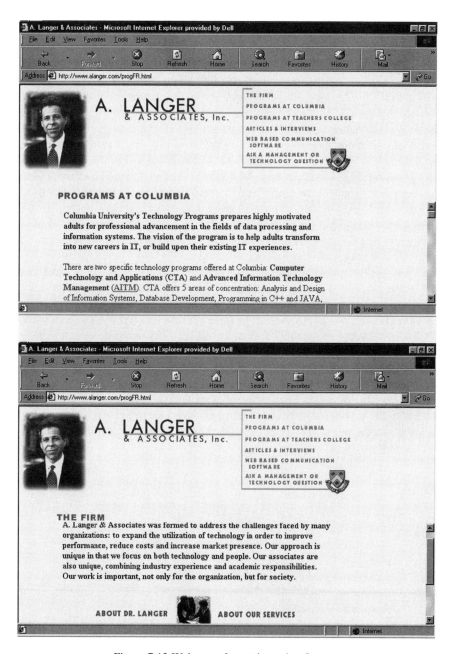

Figure 7.12 Web page formatting using frames.

to text, to graphic images that need consistent presentation for the ecommerce system to be successful.

Visuals

A Web site's visual design is often the first thing that users notice (Powell, 2000). Indeed, first impressions are lasting ones, and the impact of visuals will heavily influence a user's perception of a site's value. However, users tend to focus less on visuals as they become more familiar with using a site. There is much written about "take-away value" and "e-loyalty," which are defined as the influences that make users come back to a site. Thus, it is important to focus on the visual effect but also to recognize the site architecture and navigation as important components. Good analysts and designers understand that form is function. Design is not a battle between form and function, but rather the intertwining of them both, as great architects have always known. This section explores the challenge of how to combine great navigation and site architecture with the psychology of visual design.

If we are first to explore the psychology of design it is important to agree that for most users, the Web is a visual experience. Because of this reality, there are concepts, moods, and identities that can be portrayed through the visual affect on a site through its images. And let us not forget the old saying "You remember 50 % of what you read, but 100 % of what you see." However, understanding the visual experience is complex; it includes color, images, and backgrounds. Color must be used properly to convey the appropriate mood and cultural meaning. Images, on the other hand, can be slow to load, a factor that will affect the usability of the Web site. From a usability perspective, background contrast is critical to the way users work with the images and foreground texts. Thus, color, images, and the use of backgrounds all contribute to the success or failure of a Web design.

Color

There are three components that define color:

1. *Hue*: this represents the actual name of the color and refers to the quality itself.
2. *Value*: the degree of the lightness or darkness of the color.
3. *Saturation*: the intensity or purity of the color. The brighter the color the more saturated it is.

There are also three descriptors of color. First there are chromatic hues, which are all colors other than black, white, and gray. Second are neutral colors, which are black, white, and gray (non-chromatic hues). Third are the monochromatic combinations that represent variations of value and saturation to form a single hue. There are a number of factors relating to how these definitions of color are used in the analysis and design of ecommerce Web sites. The first significant issue is to determine the domain of colors to be supported by your Web site. This decision is directly correlated to the type of browser to be supported. Within a browser is what is known as "safe colors" or colors that are supported by most browsers. "Safe colors" also relate to the differences in the hue, saturation, and value that each type of computer and browser might display. What appears as one set of colors on one machine might look different on another computer. Sometimes such variations can affect the mood and experience of the site. In some cases, such as with logo colors, variations can confuse the brand image being presented to the user. From an analysis and design perspective, color selection is a critical step in creating mood. During interviews with users, it is important that they understand the alternatives in selecting colors, especially as they relate to the "safe" domain.

Another important analysis step is defining bit depth. Bit depth controls the number of bits used to display the image on the screen. The number of bits supported by a computer are controlled by its video card and its monitor. Users need to be aware of the type of computers needed to support the color schemes and hues they wish to attain. These issues may result either in changing the color scheme, or in requesting standardized computer interface units. Obviously, if the users are consumers, the probability of knowing this information is limited or based on market research data. In many cases decisions on color support are strategic decisions, that is, an informed decision to force users to bring their computers to a level that allows them to interface with the system. This decision is typically based on whether continuing at a lower or "safer" color level inevitably creates an inferior product. Perhaps the most important decision is to determine the browser-safe limit. The range of colors can vary from 256 and below to well over a million. Furthermore, it is important to remember that PCs and Apples have different 256 color match-ups, meaning that one blue may not match the other. In many instances the computer will attempt to "dither" if you go outside the domain of browser-safe colors. *Dithering* is a method that the computer uses to attempt to match the color selected, and it results in speckled or dotted color schemes, not the kind of look that ecommerce systems desire. Ultimately the decision about how to implement the color scheme is up to developers, but analysts should explain to all concerned parties the importance of determining the limit early in the analysis process.

Aside from physical issues and limitations, it is important to understand the meanings that colors convey to users. Colors often have different meanings in different cultures, so analysts need to focus on where the audience is, or how many different audiences are intending to use the Web system. For example, Western cultures associate black with death, but in Japan the color of death is White. On many Web sites, color is used as part of the identity and branding. Figure 7.13 represents common themes associated with color.

Furthermore, with advancements in color hand-held devices, issues surrounding color compatibilities are becoming more challenging and provide even more reason to stick within the boundaries of safe colors. However, color

Color	Theme
Red	Hot, error, stop, warning, aggression, fire, lushness, daring
Pink	Female, cute, cotton candy
Orange	Warm, autumnal, Halloween
Yellow	Happy, caution, sunny, cheerful, slow down
Brown	Warm, fall, dirty
Green	Envy, pastoral, jealousy, inexperience, fertility, newness
Blue	Peaceful, sadness, water, male
Purple	Royalty, luxury
Black	Evil, death, mourning, ghostly, night, fear
Gray	Overcast, gloom, old age
White	Virginal, clean, innocent, winter, cold

Source: *The Complete Web Reference Guide*, Powell (2000)

Figure 7.13 Common color themes.

alone can be deceiving. Contrast, particularly with hand-held devices that support only gray scales, can present another problem when designing Web sites. The more platforms supported, the more reason to have separate Web sites to support them. Of course, this means having multiple sites to support one product. Once again, having content templates and reusable components can become very attractive for portable software projects.

Images

Images represent things visually. Effective images convey thoughts, concepts and identity, with or without supporting text. Meanings can be displayed through images such as a button, a heading, or a graphic caption that helps convey an experience or a message. The difficulty with images is determining which provides the best experience for the user and conveys the message and identity that the company desires. From an architectural perspective, images can be stored in a number of different formats. Some of these formats can affect the file size and compression requirements. Size always affects the time it takes to display the image.

Analysts also need to determine the image type. There are two basic types of image storage: vector images and bitmapped images. Unless a plug-in is installed on the computer, the Web supports only bitmapped images. Vector images are discussed in Chapter 6. Bitmapped images are essentially a group of pixels of different colors that combined form the image. Because of the large number of pixels they contain, bitmaps are usually very large files. There are alternatives to compressing bitmap files, but uncompressing these files wastes more time than is saved by compression. The most popular compression image types are GIF (Graphics Interchange Format) and JPEG (Joint Photographic Experts Group). GIF are the most widely used on the Web because they work well with large areas of continuous colors. The downside of GIF images is that they support only 8-bit color for a maximum of 256 colors in a given image. Therefore, GIF files may have color loss when displaying true-type images, such as photographs. JPEG, on the other hand, is more suited for working with photographs, particularly those that have many shades of gray. JPEG is not as efficient in compression as GIF and also may display different levels of clarity depending on the color range on the computer. JPEG also does not provide good quality compression for line drawings or text. Therefore, the basic rule is for analysts to require GIF images for illustrations and JPEG images for photographs.

Backgrounds

The use of backgrounds is a tricky proposition, particularly backgrounds that contain texture. In general, busy backgrounds are not good for Web pages. When a background is desired, it is usually developed with a product like Photoshop, which can generate seamless shapes. The other problem associated with backgrounds is load time. Indeed, a background is nothing more than a large image. When using background loads, it is recommended that the software use tiles or sections; this reduces the time it takes overall to display the page.

Effective backgrounds are usually subtle images that convey a message, mood, or identity. For example, Figure 7.14 shows the *www.alanger.com* site, which has a background that identifies my association with Columbia University.

Another interesting example of background design is Figure 7.15, which is the site of the Rhode Island School of Design (*www.risd.edu*). This site shows how background can be integrated with imagery to convey a cultural view of the school.

The other issue with background is contrast with text. A fault of the Rhode Island School of Design is the difficulty in seeing the text on the site. The number of images, from this perspective, serves only to clutter the site and make it more difficult for a user to get the information they want. This kind of problem determination leads Web designers back to the original concept of approaching site design: who are the users?

Web designers will continue to be challenged in handling all of the diverse color, image, and background problems that exist in ecommerce systems. Furthermore, the movement to wireless hand-held devices will create yet another group of difficult decisions that need to be made among users, analysts, and designers. It is important to note that while Web design continues to be an art form, there are very real engineering issues that need to be discussed before the aesthetics of what is delivered to the user's desktop is decided. This is the area in which analysis and design must cooperate with the artistic element.

Figure 7.14 Enhanced image using background effects.

Figure 7.15 Use of background to represent organization culture.

Web Site Navigation and Architecture

The other important aspect of visual design is the architecture and navigation of the system itself. Indeed, the navigation and use of color, images, and background are inherently related. Navigation can be defined as the science and art of getting people or things from one place to another. While text can be pre-determined based on *what* we want to convey to the user community, visuals are strongly influenced by *how* the site is architected. The key components of Web navigation are:

- Where am I?
- Where can I go?
- How do I get where I want to go?
- How can I return from where I've gone?

Design of visuals and placement of text will be based on the answers to the above questions. Fleming (1998) offered 10 principles of successful Web navigation:

1. *Be easily learned*: Web navigation must be intuitively obvious to its users.
2. *Remain consistent*: the navigation style should be consistently represented across all Web pages.
3. *Provide feedback*: this involves creating controls that provide information to users to confirm their understanding of an image or option.
4. *Appear in context*: this relates to allowing users to get back, or to understand where they are on the site, so that the page can direct them to the next possible tasks that they might want to do.
5. *Offer alternatives*: provide as many options of things that the user might want to do, without creating a clutter effect.
6. *Require an economy of action and time*: Web designers need to be aware of how long it takes to complete a function or a task.
7. *Provide clear visual messages*: the visual guidance of the site through hierarchies of selections and icons that define functionality.
8. *Use clear and understandable labels*: common-sense and user-sensitive labels that depict the meaning of a given selection. Terminology must match users.
9. *Be appropriate to the site's purpose*: create ecommerce systems that meet the goals and objectives of the business. For example, a shopping site will be different from a site created for informational services. Mismatches between a site's purpose and navigational approach can cause user confusion.
10. *Support users' goals and behaviors*: ensure that the site is what users want it to be, not what you think it should be.

There are no easy solutions to good navigation and site architecture. The real answer lies in the user community, so it is important to explore how ecommerce analysts and designers can formulate the navigation and architecture that will work for users. This challenge, like so many others, must be faced during the user interface phase. One of the best methods of approaching the design of navigation is to categorize the type of site you are planning to deliver. There are six categories of design sites that will assist in the process of determining the style of the navigation and site architecture:

1. *Shopping Sites*: focuses on serving consumers and deals with issues of trust and security. Areas of concern include the security of financial information, protection of privacy, finding items of interest quickly, assistance for those who are unsure of what they want, preview of products for review, and dealing with problems or returns.
2. *Community Sites*: these sites need to explore creating shared spaces. Issues of concern are rules of participation, privacy of identity, obtaining feedback, authenticity of information, learning more about users from the community, and getting assistance from the community.
3. *Entertainment Sites*: focus on avoiding user distractions and attracting users to immerse themselves in the activities. Issues of concern relate to whether users know where to begin, understanding what will happen, how do they receive help, what practice do users need to have, and how will users know when they are finished.
4. *Identity Sites*: these sites need to ensure they send the right message to their users, and to create various attractions to get users onto the system. Issues to be addressed relate to knowing about the company, finding out about products, and finding contact information.
5. *Learning Sites*: must deal with multiple learning preferences and allowing users opportunities to improve their skills. Users of these sites need to know where to begin, what special knowledge they need to have, authenticity of information, obtaining information that is appropriate, and knowing how to experiment.
6. *Information Sites*: these sites must allow users to find information quickly. Therefore, they employ shortcuts for speed. Issues relating to these users are confirming whether they are on the correct site, finding the specific information they need, helping them look for what they think they want, authenticity and practicality of information, and storing information for later use.

Navigation Placement

A difficult question to answer is where on a Web site should navigation occur? There are five places to put navigation elements: top, bottom, left, right, and center. As with so many other issues in technology, there are positives and negatives of each placement.

Navigation at the Top

Placing navigation at the top of the screen ensures that users will see it first as a screen loads. Also, as with the Windows paradigm, key navigation menus appear at the top of the screen, so putting navigation capabilities at the top seems consistent and natural to the user. The largest problem with top navigation is that it can disappear off the screen as a user scrolls down. This problem can be addressed by providing navigation links that take users back to the top. A navigation palette can also be used as in Netscape, which ensures that the palette stays on the screen regardless which feature is being used. Figure 7.16 depicts the Netscape menu palette on the *www.alanger.com* site. Still another option is to provide navigation links at the bottom of the page.

Navigation as a Metaphor

Metaphor is a concept that has been used to help people understand things by using symbols, concepts, or words. A metaphor can be an important concept for learning as well as for communication. Technology has for some time used metaphors to provide simpler and more exciting definitions for users: for example, the Internet as the "information highway," or the Web as "cyberspace." Thus, a metaphor allows us to provide our view of the world as we want others to see it—a perfect concept for Web design. The navigation, along with metaphors,

Figure 7.16 Using palettes in a browser.

can be a significant component of ultimately deciding on the correct strategies and alternatives that have been offered in this chapter. Indeed, metaphors and navigation form the center of creating the kinds of experiences that we want our users to have. According to Dalgleish (2000) site metaphors include:

- *Lobby*: users are greeted by a virtual representation of a physical lobby they are familiar with.
- *Personal organizer*: users refer to the functions that a personal organizer performs to use organizational tools on the Web.
- *Desktop*: this is similar to the Windows desktop in that it represents a virtual physical desk with specific tools for different functions.
- *Folder*: a virtual folder is one that keeps data in separate files and allows users to navigate easily through each folder.
- *Briefcase*: the physical act of having a collection of information that is always available. This can be correlated to a collection of information and tools on Web sites.
- *Shopping cart*: the virtual shopping cart collects information as one "shops" through the Web site.
- *Gallery*: users can browse a virtual space in the same manner as if they were there physically. This is often done with multimedia software to enact a movement within and around a particular space.
- *Guide*: this is a virtual tour through a space, and typically provides advice on particular areas of interest to the user.
- *Neighborhood*: individuals are collected into a community where they have a role to play or a stake in what occurs.

These metaphors can be classified into three types:

1. Organizational metaphors, which relate to important concepts in the known organization. These metaphors are very useful in the development of internal or Intranet ecommerce systems.
2. Functional metaphors that attempt to match the virtual to the physical functions.
3. Visual metaphors, which virtually leverage from a user's visual recognition of known concepts.

Overall, the concept of metaphor is a fitting conclusion to the section on navigation. Indeed, it is the use of metaphor that allows analysts and designers to relate the physical world to the logical experience. Thus, I again use the concept of the logical equivalence to describe the design of virtual equivalents to what people are accustomed to experiencing. The difference in this case is the aesthetic and creative foundation that is required to provide the same experience, while at the same time creating the brand and image of the business. All this needs to be accomplished through design and navigation and represented in an intuitive, consistent, and organized manner.

Site Architecture

Web navigation needs to be finalized by ultimately developing the site architecture. The site architecture provides the blueprint for the movement from one Web page and site to another. It is the schematic of the Web design. The first purpose of this section is to define the different site organizational models. There are four main logical organizations: linear, grid, hierarchy, and web.

Linear

Linear architecture is common because it resembles the way we read a book, that is, it starts and moves forward in a linear fashion. In linear site architecture, users can move from screen to screen without jumping around in some progressive sequence. Linear Web architecture allows for bi-directionality. Figure 7.17 represents the different types of linear models.

Grid

Grid sites use a dual linear structure that provides for both horizontal and vertical relationships between pages. When properly designed, grids provide for orderly

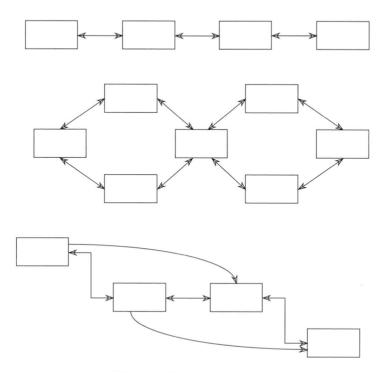

Figure 7.17 Types of linear site organization models.

movements both vertically and horizontally. While a grid allows for many options in moving around a site, it can be dangerous. Too many vertical and horizontal alternatives can create disjointed Web sites. While grids seem to be appealing, they tend to be too unstructured and often are not useful for good Web navigation designs. Figure 7.18 represents a grid architecture format.

Hierarchy

Hierarchies are one of the most common architecture structures. Indeed, the hierarchy is a visual representation of functional decomposition. In essence, the hierarchical concept is consistent with the way most common Web sites operate. Hierarchical structures are typically called trees. The concept of a tree is that as you go down the hierarchy, the number of children or nodes expands, so it horizontally becomes wider. The overall view resembles a physical tree. The other significant feature of a tree is that no node, or child, can have more than one parent. This is an excellent site concept for Web structures because it supports the "only one way back" process. Thus, the movement from a home page to other pages can be very structured and clearly represented; the way back retraces the footsteps without jumping around. Figure 7.19 represents the different types of hierarchy trees that can be designed into the site architecture.

Where there is structure, there can be violations of the pure tree model. This violation is called a "mixed" hierarchy, in which parents can talk directly to grandchildren, thus skipping over a node. Furthermore, nodes or Web pages at the same level, called siblings, can also communicate with each other. While this format is very versatile, it typically leads to similar problems as does the grid. Too much versatility destroys structure, and without structure there can be no order. Figure 7.20 is an example of a mixed or unstructured hierarchy.

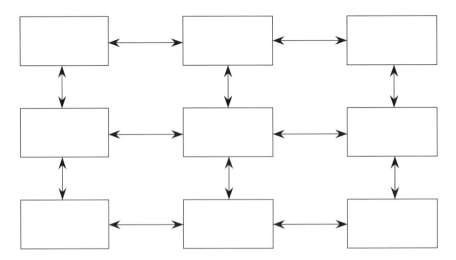

Figure 7.18 Grid site model.

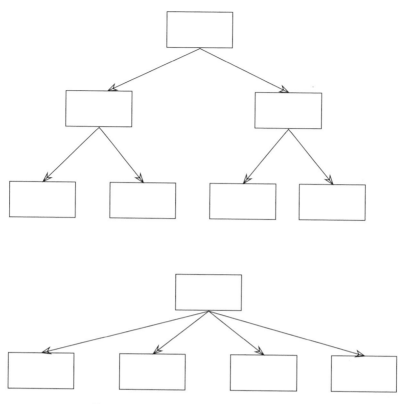

Figure 7.19 Hierarchy site organization model.

Web

Multiple permutations of Web page linkages create an unstructured model. Interestingly enough, an unstructured site is called a Web structure. Figure 7.21 represents a Web structure and shows the possible confusions that can occur when there are multiple links to the same Web page. While there is a problem

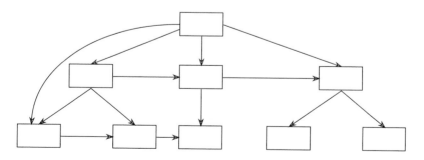

Figure 7.20 Mixed hierarchy site organization model.

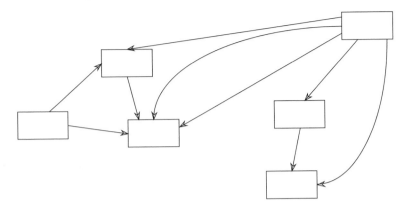

Figure 7.21 Web organization model.

with structure, the model lends itself to more expression by allowing dynamic links to be added to the site without concern of a strong mental model.

Actual site architecture diagrams can take many forms. Figure 7.22 shows some alternative completed site architecture examples.

Non-Web-Based Interfaces

While Web-based interfaces are the most popular, there are still many systems that use just GUI or character-based interfaces.

The history of GUI can be traced as far back as the early Xerox systems. Apple was the first company, through its introduction of the Macintosh computer, to effectively commercialize the concept of graphical applications using a mouse. When Microsoft Windows was introduced in the late 1980s, the use of GUI got another major boost. While there are no industry-mandated rules for GUI design, the dominance of the Microsoft Windows product line has resulted in some de facto design standards.

Character-based screens,[17] on the other hand, are often associated with mainframe applications of the 1960s and 1970s; however, many such applications still exist today and continue to be found on mid-range and personal computers. While character-based applications remain important, they are diminishing over time, especially as a result of the popularity of Web-based applications that depend on icons and graphical images. Therefore, this chapter will focus on designing the user interface with graphically driven screens.

---

[17] Character-based screens are those that are composed of only words and captions. Selection of screen options is accomplished through the entering of a code, as opposed to through an object typically called an icon. Character-based screens also do not contain built-in screen features such as drop-down menus, radio buttons, and check boxes.

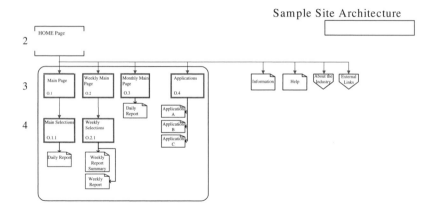

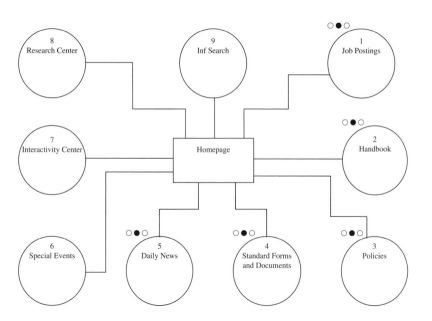

Figure 7.22 Site architecture formats.

GUI and Styles of Manipulation

A GUI is the primary mechanism that enables the user to interact with a collection of elements, called "screen objects," that are visible to the user and used by him/her to perform tasks. To accomplish these tasks, users perform various types of operations on these objects. Operations are executed using one of the two types of GUI manipulation: direct and indirect.

The term "direct manipulation" was first used by Ben Shneiderman in 1982 to describe a particular style of human interaction with a screen. Direct manipulation portrays the system as an extension of the real world where users can relate to objects and icons that remind them of real-world symbols. Direct manipulation allows the user to access and modify these symbols so that they can be used to activate tasks. Thus, selecting an icon to perform a task, such as hitting the "save" icon in a word processing program, is an example of a direct manipulation. Direct manipulation relates to the concept of WYSIWYG (what you see is what you get) and must therefore result in an immediate reaction or resultant event.

Indirect manipulation, on the other hand, represents a task that effectively executes another. Thus, selecting an icon that provides a list of other selections can be considered an indirect method for executing what is really desired. An indirect manipulation can be thought of as an easy way to select alternative direct methods. Most GUI designs use a combination of both manipulation methods.

Advantages of GUI Systems

Overall, GUI represents a simplified interface that promises to:

- reduce the need for users to remember how applications work;
- enhance the human ability to process information through a computer interface; and
- reduce the learning time to master a computer application.

Listed below are a number of specific examples of how GUI systems help users.

1. Symbols are recognized faster than text because their shapes and colors are more easily classifiable.

Different shapes   Text looks similar   Different shapes in similar circles.

2. Symbols can be easily learned. A graphical, pictorial representation has been found to aid learning.
3. Visual or spatial representations of information have been found to be easier to retain and manipulate.

4. Greater simplicity of graphics makes remembering easier.
5. Actions and visual skills developed before languages in humans. Human beings have a powerful image memory.
6. Spatial relationships are usually more quickly understood than verbal representations.
7. Concrete thinking is enhanced when objects are displayed directly in the high-level task domain. Abstract thinking is minimized.
8. Concrete thinking reduces errors.
9. Immediate feedback develops quicker reflexes. If the path of action is going in the wrong direction, then prompts to correct the path occur sooner.
10. Ability to reverse unwanted or reconsidered actions increases user control, confidence, and system mastery.
11. Icons possess more universality than text and are more easily comprehended worldwide.
12. Moving from a command language to direct manipulation is relatively easy. The reverse is not the case.

Disadvantages of GUI Systems

Some users have found the GUI to be more difficult to work with in some cases, particularly with respect to applications that require only simple data input. Furthermore, as graphical systems become more sophisticated, interfaces will become increasingly more complex. The following is a list of perceived GUI disadvantages.

1. Design complexity. Layers upon layers of options are packed into an interface.
2. When a user confronts the interface in an application for the first time, the sequence of necessary steps does not always seem intuitive.
3. Lack of thoroughly researched guidelines. Increased GUI complexity unleashes too many variables that must be controlled in order to establish meaningful cause-and-effect relationships.
4. Inconsistencies in technique and terminology occur because of copyright and legal constraints and product differentiation pressures.
5. The working domain is always in the present. Usually, icons don't have past or future tense. When users click on a button, the button takes action immediately. However, there is no reason that delay options could not be implemented.
6. Symbolic representations may not be as familiar as words or numbers.
7. There may be a limit to a human's capability to engage a more complex interface.
8. GUI interfaces are slower to act than character-based applications. There is also more application overhead.

9. Symbols cannot be clearly produced across different hardware technologies. Some are not equally legible or recognizable.
10. Inefficient for touch typists. Moving a mouse is a much slower motor movement than typing.
11. The screen can easily become more cluttered, resulting in the user having more responsibility to do screen housekeeping.
12. Requires more computer processing power.

Conclusion

Regardless of the relative pluses and minuses of GUI, the reality is that today's systems increasingly require it, and Web applications demand it. Different interface styles have different capacities. Some concepts and tasks are better suited than others for pure graphical presentation. Therefore, it is the design of the interface and not its interaction style that is the most reliable success factor. The success of a graphical system depends on the skills of its analysts and designers in following established principles of usability.

Where to Begin

Screens can be designed using a number of approaches. Under the best circumstances, the analyst should first complete data flow and process flow diagramming, creating the data dictionary, and producing process specifications. Taking these steps is an important precursor to screen design, allowing the analyst to begin mapping elements needed for screen to the data elements that exist in the data dictionary. The process specifications are also critical because they usually contain the business rules that often govern the way the elements behave during the user interface. Furthermore, the process of designing screens may even lead to process specification updates because of new requirements that get formulated during the development and approval of screen functionality. We must remember that in GUI applications, most functions are initiated through a screen program. Process flow diagrams may be extremely useful to screen design because they follow the user's sequential needs. Thus, mapping screen requirements to each process can be a useful step in beginning design. It should be understood, however, that screens and processes do not have a one-to-one relationship. While such a relationship may exist, it is totally incidental. Take the following example:

The screen of Figure 7.23 depicts three actual processes. Figure 7.24 shows the corresponding processes as they are represented in a PFD.

Another, alternative, approach to designing screens is to start with the ERD. In this case, every data element in the ERD is mapped to a specific processing point in the system. This processing point is then correlated to a screen. Unfortunately,

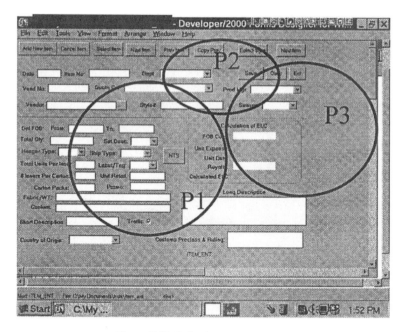

Figure 7.23 Order item entry screen.

this approach has many limitations. First, not every data element in the ERD may be required to appear on a screen. Second, there are many fields that are results of calculations that must be displayed, but are not elements in the database (remember that 3rd normal form will eliminate derived elements). Figure 7.25 depicts a screen that has been mapped to an ERD. The actual data element names are linked to the screen fields. Notice, however, that the screen fields labeled "Duty" and "Expenses" are not mapped because they must be computed each time the screen program is executed. Thus, these elements are 3rd NF failures because they are derived.

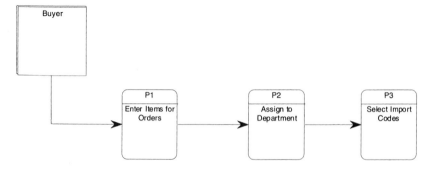

Figure 7.24 Process flow of order entry screen.

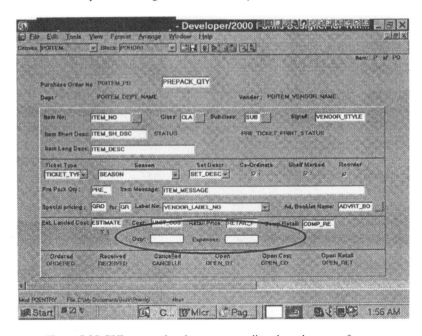

Figure 7.25 GUI screen showing corresponding data element reference.

Yet another common method is to use the screens from the legacy system as a starting point. Most software development projects are not done from scratch, meaning that there is an existing system in place. Under this procedure, the analyst obtains copies of every screen in the existing system. The screens are then modified with new GUI functionality that is needed by the new system. While this sounds very straightforward, character-based screens often do not map easily to their GUI counterparts. The analyst must be especially careful not to attempt to simply duplicate the screens in the legacy software. Figure 7.26 depicts a character-based legacy screen. Note that there can be up to four Contract/POs as shown in the upper right-hand corner. The user is required to enter each Contract/PO on a separate screen.

On the other hand, the replacement GUI screen (Figure 7.27) takes advantage of the view bar that allows for scrolling in a window. Therefore, the GUI version requires only one physical screen, as opposed to four.

Still another method of designing screens is to hold separate user interviews, with the sole focus of determining the types of screens that are needed. This process, which can be effectively done using JAD sessions, is a way of reconciling the screens against the process specifications, data dictionary, and flow diagrams (DFDs and PFDs). Often, analysts may try to develop prototype screens based on their knowledge and understanding of the requirements from the structured tools. This can at least provide users with something to critique. Screens can be quickly drawn using a number of prototype packages, although almost every development tool, such as Oracle/and Visual Basic, have easy-to-use screen

		Bill of Lading Container		Screen 1 of 4

B/L:____   SCAC: ____   VESSEL: _____   Total: ____
                        VOYAGE: _____   CTN: ____

PO Information

Contract/PO: _____   Tot Unit: _____
Item: _____   GWT: _____
Style: _____   CBM: _____
Stat: _____   O/F Chrg: _____
Orig Country: _____   Con Rate: _____

Activities

Activity	Descr	Date	Location

Figure 7.26 Character-based user screen.

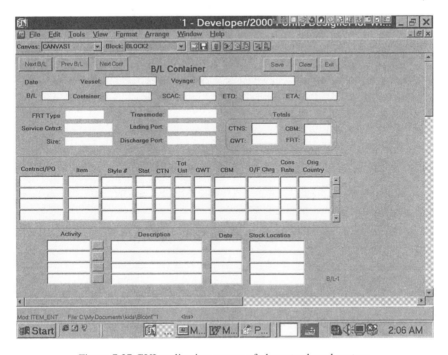

Figure 7.27 GUI replication screen of character-based system.

painter features. A screen painter is a graphic tool within a development product that allows you to design a screen quickly for prototype use. The main advantage here is that the screen painter interfaces with features that allow the prototype to be converted to a production version of the screen. The production version or compile feature of the product can typically be used by programmers after the prototype screen is passed to them for development.

Screen design is a very iterative process. It usually starts with just a drawing of the screen in pencil. The analyst then prototypes the screen for presentation. At this point, the users may need to have the screens "linked" so that they can get a sense of how the screens integrate as a product. Screen linking can be accomplished by using Microsoft's Powerpoint; still others have actual linking capabilities in their prototype feature. In any event, users need to get a sense of how the screens work. After one or two iterations of review, the analyst should then provide development with the source screens so that they can be implemented. As screens are completed, they should again be shown to users for their approval.

Components of the GUI

There are a number of parts that can go with the design of a user screen: (1) operating system; (2) application; and (3) interapplication.

An operating system component relates to the de facto universal Microsoft or Apple menus and icons that interface with the operating system itself. Examples of these controls are the Application Window Menu Bar, sizing control icons, and the Microsoft Application bar. These controls are summarized below and shown on the sample application screen in Figure 7.28

Border: Also known as a "frame," a border defines the boundaries of a window view and distinguishes it from other windows.

Title Bar: This is the top line of the window and explains the purpose or name of the window function.

Work Area: This is the portion of the screen inside the borders of the window where the user performs tasks.

System Menu Button: This button is located at the left corner of the title bar and is also called the "control menu" or the "window menu." This button is used as an aid to keyboard users and lists options for manipulating the window. This includes commands such as *Restore, Minimize, Maximize*, and, *Close*.

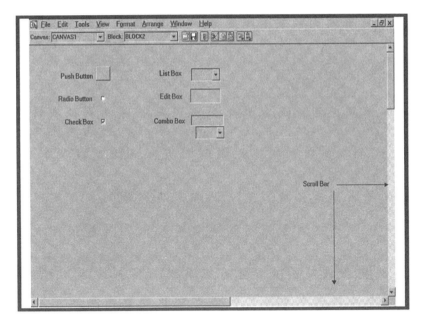

Figure 7.28 GUI screen features.

Title Bar Icon: This icon is located in the left corner of the title bar and is used to retrieve a pull-down menu of commands that apply to the object in the window.

Window Sizing Buttons: These buttons are located on the right corner of the title bar and are used to manipulate the size of the active window.

Menu Bar: This is used to organize and provide access to actions that are listed horizontally across the top of the screen and below the title bar.

Status Bar: Also known as a "message bar," the status bar provides information to the user about the state or status of the information or object inside the window.

Scroll Bars: These appear when all displayed information cannot be presented within the current window boundaries. The vertical scroll bar at the right of a window controls the up-and-down scrolling, while the horizontal scroll bar controls right-to-left movement.

Split Box/Split Bar: This is a window that is split into two or more pieces, or panes. Split boxes can be manipulated using the split bar, which is located above the vertical scroll bar.

Control Bar: This represents an array of choices and commands that need to be viewed in an accessible area of the screen and are maintained in the display area. Examples include button bars, color or pattern palettes, toolbars, rulers, and ribbons.

Size Grip: This a handle in a window that permits the window to be resized. The resizing is accomplished by dragging the grip and moving the window to the desired size. The grip is located in the lower right corner of the window. It is identified by 3 angled parallel lines.

What's This? The question mark indicates to the system that the user wishes to ask a question about the object being pointed to.

The application screen component consists of the specific data elements that are needed by the screen application program. One can visualize that the application component interfaces with the data elements in the ERD. The application component is the most free-flowing and involves the most design issues. There are a limited number of application screen tools such as buttons, check boxes, and drop-down selections. The specific component controls within an application screen are depicted below:

O   *Radio Button:* This is used when there are two or more mutually exclusive options. A dot in the circle indicates that the option has been selected.

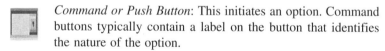 *Command or Push Button:* This initiates an option. Command buttons typically contain a label on the button that identifies the nature of the option.

Check Box: This used when you have one or more options that are independent of each other. A checked box indicates that the option is selected.

Scroll Bar: A scroll bar scrolls the screen either horizontally or vertically. The purpose of the scroll bar is to allow users to input or view more information than is available on the normal screen view.

 List Box: These are used to display several choices. There are two types of list boxes. Single selection list boxes force the user to choose one selection. Multiple selection list boxes allow the user to make several selections. Multiple selections is a useful option if the user is choosing several items that will be acted upon the same way.

Combo Box: This is used when you want to provide the user with the ability to either select from a list or enter a value. A good example is the "Save As" feature in Windows, where a user can either leave the default value or change the name by overwriting it. Combo boxes are also useful for ensuring that the insert of a foreign key points to a valid parent value (see the Chapter 6 section titled "Business Rules").

Text or Edit Box: This is used simply to enter or edit data. Text boxes are used frequently for screens that require data entry and for display of data. Data that is only displayed is often shown as gray without a black outline. Thus, just the text appears on the screen.

Database Design

The database design of Web-based software is particularly challenging when an Internet/Intranet architecture is desired. As discussed above, security of data becomes a major issue in two areas. First, data must be encrypted in some fashion for users from within the company that are accessing internal sensitive data. While these elements are traveling via an Internet connection, they are vulnerable to illegal access. The only method to secure such data is to encrypt it, meaning that the data is scrambled using a sophisticated algorithm. Even if the data is illegally accessed or copied, it would have to be decrypted, or unscrambled, to be understood. Offenders would thus need to be sophisticated enough to know how to "break" the encryption code scheme.

Second, and more challenging, is the allowing of certain data information to be available to the general public while other data elements are secured from outside access. Data made available to the public through the Internet is said to reside outside the firewall. A firewall is a hardware server that protects organizations from illegal access from unauthorized users who could corrupt or steal data. Analysts are therefore challenged to design database systems that have data outside the firewall and available to all, and data inside and secured against those who do not have correct access security. This challenge creates a comprehensive database design issue. There may need to be a way that data on either side of the firewall can communicate. Data that resides outside the firewall may need to be refreshed from time to time with data from the internal system. There must also be a way of obtaining new data or updates from the data residing outside the firewall. Finally, and most important, there is the reality that two or more databases may indeed need to coexist. Multiple databases that contain some of the same data elements create redundancy and integrity problems. Thus, analysts need to provide a solution to what appears to be a direct design need with the concept of normalization. Further complications are the challenges of maintaining the performance of internal production data, and the impact of potentially massive amounts of access from the general public. While there is no single right answer, there are a few ways to address these issues.

1. *Maintain One Database*: This is certainly not easy, but it provides the best control over redundancies and integrity issues. The analyst has little to do with respect to design, but a lot to address as to which data may be accessed by external users. This means that data access outside the firewall must be completely controlled by an application program that filters requests to the main database server. Outside requests must be guarded by special screen programs that operate over the Internet and control which elements are available to users. Furthermore, elements that are added or updated outside the firewall must be received by the database system and handled under the auspices of the product's database manager, as shown in Figure 7.29.

2. *Database Replication and Synchronization*: This provides more security over the internal data by allowing the specific database product to use its replication capabilities to generate a mirror database. Thus, all the database changes outside the firewall would need to be synchronized back to the internal copy. The external database would still allow access only to certain data elements deemed accessible to external users, as shown in Figure 7.30.

3. *Separate Databases*: This design concept creates two separate databases. The synchronization between the databases is delayed and occurs through an application that ensures that the elements are updated in a batch mode. This means that the production database, which resides behind the firewall, goes through a number of replications and updates a subset database for the general Internet user. The second database contains only the elements that are deemed accessible to external users. The separate database method establishes two separate systems. The second, or external, database serves the Internet portion of the system

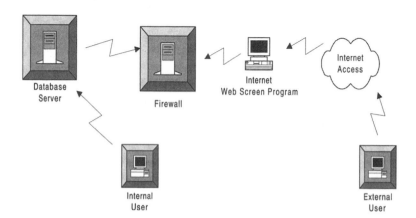

Figure 7.29 Internet/Intranet central database diagram.

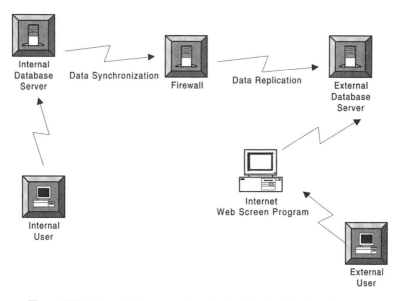

Figure 7.30 Internet/Intranet synchronized replication database diagram.

and is not a copy of the latest data. This approach almost certainly requires that the external data be used only for decision support information, in that changes to the external database would be very difficult to bring back to the production system. Thus, synchronization goes only from production to external, not vice versa. External databases of this design are often implemented using data warehouses, because the data need not be in a normalized form as a read-only provider of data. Unfortunately, this design is not effective for systems that require the Internet data to update the internal production system.

E-Commerce Application Requirements

Designing application programs that support the Internet/Intranet database design poses a major challenge for the analyst. On first consideration, it might appear that the database design must be completed before applications analysis begins. In fact, though, these two processes take place in a more parallel fashion. The reason for this parallel development is that decisions about the way the database will function are inevitably shaped by the needs of the application, especially those outside the firewall. For example, if an Intranet application is required directly to update elements in the production database, then the analyst should not prescribe the separate database design approach. Even more important is the need to have users involved in decisions about how e-commerce in their organization should function. User input may be ongoing and will certainly shape the development process. However, as in other areas of analysis, users cannot be left to determine what they want entirely on their own. The constraints of applications, security issues, and performance limitations must be discussed with users so that they fully understand the implications of their decisions both for themselves and for other parts of the organization. Without benefit of such discussions, users may demand Web functionality that could create problems for the system as a whole.

Many Internet/Intranet development projects utilize Web applications to create a new form of business known as e-commerce (electronic commerce). E-commerce creates a virtual interface for consumers to interact with an organization, and this interface may differ from the way the business typically operates in the real world. In e-commerce analysis, the "user" becomes the "consumer." This transformation is an important issue for the analyst. The most well developed e-commerce models are usually those relating to retail operations, where defining users as consumers seems natural. Through these e-commerce retail sites, consumers can actually order, purchase, and track products from a company via the Web interface.

However, e-commerce from a data processing perspective is not just about product fulfillment via a Web interface—it also encompasses the challenges of creating a user interface that relies on forms of artificial intelligence (AI). While I am not suggesting that Web systems are full-fledged AI products, they are systems that need to allow users to enter "*what ifs*." These "*what ifs*" allow consumers to receive results about their needs based on their own input. For example, if I want to search for a particular type of exercise equipment, an e-commerce Web application might ask me to provide information about my height, weight, exercise habits, age, etc. This information would then be utilized by the application to *suggest* or *recommend* what equipment might best fit my personal needs. Thus, e-commerce systems attempt to replace the store attendant, who would typically provide this consultation to a potential buyer at an exercise storefront, with an intelligent interface. This example is certainly not limited to retail, as many e-commerce Web sites provide consulting services through a similar question and answer interface. This concept of processing is the component that represents the AI aspect of Web development.

Using AI skills, then, analysts need to develop procedures that emulate the behavior patterns of users as consumers, so that they can design systems that respond well to these behavior patterns. Unlike most traditional software development situations, it is the marketing wing of the organization that will have perhaps the greatest input in the design of the system, because of its focus on consumers. Analysts therefore need to work closely with the organization's marketing operations to gain an understanding of what consumers/users need. Rather than interviewing consumers directly, analysts will learn about their needs indirectly from the perspective of the marketing department. *This kind of learning is not an easy task.* Therefore, the following phases are recommended to help the analyst generate appropriate specifications for e-commerce systems.

Phase One of the process is to identify the types of products and services to be marketed on the e-commerce system.

Phase Two involves the prepurchase interaction with consumers. This process involves comparison shopping and/or product selection based on competitive variables and attributes.

Phase Three is the pricing, leasing, charging interface, where the consumer has the ability to understand and determine the payment plan and process of goods and/or services.

Phase Four is the consumer's actual placement of the order and its authorization and confirmation of. Delivery date is also a part of this phase of e-commerce processing.

Phase Five involves issuing the consumer some form of receipt or confirmation of the order.

Phase Six involves the postpurchase process interaction, where the customer is serviced and supported based on various plans offered by the organization.

The analyst will need to develop specifications for each of these phases by working with the marketing department to gain an understanding of the user community. The marketing department must provide an action plan to support each of these processes. Below are the proposed analysis and organizational steps that should be taken to ensure successful e-commerce development.

Phase One

This phase requires that the branding of the business's image be completed. Branding means that the marketing department must first define the image it wants the Web site to convey. Indeed, it is critical first to define the mission and image of the organization before determining the products and services that are to be offered on the Web. It is also important to have a detailed understanding of the needs and demographics of targeted consumers. Buying patterns are changing with the increasing numbers of time-strapped, two-career couples, as well as the aging American population. Recent data suggests that Americans are spending less time in shopping malls and storefronts.[18] Therefore, understanding the implications of time constraints and other issues on the way consumers shop is crucial for the development of an e-commerce site that suits this population's buying preferences. Analysts should take an active role in this research process, not so much from a market definition perspective, but rather as a manager of the on-line consumption processes. This implies that the analyst will define the *kind* of information that is needed, rather than the *content* of that information.

---

[18] Ravi Kalakota and Andrew B. Winston, *Electronic Commerce: A Manager's Perspective*, Addison-Wesley Publishing Co., 1997.

Phase Two

This process involves determining what constitutes an effective consumer user interface. During this phase, the design of the e-commerce screens in accordance with the entire Web site must provide the features that make using the Web easy for on-line purchases. Thus, Phase Two requires the design of the features and functions that must be available to consumers, and these must be designed for effectiveness and simplicity. Software development decisions, Web browser requirements, multimedia versus dynamic screens and pictures are all components of making the appropriate design decisions.

Software product decisions must also be made during this phase. Technical architecture of the Web infrastructure, including network topology and security, use of CGI tools and interactive Web applications, as well as database integration must all be considered. Network topology decisions include selecting the hosting architecture and firewall hardware. CGI scripting will be necessary to ensure standard interfaces between other Web servers and applications. Interactivity must also address four distinct forms:

- ability to link data provided by different servers or hyperlinks and anchors.
- ability to provide customers with data from diverse sources including external systems and databases.
- ability to encompass new types of data including HTTP protocols and Internet mail extensions (MIME).
- ability to integrate new helper or plug-in applications.

The integration of a back-end database will be crucial to the overall e-commerce design. Issues surrounding the centrality of the data, and its interface with existing production systems, will require the analyst to provide an intricate design. Data warehousing alternatives for quick search results might be another alternative. In any case, a detailed database interface analysis must be completed.

Phase Three

This phase essentially creates the virtual store. The analyst must ensure that consumers are provided with systems that can determine the pricing of products and/or services, and that allow them to pursue different scenarios—in other words, an AI interface. The creation of this kind of virtual store often requires the creation of a separate business entity within the organization. This can have a profound effect on the culture of the organization. Therefore, it may be wiser to develop the Web e-commerce system as a separate and distinct business.

Some of the consumer interface design challenges involve enabling consumers to receive the answers they need to make a well-informed decision. For the selling of some items, Web sites must allow consumers to select among different options or components and thus to create different product configurations. Furthermore, the Web must offer consumers help in determining what product or service best fits their needs. This can be accomplished by creating interfaces that request specific data from the consumer. The data in turn generates advice for the online consumer. In essence, the traditional steps that typically occur during the in-store sales process need to be replicated using a virtual interface.

Phase Four

This phase requires that the new e-commerce system be incorporated into the back-end processing and delivery procedures of the organization. Again, analysts will need to decide whether to blend e-commerce processing with the existing internal system or to create a new, stand-alone, business. Analysts will also need to provide some form of on-line tracking systems that allow electronic users to receive confirmation of their orders, acknowledgment of product shipments, and a confirmed delivery date. These systems must also provide for security of on-line charge accounts.

Another challenge may be the requirement to blend production software with administrative products, such as e-mail. E-commerce transactions must be monitored and confirmations sent out to consumers. Internal e-mail accounts must be created so that a system operator responsible for the Web can receive communication from both customers and internal parties about problems and questions.

Phase Five

This process involves the actual delivery of product, and the need to have the Web interface capable of communicating this delivery. During many transactions, the normal retail issues of refunds and disputes will arise. Therefore, software must be developed that provides an e-commerce system that can handle account activity, statements, and credit handling to facilitate the resolution of postpurchase problems. Other aspects of improving delivery issues are:

- administrative software that allows staff to handle e-commerce-related issues.
- access for customers to automated support information, such as product sheets and frequently asked questions.
- providing timely information via the Web so that customers would rather check the Web page than call the office.

Also involved in this phase is the method marketing the Web site itself. This process involves developing strategies to ensure that the site receives "hits." The system must also have capabilities to capture and track user information such as the number of hits, what features and functions are being used, and how many visitors to the site are actually ordering products and services.

Phase Six

This process involves postsupport after product delivery. It addresses the issues of ongoing customer relations and activities that can be organized as installed-based sales opportunities. Existing customers and prospects represent the best opportunity for cross-selling installed customers and "upselling" product lines. The most important requirement of the technology will be to effectively gather information that aids in defining user needs. These needs can be determined by having software that records demographic information and buyer habits, and thus builds customer profiles. Such information must therefore be part of the e-commerce system. This might be a good time to discuss privacy issues with users.

Help-desk management must also interface with the e-commerce data to allow personnel to provide accurate help to callers. Calls will come in, especially from unsophisticated Web users who are not familiar with using electronic means to generate orders. Phone and e-mail interfaces should also be considered to provide maximum customer support.

We can see from the processes outlined above that constructing an e-commerce Web model involves analysts in a more expanded role than other tasks.

Problems and Exercises

1. Explain the challenges of Web-based development as it relates to end-user satisfaction.
2. What specific advantages does using a browser product provide to software development and user operation?
3. Discuss the database design challenges for Web-based applications development.
4. What is data replication and data synchronization?
5. What is the purpose of a firewall?
6. Explain the different design techniques for developing Internet/Intranet database products.
7. What is the difference between an Internet and an Intranet?
8. How do batch updates operate within a Web-based database application?
9. Describe the six phases involved with developing e-commerce systems.
10. How are artificial intelligence (AI) concepts used in e-commerce analysis and design?
11. Define what is meant by a GUI.

12. Explain the differences and similarities between character-based screens and GUI-based screens.
13. Describe the differences between direct manipulation and indirect manipulation.
14. Provide 10 advantages of GUI systems and 10 disadvantages. Explain your support for each pro and con.
15. How do GUI screens interface with a PDF? a DFD?
16. How do GUI screens interface with the ERD?
17. Explain how derived data elements exist between screens and the ERD.
18. List and explain five unique components of a GUI screen.
19. What is the functional difference between a check box and a radio button?
20. Explain the relationship among a derived data element, the ERD, and the process specification.

8
XML in Analysis and Design

Introduction to XML

The Extensible Markup Language (XML) is a significant development that adds flexibility and richness to the exchange of data on the Net. Specifically, XML and its related standards improve Web data exchange by providing a method for structured data transfer. This structured data transfer allows different systems to exchange data through standard or agreed upon formats. Furthermore, XML supports an object model that allows for the sorting, selecting, and manipulating of data in documents, regardless of whether the data resides on the server or on the client computer.

The purpose of XML is to allow for data exchange across multiple tiers of Web applications. Like HTML, XML is a subset of SGML (Structured Generalized Markup Language), optimized for delivery over the Web. HTML, however, restricts developers to a finite set of tags designed to describe Web pages for presentation, as opposed to exchange of reusable information or data. Unlike HTML, which tags only elements in Web pages for presentation by a browser, XML tags elements and stores them as data. This means that XML can be used to identify text or numeric elements within a Web page, allowing text to be passed into the page as data. This is accomplished by a coding system that makes use of data tags that precede the value. For this reason, XML can be defined as a *metalanguage*—a language used to define new markup languages. With XML, developers can create languages or documents specifically for an application.

The ecommerce applications that have the most to gain from using XML are obviously those that cannot accomplish what they need to do with HTML. The types of applications that can maximize their benefit from XML fall into one of four categories:

1. Applications that require a Web client to utilize data between two or more related databases.
2. Applications that have more processing on the client tier than on the server tier.
3. Applications that require Web pages to be presented differently depending on the user and device accessing the ecommerce system.

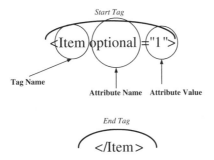

Figure 8.1 XML text format.

4.   Applications that allow intelligent Web agents to dynamically tailor the information provided to users depending on the environment or Web client that the information must reside on.

In practice, then, XML is suitable for storing and exchanging data that can be plausibly coded as text (Harold & Means, 2001). On the other hand, it is unsuitable for multimedia data, such as photographs, sound, and video.

XML Structure

As stated earlier, XML can be considered a metalanguage. It is essentially text that can represent an element, tag, or character data. An element defines the existence of a data field, the tag delimits its beginning and ending, and the character data represents the element's actual data. Sometimes the data is an actual value; other times it is a text string. This depends, of course, on the definition of the element's attributes. An example of an XML text structure is shown in Figure 8.1.

Because XML can have multiple types of definitions, it is said to contain mixed content. The mixed content can be represented in the form of a tree structure as shown in Figure 8.2.

In figure 8.2, the contents of the F-Name and L-Name are character data, whereas name and profession are elements that have tags to delimit the definition values.

XML Parsing

From a process perspective, there are a number of related components or tools that provide XML with the ability to connect to various applications. The first component is called the XML Parser. In many ways a parser is similar to a compiler in that it is charged with the responsibility to translate source data into an object or target machine form. The XML Parser is responsible for editing

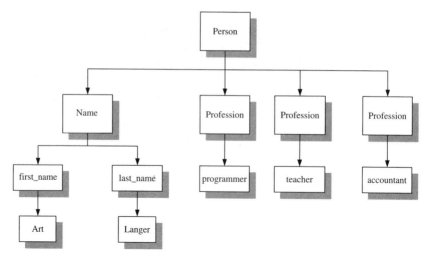

Figure 8.2 An XML tree.

an XML document and breaking it down to its elements for transfer to various application programs. These programs could be Web browsers, word processing editors, database systems for storage of the source, spreadsheet, Java or C++ programs, or miscellaneous third-party products. The transferring process is known as "parsing out" the data. From an edit perspective, the XML Parser is responsible for validating the input data to ensure that there are no errors. This is accomplished by interfacing with a document type definition (DTD) file. The DTD contains the master list of data rules and document constraints. The data rules include the list of fields that can be used in an XML document. If the DTD does not contain a definition, an error will be generated. Error messages can have varying levels of significance, similar to the way compilers issue warning and fatal errors when editing source code.

Once an XML document has completed the parser, it can be generated to a number of different applications as shown in Figure 8.3.

What XML Is Not

XML is just a markup language, meaning that it is limited to the manipulation and presentation of data as text. Therefore, XML is not truly a programming language *per se*. Furthermore, XML is not a network protocol and therefore cannot be used to send data across a network without the assistance of other network protocols like HTTP and FTP (File Transfer Protocol). Finally, it is important to recognize that XML is not a database and cannot replace the functionalities of databases. XML can be stored within a database and provides a reuse function by providing an XML format to many different types of applications on many hardware platforms. The format is stored as data only.

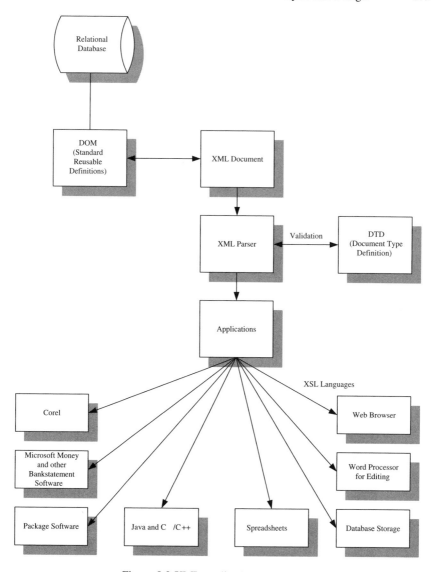

Figure 8.3 XML application generation.

Other XML Interfaces

There are other application interfaces that are used when the target is a Web browser. The functionality of these applications is to provide better formatting features that allow XML to better integrate with a Web browser screen or what is called a "stylesheet." The Extensible Stylesheet Language (XSL) is an XML application that transforms XML documents into Web browser form. This

application has been decomposed into two more specific programs: XSL Transformations (XSLT) and XSL Formatting Object (XSL-FO). XSLT is general-
purpose in that it allows one XML document to be displayed in a Web browser,
whereas the XSL-FO feature describes the layout of the text data. Another
enhancement is that the Extensible Linking Language (XLL) is a more powerful
linking construct that has greater capabilities than HTML's A tag. XLL is
comprised of two separate standards: Xlink, which describes the connections
between XML documents, and Xpointer, which addresses the individual components within an XML document.

   Another application that can be used to format Web browser pages is
Cascading Style Sheets (CSS). CSS is usually utilized as a lower-level formatter
for HTML. CSS does allow styles to be reused within documents without the
need to redefine them. In addition, CSS allows for the definition to be changed
anywhere in the document file.

XML and Ecommerce Applications

Ecommerce systems are all about the interfacing of systems across the Web
to conduct business transactions. A number of years ago, a communication
standard called Electronic Data Interface (EDI) was developed. EDI is essentially a standard file format that allowed companies to provide a consistent
way for vendors to interface with their systems. For example, the publications
industry has a standard file format for vendors who submit invoices to them.
The EDI standard became part of most internal systems in the publications
industry because it saved costly custom modifications for each system for both
the company and its vendors. XML provides a great deal more functionality than
EDI; however, it works on the same principle of allowing standard interfacing
and exchange of data. What makes XML so exciting is that the data, unlike in
EDI, can also be used as text to populate applications, as well as passing over
the Web so that businesses can exchange information without standard network
protocols. Thus, an EDI-like data interchange can be accomplished by combining
data requirements and applications; the Web page combines application interface
and data interface in one package. By using XSL capabilities, an XML file can
be translated into HTML and be propagated into an operational Web application
in a Web browser as shown in Figure 8.4.

Document Object Model

The Document Object Model (DOM) represents the most important component
application for the ecommerce analysis and design function. Indeed, ecommerce
analysts must decide which portions of the system will utilize XML applications,
and more important how these XML documents should be defined. The DOM
is a powerful tool that allows XML documents (as well as other documents)

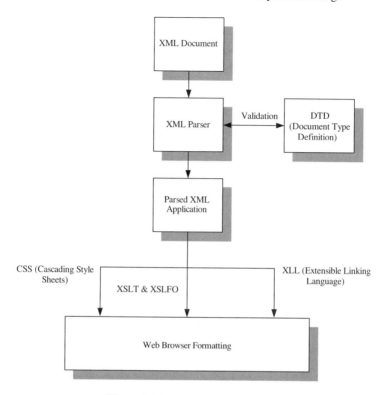

Figure 8.4 XSL Web page creation.

to be manipulated as objects. This means that the DOM can access an XML document, reformat it, and preview it visually as an object tree-structure. Given that XML is structured hierarchically, any XML document can be displayed in a tree structure as depicted in Figure 8.5.

Figure 8.5 reflects a recipe as a tree of document tags. This structure makes it easier to understand—and to update—any XML design. The tree structure is also consistent with a class diagram structure, so the model is well suited for interface with object-oriented systems. Thus, the DOM allows developers to make modifications to the structure, which will then be automatically translated back to the XML document as shown in Figure 8.6.

Furthermore, the DOM can be used to create XML documents from scratch, so it is truly full-duplex in its relationship with XML documents. Thus, with the DOM, XML documents can be manipulated as objects, instead of only as streams of text. Having a visual representation of an XML document makes it easier to edit the information. Furthermore, the DOM is compatible with the Interface Definition Language used in CORBA (Common Object Request Broker Architecture), often used to implement object middleware applications.

The DOM also plays a pivotal role in the interface of XML with relational databases. This is accomplished by thinking of the relational database as a set

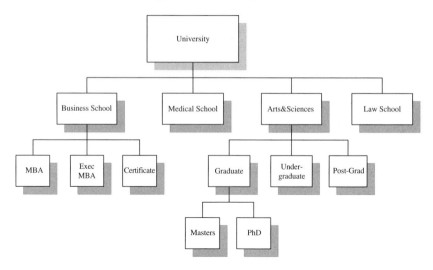

Figure 8.5 XML tree structure design.

of DOM objects. If an ecommerce analyst wants to design a document that represents a particular schema of data, it can be described by the DOM and then translated into an XML document. The XML document can then be formatted using XSL into an HTML Web application. SQL can be used and mapped via XML to the backend relationally modeled data. Thus, database schemas can be brought together in a rather robust way using the DOM as shown in Figure 8.7.

XML as a Common Data Format

In Chapter 9, I discuss the different methods of linking legacy applications with ecommerce systems. Two methods, "Leave As Is" and "Enhance," both required some form of data linkage. The format alternatives were parameter passing and database. While these options had value, XML provides yet another interesting

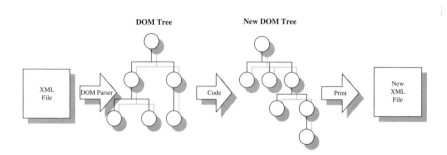

Figure 8.6 DOM document transformation system.

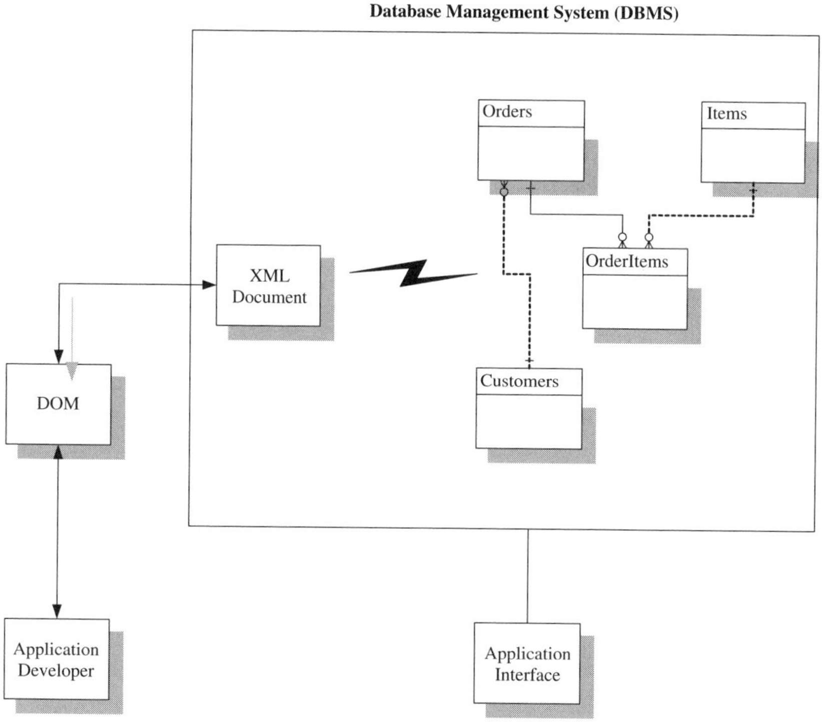

Database Management System (DBMS)

Figure 8.7 DOM interface with databases.

alternative, especially in cases where the legacy link does not have a database interface. XML, as previously stated, provides linkages without concern for the hardware platform. While relational databases provide for application and platform independence, there is huge overhead associated with using a database as a method of intercommunication among application programs.

With the rapid proliferation of ecommerce interfaces, free XML tools can represent another method of providing platform-independent and database-independent program communications. The unique strengths of using XML as a software data communication method include:

- *Simple Syntax*: XML is easy to generate using the DOM, and easy to parse using XSL.
- *Support for Nesting*: the tree format allows for programs to represent data structures with nested elements—required by many program formats.
- *Easy to Debug*: XML is easy to format, especially with the DOM.
- *Language and Platform Independent*: an XML data file is completely transportable across different architectures and database products.

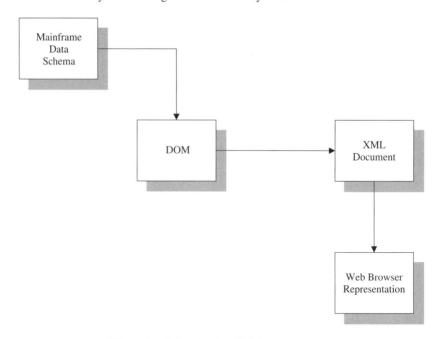

Figure 8.8 Using XML to link legacy systems.

Thus, XML is becoming a popular format for enterprise data sharing, especially when there are mixed platform environments. For example, suppose a typical organization needs to take information from an IBM mainframe and display it on a Web site. Using XML, the mainframe schema of data can be accessed by the DOM, which in turn would format the output as an XML document. Using XSL, the Web server could then transform the XML into HTML, which could then be loaded into a Web browser template (Figure 8.8). It is important to note that I am not suggesting that XML replace relational database technologies. Indeed, XML is too slow to handle high-volume transactions. However, XML can be used to work with database subsets, called sub-schemas, in which a small picture of the data needed can be downloaded and formatted in a class structure for use by an ecommerce object application.

XML Applications with Database Systems

A significant issue addressed by XML is the ability to create consistent representation of data. While normalized databases were supposed to provide this consistency, most do not because they violate certain normal form rules. These violations ultimately create problems with the transportability of the data. Furthermore, stored procedures tend to be proprietary at the vendor database level, and therefore further complicate the task of providing seamless portability among databases. XML, on the other hand, creates a portable structure that allows ecommerce systems to connect multiple databases across different hardware platforms. Indeed, in some situations an XML-based representation of data and the http protocol might be the only method of connecting legacy systems with ecommerce technology. Figure 8.9 illustrates a sample ecommerce system that uses XML to provide application integration. This integration is provided via the linking of various databases using an XML interface.

Figure 8.9 reflects that XML, over the Web, provides the data integration between the Oracle and SQL Server systems. If XML were not used, the application developer would need to use separate SQL-based languages (SQL-7 for SQL Server and PLSQL for Oracle) to provide data access to each program. XML provides a means of using a central repository that can generate its own SQL necessary to access its data. This means that each database vendor supplies an SQL-XML interface that can generate (output) and access (read) XML formats. Thus, just knowing and using XML allows for access to multiple proprietary SQL coding.

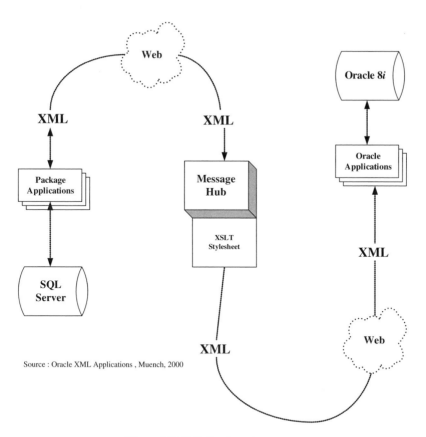

Source : Oracle XML Applications , Muench, 2000

Figure 8.9 XML/database integrator.

The key to integrating XML and SQL is making the information in the query results easy to transform, transport, and transcribe. Figure 8.10 shows the architecture of integrating XML and SQL to produce multiple applications. Note that XSLT is used to transform the parsed XML data pages to multiple applications such as Web pages, Wireless Markup Language (WML) for cell phones, and handheld devices.

Therefore, publishing XML diagrams from relational databases allows for proven portability, scalability, manageability, and performance.

Using the Oracle product as an example, we can see a more detailed view of how a relational database and XML are integrated to provide portability between XML and SQL technologies. Figure 8.11 shows how Oracle has implemented XML in its product.

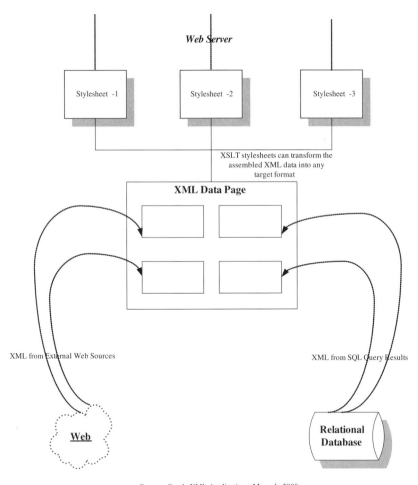

Source : Oracle XML Applications, Muench, 2000

Figure 8.10 XML/SQL integrated architecture.

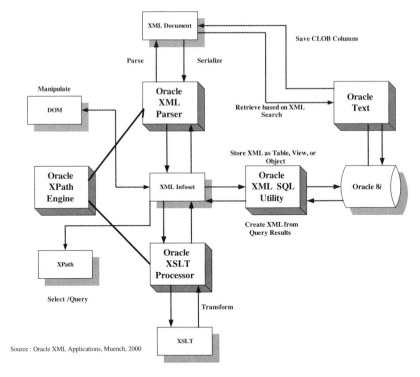

Figure 8.11 Oracle XML architecture.

Using the Oracle XML parser, XML documents can be manipulated and modified with the DTD, which Oracle calls the information set or Infoset. The Oracle XSLT processor transforms XML into HTML or other structures. While these components are somewhat standard XML applications, Oracle adds an XPath engine that enables the querying of XML documents. The Oracle XML SQL utility then automates the tasks of producing XML from SQL query results and vice versa (that is, storing XML documents into tables in the database). The Oracle Text application provides a method of creating indexes of the XML structure to support SQL queries. Figure 8.12 provides a summary of the Oracle XML infrastructure.

Analysis and Design of XML Documents

The ecommerce analyst must provide XML specifications as part of the overall engineering architecture. To do so, the analyst must determine the XML components that will be used for data interface and what portions will be used for ecommerce application reuse. Therefore, the first step in designing an XML interface is to decide what will constitute an XML document. The second step

Oracle Feature/Function	Description
XML Parser	Edits and validates XML documents
XPath Engine	Searches for XML documents
XSLT Processor	Transforms XML documents to other output formats
XML SQL Utility	Produces XML from SQL and inserts XML into tables
XSQL Pages	Assembles XML data for use by XSLT
Oracle Text	Indexes and searches XML documents using native structure
Object Views	XML-enabled view of relational data
Oracle JVM	Java implementation on the database
JDeveloper	Java development for XML, XSLT, and XSQL
Advanced Queuing	Queues XML messages

Figure 8.12 Oracle XML infrastructure component definitions.

is to determine what elements, text, or code will comprise the XML document. The third step is to determine the reuse and propagation of the XML document data into the various ecommerce applications.

Step 1: Determining XML Documents

The process of determining what will be an XML document relates to two factors mentioned above: (1) what data will be used as an EDI application and (2) what will be used to populate Web applications. Regardless of which factor is used, an ecommerce analyst must determine the actual data structure for the XML tree. This data structure can be defined as a vocabulary of XML elements and attributes. The elements and attributes are the text in the vocabulary that enables communication of information.

An example of choosing the right reuse is the function provided by a search engine. A search engine is typically used for general search requirements to locate specific information in the database. An XML document can be created that identifies the database elements that are required for the search application. This is then coded in the DOM, and outputted as a XML document. The XML design allows a user to search for a particular type of product, similar to the way Amazon.com allows a user to search for a particular product offering like a book or a DVD (see Figure 8.13). Thus, the root of the XML document tree is the "Type Identifier" of the product. The DOM would then structure the XML tree as shown in Figure 8.14.

Thus, the "Type Identifier" element identifies a type of product that is needed to display the results of the search. The data can then be transformed into various HTML Web browser applications. The data interface can be accomplished via an SQL interface engine. So when a user wants to query the product database, he/she will use the search engine XML document. This document interfaces with the Oracle Text application, which created indexes on the related database

Figure 8.13 Amazon search engine options.

elements that were defined in the XML document. When the query is created by the application driving the ecommerce activity, the stylesheet created from the XML document will issue an SQL call to the XML SQL interface (Oracle), which will retrieve the necessary data and convert it back to the XML format as shown in Figure 8.15.

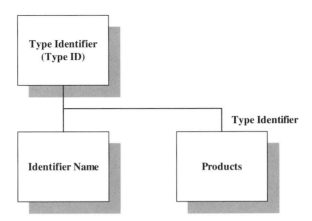

Figure 8.14 XML search tree.

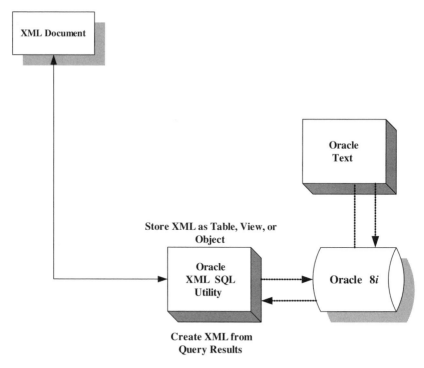

Figure 8.15 XML and SQL execution.

XML as an EDI

Earlier in this chapter it was mentioned that XML is an effective application to replace the EDI traditionally used to handle standard file interfaces between clients and vendors. EDI in legacy applications was typically implemented by designing a standard file format that would be required for any entity to interface with an ecommerce system. This file format was usually delivered in a comma-delimited record (CSV file) that matched with a standard database format required by the accepting system. A special application was then programmed that was designed to read the standard CSV file and convert it into the target database format. The program operated in a batch mode and included an edit program that reported errors as appropriate and determined the validity of the input transactions.

XML can be used to create a much more robust and portable EDI. The data structure required would be converted as an object-tree structure using the DOM (or coded directly as an XML document). The DOM would then generate the XML document, which would be parsed against the DTD. An XSLT application would then create a Web browser program that would accept the required input data.

The XML solution could also be adapted to accept a file input, instead of an input screen over the Web. In this situation, the vendor would be provided with

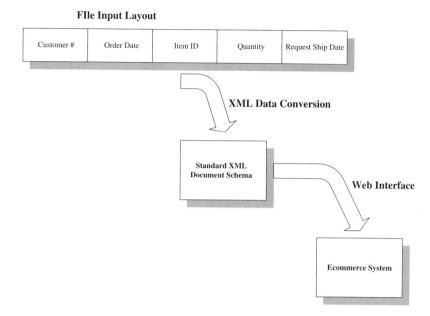

Figure 8.16 EDI/XML interface configuration.

the XML schema and asked to create their data using the same XML document. Should an EDI standard exist in a particular industry group, then all parties would incorporate the XML format into their respective systems. Of course this requires all parties to agree about what that format should be. Figure 8.16 depicts the EDI XML configuration interface.

In a nutshell, the ecommerce analyst must know whether an industry standard exists, or whether the organization must create a standard for its own use and hope others will adhere to it. Typically the latter is the case, and the EDI standard format will evolve over time.

XML and Populating Web Applications

While XML can be used as a method of data interchange among applications, it is also useful to provide data that is part of a Web application. Thus, the ecommerce analyst needs to provide information about what portions of a particular application can receive data that can be used to populate its content. For example, suppose there is a particular phrase or logo that is used on multiple screens in an application. The ecommerce analyst needs to determine if this phrase or logo should be stored in a database and then formatted as an XML document. This process greatly reduces duplication of static coding on a Web page. More important, the concept of storing literals as data allows for better maintenance of text that can change over the life of a Web application. Indeed, the content in ecommerce systems is much more dynamic. Thus, XML can provide the standard

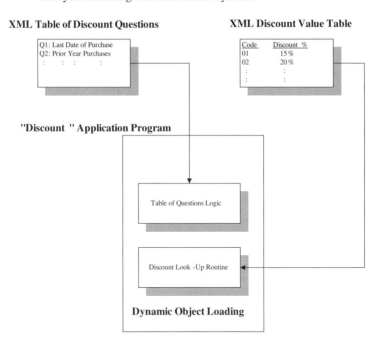

Figure 8.17 XML discount data architecture.

format to propagate content for Web applications. In Chapter 16, we will see how XML, along with content management products, provides significant maintenance capabilities by storing content as data and incorporating it into template systems.

In addition, XML can be used to provide data that is stored inside program applications. This data could be in the form of an internal array, or multidimensional tables that are used by an application to complete an algorithm, or as a component of some conditional selection logic. Internal data structures are very common, particularly in object component programming. Once again, XML can be used to provide the data structure and allow programmers to use it in many different applications. This allows for the creation of standard data structures that can be dynamically loaded into an application. The capability to dynamically load data structures can have a profound impact on program maintenance. Not only can the data structure be stored, its values associated with the structure can also be included in the XML document. Remember, XML can store both element definitions and values. Suppose, then, that an XML document contained a table that calculated discounts for book purchases. Such a calculation could have many tiers of logic, and could be dependent on how many books have been purchased and where. The XML document could store the table of questions, as well as the questions themselves. Furthermore, the "discount codes" could be stored as values. Thus, when the XML document is propagated into the application program, it not only has the algorithm structure, but also the actual codes that it needs to formulate the final discount amount. Should any of the questions or codes change, which normally will occur, the developer need only update the XML document, changing its data structure or values, as necessary. These changes would then be reloaded into the application upon its next instance (or next execution of the program in the Web application). Figure 8.17 depicts the XML data structure for the discount algorithm.

Embracing XML goes beyond just agreeing to use it; it also means engineering applications that assume a component will change. This greatly affects the architecture of the applications. Thus, the ecommerce analyst must work closely with developers to ensure that specifications clearly establish information on what components will be stored as XML documents. Ecommerce analysts must also be aware how text (or content) will be stored in the relational database. This topic will be discussed further in Chapter 13. As previously mentioned, the reuse aspect of XML is consistent with object technologies. These aspects are discussed in greater detail in Step 3 of this section.

Step 2: XML Data Schemas

A schema is defined as a way of describing the characteristics of data. The DTD, in many ways, constitutes the basis of the XML schema. Unfortunately, the DTD falls short in relation to some required processing needs. An XML schema must provide three important benefits: (1) functionality and power, (2) ease of use, and (3) compatibility.

Functionality

The DTD alone provides limited semantic checking of XML. This means that there can be errors in the syntax of the code that will not be caught by the DTD. So it is possible to produce an XML document that will be authorized by the DTD, yet have some problems with syntax. Incorrect syntax can affect a statement's semantics or meaning.

Ease of Use

Unfortunately, good DTDs are difficult to write because of the limited infrastructure support provided by their design. Furthermore, DTDs are not easy to read and edit. The result is that it can be difficult to produce XML that correctly matches the DTD. DTDs also lack extensibility and have poor version control mechanisms. Finally, there are syntactical differences between XML and DTD, which makes it even more difficult to match the two scripts.

Compatibility

The DTD is part of the first version of XML. There are many later versions of XML that have difficulty communicating with earlier versions. Ultimately this means that the relationship between XML documents and DTDs is very version sensitive, and system personnel must ensure that versions are kept consistent. While this requirement sounds straightforward, it is difficult to enforce after the initial installations of ecommerce systems. Indeed, version control becomes progressively more challenging as the system is updated.

The weaknesses of DTD can be summarized below:

- Poor support for semantic checking
- No data typing
- No relational support
- No support for objects features such as inheritance
- Cannot use parts of other DTDs
- Difficult to write
- No extensibility
- No version control mechanism
- Unique syntax

(Source: Spencer, 1999)

The schema method is obviously designed to address the DTD weaknesses summarized above. There are a number of product schemas designed to complement the DTD. A document content description (DCD) mechanism has been implemented as a schema in a number of products such as Internet Explorer 5. Internet Explorer 5 implements a schema that contains a more extensible and robust method for providing constraints on the structure and contents of XML documents. The importance of an enhanced DCD is that it can provide more advanced metadata, or data about data. The ecommerce analyst needs to be aware of whether specific DCDs are available, since this information can affect how XML documents are designed. Specifically, the more DCD capability, the more advanced the XML applications can be used in the overall engineering of the ecommerce system. More important is that the DCD has a significant influence on what data elements and structures can be included in the XML document. If the DTD edit abilities are limited, then certain data structures may be deemed too risky (from a quality perspective) for inclusion in an XML document.

No matter how ambitious the XML structure designed, the ecommerce analyst must provide a specification that defines the data elements and specific data types to be included in the XML tree structure. While the data elements should correspond to the definitions stored in the relational database, their syntax can be different from an SQL data type and type qualifier. Figure 8.18 represents the list of data types supported by XML.

Thus, an XML specification must list the actual names and XML definitions. One method of accomplishing this is for the ecommerce analyst to establish the corresponding XML name and attributes when building the data dictionary. Thus, an XML definition should be included for every data element that is a candidate for an XML solution. Another approach is to provide an XML definition for all data dictionary data elements. The advantage of the latter approach is that it prepares all data elements for possible inclusion in an XML document.

Name	Description	Storage Type	Example
string	Alphanumeric data	string	Art Langer
number	A number that has no limits on digits	string	18, 54.596, .01
char	string	1 Unicode character (16 bits)	A, Z
int	Whole number, optional sign value	32-bit signed binary	7, 45302, -87
float	A number that has no limits on digits	64-bit IEEE 488	.3258798554E+3
Fixed 14.4	A number with a limit of up to 14 digits to the left of the decimal point, and no more than 4 decimal places to the right	64-bit signed binary	188.0458
boolean	"1" or "0"	bit	0, 1 (0="false")
dateTime.iso8601	A date in ISO 8601 format with optional time and no optional zone	Structure that contains year, month, hour, minute, second, nanosecond	20011204T09:25:01501
dateTime.iso8601tz	A date in ISO 8601 format with optional time and optional zone	Structure that contains year, month, hour, minute, second, nanosecond, zone	20011204T09:25:01501+02
date.iso8601	A date in ISO 8601 format only	Structure that contains year, month, day	20011225
time.iso8601	A time in ISO 8601 format only	Structure that contains day, hour, minute	251548
time.iso8601.tz	A time in ISO 8601 with no date but optional time zone	Structure that contains day, hour, minute, zonehours, zoneminutes	09:25-05:00

Figure 8.18 XML data types.

Step 3: XML Reuse

XML documents can be designed to provide reusable components that can be part of different Web applications. In order to design such components, ecommerce analysts must track the number of operations that are reused in applications, similar to the example of the Search Engine. An example of application reuse can be described with a function that adds a new customer. Let's say that this function is used when a caller wants to sign up as a customer to order a product. An XML document could be designed that would be comprised of the data elements necessary for inserting a new customer. The XML document would then be used through XSLT to generate an HTML screen. There is another operation that allows for entering new orders. This application requires the entry of the customer who has placed the order. Sometimes a new order is placed by a caller who has not yet signed up as a customer and is therefore not in the Customer database. Users would like the order entry screen to allow the customer to be added while the new order entry screen is operating. This is accomplished by allowing a pop-up window to be invoked when a new customer needs to be inserted during the order entry process. Instead of writing a new screen, the application can use the same XML document that was used to generate the new customer application. Thus, the XML document serves to provide a reusable application that is generated into more than one application screen. Analysts should seek to design XML documents that link up with object classes. The purpose of this approach is to provide matching data for classes that are designed by nature to be reusable. This means that the need for reusable XML documents for applications can be mapped to classes designed to become reusable object components. Of course, this approach assumes that the host system is based on object development. In legacy systems, or even those that contain hybrid combinations (a high probability in ecommerce systems), the likelihood of using this approach to identify all reusable components is slim. XML and its relation to object components are shown in Figure 8.19.

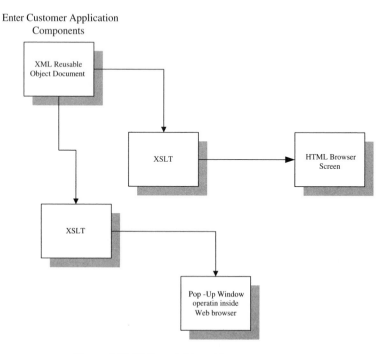

Figure 8.19 XML matching object components.

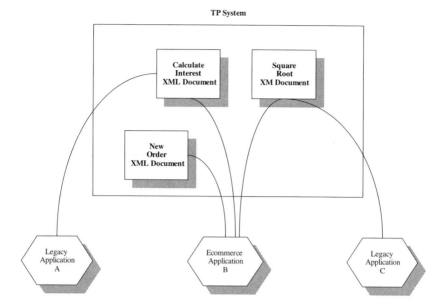

Figure 8.20 Implementation of XML in a TP system.

Another area that can assist in determining the need for XML reuse application is in a TP system. You might recall that the TP system was designed as a middleware application repository. The TP monitor component was designed to provide consistent operation and data integrity among many "linked" programs from different systems. Thus, the TP monitor was the center of traffic among different system components and reduced the need to program the same logic in different program languages and for different file systems. XML can become the data vehicle to operate within the TP system. Instead of requiring the TP system to format and update data in different file systems, XML can be used to send a standard format of the data needed to multiple applications across the network. Each system would have the ability to read the data and reformat it as necessary into their respective applications and file schemas. Figure 8.20 reflects the use of XML in a TP system.

Storing XML Documents in a Database

External XML document files can be loaded into a database system so that it can be better integrated with the SQL-based relational system. Notwithstanding the fact that there is a difference in file format, most of the physical data will remain stored in the database. The significant issue to remember is that the relational model is built under third-normal form and referential integrity rules. This, of course, focuses on a production-oriented database management component that contains a high volume of transactional processing as opposed to a data warehouse implementation (see Chapter 15). However, it is possible in a database system such as Oracle actually to store an XML document in the database without it being part of the traditional normalized schema. This means that the XML document may contain data elements unique to the document itself, thus not propagated into a particular entity. A database system like Oracle provides an XML parsing utility, which allows the XML document to be accessible via normal SQL queries and stored procedures. Thus, the XML document retains its own format while being assimilated into the database infrastructure. Accessing a data element within the XML document or in the relational database can be transparent to the user community. Figure 8.21 reflects the concept of XML and relational database schema integration.

The question arises from a design perspective of whether an XML document should contain data elements that have not originated from the relational part of the database. This certainly is a question that must be answered by the ecommerce analyst. The most logical support for this occurrence is when a data element in an XML document is unique to a particular application. Therefore, the XML document has been designed to use in a one-on-one relationship with a specific Web program or application. To propagate the data element into the relational database under these circumstances would create unnecessary overhead and the ongoing need for data synchronization. On the other hand, leaving the data elements in XML structure eliminates the need for dual storage and allows access from multiple sources, including traditional SQL-based applications.

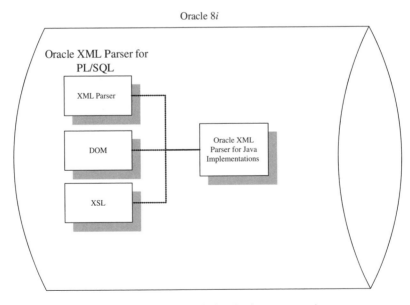

Figure 8.21 XML and relational schema generation.

From a specification perspective, an ecommerce analyst needs to understand how to design the XML-relational model. This task is easier if the analyst knows the physical database features and functions that are designed to support the product's architecture. For example, Oracle supports the creation of an element known as a CLOB. "CLOB" stands for *Character Large Object*. In Oracle, a CLOB can hold character-based data like XML documents as large as four gigabytes (4GB). A CLOB column is stored in the database and is fully readable and writable. Using Oracle Text, CLOB files can be indexed for fast XML document searching across millions of rows. Obviously, Oracle needed to establish an XML/SQL API (Application Program Interface) to allow for the parsing and integration of both models within the database. Essentially it allows for the coexistence of the two.

Should the physical database vendor, like Oracle, support XML document storage within their database, ecommerce analysts still must be aware of the following challenges:

1. If an XML document is used by multiple databases vendors, will there be compatibility in the XML/SQL integration, or should the XML document be stripped out from one of the databases so that it is resident in only one file?
2. There cannot be any "external" references within the XML document that allow for insertion of data elements that exist, let's say, in a URL. This would be problematic since there is no existing infrastructure in Oracle that allows for the external linking outside the confines of the database infrastructure.
3. There needs to be documentation and control among the different versions of XML and DTD used in all systems. Different versions between XML and DTD could cause serious problems in the quality of the parsing process as well as the validity of the applications generated through the XSLT.

XML-Based File Types in Oracle *i*FS

Oracle provides an Internet file system (*i*FS) that supports the infrastructure for defining XML documents. The file system essentially assigns descriptors that specify the XML structure and store the schema in the database. As stated above, the CLOB allows an entire XML file to mix structured data and text markup in the same document. For example, an "Order" file type may map to an OrderHeader and OrderLines table, while a "BenefitsClaim" file type can mix the methods of data and text by actually structuring text markup for a Summary Report and combining it with a Payments Report. In this case the data is stored in the traditional database, whereas the text stored as a CLOB. Figure 8.22 shows the contents of a sample BenefitsClaim.

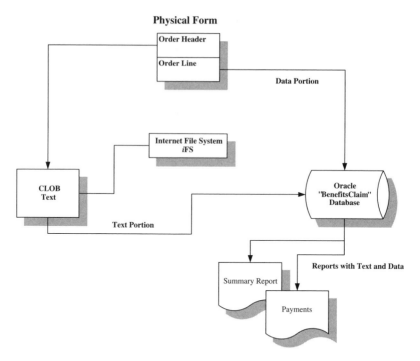

Figure 8.22 BenefitsClaim as a mixture of structured data and text.

XML as a Centralized Data Search Engine

Another application of XML is as a central search engine. A central search engine is one that can be used to collect information over several different systems and provide summary information on the collective meaning of the information. This can be a difficult task in large organizations that have a proliferation of legacy applications running across different hardware platforms. While Chapter 9 provided guidance on ways of integrating legacy applications, it did so with approaches that have high overhead and require significant time to install. With XML, on the other hand, the goal of centralizing information quickly and cheaply is attainable. This can be accomplished by allowing each proprietary application to generate a standard XML document that holds the data and text needed. Each XML output could then be merged together in a database CLOB or integrated in a table relational format for querying of data. Furthermore, the searching could be accomplished via the Web, using the index utilities provided by the database vendor. While this "central" repository of data is similar in concept to data warehousing, it involves far less complexity in overhead, coding, and maintainability. Most important is that it can be accessed over the Internet using portable application programming. Thus, the ecommerce analyst should consider XML for all multi-data analysis requirements.

The importance of having a central repository for searching has further benefits. Common ecommerce initiatives involve accessing text documents on the Web for research, analysis, and business. Indeed, users would love to be able to query text in a document and pull out all relevant information and citations that they need, as opposed to being forced to print the entire document and find the information they need manually. We say then that such data needs to be stored as metadata. For example, suppose a user needed to access a Web site to review information about a particular subject. If the document were created in XML, it could be searched for matches on the subject, which would be looking at multiple XML documents from many systems. If a match is found, instead of just printing or copying the text, a portion of the data could be extracted from the document in order to populate another application. This application could be a spreadsheet program, or database system, that would capture the data or text and categorize it as appropriate. Thus, the text document has become metadata, and the user can select what portions of the text are useful for other applications.

XML Query Usage

Database products such as Oracle and Microsoft's SQL Server must provide a set of query functions that support the manipulation of data as provided by SQL on the relational model. Obviously, with a hybrid model of XML integrated with the database, not all typical SQL queries can be supported. Ecommerce analysts need to understand the extent of query functionality available in XML documents and the types of documents that can be queried before making final design decisions relating to what will be stored as XML and what will be stored as a traditional data element. W3C (World Wide Web Consortium) has issued "query usage scenarios" that provide guidelines on the query usage for XML documents as follows:

1. *Human-Readable Documents*: perform queries on structured documents and collections of documents, such as technical manuals, to retrieve individual documents, to generate tables of contents, to search for information in structures found within a document, or to generate new documents as the result of a query.

2. *Data-Oriented Documents*: perform queries on the XML representation of database data, object data, or other traditional data sources to extract data from these sources, to transform data into new XML representations, or to integrate data from multiple heterogeneous data sources. The XML representation of data sources may be either physical or virtual; that is, data may be physically encoded in XML, or an XML representation of the data may be produced.

3. *Mixed-Model Documents*: perform both document-oriented and data-oriented queries on documents with embedded data, such as catalogs, patient health records, employment records, or business analysis documents.

4. *Administrative Data*: perform queries on configuration files, user profiles, or administrative logs represented in XML.

5. *Filtering Streams*: perform queries on streams of XML data to process the data in a manner analogous to UNIX filters. This might be used to process logs of email messages, network packets, stock market data, newswire feeds, EDI, or weather data to filter and route messages represented in XML, to extract data from XML streams, or to transform data in XML streams.

6. *Document Object Model (DOM)*: perform queries on DOM structures to return sets of nodes that meet the specified criteria.

7. *Native XML Repositories and Web Servers*: perform queries on collections of documents managed by native XML repositories or Web servers.

8. *Catalog Search*: perform queries to search catalogs that describe document servers, document types, XML schemas, or documents. Such catalogs may be combined to support search among multiple servers. A document-retrieval system could use queries to allow the user to select server catalogs, represented in XML, by the information provided by the servers, by access cost, or by authorization. Once a server is selected, a retrieval system could query the kinds of documents found on the server and allow the user to query those documents.

9. *Multiple Syntactic Environments*: queries may be used in many environments. For example, a query might be embedded in a URL, an XML page, or a JSP or ASP page; represented by a string in a program written in a general-purpose programming language; provided as an argument on the command-line or standard input.

XML versus the Database

XML appears to provide many storage and content benefits. However, I have not meant to suggest that the relational database model is no longer necessary and should be scrapped for total XML-based storage. The reality is that XML deals much better with content than storage. During complex searches on large databases, XML searches for data elements will be considerably slower than through the relational model. Furthermore, relational databases provide better facilities for security and the maintainability of the data itself.

However, databases have their downsides also. Their content cannot easily be shared, and the standardization of their design is questionable; therefore, exchanging data between two different database systems can be very difficult. Furthermore, field value among multiple systems may not map well, and as a result there can be significant incompatibilities when passing data among applications. XML addresses this shortfall by providing a neutral data format that supports easy data exchange.

The result of this chapter's discussion on XML is that, like so many other system components, XML is best integrated within a framework, in this case the traditional relational database. Indeed, XML works best when it is integrated with the relational model, where each component can be used to the fullest extent of its design advantages. Thus, it is not XML versus the database; it is XML *and* the relational database as a new hybrid storage model.

XML and SVG

SVG or Scalable Vector Graphics is a language for describing two-dimensional graphics in XML. SVG allows for three types of graphic objects: vector graphic shapes (images consisting of straight lines and curves), images, and text. Graphic objects can be grouped, styled, transformed, and composited into previously completed objects, meaning that they can be exported to XML and then imported back as an XML version of the original graphic. Text can be included as part of the XML SVG, which enhances the document's searchability and the accessibility of the SVG graphics within the document. Therefore, SVG enables the creation of resolution- and media-independent graphics in a text-based format that permits integration with XHTML, XSL and XSLT, XLink, DOM, and other W3 specifications, including support for CSS, scripting, and animation.

SVG drawings can be dynamic and interactive. The Document Object Model (DOM) for SVG, which includes the full XML DOM, supports vector graphics animation through scripting languages. The power of this model is that it allows for scripting to be used for both XML text and XML SVG drawings within the same document simultaneously. This means that one search will examine both text and graphic images within the domain of the search. Furthermore, SVG files are not proprietary binary data files as are many other graphic formats. Because SVG files use XML, their syntax is readable as text files. This means that developers can easily create scripts that dynamically modify content as well as exchange designs between tools. XML also describes information in terms of a structured data format thus allowing applications to process the same SVG image differently.

SVG is currently a W3C candidate for recommendation, meaning that it has not yet been authorized as a W3C standard. However, SVG is expected to undergo widespread testing and eventual acceptance as a standard shortly. The ability of XML to be extended beyond just text-based documents allows for much greater use within Web applications. In Chapter 6, I described the complex and extensive features of animation and interactivity being used in today's Web applications. The inclusion of XML into graphics establishes much greater capabilities to combine database operations with interactive objects using XML as the standard delivery medium.

SVG Formats

Defining objects, such as text and shapes, in an SVG image is relatively straightforward. While a software developer can code most SVG formats directly, there are a number of third-party products such as Adobe® and Illustrator® 9.0 that allow designers to generate complex images easily by simply exporting the files as SVG. However, an ecommerce analyst must have a general understanding of how SVG objects are defined, and what the various coordinates and elements refer to in the syntax when considering animation and interactivity in any Web design project. Listed below is some important information about the types of graphics supported by SVG and the most common data type formats. This information may need to be identified in the DOM and possibly the database system. Most important, it needs to be described in the repository of data, meaning that graphic images and their formats need to be organized in a central place so that they can be reused in the same manner as data and applications.

SVG supports three fundamental types of graphics elements that can be rendered onto the canvas:

1. *Shapes:* representing combinations of straight line and curves
2. *Text:* representing combinations of characters
3. *Raster Images:* representing an array of values that specify the paint color at a series of points on a rectangular grid.

The common data types for SVG properties and attributes fall into the following categories:

- <integer>: a whole number.
- <number>: real number value.
- <length>: a length is a distance measurement.
- <coordinate>: represents a length in the user coordinate system that is the given distance from the origin of the user coordinate system along the relevant axis (the x-axis for X coordinates, the y-axis for Y coordinates).
- <angle>: an angle value is a number optionally followed immediately with an angle unit identifier. Angle unit identifiers are: deg, degrees; grad, grads; rad, radians.
- <color>: the basic color type.
- <paint>: specifications of the type of paint to use when filling or stroking a given graphics element.
- <percentage>: the format of a percentage value is a number immediately followed by a "%". Percentage values are always relative to another value, for example a length.
- <uri>: Uniform Resource Identifiers [URI] references. A URI is the address of a resource on the Web.
- <frequency>: a frequency value is a number immediately followed by a frequency unit identifier. Frequency unit identifiers are: Hz, hertz ; kHz, kilohertz.
- <time>: a time value is a number immediately followed by a time unit identifier. Time unit identifiers are: ms, milliseconds; s, seconds.

Summary of SVG Features

SVG has many advantages over other image formats, and particularly over JPEG and GIF, the most common graphic formats used on the Web today. Listed below is a summary of SVG features that the ecommerce analyst should keep in mind when considering the integration of animation and graphics as an XML extension.

- *Plain text format:* SVG files can be accessed by a number of software tools and are usually smaller and more compressible than JPEG or GIF images.
- *Scalable:* unlike bitmapped GIF and JPEG formats, SVG is a vector format, which means that SVG images can be printed with high quality at any resolution.
- *Zoomable:* images can be zoomed in on any portion of an SVG image without any visible degradation.
- *Searchable and selectable text*: unlike bitmapped images, text in SVG text is selectable and searchable. For example, you can search for specific text strings, like city names in a map.
- *Scripting and animation*: enables dynamic and interactive graphics far more sophisticated than bitmapped or Flash images.
- *Works with Java technology:* SVG complements Java technologies' high-end graphics engine.
- *Open standard*: SVG is an open recommendation developed by a cross-industry consortium. Unlike some other graphics formats, SVG is not proprietary.
- *True XML*: as an XML grammar, SVG offers all the advantages of XML.

9
Design Specification Tools

Chapter 4 discussed specification formats that can be used to communicate information to both users and technical development personnel. Chapter 5 focused on the specific tools to create the logical equivalent. A diagram was used to show how an architect created a drawing for the user and a blueprint for the builder. This example was expanded to relate to the analyst:

In this chapter, we will focus on the process specification portions of the system, both from a user and a development perspective. The process specification is a component of every modeling tool.

Business Specifications

The ultimate purpose of the *business specification* is to confirm with the user the requirements of the system. In the picture in Figure 9.1, this confirmation is shown in the form of a prototype. Although this is the best way to confirm requirements with a user, there is always a need to have certain logic and flow documented in the form of a business specification. Chapter 5 presented the business specification in Figure 9.2 and defined it as a summary of the overall requirements of the system.

The business specification was written in a prose format so users could be comfortable with its meaning and intent, so that they could approve it. Although an overview like the one above is helpful, it is often incomplete and may not actually provide sufficient information for the user to approve. In order to provide more detail, the analyst should include the following components with many business specifications given to a user.

Functional Overview Sections

Functional overviews effectively take the business view a notch down in detail. A function can be considered a subset portion of the whole specification. For example, suppose a business specification was designed to handle order processing. Order processing would be considered the overall business specification goal; however, a subset function of the overall project could be picking order items from the warehouse. The subset description of the process is similar

Designing the System

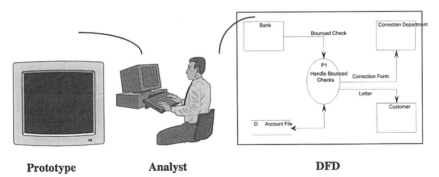

| Prototype | Analyst | DFD |

Figure 9.1 Analyst interfaces.

Client: XYZ Corporation	Date: 9/5/2006
Application: Operations Database	Supersedes:
Subject: Contact Management	Author: A. Langer
Process: Overview -- Business Spec	Page: 1 of 2

Overview

The contact management process will allow users to add, modify, or delete specific contacts. Contacts will be linked to various tables including Company. A contact refers to a person who is related to XYZ for business reasons. It can be a client, a vendor, a consultant, a person involved in a negotiation, etc.

Contact General Information:

The database must allow for the centralization of all the contacts handled by all the departments in XYZ. The database and screens will be focused on the following information component groupings:

Basic Information

This is the minimum data requirement and includes such elements as Name, Title, Organization, Phone, Fax, Address, Country, etc.

Contact Profile Information

Further qualification and related elements. Relations include:

- department
- type of client
- nature of client (primary, technical)
- interest of prospect
- importance of client
- memberships (FTUG)
- FT employee

This is a business specification that reflects the overall requirements in prose format. Its focus is to provide the user who is not technical with a document that he or she can authorize. This business specification should then point to detailed programming logic.

Figure 9.2 Sample business specification.

to the general overview and simply puts the subset functionality into perspective using prose format. After each subset functional overview is completed, the user should have enough information to understand the requirements of the system. It is important that the analyst make every attempt to keep the general and functional overviews as short as possible yet accurate and complete. This may sound contradictory; however, users typically do not like to read long documents summarizing all the detailed events of a system. Although Figure 9.3 looks like an overview, it is focused solely on a subprocess called Discounts.

Functional Flow Diagrams

Wherever possible it is important to use graphical representations to verify the accuracy of a specification. A high level data flow is suggested to allow the

Company: XYZ	Date: 9/27/2006
Application: Discounting	Supersedes:
Subject: Discounting Plan	Author: A. Langer
Process: Functional Business Spec	Page: 2 of 2

Year-End Reconciliation

The XYZ discount is guaranteed at the starting discount level. Therefore, should the bookstore not meet last year's order level, the discount cannot be lowered during the year. The only time the discount can be lowered is at the end of the year. At year-end, a process runs which reevaluates all the customers based on the current year's and last year's sales. This procedure is used only to create the new level for next year.

Screens & Reports

> *Although Figure 9.3 looks like an overview, it is focused solely on a subprocess called Discounts*

The order entry screen and all customer inquiry screens need to display the current Book and Bible discount for these customers. The amount used to determine the discount should be available on a customer inquiry screen as well as a report. The current system displays the month-to-date, current quarter, and current year's sales, as well as last year's sales. Total net sales and returns are listed, as well as net sales and returns of the discount items.

Chain Stores

Another major difference between this plan and others is that for chain stores, all sales for each branch store are added together, and they all receive the discount based on the total net sales for the chain. There can be situations where one of the branches does not qualify to receive the discount, but their sales are still added into the total for the chain.

If two stores become a chain mid-year, their individual annual net sales are added together, and their discount is increased if applicable.

Figure 9.3 A functional business specification summarizing the requirements for a discount component of the entire business specification.

user to see a graphical representation of the overall requirement (see Figure 9.4). Analysts should be encouraged to educate users so that they understand simple modeling concepts and tools.

Screens and Reports

The business specification should also include sample screens and reports. The level of detail of the screens and reports will vary depending on the prototype tools being used and the available time framed that the analyst has to get user sign-off on the requirements. CASE can be used where screen and report interface are available (see Figure 9.5). Analysts should avoid CASE products that contain drawing capabilities as opposed to true screen and report generators. Today's programming tools typically have prototype capabilities. The advantage here is that part of the development work is being accomplished during analysis and design. Using actual development tools during analysis and design is yet another form of Rapid Application Development (RAD).

Company: XYZ	Date: 5/27/2006
Application: Discounting	Supersedes:
Subject: Discounting Plan	Author: A. Langer
Process: Data Flow Diagram	Page: 1 of 1

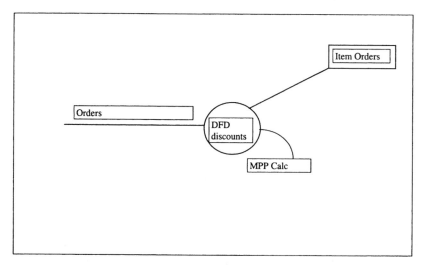

Figure 9.4 High Level DFD. Although a DFD, it is designed at a very simple level to allow a user to confirm flow.

Contact Management General							

Criteria and Basic Info

	Last Update	Company Name					Company
Contact-ID		Last-Name					
Area Number Ext		First-Name					
Telephone		Title					
Area Number		Address1			Contact Date		
Fax		Address2					
Telex		Address3					
E Mail							
		City		State	Zip Code		

Clear   Delete   Close   Security   Query   Add / Modify

Last-Name	First-Name	Company	Title	Telephone	User Last Name

Notes   Detail   Editions

Figure 9.5 CASE screen design. The above screen was created in System Architect and contains connectivity to physical application products such as Powerbuilder.

Therefore a good business specification should include the following component documents:

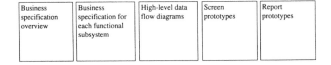

Business specification overview	Business specification for each functional subsystem	High-level data flow diagrams	Screen prototypes	Report prototypes

Programming and Technical Specifications

Once the business specifications are completed and agreed upon by the users, the information must be mapped into a programming or technical specification. These specifications effectively provide all of the algorithms that are required by the functional primitive DFDs and STDs. That is, each functional primitive must point to a technical programming specification. This programming specification will define all algorithms which affect the process. The programming specification must also, however, point back to its original functional business specification as shown in Figure 9.6.

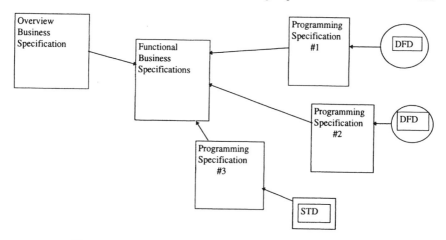

Figure 9.6 Relationship of specifications with DFDs and STDs.

Another way of explaining the relationship is to say that an overview business specification can have many functional business specifications. Functional business specifications can have many programming specifications and each programming specification should be associated with one or many functional primitive DFDs or STDs. The example of a technical/programming specification contained in Figure 9.7 initially appeared as Figure 5.11 of Chapter 5.

The programming specification in Figure 9.7 utilizes the pseudocode method discussed in Chapter 5 and provides the necessary information for a programmer to develop the application. Many IT professionals often feel the need for programmers to understand the business specification. If the program specifications are developed using the methods recommended herein, then there is no such requirement placed on the programming team. Good programming specifications stand alone, like a good blueprint that will allow a contractor to build a house without ever being part of the development and confirmation phases with the buyer. Programmers who can focus on the engineering issues rather than user requirements will be much more productive. Therefore, IT professionals who share both roles, that is, those with the title "Programmer/Analyst," will always be susceptible to doing both system requirements and engineering development simultaneously. Doing both "as you go" poses a real danger in that the individual has to continually change hats without really separating the tasks. In addition, when the two tasks are combined it typically results in a longer development life cycle and one that has less quality because neither task is ever really completed. Furthermore, the skill sets of analysts tend to conflict with those of programmers. For example, analysts should enjoy interacting with users and need to develop skills that allow them to gather the information they need. Programmers, on the other hand, often are not comfortable with user interaction and are more focused on their technical knowledge of software and hardware products.

Client: XYZ Company	Date: 9/15/06
Application: Contact Management	Supersedes: 9/5/06
Subject: Program Specification Detail	Author: A. Langer
Spec-ID FTCM01 - Add/Modify Screen Processing	Page: 1 of 1

Process Flow Description:
The user will input information in the top form. At a minimum, at least the Last Name or Contact ID will be entered. The system must check a Security indicator prior to allowing a user to modify a Contact. The Security will be by Department or Everyone. Therefore, if the Modify button is selected and the user is restricted by a different department, Display:
" Access Denied, not eligible to modify, Department Restriction"

If Security authorized, the Add/Modify Button will activate the following business rules:

If Contact-ID (cntid) not blank
Find match and replace entered data into record
If no match display "Invalid Contact-ID" and refresh cursor

> This area actually states the algorithm required by the program. It is in a format called Pseudocode" meaning "false code." This type of logic resembles Cobol format. (see Chapter 4)

If Contact-ID (cntid) Blank and Last-Name (cntlname) Blank then
Display " Contact-ID or Last-Name must be entered"
Place Cursor at Contact-ID (cntid) entry.

If Contact-ID (cntid) Blank and Last-Name (cntlname) + First-Name (cntfname) is Duplicate
Display Window to show matches so that user can determine if contact already in system
If user selects the Add Anyway button
assume new contact with same name and assign new Contact-ID (cntid)
else
upon selection bring in existing data and close window.
Else
Create new record with all new information fields and assign Contact-ID (cntid)

If Company button activated
Prompt user for Company-ID (cmpcd) and/or Company-Name (cmpna)
If duplicate
link foreign-key pointer to matched company
else
add Company-Name (cntcmpna) to Contact Table only
Display "You must use Company Screen to Link, Company Master File Not Updated"

Figure 9.7 Technical/Programming Specification.

Screen Specifications

Another method of creating specifications, particularly when data flow diagrams and process diagrams are not used, is to create them directly from the screens themselves. This is usually accomplished by having two levels of screen processing specifications. The first type of specification is used to describe the functionality of the screen, especially as it relates to its execution options. The second type of specification relates to how the data elements on the screen are to be processed. By process we mean the business rules that govern how the data element is treated by the screen program. For example, a data element in one screen program may be used only in display mode and not allow its value to be modified. Yet in another screen, the very same data element may require modification.

Therefore, a screen specification has three components: (1) the screen itself; (2) screen processing specifications; and (3) data element specifications. There should be one data element specification for every data element that appears on a screen. Good specifications will even use the same data element definition across multiple screen specifications just to ensure that there are no elements that are left undefined in any screen definition documentation.

Figure 9.8 shows a screen designed using Oracle Developer 2000. Figure 9.9 depicts the screen processing requirements. Specifically, the screen processing specifications provide a description of the purpose and functionality of the screen, as well as stating how each function button is to be handled by the program. Figure 9.10 is an example of a screen data element definition in which Vendor_No is used to fetch and display Vendor, which is the vendor's name. Note that the form is designed to state specific information necessary for a programmer to complete development, including the domain of values of the data element, its definition in terms of processing, and whether the value can be added, deleted, or modified from the database.

Screens and Derived Elements

In Chapter 6, the handling of derived data elements in normalization was defined as a type of 3rd normal form failure. That is, derived data elements, commonly known as calculated fields, were eliminated as a stored attribute in an entity. However, screens often need to calculate and display these derived elements. For example, the screen in Figure 9.8 has a field called "ELC" standing for "Estimated Landing Cost." This element is calculated, both for the season and for year-to-date. The calculations for "ELC Season" and "ELC YTD" are

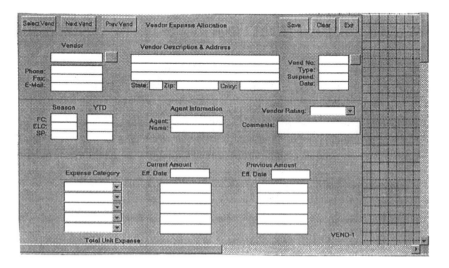

Figure 9.8 GUI screen using Oracle Developer/2000.

Client:	Date: 2/28/06
Application: **Vendor Expense Allocation**	Supersedes: 12/28//06
Process: **Screen Processing**	Author: **A. Langer**

Description & Source:
This screen allows for the entry of expenses and other pertinent information about vendors. The screen can also be executed in edit mode and allows users to browse sequentially by Vendor. The screen allows for up to three (3) expense allocations. The expense allocation is used to calculate the ELC (see Item-1)

ANALYSIS OF SCREEN FUNCTIONS

Button Function:	Process Definition:
Select Vendor	Locates a particular vendor to add or edit information.
Next Vend	Displays next sequential Vendor stored in the database
Previous Item	Displays previous Vendor in database
Save	Saves contents of screen to database
Clear	Clears screen values (only in Add New Item mode)
Exit	Cancel execution of screen program and display calling screen

Figure 9.9 Screen processing requirements.

defined in their corresponding Screen Data Element Definition forms as shown in Figures 9.11 and 9.12 respectively. Thus, every data element in the data dictionary that appears on a screen must have a corresponding Screen Data Element Definition form, regardless of whether it is a stored attribute in an entity or a derived element that requires dynamic calculation.

Problems and Exercises

1. What is the purpose of business specifications?
2. How do functional overview sections relate to the entire business specification?

Client:	Date: 12/28/06
Application: **Vendor Expense Allocation**	Supersedes:

Process:
    Screen data Element Definition
	Author:
	    A. Langer

Data Element:
    Vendor
	SQL Data Type and Qualifier
	    Varchar18

Description:
This element represents the Vendor Name. Vendors can be created only from Unisys. Therefore, they may be assigned to only for further editing with respect to expenses and other imports-specific information. The changes do not update the Unisys system.

ANALYSIS OF DATA ELEMENT

Values:
Value is assigned from advanced selection button.

Definition:
Search/Select from table. New Vendor may not be added. Entry required.

✓	Data Element Action	Table Action	Name / Value
✓	ADDED	Assign from Vendor Table	Vendor_No
	DELETED		
✓	MODIFIED	Assign from Vendor table:	Vendor_No

Copyright A. Langer 1994-2006
Form xxxd01

Figure 9.10 Screen data element definition.

3. What is the use of a functional flow diagram? Which modeling tool is used?

4. What are the five most common components of the business specification?

5. How does the business specification relate to the programming specification?

6. How does the programming specification interface with DFDs and STDs?

7. Define the three components of a screen specification.

8. Explain the purpose of a "Screen Data Element Definition."

9. What is the purpose of having "Screen Processing" instructions?

Form: Venddl1

Client:	Date: 12/28/06
Application: **Vendor Expense Allocation**	Supersedes:
Process: **Screen data Element Definition**	Author: **A. Langer**
Data Element: **ELC Season**	SQL Data Type and Qualifier **Number 15,2**

Description:
This element represents the calculated Estimated Landing Costs Season-to-Date.

ANALYSIS OF DATA ELEMENT

Values: ·
Must be a calculated from all ELC from Vendor items season to date.

Definition:
Calculated field IMP_ELC_SN. Add all Item ELCs for Vendor for season. See Item-Ent.

✓	Data Element Action	Table Action	Name / Value
	ADDED	Add	
	DELETED	Delete	
	MODIFIED	Modify:	

Copyright A. Langer 1994-06
Form xxxd01

Figure 9.11 Screen data element definition for ELC season calculation.

Form: Vendd11a

Client:	Date: 2/27/06
Application: **Vendor Expense Allocation**	**Supersedes: 12/28/06**

Process:
    Screen data Element Definition
	Author:
	    A. Langer

Data Element:
    ELC Year
	SQL Data Type and Qualifier
	    Number 15,2

Description:
This element represents the calculated Estimated Landing Costs Year-to-Date.

ANALYSIS OF DATA ELEMENT

Values:
Must be a calculated from all
ELC from Vendor items year to
date.

Definition:
Calculated field IMP_ELC_YR. Add all Item ELCs for Vendor for
year. See Item-Ent.

✓	Data Element Action	Table Action	Name / Value
	ADDED	Add	
	DELETED	Delete	
	MODIFIED	Modify:	

Copyright A. Langer 1994-06
Form xxxd01

Figure 9.12 Screen data element definition for ELC YTD calculation.

Mini-Project

The process specifications and GUI screens are part of the requirements of a contact management system. Based on this specification, design the ERD in 3rd normal form.

Client:	Date: 9/5/06
Application: **Operations Database**	Supersedes:

Subject:
    Contact Management
	Author:
	    A. Langer

Process:
    Overview - Business Spec
	Page:
	    1 of 2

Overview

The Contact Management Process will allow users to add, modify, or delete specific contacts. Contacts will be linked to various tables including Company. A Contact refers to a person who is related to the business. It can be a Client, a Vendor, a consultant, a person involved in a negotiation, etc.

Contact General Information:

The Database must allow for the centralization of all the contacts handled by all departments.
The database and screens will be focused on the following information component groupings:

Basic Information
This is the minimum data requirement and includes such elements as Name, Title, Organization, Phone, Fax, Address, Country.

Contact Profile Information
Further qualification and related elements. Relations include:

- department
- type of client
- nature of client (primary, technical)
- interest of prospect
- importance of client
- memberships (FTUG)
- FT employee

Client:	Date: 9/5/06
Application: **Operations Database**	Supersedes:

Subject:
    Contact Management
	Author:
	    A. Langer

Process:
    Overview - Business Spec
	Page:
	    2 of 2

Mailing Information

Mailing selections to produce labels include:

- Selected Mailing Groupings via Query
- Source of Lead
- The Region
- Description of the salutation for the contact

Log Information:

This will include general information in the form of comments and a related date of entry.

Contact-Specific Information:

In addition to the groupings listed above, there is specific information required:

Market Observation/Business Development Information:

This involves activity of a visit and requires linkage to the main contact database. Elements needed are:
- Objective of Visit
- Date of Visit
- Place of Visit
- Visit Report

Press Information:

This includes:
- related contact publication
- areas of expertise
- circulation

Client:	Date: 9/5/06
Application: Contact Management	Supersedes:
Subject: Specification Detail	Author: A. Langer
ID FTCMSDR	Page: 1 of 1

REQUIREMENTS INDEX	SPEC-ID
Add / Modify Button	FTCM01
Query Button	FTCM02
Delete Button	FTCM03
Clear Button	FTCM04
Detail Button and Screen	FTCM05
Notes Button	FTCM06

Client:	Date: 9/15/06
Application: Contact Management	Supersedes: 9/5/06
Subject: Program Specification Detail	Author: A. Langer
Spec-ID FTCM01 - Add/Modify Screen Processing	Page: 1 of 1

Process Flow Description:

The user will input information in the top form. At a minimum, at least the Last Name or Contact ID will be entered. The system must check a Security indicator prior to allowing a user to modify a Contact. The Security will be by Department or Everyone. Therefore, if the Modify button is selected and the user is restricted by a different department, Display:

> "Access Denied, not eligible to modify, Department Restriction"

If Security authorized, the Add/Modify Button will activate the following business rules:

    If Contact-ID (cntid) not blank
            Find match and replace entered data into record
            If no match display "Invalid Contact-ID" and refresh cursor

    If Contact-ID (cntid) Blank and Last-Name (cntlname) Blank then
            Display " Contact-ID or Last-Name must be entered"
            Place Cursor at Contact-ID (cntid) entry.

    If Contact-ID (cntid) Blank and Last-Name (cntlname) + First-Name (cntfname) is Duplicate
            Display Window to show matches so that user can determine whether contact already in
            system
            If user selects the Add Anyway button
                    assume new contact with same name and assign new Contact-ID (cntid)
            else
                    upon selection bring in existing data and close window.
    Else
            Create new record with all new information fields and assign Contact-ID (cntid)

    If Company button activated
            Prompt user for Company-ID (cmpcd) and/or Company-Name (cmpna)
            If duplicate
                    link foreign-key pointer to matched company
            else
                    add Company-Name (cntcmpna) to Contact Table only
                    Display "You must use Company Screen to Link, Company Master File Not
                    Updated"

Client:	**Date 9/15/06**
Application: Contact Management	**Supersedes: :** 9/5/06
Subject: Program Specification Detail	**Author: A. Langer**
Spec-ID FTCM02 - Query	**Page:** 1 of 1

Process Flow Description:

The user will have the ability to select the Query Button after entering information in upper portion of the screen. The Query button will activate a search on the Contact database for matches based on entered information.

   If Matches (Based on Access Authorization, if not authorized, display in gray without Company
   Name):
         Display matched records (see screen format)
   else
         Display "No Matches Found"

   If Matches and User enables Edition buttons
         select appropriate option for labels or ASCII File creation on matched query records

   If user highlights specific match and double clicks
         Display General and Detail and allow user to activate Modify to make changes

Client	Date 9/15/06
Application: Contact Management	Supersedes: : 9/5/06
Subject: Program Specification Detail	Author: A. Langer
Spec-ID FTCM03 - Delete	Page: 1 of 1

Process Flow Description:

The user will have the ability to select the Delete Button in order to delete a Contact. Only certain users will have authorization to perform this function. Therefore, this process must interface with a security table.

To preserve referential integrity on Company, the user must be prompted to delete the Company based on the following rules:

>   If Company Name in Contact database (meaning that Company database was not updated)
>> delete Contact record only (no foreign key pointer)
>   else
>> do not delete related Company in Company database

Client	Date 9/15/06
Application: Contact Management	Supersedes: : 9/5/06
Subject: Program Specification Detail	Author: A. Langer
Spec-ID FTCM05 -Detail	Page: 1 of 1

Process Flow Description:

The user will have the ability to select the Detail Button in order to activate the Contact Management Detail Screen (see sample). The following rules apply:

1. Basic Information = Basic Information from General Screen. This data cannot be modified from Detail Screen.

2. Mailing Information includes pick lists for Sources, Leads, and Regions

3. Press Information includes pick list for Expertise

4. Contact Profile includes Departments, CTC types, CTC nature, Interest Level, and Importance Level

5. Activating the Cancel Button at any time will cancel any new input/modifications and link back to the General Screen.

6. Activating the OK button will save all Detail Screen Data to record and return to General Screen.

Client	Date 9/15/06
Application: Contact Management	Supersedes: : 9/5/06
Subject: Program Specification Detail	Author: A. Langer
Spec-ID FTCM05 -Detail	Page: 1 of 1

Process Flow Description:

The user will have the ability to select the Detail Button in order to activate the Contact Management Detail Screen (see sample). The following rules apply:

1. Basic Information = Basic Information from General Screen. This data cannot be modified from Detail Screen.

2. Mailing Information includes pick lists for Sources, Leads, and Regions

3. Press Information includes pick list for Expertise

4. Contact Profile includes Departments, CTC types, CTC nature, Interest Level, and Importance Level

5. Activating the Cancel Button at any time will cancel any new input/modifications and link back to the General Screen.

6. Activating the OK button will save all Detail Screen Data to record and return to General Screen.

Client:	Date: 9/5/06
Application: Contact Management	**Supersedes:**
Subject: Program Specification Detail	**Author: A. Langer**
Spec-ID FTCM06 -Notes	**Page:** 1 of 1

Process Flow Description:

The user will have the ability to select the Notes Button in order to enter free-form about the Contact.

1.The System should record the date of each note when entered.

2. There is no limit to the number of Notes.

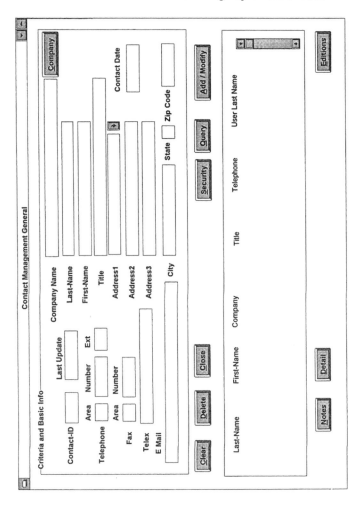

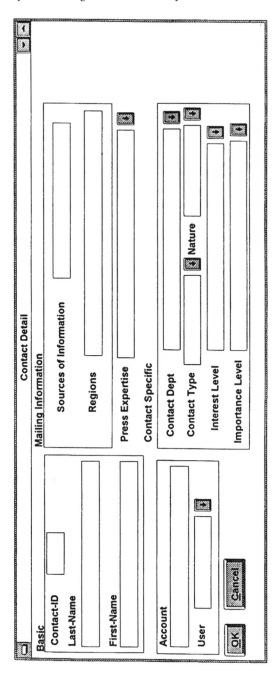

10
CASE and Automated Techniques

CASE Defined

We have mentioned CASE (Computer-Aided Software Engineering) in previous chapters. Although its meanings can vary, CASE is traditionally defined as "a comprehensive label for software designed to use computers in all phases of computer development, from planning and modeling through coding and documentation. CASE represents a working environment consisting of programs and other development tools that help managers, systems analysts, programmers, and others automate the design and implementation of programs and procedures for business, engineering, and scientific computer systems."[19] CASE became popular during the late 1970s as a way of automating and integrating modeling tools. It also allows for the creation and maintenance of data repositories which provide organizations with a tool to establish a central place to store all of their data elements. Figure 10.1 shows the common components of most integrated CASE products.

Data Repository Inputs

The design of CASE is based on inputs which create entries into the data repository. A data repository can be defined as a "robust data dictionary." A data dictionary essentially provides the definition of the data element itself. A data repository, on the other hand, stores information relating to the data element's behavior. This can include the element's stored procedures, descriptions, and documentation about how and where it is used. Therefore, the data dictionary can actually be considered a subset of the data repository. Inputs to the data repository are typically the modeling tools discussed in Chapter 5: DFDs, ERDs, STDs, and process specifications as well as the object oriented analysis discussed in Chapter 11. These input capabilities can be summarized as follows.

---

[19] Microsoft Press, *Computer Dictionary*, 2nd ed., p. 66.

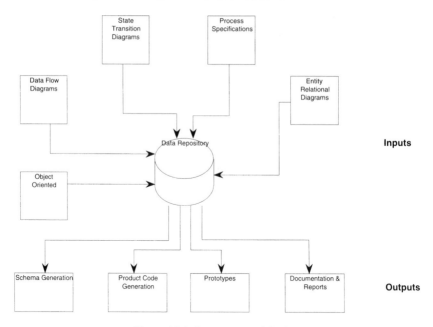

Figure 10.1 Components of CASE.

Data Flow Diagrams (DFD)

Every named data flow will automatically require an entry into the data repository. This named flow may consist of other elements and therefore require functional decomposition down to the elementary data element level. Unique data elements that are components of data stores will also generate entries into the data repository. Figures 10.2 and 10.3 show these interfaces in the Popkin System Architect CASE product.

Entity Relational Diagrams (ERD)

The ERD interfaces with the data repository by mapping an element to particular tables (entities), that is, each unique data element within an entity points to a data repository definition (see Figure 10.4).

State Transition Diagram (STD)

The STD interfaces with the data repository via the "conditions that cause a change in state." These condition arrows map to the data repository and allow component elements to be defined as shown in Figure 10.5.

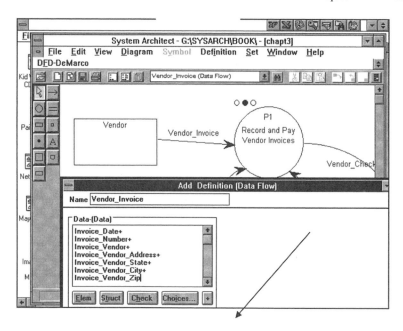

Figure 10.2 CASE flow elements. The above diagram shows how a data flow is defined by its elementary data elements.

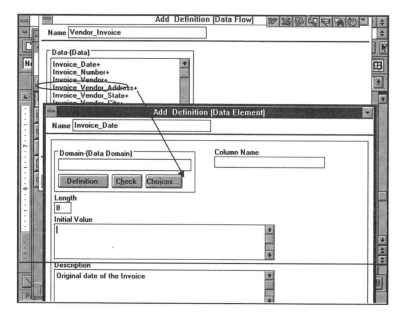

Figure 10.3 CASE data flow definition. The above diagram shows how the data components of the Vendor_Invoice flow define each data element in the repository.

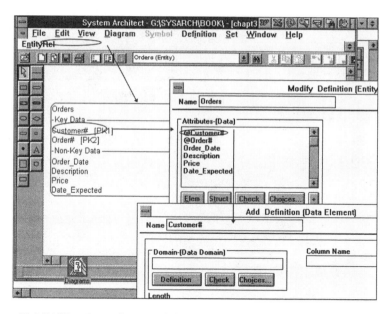

Figure 10.4 CASE entity attributes. This figure reflects how the Orders entity is defined by its component data attributes. These attributes then point to their respective data elements in the data repository.

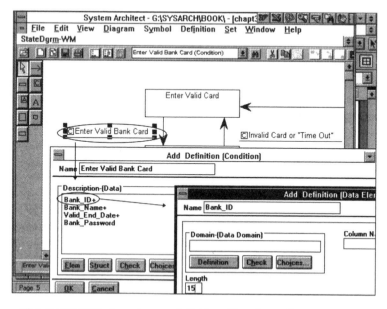

Figure 10.5 CASE STD data element definition. The above diagram shows how the condition-arrow "Enter Valid Bank Card" in an STD points to its component data attributes. These attributes are then defined as data elements in the data repository.

Process Specifications

Process Specifications are typically defined via the functional primitive process of the DFD or a particular state in an STD. The example in Figure 10.6 reflects how this is done using a DFD. Once the process specification is defined, data elements embedded in the application logic are mapped to the data repository.

The OO paradigm is also supported by CASE where objects can store both attributes and methods and point data element definitions into the data repository (Figure 10.7).

Data Repository Outputs

CASE outputs provide links to physical products and services. Its capabilities therefore allow for the storage of various design-specific features that can automatically produce output that can then be used by other products. The rest of this section describes the features in each of the areas shown in Figure 10.1 schema generation; product code generation; prototypes; and documentation and reports.

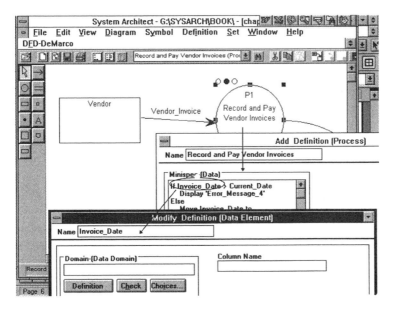

Figure 10.6 CASE process specification. The process specification above in System Architect is mapped to a process in a DFD called "Record and Pay Vendor Invoices." The algorithm of the process is defined and any elements used in the process specification must point to its data element definition in the data repository.

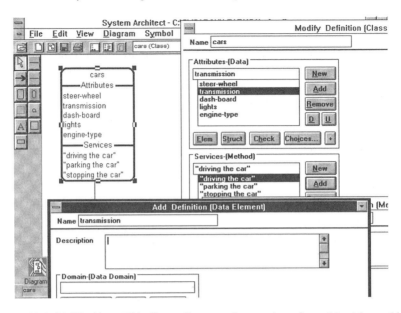

Figure 10.7 CASE object. This figure diagrams the creation of an object/class which points to an attribute of an object that then points to the data repository definition of the element itself.

Schema Generation

The schema generation facility in CASE allows various interfaces with physical database products. These schemas include support for most of the popular database products such as Oracle, Sybase, Informix, Microsoft's SQL_Server, and DB2. A *schema* is defined as the description of the data elements in the format necessary for a particular RDBMS product. Most of the databases just mentioned support SQL (Structured Query Language) data type identifiers as shown in Figure 10.8.

Product Code Generation

Product Code Generation relates to storing specific information needed by programming products such as Powerbuilder and C++ (see Figure 10.9). This information, similar to the process in schema generation, allows the analyst to export information directly into the intended product. The ability to store multiple product definitions also provides a central capability to provide information about a data element for different product languages. This translates to providing a mechanism to support multiple development environments and languages without the need to have the definition given only in the programming language code.

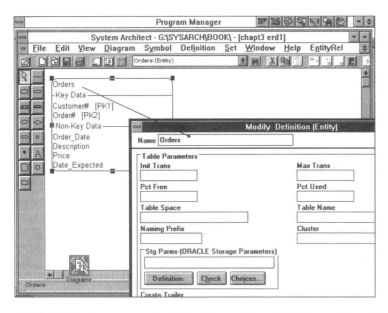

Figure 10.8 CASE schema generation. This diagram shows the Orders entity and how definitions specific for Oracle schema generation can be stored.

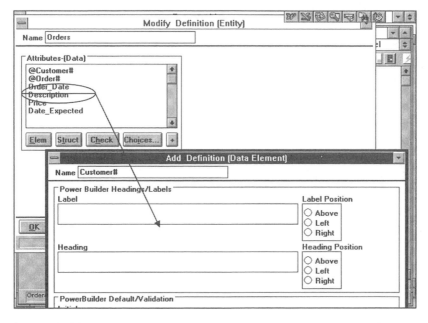

Figure 10.9 CASE program interface. This is an example of how CASE can store data element information for the Powerbuilder programming product.

Prototypes

Prototypes are usually screens and reports that are produced so that users can get a visual view of the system. Prototypes do not actually work; they are like cars with no engines. CASE prototypes can range in capabilities from simple views of the way a screen or report will look to an actual demonstration of the application's functional capabilities. These demonstration capabilities can provide a way of linking screens with the data repository to show the "look and feel" of the application to the user. In addition, certain CASE products allow screen and report information to be directly ported into a development language (see Figure 10.10).

Documentation and Reports

CASE provides both documentation and reports to reflect the information stored in the data repository. The information can range from a simple data element report to more sophisticated comparison information (e.g., missing data element descriptions), as Figure 10.11 illustrates.

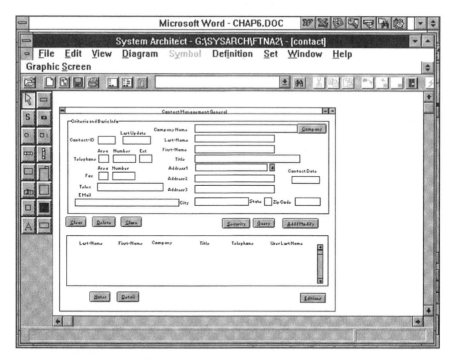

Figure 10.10 CASE screen painter. The above diagram shows the screen painter properties of System Architect. The data elements contained in the screen are mapped to the data repository and therefore contain their appropriate definitions.

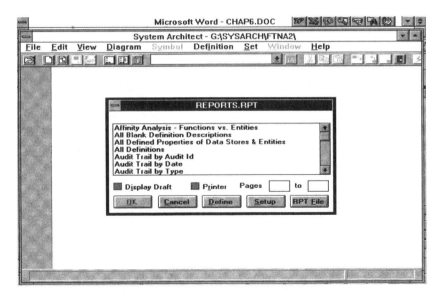

Figure 10.11 CASE report writer. The above screen shows the report menu from System Architect.

The data repository of CASE is therefore the central component of the product and serves to store all related information of a particular data element. A data element in the data repository does not necessarily need to belong to any entity, schema, prototype or program product, but rather it may be an independent piece of information. However, CASE provides an easier way to make a data element associated with an entity, schema, prototype, and so on, without losing this independence. The integration facility of CASE allows analysts to modify the definitions of a data element and have that change propagated throughout the data repository.

Why Does CASE Fail?

Unfortunately, many of the implementations of CASE during the 1980s were not successful. Information systems professionals began to shy away from its use. The reasons for this are very straightforward:

- Organizations were not properly trained how to use structured tools.
- CASE products did not comply with GUI (Graphic User Interface) and therefore were not robust.[20]

---

[20] The term robust or robustness is defined as the ability of a program to function, or to continue functioning well, in unexpected situations. Microsoft Press, *Computer Dictionary*, 2nd ed., p. 342.

- CASE products were methodology driven, and therefore required the organization to commit to a particular approach. Such approaches did not typically conform to the organization's culture.
- There were limited third party product interfaces to enable efficient transfer from logical models to physical products and databases.

Perhaps the CASE transition was bound to occur in a slow and methodical manner. Many organizations could not afford to buy the popular CASE products then that included Knowledgeware, Excellerator and IEF (Information Engineering Facility). Those who did buy them still feel scarred, and even today CASE is considered a bad word in some circles.

A key factor in the success of CASE is understanding where and when to use it in the software implementation cycle. To determine this point, the table in Figure 8.3 is a replication of the table of the Tiers of Analysis and Software Application Development developed in Chapter 1. This table can also be used to *compare* or *map* the analyst's proficiency level to that of the software development process being used.

The table shows that CASE should not be considered until tier 3, that is, until an analyst is proficient with the user interface and the structured tools. CASE can then be used as a way of automating the analysis process. By automating portions of the analysis functions, organizations can thus become more productive when modeling systems.

Why CASE Should Succeed

Using CASE is the only means of creating and maintaining any central storage of information for enterprise level systems. Today, the CASE products are far more robust, contain the GUI interface and allow for the handling of multiple analysis methodologies. Analysts can therefore create data repositories as they see fit for their organizations. In addition, there are many database and development third party products that can be linked to CASE. Many companies like Oracle now produce their own CASE products (Oracle Designer/2000) that are focused on creating even more interfaces between data repositories and the Oracle RDBMS. Frankly, an IT organization that does not consider CASE cannot provide the long-term support for many of the features and capabilities required by the applications of the future. These applications will be based on the OO paradigm and client/server computing. Perhaps the most significant advantage to CASE is in the area of maintenance. Definitions of quality software have included the word "maintenance" for decades: systems that are difficult to maintain will not be considered quality systems. When there is a central repository of data as well as defined processes, the maintenance of both databases and applications becomes easier and more productive. The data repository also allows both analysts and developers to use CASE as a means of training and documenting existing systems. Having new programmers use an automated tool to see the contents of each entity and how the data is used in an application provides IT organizations with greater flexibility and productivity for future enhancements.

Open Systems Requirements and Client/Server

Perhaps the most significant support for today's use of CASE is Open Systems architecture. Open systems architecture can be defined as a set of standards for both hardware and software that allows portability of applications and databases. Open systems architecture includes such operating systems as UNIX, LINUX, Windows and Windows NT, DOS and Netware. These operating systems support the standards in application software that allow such software to run across one another's operating systems. Although this concept is not fully transparent, application developers have enjoyed more portability of their code than ever before. The software industry will continue to support open systems, especially through the use of OO technology. Essentially, without CASE it is impossible to support the open systems model. In order for an IS organization to be compliant with open systems, it must have the ability to store data elements free from specific hardware and software products, that is, it must not be proprietary.

Client/server even further strengthens the need to use CASE. Built on the basis of open systems and OO, client/server establishes the need for additional standards in the area of object interfaces across LANs and WANs. The use of the Internet as a key component of the future for IT processing is also constructed on the basis of OO and client/server concepts. The analysis proficiency skills tiers (Figure 10.12) showed us that CASE is a prerequisite for OO and client/server. Chapter 11 will demonstrate that OO is constructed via the structured tools and that client/server is developed after determining the appropriate objects and classes. None of these links can be accomplished without a central point of control, evaluation and reconciliation, all of which CASE provides to us.

We mentioned above that client/server established new needs for standards for communicating among and WANs. Much of this interface is called

Tier	Analyst Proficiency
6	Internet/Intranet – Web-based transaction processing, media, and graphics
5	Client/Server – breaking down objects to their client and server applications
4	Object orientation – selection of objects and classes
3	CASE – automation and productivity of Tier 2
2	Structured Tools – DFD, PFD, ERD, STD, process specification, data repository
1	User Interface – interviewing skills, JAD, RAD

Figure 10.12 Analyst Proficiency Skills Correlation.

middleware. Middleware contains the necessary APIs (application program interface), protocols, metadata, gateways and object messaging necessary to provide communication across client/server networks. The driving force behind middleware is that today's applications must communicate with other applications and databases without knowing one another's hardware and software configurations. This means that the middleware must contain information for the client or server about what data is being sent or received respectively. For example, without knowing the receiving application's programming language, middleware must provide the details of the layout of data being sent. This data layout is defined in the metadata (data about the data) facility of the middleware. The components of open systems and client/server architecture are shown below in the client/server three tier architecture depicted in Figure 10.13.

Our discussions of CASE can be mapped to every tier of the client/server architecture. CASE thus provides the underlying facility to record information and data to build such systems.

Types of CASE Tools

The CASE components which comprise analysis and design capabilities are typically known as Upper-CASE. Many CASE products may provide only the

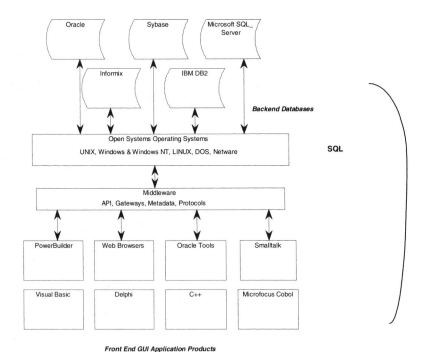

Figure 10.13 Client/server three tier architecture.

input side that has been shown. CASE products that also provide for output to the physical product side are known as *Lower*-CASE. Once again, there are CASE products that do not provide the analysis tools but rather only a data repository to create outputs. These CASE products are also known as *Code Generators*. CASE products that do both the input analysis and output generation are known as *I-CASE* or *Integrated CASE*. I-CASE tools will continue to become more popular as open systems and client/server architectures become more widely used.

CASE tools should also support multiple data repositories. This means that some repositories can be either mutually exclusive or dependent as children in a tree structure. *Mutually exclusive* repositories simply mean that there are multiple libraries of data elements that have no relationship with each other. This situation can occur in organizations that have different business lines or subsidiaries that are in different businesses. Mutually exclusive libraries should be created only if the analyst is sure that there is no need for an enterprise model.

Tree structure libraries are used more often. The tree of repositories allows an organization to have a central parent repository with all common data elements of the enterprise. *Child libraries* inherit the global definitions. Locally defined data elements will become only global if they are needed by at least two entities in the organization. Another use of the tree structure repositories is *work-in-process*. Specifically this means that new projects may create potentially new data elements to be added to the global data repository. This allows the IT organization to properly control any new entries into the global data repository until the project is completed or the data element candidate is approved by the appropriate people in the organization. In any event, good CASE products allow for this versatility, and it is recommended that analysts utilize such capabilities.

Reverse Engineering

Analysts will often be confronted with a system that is not in any existing CASE product. The issue then becomes the chicken- and-egg paradox: how do I create a data repository if the product already exists? Advanced CASE products typically contain a module that allows for *reverse engineering*. "Reverse Engineering is the process of analyzing existing application programs and database code to create higher-level representations of the code. It is sometimes called *design recovery*."[21] For example, reverse engineering features would allow for the input of an existing Oracle table into the CASE product. This input would result in the creation of a logical ERD and the creation of all the data elements into the data repository. In addition foreign key links, triggering operations and other stored procedures would automatically populate the appropriate repository areas. Reverse engineering therefore allows analysts to "start somewhere" and

---

[21] Jeffrey Whitten, Lonnie Bently, Victor Barlow, *Systems Analysis & Design Methods*, 3rd ed., p. 181.

eventually to get the organization into forward engineering, that is, building physical products and databases directly from the CASE tool.

Problems and Exercises

1. Define the applications of a CASE tool.
2. What are the benefits of the input facilities of CASE? Of the output facilities?
3. Explain the concept of a data repository. How does it relate to the dictionary?
4. What is schema generation? Why is this important for forward engineering?
5. How does the data repository assist in the development of screen prototypes?
6. What is I-CASE? Explain.
7. What are the most important issues to ensure the success of CASE?
8. What are the five analysis proficiencies?
9. How does CASE relate to the implementation of object and client/server system?
10. What is a three tiered architecture?
11. Why is reverse engineering so prevalent in most IS organizations?

11
Object-Oriented Techniques

What Is Object-Oriented Analysis?

Object-oriented analysis has become a key issue in today's analysis paradigm. It is without question the most important element of creating what may be called the "complete" requirement of a system. Unfortunately, the industry is in a state of controversy about the approaches and tools that should be used to create object systems. This chapter will focus on developing the requirements for object systems and the challenges of converting legacy systems. Therefore, many of the terms will be defined based on their fundamental capabilities and how they can be used by a practicing analyst (as opposed to a theorist!).

Object orientation (OO) is based on the concept that every requirement ultimately must belong to an object. It is therefore critical that we first define what is meant by an object. In the context of OO analysis, an *object* is any cohesive whole made up of two essential components: data and processes.

Classic and even structured analysis approaches were traditionally based on the examination of a series of events. We translated these events from the physical world by first interviewing users and then developing what was introduced as the concept of the logical equivalent. Although we are by no means abandoning this necessity, the OO paradigm requires that these events belong to an identifiable object. Let us expand on this difference using the object shown in Figure 11.1, an object we commonly call a "car."

The car shown in Figure 11.1 may represent a certain make and model, but it also contains common components that are contained in all cars (e.g., an engine). If we were to look upon the car as a business entity of an organization, we might find that the three systems shown in Figure 11.2 were developed over the years.

Figure 11.2 shows us that the three systems were built over a period of 11 years. Each system was designed to provide service to a group of users responsible for particular tasks. The diagram shows that the requirements for System 1 were based on the engine and front-end of the car. The users for this project had no interest in or need for any other portions of the car. System 2, on the other hand, focused on the lower center and rear of the car. Notice, however, that System 2 and System 1 have an overlap. This means that there are parts and procedures common to both systems. Finally, System 3 reflects the upper center and rear of the car and has an overlap with System 2. It is also important to note

Figure 11.1 A car is an example of a physical object.

that there are components of the car that have not yet been defined, probably because no user has had a need for them. We can look at the car as an object and Systems 1 to 3 as the software which has so far been defined about that object. Our observations should also tell us that the entire object is not defined and more important, that there is probable overlap of data and functionality among the systems that have been developed. This case exemplifies the history of most development systems. It should be clear that the users who stated their requirements never had any understanding that their own situation belonged to a larger composite object. Users tend to establish requirements based on their own job functions and their own experiences in those functions. Therefore, the analyst who interviews users about their events is exposed to a number of risks:

- Users tend to identify only what they have experienced, rather than speculating about other events that could occur. We know that such events can take place, although they have not yet occurred (you should recall the discussion of using STDs as a modeling tool to identify unforeseen possibilities). Consider, for example, an analysis situation in which $50,000 must be approved by the firm's Controller. This event

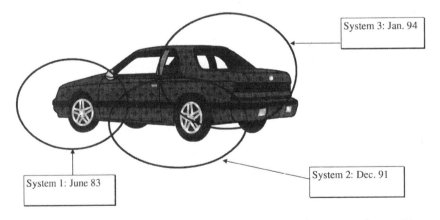

Figure 11.2 This diagram reflects the three systems developed to support the car object.

might show only the approval, not the rejection. The user's response is that the Controller, while examining the invoices, has never rejected one and therefore no rejection procedure exists. You might ask why. Well, in this case the Controller was not reviewing the invoices for rejection but rather holding them until he/she was confident that the company's cash flow could support the issuance of these invoices. Obviously, the Controller could decide to reject an invoice. In such a case, the software would require a change to accommodate this new procedure. From a software perspective we call this a system enhancement, and it would result in a modification to the existing system.

- Other parts of the company may be affected by the Controller's review of the invoices. Furthermore, are we sure that no one else has automated this process before? One might think such prior automation could never be overlooked, especially in a small company, but when users have different names for the same thing (remember Customer and Client!) it is very likely that such things will occur. Certainly in our example there were two situations where different systems overlapped in functionality.
- There will be conflicts between the systems with respect to differences in data and process definitions. Worst of all, these discrepancies may not be discovered until years after the system is delivered.

The above example shows us that requirements obtained from individual events require another level of reconciliation to ensure they are complete. Requirements are said to be "complete" when they define the whole object. The more incomplete they are, the more modifications will be required later. The more modifications in a system, the higher the likelihood that data and processes across applications may conflict with each other. Ultimately this results in a less dependable, lower quality system. Most of all, event analysis alone is prone to missing events that users have never experienced. This situation is represented in the car example by the portions of the car not included in any of the three systems. System functions and components may also be missed because users are absent or unavailable at the time of the interviews, or because no one felt the need to automate a certain aspect of the object. In either case, the situation should be clear. We need to establish objects prior to doing event analysis. The question is how?

Before we discuss the procedures for identifying an object, it is worth looking at the significant differences between the object approach and earlier approaches. This particular example was first discussed with a colleague, Eugene O'Rourke, on the generations of systems and how they compare to the object methodology:

The first major systems were developed in the 1960s and were called Batch, meaning that they typically operated on a transaction basis. Transactions were collected and then used to update a master file. Batch systems were very useful in the financial industries, including banks. We might remember having to wait until the morning after a banking transaction to see our account balance because a batch process updated the master account files overnight. These systems were built based on event interviewing, where programmer/analysts met with users and designed the system. Most of these business systems were developed and maintained using COBOL.

In the early 1970s, the new buzz word was "on-line, real-time" meaning that many processes could now update data immediately or on a "real-time" basis. Although systems were modified to provide these services, it is important to understand that they were not reengineered. That is, the existing systems, which were based on event interviews, were modified, and in many cases portions were left untouched.

In the late 1980s and early 1990s the hot term became "client/server." These systems, which will be discussed later, are based on sophisticated distributed systems concepts. Information and processes are distributed among many Local and Wide Area Networks. Many of these client/server systems are re-constructions of the on-line real-time systems which in turn were developed from the 1960s batch systems. The point here is that we have been applying new technology to systems that were designed over 30 years ago without considering the obsolescence of the design.

Through these three generations of systems, the analyst has essentially been on the outside looking in (see Figure 11.3). The completeness of the analysis was dependent upon—and effectively dictated by—the way the inside users defined their business needs.

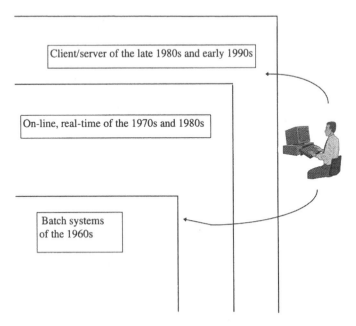

Figure 11.3 Requirements are often developed by analysts from an outside view. The specifications are therefore dependent on the completeness of the user's view.

Object-orientation, on the other hand, requires that the analyst have a view from the inside looking out. What we mean here is that the analyst first needs to define the generic aspects of the object and then map the user views to the particular components that exist within the object itself. Figure 11.4 shows a conceptual view of the generic components that could be part of a bank.

Figure 11.4 shows the essential functions of the bank. The analyst is on the inside of the organization when interviewing users and therefore will have the ability to map a particular requirement to one or more of its essential functions. In this approach, any user requirement must fit into at least one of the essential components.. If a user has a requirement that is not part of an essential component, then it must be either qualified as missing (and thus added as an essential component) or rejected as inappropriate.

The process of taking user requirements and placing each of their functions into the appropriate essential component can be called mapping. The importance of mapping is that functions of requirements are logically placed where they generically belong, rather than according to how they are physically implemented. For example, suppose Joseph, who works for a bank, needed to provide information to a customer about the bank's investment offerings. Joseph would need to access investment information from the system. If OO methods were used to design the system, all information about banking investments would be grouped together generically. Doing it this way allows authorized personnel to access investment information regardless of what they do in the bank. If event analysis alone was used, Joseph would probably have his own subsystem that defines his particular requirements for accessing investment information. The problem here is twofold: first, the subsystem does not contain all of the functions relating to investments. Should Joseph need additional information, he may need an enhancement or need to use someone else's system at the bank.

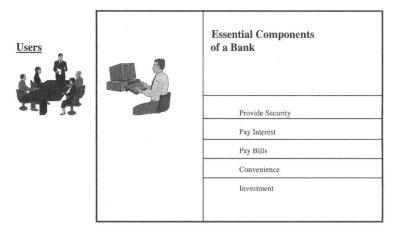

Figure 11.4 Using the object approach, the analyst interviews users from the inside looking out.

Second, Joseph's subsystem may define functions that have already been defined elsewhere in another subsystem. The advantage of OO is that it centralizes all of the functions of an essential component and allows these functions to be "reused" by all processes that require its information. The computer industry calls this capability Reusable Objects.

Identifying Objects and Classes

The most important challenge of successfully implementing OO is the ability to understand and select Objects. We have already used an example which identified a car as an object. This example is what can be called the tangible object, or as the industry calls them "physical objects." Unfortunately, there is another type of object called an "abstract" or intangible object. An intangible object is one that you cannot touch or as Grady Booch describes: "something that may be apprehended intellectually . . . Something towards which thought or action is directed."[22] An example of an intangible object is the security component of the essentials of the bank. In many instances OO analysis will begin with identifying tangible objects which will in turn make it easier to discover the intangible ones.

Earlier in the book, we saw that systems are comprised of two components: Data and Processes. Chapter 6 showed how the trend of many database products is toward combining data and processes via stored procedures called triggers. Object orientation is somewhat consistent with this trend in that all objects contain their own data and processes, called *attributes* and *services*, respectively. Attributes are effectively a list of data elements that are permanent components of the object. For example, a steering wheel is a data element that is a permanent attribute of the object "Car." The services (or operations), on the other hand, define all of the processes that are permanently part of or "owned" by the object. "Starting the Car" is a service that is defined within the object Car. This service contains the algorithms necessary to start a car. Services are defined and invoked through a method. A method is a process specification for an operation (service).[23] For example, "Driving the Car" could be a method for the Car object. The "Driving the Car" method would invoke a service called "Starting the Car" as well as other services until the entire method requirement is satisfied. Although a service and method can have a one-to-one relationship, it is more likely that a service will be a subset or one of the operations that make up a method.

Objects have the ability to inherit attributes and methods from other objects when they are placed within the same class. A *class* is a group of objects that have similar attributes and methods and typically have been put together to

---

[22] Grady Booch, *Object Solutions: Managing the Object-Oriented Project*, Addison Wesley Publishing Co., p. 305.

[23] James Martin and James Odell, *Object-Oriented Methods*, Prentice-Hall, p. 158.

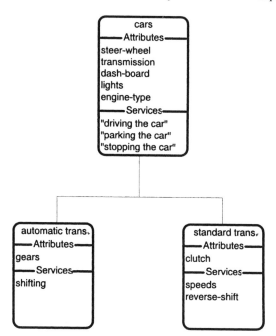

Figure 11.5 Class Car Transmissions.

perform a specific task. To further understand these concepts, we will establish the object for "Car" and place it in a class of objects that focuses on the use of transmissions in cars (see Figure 11.5).

Figure 11.5 represents an object class called Car Transmissions. It has three component objects: cars, automatic trans, and standard trans. The car object is said to be the parent object. Automatic trans and standard trans are object types. Both automatic trans and standard trans will inherit all attributes and services from their parent object, Cars. Inheritance in object technology means that the children effectively contain all of the capabilities of their parents. Inheritance is implemented as a tree structure[24]; however, instead of information flowing upward (as is the case in tree structures), the data flows downward to the lowest level children. Therefore, an object inheritance diagram is said to be an inverted tree. Because the lowest level of the tree inherits from every one of its parents, only the lowest level object need be executed, that is, executing the lowest level will automatically allow the application to inherit all of the parent information and applications as needed. We call the lowest level objects concrete, while all

---

[24] A data structure containing zero or more nodes that are linked together in a hierarchical fashion. The topmost node is called the root. The root can have zero or more child nodes, connected by links; the root is the parent node to its children. Each child node can in turn have zero or more children of its own. Microsoft Press, *Computer Dictionary*, 2nd ed., p. 397.

others in the class are called abstract. Objects within classes can change simply by the addition of a new object. Let us assume that there is another level added to our example The new level contains objects for the specific types of automatic and standard transmissions (see Figure 11.6).

The above class has been modified to include a new concrete layer. Therefore, the automatic trans object and standard trans object are now abstract. The new four concrete objects not only inherit from their respective parent objects, but also from their common grandparent, cars. It is also important to recognize that classes can inherit from other classes. Therefore, the same example could show each object as a class: that is, cars would represent a class of car objects and automatic trans another class of objects. Therefore, the class automatic trans would inherit from the cars class in the same manner described above. We call this *class inheritance*.

We mentioned before the capability of OO objects to be reusable (Reusable Objects). This is very significant in that it allows a defined object to become part of another class, while still keeping its own original identity and independence. Figure 11.7 demonstrates how Cars can be reused in another class.

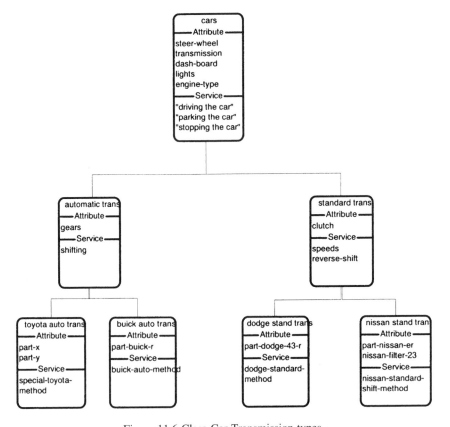

Figure 11.6 Class-Car Transmission types.

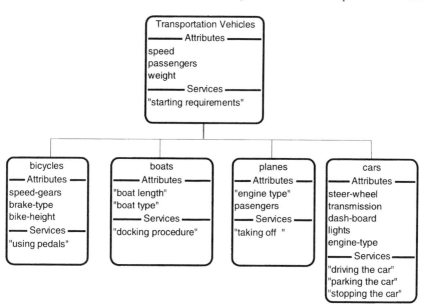

Figure 11.7 Class: Transportation Vehicles

Notice that the object Car is now part of another class called Transportation Vehicles. However, Car, instead of being an abstract object within its class, has become concrete and thus inherits from its parent, Transportation Vehicles. The object Cars has methods that may execute differently depending on the class it is in. Therefore, Cars in the Transportation Vehicle class might interpret a request for "driving the car" as it relates to general transportation vehicles. Specifically, it might invoke a service that shows how to maneuver a car while it is moving. On the other hand, Cars in the Transmission class might interpret the same message coming from one of its children objects as meaning how the transmission shifts when a person is driving. This phenomenon is called *polymorphism*. Polymorphism allows an object to change its behavior within the same methods under different circumstances. What is more important is that polymorphism is dynamic in behavior, so its changes in operation are determined when the object is executed or during run time.

Because objects can be reused, keeping the same version current in every copy of the same object in different classes is important. Fortunately, objects are typically stored in dynamic link libraries (DLL). The significance of a DLL is that it always stores the current version of an object. Because objects are linked dynamically before each execution, you are ensured that the current version is always the one used. The DLL facility therefore avoids the maintenance nightmares of remembering which applications contain the same subprograms. Legacy systems often need to relink every copy of the subprogram in each module where a change occurs. This problem continues to haunt the COBOL application community.

Another important feature in object systems is *instantiation* and *persistence*. Instantiation allows multiple executions of the same class to occur independent of another execution. This means that multiple copies of the same class are executing concurrently. The significance of these executions is that they are mutually exclusive and can be executing different concrete objects within that class. Because of this capability, we say that objects can have multiple *instances* within each executing copy of a class to which it belongs. Sometimes, although class executions are finished, a component object continues to operate or *persist*. Persistence is therefore an object that continues to operate after the class or operation that invoked it has finished. The system must keep track of each of these object instances.

The abilities of objects and classes to have inheritance, polymorphic behavior, instantiation and persistence are just some of the new mechanisms that developers can take advantage of when building OO systems.[25] Because of this, the analyst must not only understand the OO methodology, but must also apply new approaches and tools that will allow an appropriate schematic to be produced for system developers.

Object Modeling

In Chapter 5, we discussed the capabilities of a state transition diagram (STD) and defined it as a tool useful for modeling event driven and time dependent systems. A state very closely resembles an object/class and therefore can be used with little modification to depict the flow and relationships of objects. There are many techniques available such as Rumbaugh's Object Modeling Technique (OMT) and Jacobson's Object-Oriented Software Engineering (OOSE) that can also be applied. However, be careful, as many of the methodologies are very complex and can be overwhelming for the average analyst to use in actual practice.

The major difference between an object and a state is that an object is responsible for its own data (which we call an attribute in OO). An object's attributes are said to be *encapsulated* behind its methods, that is, a user cannot ask for data directly. The concept of encapsulation is that access to an object is allowed only for a purpose rather than for obtaining specific data elements. It is the responsibility of the method and its component services to determine the appropriate attributes that are required to service the request of the object. For this reason, object relationships must include a cardinality definition similar to

---

[25] This book is not intended to provide all of the specific technical capabilities and definitions that comprise the OO paradigm, but rather its effects on the analyst's approach. Not all of the OO issues are analyst responsibilities, and many of them are product-specific. Because OO is still very controversial, OO products are not consistent in their use of OO facilities. For example, C++ allows multiple inheritance, meaning that a child can have many parent objects. This is inconsistent with the definition of a class as a tree structure, since children in tree structures can have only one parent.

that found in the ERD. An object diagram, regardless of whose methodology is used, is essentially a hybrid of an STD and an ERD. The STD represents the object's methods and the criteria for moving from one object to another. The ERD, on the other hand, defines the relationship of the attributes between the stored data models. The result is best shown using the order processing example contained in Figure 11.8.

The object diagram in Figure 11.8 reflects that a customer object submits a purchase order for items to the order object. The relationship between customer and order reflects both STD and ERD characteristics. The "submits purchase order" specifies the condition to change the state of or move to the order object. The direction arrow also tells us that the order object cannot send a purchase order to the customer object. The crow's-foot cardinality shows us that a customer object must have at least one order to create a relationship with the order object. After an order is processed, it is prepared for shipment. Notice that each order has one related shipment object; however multiple warehouse items can be part of a shipment. The objects depicted above can also represent classes suggesting that they are comprised of many component objects. These component objects might in turn be further decomposed into other primitive objects. This is consistent with the concept of the logical equivalent and with functional decomposition (see Figure 11.9).

It is important that the analyst specify whether classes or objects are depicted in the modeling diagrams. It is not advisable to mix classes and objects at the same level. Obviously the class levels can be effective for user verification, but objects will be inevitably required for final analysis and engineering.

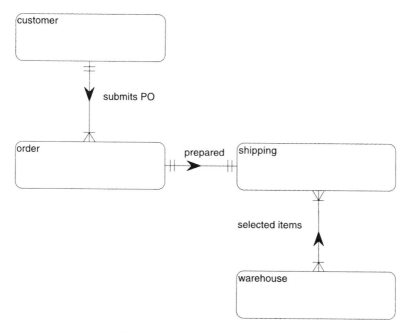

Figure 11.8 An object/class diagram.

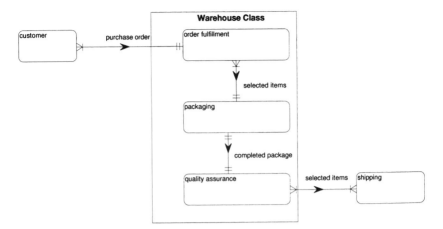

Figure 11.9 The component objects of the Warehouse class.

Relationship to Structured Analysis

Many analysts make the assumption that the structured tools discussed in Chapter 4 are not required in OO analysis. This simply is not true, as we have shown in the previous examples. To further emphasize the need to continue using structured techniques, we need to understand the underlying benefit of the OO paradigm and how structured tools are necessary to map to the creation of objects and classes. It is easy to say: "find all the objects in the essential components"; actually to have a process to do so is another story. Before providing an approach to determine objects, let us first understand the problem.

Application Coupling

Coupling can be defined as the measurement of an application's dependency on another. Simply put, does a change in an application program necessitate a change to another application program? Many known system malfunctions have resulted from highly coupled systems. The problem, as you might have anticipated, relates back to the analysis function, where decisions could be made as to what services should be joined to form one single application program. Coupling is never something that we want to do, but no system can be made up of just one program. Therefore, coupling is a reality and one that analysts must focus on. Let us elaborate on the coupling problem through the example depicted in Figure 11.10.

The two programs A and B are coupled via the passing of the variable Y. Y is subsequently used in B to calculate R. Should the variable Y change in A, it will not necessitate a change in B. This is considered good coupling. However, let us now examine X. We see that X is defined in both A and B. Although the value of X does not cause a problem in the current versions of A and B, a subsequent change of X will cause a programmer to remember to change the value in B.

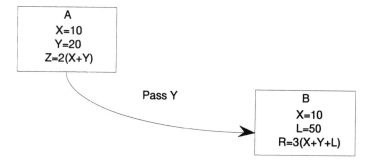

Figure 11.10 Application coupling.

This is a maintenance nightmare. In large enterprise level systems, analysts and programmers cannot "remember" where all of these couples have occurred, especially when the original developers are no longer with the organization. The solution to this problem is also to pass X from program A (see Figure 11.11).

We now see that both X and Y are passed and programs A and B are said to have *low coupling*. In addition, program A is said to be more cohesive.

Application Cohesion

Cohesion is the measurement of how independent a program is on its own processing. That is, a cohesive program contains all of the necessary data and logic to complete its applications without being directly affected by another program; a change in another program should not require a change to a cohesive one. Furthermore, a cohesive program should not cause a change to be made in another program. Therefore, cohesive programs are independent programs that react to messages to determine what they need to do; however they remain self-contained. When program A also passed X it became more cohesive because a change in X no longer required a change to be made to another program. In addition B is more cohesive because it gets the change of X automatically from A. Systems that are designed more cohesively are said to be more maintainable. Their codes can also be reused or retrofitted into other applications as components

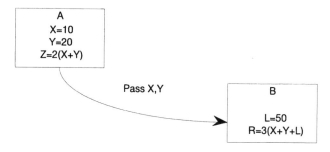

Figure 11.11 Application coupling using variables X and Y.

Figure 11.12 Coupling and cohesion relationships.

because they are wholly independent. A cohesive program can be compared to an interchangeable standard part of a car. For example, if a car requires a standard 14-inch tire, typically any tire that meets the specification can be used. The tire, therefore, is not married to the particular car, but rather is a cohesive component for many cars.

Cohesion is in many ways is the opposite of coupling. The higher the cohesion, the lower the coupling. Analysts must understand that an extreme of either cohesion or coupling cannot exist. This is shown in the graph in Figure 11.12.

The graph shows that we can never reach 100 % cohesion; that would mean there is only one program in the entire system, a situation that is unlikely. However, it is possible to have a system where a 75 % cohesion ratio is obtained.

We now need to relate this discussion to OO. Obviously OO is based very much on the concept of cohesion. Objects are independent reusable modules that control their own attributes and services. Object coupling is based entirely on message processing via inheritance or collaboration.[26] Therefore, once an object is identified, the analyst must define all of its processes in a cohesive manner. Once the cohesive processes are defined, the required attributes of the object are then added to the object. Figure 11.13 contains a table showing how processes can be combined to create the best cohesion:

Tier	Method	Method Description
1	By function	Processes are combined into one object/class based on being a component of the same function. Examples include: Accounts Receivable, Sales, and Goods Returned are all part of the same function. A sale creates a receivable and goods returned decreases the sale and the receivable.
2	By data	Processes are combined based on their use of the same data and data files. Processes that tend to use the same data are more cohesive.
3	By generic operation	Processes are combined based on their generic performance. Examples could be "editing" or "printing."
4	By lines of code	Processes are created after an existing one reaches a maximum number of lines in the actual program source code.

Figure 11.13 Methods of selecting cohesive objects.

---

[26] *Collaboration* is the interaction between objects and classes where inheritance is not used. Inheritance can operate only in hierarchical structures; however, many object and class configurations can simply "talk" to one another through messaging systems.

The tiers above are based on best to worst, where the by function method is the most desirable and by lines of code method the least desirable. Tiers 1 and 2 will render the best object cohesiveness. This can be seen with the example in Figure 11.14.

Figure 11.14 depicts a four-screen system that includes four objects, that is, each screen is a separate object. The Transaction Processing object has been designed using tier 2, By Same Data since it deals only with the Transaction File. The object is cohesive because it does not depend on or affect another module in its processing. It provides all of the methods required for transaction data.

The Financials object is an example of tier 1, the by function method since a Balance Sheet is dependent on the Income Statement and the Income Statement is dependent on the Trial Balance. The object therefore is self-contained within all the functions necessary to produce financial information (in this example).

The System Editor, on the other hand, being an example of tier 3, shows that it handles all of the editing (verification of the quality of data) for the system. Although there appears to be some benefit to having similar code in one object, we can see that it affects many different components. It is therefore considered a highly coupled object and not necessarily the easiest to maintain.

We can conclude that tiers 1 and 2 provide analysts with the most attractive way for determining an object's attributes and services. Tiers 3 and 4, although practiced, do not provide any real benefits in OO and should be avoided as much as possible. The question now is what technique do we follow to start providing the services and attributes necessary when developing logical objects?

The structured tools discussed in Chapter 5 provide us with the essential capabilities to work with OO analysis and design. The STD can be used to determine the initial objects and the conditions of how one object couples or relates to another. Once the STD is prepared it can be matured into the object model discussed earlier in this chapter. The object model can be decomposed to its lowest level; the attributes and services of each object must then be defined. All of the DFD functional primitives can now be mapped to their respective objects as services within their methods. It is also a way of determining whether an object is missing (should there be a DFD that does not have a related object).

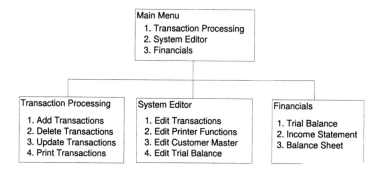

Figure 11.14 Applications with varying types of object cohesion.

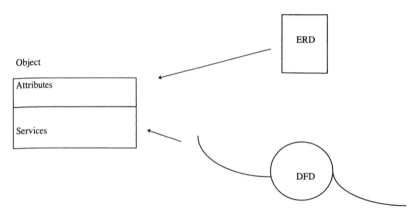

Figure 11.15 The relationships between an object and the ERD and DFD.

The analyst should try to combine each DFD using the tier 1, by function approach. This can sometimes be very difficult depending on the size of the system. If the tier 1 approach is too difficult, the analyst should try tier 2 by combining DFDs based on their similar data stores. This is a very effective approach; since tier 1 implies tier 2,[27] it is a very productive way to determine how processes should be mapped to their appropriate objects. This does not suggest that the analyst should not try tier 1 first.

The next activity is to determine the object's attributes or data elements. The ERD serves as the link between an attribute in an object and its actual storage in a database. It is important to note that the attribute setting in an object may have no resemblance to its setting in the logical and physical data entity. The data entity is focused on the efficient storage of the elements and its integrity, whereas the attribute data in an object is based on its cohesiveness with the object's services.

The mapping of the object to the DFD and ERD can be best shown graphically, as in Figure 11.15.

Thus, the functional primitive DFDs and the ERD resulting from the normalization process provide the vehicles for providing an object's attributes and services.

Object-Oriented Databases

There is a movement in the industry to replace the traditional relational database management systems (RDBMS) with the object-oriented database management

---

[27] We have found that application programs that have been determined using tier 1 will always imply tier 2. That is, applications that are combined based on function typically use the same data. Although the converse is not necessarily true, we believe it is an excellent approach to backing-in to the functions when they are not intuitively obvious.

system (OODBMS). Object databases differ greatly from the relational model in that the object's attributes and services are stored together. Therefore, the concept of columns and rows of normalized data becomes extinct. The proponents of OODBMS see a major advantage in that object databases could also keep graphical and multimedia information about the object, something that relational databases cannot do. The answer will come in time, but it is expected that the relational model will continue to be used for some time. However, most RDBMS products will become more object-oriented. This means they will use the relational engine but employ more OO capabilities, that is, build a relational hybrid model. In either case, analysts should continue to focus on the logical aspects of capturing the requirements. Changes in the OO methodologies are expected to continue over the next few years.

Problems and Exercises

1. What is an object?
2. Describe the relationship between a method and a service.
3. What is a class?
4. How does the object paradigm change the approach of the analyst?
5. Describe the two types of objects and provide examples of each type.
6. What are essential functions?
7. What is an object type and how is it used to develop specific types of classes?
8. What is meant by object and class inheritance?
9. How does inheritance relate to the concept of polymorphism?
10. What are the association differences between an ERD and an object diagram?
11. How does functional decomposition operate with respect to classes and objects?
12. What is coupling and cohesion? What is their relationship with each other?
13. How does the concept of cohesion relate the structured approach to the object model?
14. What four methods can be used to design a cohesive object?
15. What are object databases?

12
Documentation and Acceptance Testing

Documentation

Many IS organizations are faced with the ongoing issue of good product documentation. Documentation has been classically defined as having two components: *user documentation* and *technical documentation*. User documentation consists of the necessary instructions required for users to operate and maintain the system. Technical documentation, on the other hand, contains detailed information about the inner components of the product itself. Technical documentation should be designed to provide developers with the ability to support and maintain the system from a programming and engineering perspective.

Once analysis and design are completed, user documentation can be developed as a parallel function with the rest of the product life cycle components. This means that the screens and reports can be used from the design phase to build the documentation on the inputs, queries and output reports of the system. If the software is a GUI product, then the user documentation must also adhere to the standard Help facility which is included in these types of products. Although analysts may be involved with providing information to the documentation team, it is not their responsibility to produce user documentation.

A major part of the technical documentation should be the product of the analyst's work. All of the tools used by the analyst to formulate the logical equivalent must remain as the schematic or blueprint of the product. It is not advisable to try to provide other documentation. First, there rarely is enough time, and second, it should not be necessary. Remember, the concept of using modeling tools was compared to the creation and maintenance of an architect's blueprint in which the schematic had to be self-documenting. There are, however, other components of technical documentation. This technical documentation relates to the physical software development itself. Programming source code, product libraries and version control are examples of technical product documentation that should be the responsibility of the programming team.

Acceptance Test Plans

Acceptance Test Plans can be defined as the set of tests that if passed will establish that the software can be used in production. Acceptance tests need to be established early in the product life cycle and should begin during the analysis phase. It is only logical then that the development of acceptance test plans should involve analysts. As with requirements development, the analyst must participate with the user community. Only users can make the final decision about the content and scope of the test plans. The design and development of acceptance test plans should not be confused with the testing phase of the software development life cycle. Testing should be defined as the carrying out or execution of the acceptance test plans themselves.

The analysis and design of acceptance test plans is often overlooked in many IS organizations. This is because it is viewed inappropriately as a testing method rather than as a way of developing better systems. The question then is: Why and how do acceptance test plans improve software quality?

Quality During Analysis

If acceptance test planning is conducted as a step in analysis, then the issue of how to best test the requirements becomes part of making decisions about overall system requirements. Specifically, if a user wants something that can be difficult to test and maintain, it may force them to rethink the requirement and alter its focus. What better time to do this than when the requirement itself is being discussed? Remember, a strong part of quality software is how easy that software is to maintain.

How Much Can Be Tested?

One must work with the understanding that no new product will ever be fault-free. The permutations of testing everything would make the timetable for completion unacceptable and the costs prohibitive. The acceptance test plan is a strategy to get the *most important components tested completely enough for production*. The testing of software can be compared to the auditing of a company. Accounting firms that conduct an audit for a public company must sign a statement that the books and records of their client are materially correct, meaning that there are no significant discrepancies in the stated numbers. Accounting firms know that they cannot test everything in their client's books and records to be 100% confident that the numbers are correct. Therefore, auditors apply strategic methods like statistical sampling in order to be "comfortable" that the risk of a significant difference is improbable. Software verification is no different. Analysts and users must together decide on the minimum tests necessary to provide comfort to going live with the system. It is unfair to leave this responsibility solely with the user. Having the analyst or programmer do this alone is equally unfair. The wise strategy is to have acceptance test plans developed by the analyst along with input from the user and verification by programming as follows:

1. As each part of a system is functionally decomposed using the various modeling tools, the analyst should develop generic test plans that are based on typical standard logic tests (e.g., Account_Number must be numeric). The analyst and users should then meet to refine the test plans by focusing on how many permutations are required for each logical test. Users should also be encouraged to establish new tests that are missing from the plan. It is highly recommended that the analyst not wait for the entire analysis to be completed before working with acceptance test plan generation Tailoring an acceptance test plan specifically to the needs of a group of users is a good technique. This means that as the analyst completes the interviews with each user or user group, the acceptance test plans should be completed for the specifications developed for them. This philosophy is also good because it avoids the process of meeting again and rehashing old information.

2. The analyst develops interpart tests necessary to ensure that each component properly links with the other.

3. Once the acceptance test plans are approved by users, development must design tests that focus on product-specific validation. These include operating system and program tests to ensure that the operating environment is working correctly. Users and analysts need not be involved with this step as it represents the testing from an engineering perspective. Quality assurance personnel who are part of the development team should be involved in these test designs as these professionals are specifically trained to provide intricate testing that involves the mathematical aspects of finding errors. Once again, quality assurance and testers should not be confused or combined with the role the analyst and users play in the design of acceptance test plans.

More Efficient Development

Providing development personnel with the acceptance test plans is a somewhat controversial idea. Many IS professionals would object to doing so, arguing that the testing of software quality should not be carried out by programmers. However, programmers who are given the test plans are not being asked to do the testing but rather to understand what the user perceives as the most important operational qualities of the system. If the programmer is aware of the specific focus of the tests, then he/she should direct the development to ensure that such errors do not occur. In essence, we are trying to focus the programmer on the most important aspects of the system. To ask programmers to treat each component of a program in an equal manner is unfair, especially since they have no perspective on how to make the decision. If the programmer is especially focused on the tests, there should be fewer errors detected during the test review, thus supporting a more efficient development effort. Focusing on the tests does not suggest, however, that the programmer is free to ignore the other quality areas of the program.

Now that we have established the reasons and processes of developing acceptance test plans, the analyst must provide a format for its use. The format must be user-friendly so that users can participate. The format must include a record of each iteration of the test, allowing for better documentation and audit trail. The test plans should be in a machine readable format so that changes can be made. Figure 12.1 contains a sample acceptance test plan.

The acceptance test plan in Figure 12.1 reflects a group of tests to be applied to the contact screen shown in Figure 12.2. This particular test plan assumes that no data is on the screen and that the operator will only use the enter key (as opposed to a mouse). Each condition to be tested and its expected result must be listed. The tester will then execute each test number and fill in the results along with any comments. The test plan is then reviewed for completeness. If the test plan fails, the test will be performed again after the software is fixed. Each test iteration is part of the documentation of the testing process. Users and analysts should periodically review the test plans when the system goes live. This procedure will allow the test plans to be "fine-tuned" should any critical errors occur when the system goes into production.

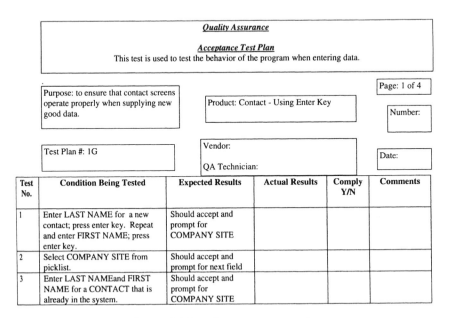

Quality Assurance
Acceptance Test Plan
This test is used to test the behavior of the program when entering data.

Purpose: to ensure that contact screens operate properly when supplying new good data.	Product: Contact - Using Enter Key	Page: 1 of 4
		Number:
Test Plan #: 1G	Vendor:	Date:
	QA Technician:	

Test No.	Condition Being Tested	Expected Results	Actual Results	Comply Y/N	Comments
1	Enter LAST NAME for a new contact; press enter key. Repeat and enter FIRST NAME; press enter key.	Should accept and prompt for COMPANY SITE			
2	Select COMPANY SITE from picklist.	Should accept and prompt for next field			
3	Enter LAST NAMEand FIRST NAME for a CONTACT that is already in the system.	Should accept and prompt for COMPANY SITE			

Figure 12.1 Sample acceptance test plan.

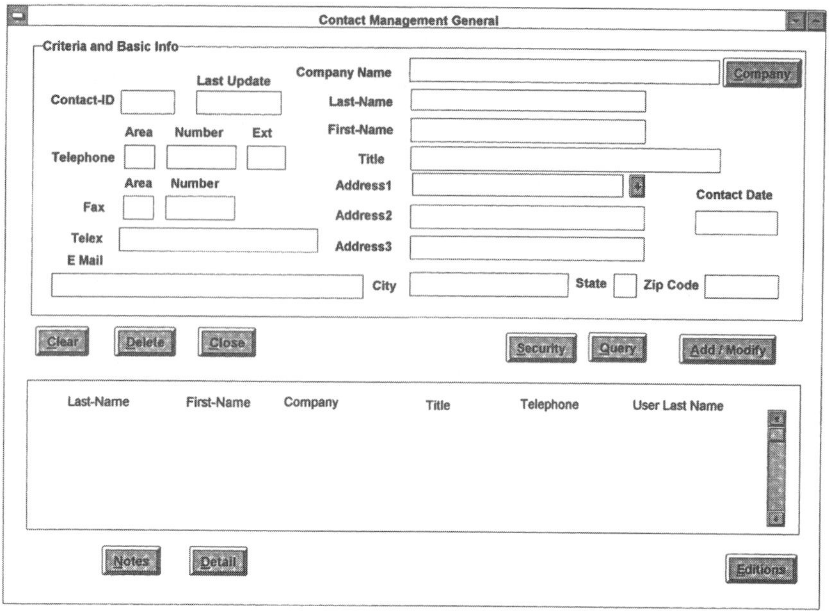

Figure 12.2 Contact Management screen.

Designing acceptance test plans is not a trivial task, for either the user or the analyst; however, good test plans can make the difference in the ultimate quality of the software. When GUI products are tested, the number of test iterations increases substantially. For example, the test plan in Figure 12.1 is focused only on data entry (as opposed to changing existing data), and when the operator uses the enter key. Because this is GUI, operators can enter data by using the enter key, a mouse or the tab key. Therefore, the analyst will need to repeat the same test plan two more times, once when the operator uses a mouse and the other when a tab key is used.

Budget Process

We have continued to expand the role of the analyst in the life cycle of systems development. Analysts must develop the ability to view an upcoming project and submit an accurate budget for their time and effort. The best approach here is to list the generic tasks that are typically performed by an analyst and then attempt to provide an estimate of the requirements not only for each task, but also for each system component within the task. Below is a step-by-step process that can be followed.

Establish the Task List

The analyst should begin the budget by listing the three standard tasks:

- interviewing;
- modeling;
- acceptance test planning.

Each of these tasks will then need to be expanded depending on the scope of the project.

Interviewing

The analyst will need to assess the number of users on the project and whether there will be a need for JAD sessions. Once this schedule is put together, the analyst should arrange for pre-meetings to assess the user skill sets, as this will affect the strategy and time frame of the user interface process. Analysts should employ a weighted criterion when budgeting time. Although there is no exact science to doing this, Figure 12.3 contains a suggested template to follow.

This table does not include the specific budget for each session, as this would require the analyst to have pre-meetings to assess the number of functions in each component and then budget the time necessary. The user interviewing tasks should take into consideration an estimate for the number of iterations. More detailed sessions can require three to four iterations before final approval is accomplished. The number of hours (or whatever time period is chosen) should be based on a novice user. Note that if the user(s) is knowledgeable, there may actually be a reduction in the budgeted time whereas amateurs (those that know a little) may substantially increase the time frame. The latter situation is due to the likelihood that amateur users will tend to get off track and in general have more questions. The ultimate budget for JAD sessions must be based on a composite of the levels of involved users for each JAD session.

Task: User Interviewing

Sub-Task	Expected Hours	User Skill Set Weight .75—Knowledgeable 1.75—Amateur 1.00—Novice	Weighted Hours
Selection of Users			
Determine JAD Sessions			
Pre-Meetings			
Individual Meetings			
JAD Sessions			

Figure 12.3 User interview budget worksheet.

Modeling

Once the interviewing budget has been determined and there is an established understanding of the scope, objectives, constraints and assumptions of the project, the analyst can begin to determine the time period for modeling the system requirements. Some guidelines are listed in Figure 12.4.

Analysts will need to get a sense during the pre-interviews of the likely number of processes (or data elements with respect to the repository) and how many diagrams might be included. Once this is established, then the budget can be developed. Note that the weight factors are based on the level of integrated automation. Integrated automation refers to the extent of computerization (e.g., a CASE tool) that will be used to develop the models. Non-integrated, which is the non-weighted factor, represents computerized diagramming without intelligent interfaces (which would exist with a CASE product).

Acceptance Test Plans

Acceptance test plan budgeting must take into consideration two key factors: the user interviews and the type of product. The user interview portion should be based on the original budget for user interviews applying a factor based on the modeling budget (see Figure 12.5).

Essentially the above matrix reflects that budget hours for acceptance test plans are approximately 10% of the original interview budget hours factored by the estimate of the number of diagrams and the level of automation. The 10% represents the portion of the interview time that is perceived to be spent discussing testing issues with the user. The final factor is the GUI. Because of the event-driven nature of GUI screens, the number of tests to be performed is dramatically increased. Many IS professionals would feel that a 2.00 factor is too low, since many favor 3.00.

Task: Modeling

Modeling Type	Estimated Hours Based on Number of Diagrams or Data Elements	Automation Factor .75—Integrated CASE 1.00—Nonintegrated 3.00—Manual	Factored Hours
Data Flow Diagram			
State Transition			
Data Repository			
Entity Relational Diagrams			
Process Specifications			
Object Orientation			

Figure 12.4 Modeling budget worksheet.

Task: Acceptance Test Plan

Sub-Task	10 percent of User Interview Weighted Budget Hours	Estimated Hours Based on Number of Diagrams or Data Elements (from Modeling budget)	Type of User Interface Factor 2.00—GUI 1.00—Character	Estimated Acceptance Test Plan Hours
Individual Meetings				
JAD Sessions				

Figure 12.5 Acceptance test plan budget worksheet.

Problems and Exercises

1. How does modeling provide the input of the system's documentation?
2. What is an acceptance test plan?
3. Comment on the statement, "Cannot test 100 % of everything."
4. How does strategic testing relate to risk management?
5. What is meant by the concept of self-documentation and quality?
6. How do acceptance test plans facilitate productivity and quality of the programming phase?
7. Why is it important for the analyst to provide a budget for his/her tasks?
8. How can acceptance test plans strengthen the relationship with users?
9. Why does acceptance test planning assist the budget process?
10. When should acceptance test plans be developed and by whom?

13
Business Process Reengineering

Business process reengineering (BPR) is one of the more popular methodologies used to redesign existing applications. A more formal definition of BPR is "a requirement to study fundamental business processes, independent of organization units and information systems support, to determine if the underlying business processes can be significantly streamlined and improved."[28] BPR is not just rebuilding the existing applications for the sake of applying new technology to older systems, but also an event that allows for the application of new procedures designed around the OO paradigm. Remember, it is the OO paradigm that focuses on the essential components that were outlined in Chapter 9. The essential components first require the establishment of the core business requirements and then the mapping of the functionality of the organization or business unit to these components.

You might recall that existing applications were referred to as legacy systems in Chapter 3. Many chief information officers (CIOs) today are confronted with a corporate mission to reengineer their existing applications and apply a more sophisticated and structured approach to developing what is known as the *enterprise system*. The enterprise system is composed of one common data repository for all of the organization's data. The typical enterprise configuration includes the OO paradigm and the client/server model that was developed in Chapter 9 and is repeated here as Figure 13.1.

The mission of BPR is to take an existing system, which is typically based on older technology and developed on the basis discussed in Chapter 9 (where the analyst is on the outside looking in), and reengineer it into one integrated system. Much has been written about the approaches or methodologies to use when applying BPR, especially by Ivar Jacobson.[29] The focus of this book is to provide direction from a practitioner's perspective, that is, something that can realistically be applied within the typical resources and constraints that exist in most IS organizations of today.

---

[28] Jeffrey Whitten, Lonnie Bentley, Victor Barlow, *Systems Analysis & Design Methods*, 3rd ed., p. 238.

[29] Jacobson's book, *The Object Advantage* (1995, Addison-Wesley), focuses on business process reengineering using object technology.

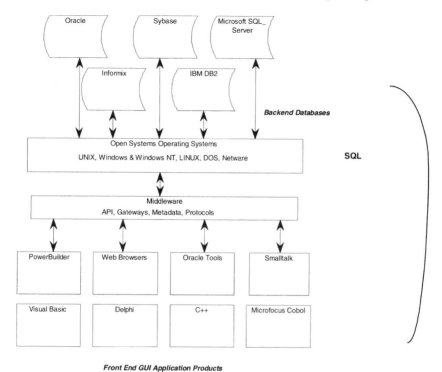

Figure 13.1 Client/server three-tiered architecture.

Analyzing Legacy Systems

The first step to applying successful BPR is to develop an approach to defining the existing system and extracting its existing data elements and applications. Once again, this is similar to the process described in Chapter 3 in that the data needs to be captured into the data repository and the applications need to be defined and compared to a new model based on essential components. Our assumption in this section is that the legacy system resides on an IBM mainframe computer. The data is stored in a VSAM format (non-database files) and the applications have been developed in COBOL. There are no central libraries or repositories of data or programs.

Data Elements

The analyst team will need to design conversion programs that will access the data files and place them in a data repository. The simplest approach is to use a repository from a CASE product. Once this has been accomplished, the analyst can utilize a reverse engineering tool to access the converted data based on the same procedures outlined in Chapter 3. Once all the data elements are loaded, the more rigorous process of identifying duplicate elements becomes the major effort. Duplicate elements may take on different forms. The most obvious is the same element with the same name and attributes. Another type is the same element name, but with different attributes. The third type, and the most challenging, is the duplicate elements that have different names and different attributes. This third type can be related to our discussion about combining user views (see Chapter 4). In any event, users and analysts will need to begin the laborious process of taking each element and building a data repository.

Applications

Application documentation is more problematic but again resembles the procedures followed in Chapter 3. This means that each existing application must be flowed and included as part of a new reengineered processes. Although this procedure may sound straightforward, it is not. BPR typically involves a methodology called Business Area Analysis (BAA). The purpose of BAA is to:

- establish various business areas that make up the enterprise.
- break down the business areas to their required data and process portions.
- reengineer the new and old requirements of each business area,
- develop requirements that provide an OO perspective of each business area, meaning that there is no need to map its needs to the existing physical organization structure,
- define the links that create relationships among all of the business areas.

A business area should be developed in the same manner as depicted in Chapter 9, where we established the essential components of a bank. Each component is a business area that needs to be reengineered into its equivalent OO and client/server enterprise system. Therefore, each essential component must be functionally decomposed to its reusable parts.

Combining Structured and Object Techniques

Once the essential components or business areas have been completed and agreed to by the user community, it is time to develop the actual architecture of the new reengineered system. What modeling tools should we use? The answer is that we should be ready to use all of them when required. Figure 13.2 is a schematic of the reengineering process within a business area.

Like OO, BPR also uses the object concept to develop cohesive and reusable processes. We use the example from Chapter 9 to demonstrate how this maps to business areas. Once the business areas are defined, the structured tools should

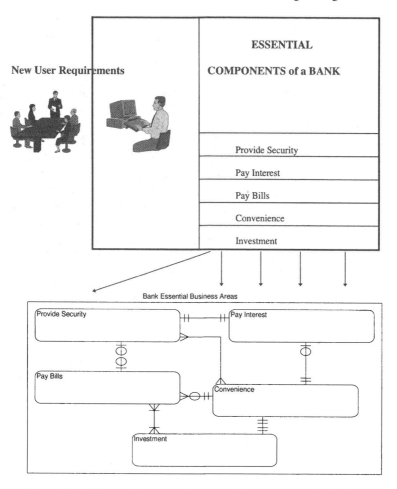

Figure 13.2 BPR modeling using the essential components of a bank.

be used to define all data and processes. BPR supports the concept that the data for a business area should be determined before the processes. You may recall that the same data represented an excellent method for creating cohesive modules. By using the same data, functional primitive DFDs and STDs can be mapped to their appropriate business area.

Logical data modeling and the ERD will need to be completed prior to creating the permanent objects and classes that belong to each business area. Normalization must be applied to the required entities, which will not only have the legacy data elements but also those added as part of the reengineering analysis process.

Prior to mapping the processes and data to their logical objects, the analyst can use another tool to assist in the reconciliation that all data and processes have been found. The tool is called an *association matrix* or a *CRUD diagram*.

"CRUD" stands for the four functions that can be performed on any entity: create, read, update or delete (archive). The importance of the CRUD diagram is that it ensures:

- that an object has complete control over its data,
- that a data file is accessed by at least one process, and
- that processes are accessing data.

The CRUD matrix in Figure 13.3 tells us a lot about the status and activities of our business area data and processes:

- Only the Items entity has enough component processes to control its objects data, that is, by spelling CRUD its processes have the minimum capabilities to control the cycle of any data element. Although this does not ensure that processes are not missing, it is a good indicator that the analysis has covered the life cycle of an entity.
- The Expense Category is not accessed by any process. This means that we have a file that the system is not using. This is an excellent indicator that processes are missing.
- The Customer, Expense Category and Salesperson data are created and deleted by some other processes or business area. This could be a situation where the physical location of a business function is not where it logically should be processing. The analyst should look for the missing processes to complete the spelling of CRUD before finalizing both the processes and data of any business area.

Even if BPR is not used, the CRUD diagram is an excellent tool to use to determine the processes and data needed for an object. Once the CRUD diagram is finalized, the objects and classes can be created, as Figure 13.4 displays.

It is important to recognize that many of the objects that are developed during BPR may become reusable components of other business area classes. If there

Data Subject or Entity \ Processes or Business Function	New Orders	New Products	Shipping	Sales Commission
Customers	R		R,U	
Orders	C, U		U	R
Items	R	C,U,D	R	R
Inventory	R,U	C,U	U	
Expense Category				
Salesperson	R			U

Figure 13.3 Sample CRUD diagram.

Bank Essential Business Areas

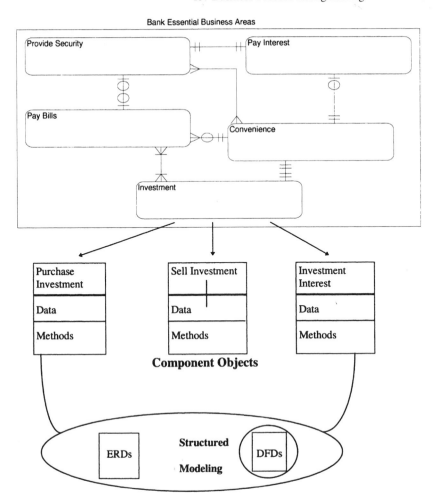

Figure 13.4 Business area component objects and diagrams.

are additions to an object as a result of reviewing a new business area, then the object's data and methods may need to be updated. The best approach to tracking these objects is through an integrated CASE tool, although any level of automation can be feasible.

Dealing with End Users

When applying BPR, analysts need to formulate a plan for how users and user groups will be interviewed. Most important, since reengineering implies change, change means discussions that must lead to decisions. Coordination of these decisions is critical, and it can get out of hand quickly. For this reason the analyst should attempt to organize BPR using multiple JAD sessions. The sessions should be focused first on each individual business area. Prior to actually holding the session, analysts and facilitators should educate users on the techniques and reasons for BPR. Analysts should not be afraid to show users the business area schematic and explain the concepts of essential components and how they eventually can become reusable objects. This means that there may be a need to hold a one-day training session for the users who will be involved in the JADs. This suggestion is consistent with the concept of having users prepared before they attend a meeting.

JAD sessions should be organized to have session leaders who can provide walkthroughs of the existing functions. While these walkthroughs take place, the adjustments and missing functionalities can be added to the business area. The issues concerning the selection of key personnel as they were outlined in Chapter 1 are extremely important, especially when selecting decision makers. Because of the volume of information being discussed, it is advisable to have more than one scribe available. This minimizes the risk of not capturing important business rules.

After each business area is completed, the links to the other business components must be handled. These should also take place via JADs and typically use the session leaders as attendees. Session leaders tend to have enough information at this point from the JAD sessions to determine the necessary links for each business area.

The use of prototypes for each JAD is highly recommended because it will provide the best vehicle to get agreement on the new system. This suggests that an integrated CASE product is almost a necessity for creating a successful BPR project.

Information Systems Issues

BPR is implemented on existing systems. Existing systems have IT staffs and constraints that must be addressed as part of the process. Since the current view of BPR is to create an open systems client/server enterprise system, the physical requirements of the network are critical during analysis. Remember, RAD means the combining of analysis, design and development into multiple iterative steps. In order to take the objects and classes developed from the JAD sessions, the analyst must start breaking up the data and methods of the classes into its related client and server functions. You may recall that if the client and server processing portions of an object must reside on separate hardware components then the object/class must be separated or further decomposed into separate physical modules (see Figure 13.5).

We have emphasized the importance of analysts being involved with the network design for client/server systems. BPR thus requires that the network design be completed as soon as possible and ideally before analysis starts. This

Client/Server Hybrid Object

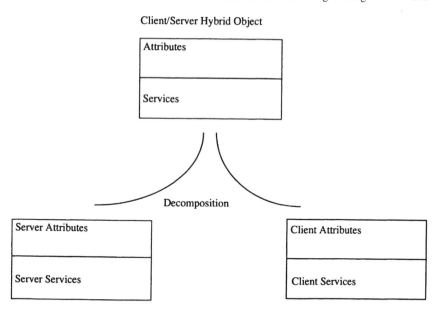

Figure 13.5 Client/server hybrid model.

will be difficult since many of the network decisions may be altered depending on how the objects become distributed across the network. In addition, the back-end database stored procedures (business rules, triggers, etc.) and middleware software components must be defined while the analysis specification is being finalized.

IS personnel must also be heavily involved in the JAD sessions to clarify questions about the existing system processes. This will involve discussions about the amount of data processed, as well as the difficulty or ease of getting additional information from the suggestions brought up during the JADs. IS can also disclose the details of the equipment choices and how these may affect the requirements being discussed. Such input may enable quicker decisions based on predetermined IS constraints.

Finally, IS will be required to establish the information about the existing data and processes. They will most likely be responsible for the conversion of the data as well as for clarifying the meaning of many of the data elements in question. You may assume that many of the legacy data element definitions will be unknown, and as a result analysts and programmers will be spending time together figuring out what such elements do in the system. Existing process review means looking at the current application programs and how they function in the system. Most of this work will be required from IS programmers and legacy designers (if they are still around!). Since our assumption was that the existing system was developed under COBOL, there will be a more difficult mapping of how a 3GL (third generation language[30]) is designed as opposed to today's 4GL (fourth generation language[31]) products.

System Development Life Cycle (SDLC)

BPR changes the steps in the typical IS SDLC. The traditional SDLC is based on the waterfall approach as was shown in Chapter 1 and is repeated here as Figure 13.6.

The problems with the waterfall approach are that it is unrealistic (as discussed in Chapter 1) and that it does not conform to the requirements of the OO life cycle. Therefore, IS must modify its SDLC to conform to the OO and client/server needs of BPR. The OO client/server life cycle resembles a spiral as shown in Figure 13.7.

The spiral life cycle reflects a much larger allocation of time spent on design than in the traditional life cycle, because much of the development time is spent designing the objects for product reuse. Although this may appear unduly time-consuming, there is a heavy payback in BPR if it is done correctly. Remember that the spiral life cycle is applied to the development of each object since it is a cohesive component within itself. The more reusable the object, the more spiral the effort becomes with a particular emphasis on the analysis/design phase.

Activity		March	April	May	June	July	August	Sept	Oct
Feasibility		▭							
Analysis			▭						
Design				▭					
Development					▭				
Quality Assurance							▭		
Implementation									▭

Figure 13.6 The classic waterfall SDLC, showing each phase dependent on the completion of the previous one.

---

[30] A *generation language* refers to the level of the programming language. Thirdgeneration languages were considered high-level development systems that included C, Pascal and COBOL

[31] Fourth-generation languages typically include programming languages that work directly with database systems and contain simpler program instructions than its predecessor languages.

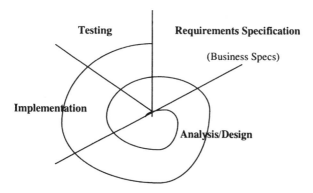

Figure 13.7 Object-oriented software life cycle.

Pilot Applications

Many analysts opt to have a pilot application as part of the BPR effort. The purpose of the pilot is to get users excited about the benefits of creating the new system. Because an actual application is developed, IS must be involved to ensure the pilot is successful. How can success be evaluated? The first real decision in a pilot is to select an existing application that is not working favorably and one that can demonstrate enough advantages of the OO GUI and client/server environment to pique the interest of users. Below is a suggested strategy:

- Focus on an application that can demonstrate the flexibility of the GUI front end.
- Select an application that accesses existing corporate data to show the users how easily the data can be reached. Analysts should avoid an application that gets involved with massive updates or large data queries, as this is inviting an unexpected delay in processing. Such exercises tend to involve much study and experience with the corporate network of information, and this expertise may not be available.
- Select an application that has a relatively short development time when using a GUI product. Do not try an application which might be more involved when using a client/server model.

The pilot application not only has the potential to generate more interest, but it also allows users to be more creative and understanding of the requirements of BPR.

Downsizing System Components

After the business areas and interfaces among them have been completed, the analyst and development must decide on a strategy for implementation. To attempt to convert an entire enterprise level system in one project is very dangerous and very unlikely to succeed. The user community also needs to be involved with this decision since many business units can convert only at certain times of the year due to various seasonal business requirements. Therefore, the analyst must plan to migrate applications in pieces. It is only logical to do this migration by business area and to develop temporary legacy links back to the main system. Most organizations are doing just this by purchasing open systems hardware and moving complete self-contained business areas independently onto the new platforms (see Figure 13.8).

As each business area is converted to the open systems architecture, the temporary legacy links will be deleted and incorporated in the new system.

Transactions Versus Data Warehousing

Our sample system is categorized as a *transaction-based operation*, that is, the system was designed to maximize its performance based on the processing of transactions. This type of systems must perform under the stress of many users

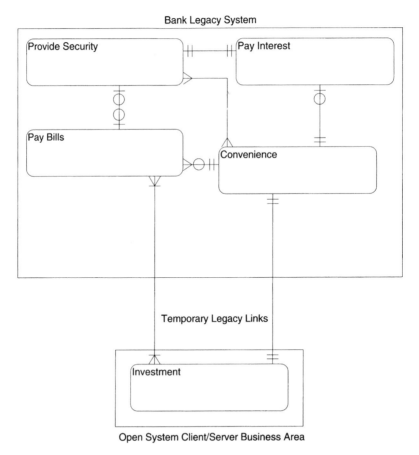

Figure 13.8 Legacy links of a business area.

who are using the system for production purposes. The limit of these systems is that they do not provide the end-user with on-line data comparisons and what-if analysis in a productive and robust environment. Such systems were designed in the early 1980s and were called decision support systems (DSS). Today's robust software goes even further than the awkward DSS systems, and users want the same level of flexibility with their enterprise solutions. The problem is simple: You cannot maximize your transactions performance while maximizing your DSS functionality. The result is many client/server systems have had trouble performing at the same level as the legacy systems. SQL-based queries that are issued during peak time enterprise processing can cause significant slow-down in processing. In most cases such delays are simply unacceptable. In fact, GUI applications will never outperform VSAM transaction-based mainframe systems. This sounds like a disappointing state of affairs for users. The remedy is to separate the transaction processing from the DSS functionality and improve transaction processing to an acceptable user level. This is accomplished by creating a *data warehouse environment* (see Figure 13.9). A data warehouse is an archive of the database off-loaded usually to a separate machine to provide DSS capabilities to those that need to query information.

The problem with data warehousing is the currency of the data, since off-loaded information is typically not performed real-time. Therefore, users must agree to use "old" data. Many organizations have provided data warehousing capabilities within hours of the input or update of information. Nevertheless,

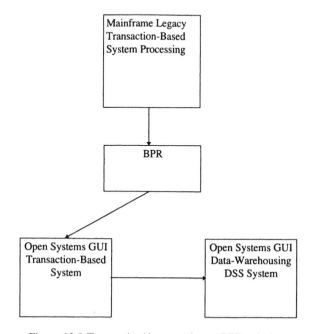

Figure 13.9 Transaction/data warehouse BPR solution.

data warehousing can work only if the user community can settle on aged data that they cannot change. There are products such as SAS that provide specific tools to create data warehouse databases. Often the data is not fully normalized because the user cannot change the information. This results in a more efficient and accessible database because the information is stored in a flatter format (fewer database files). Almost every database manufacturer will be providing data warehouse capabilities in their next release. The analyst must be involved in determining which applications (usually reporting and inquiry operations) are candidates for the warehouse function. Analysts and IS personnel must take care in explaining the role of the data warehouse to the users so that they can use it effectively.

Problems and Exercises

1. Explain the objectives of BPR.
2. How is BPR consistent with the object and client/server models.
3. What is a business area?
4. Explain the relationship between BPR and structured tools.
5. What is a CRUD diagram?
6. How should BPR be introduced to users and IT personnel?
7. What is the SDLC? Why is it called a waterfall approach?
8. Compare the SDLC with the OOLC.
9. What is the significance of the spiral approach and how does it support the development of reusable objects?
10. Describe the procedures to implement a pilot application. Why is this so important in BPR?
11. Describe the philosophy of reengineering an enterprise system.
12. What is the difference between a transaction database and a data warehouse?

14
Security

Introduction

Analysts should be involved with the security of database and network systems. Security responsibility covers a number of areas. The primary involvement is in application security, which includes access security, data security, and functional screen security. Access security regulates who is authorized to use an application. Data security covers transaction data and stored data across the Web system, and how to validate and secure it. Functional screen security involves determining what features and functions are made available to which users *within* an application. In addition, the analyst must also participate in network design decisions and decisions about what hardware and operating system conventions should be implemented to help protect the systems from vulnerabilities in browsers, servers, protocols, and firewalls.

Obviously, Web systems need to provide security architectures similar to those of any network system. But Web services are designed somewhat differently from those of regular Internet networks. Specifically, Web systems require verification of who is ordering goods and paying for them and have an overall need to maintain confidentiality. Finally, the issue of availability and accountability of Web systems to generate revenues and services to customers and consumers goes well beyond the general information services offered by traditional public Internet systems.

Figure 14.1 reflects the dramatic growth in Internet usage from its core beginnings in the early 1990s over a 10-year period. The result of this increase is that users will be downloading and executing programs from within their own Web browser applications. In many cases, users will not even be aware that they are receiving programs from another Web server.

Since the frequency of downloading software has risen, analysts need to ensure that applications operating over the Internet are secure and not vulnerable to problems associated with automatic installation of active content programs. Furthermore, analysts need to participate in deciding whether the Web system will provide active content to its users. This means that user systems, especially external ones, may have safeguards against downloading active contents on their respective network system. Thus, Web applications that rely on downloaded

Internet Usage

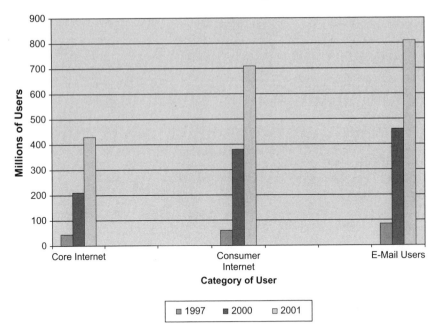

Figure 14.1 Internet usage.

animation and other configuration software may not be compatible across all user environments—certainly a problem for consumer-based Web systems.

Examples of Web Security Needs

This section presents some examples to demonstrate the crucial importance of verification, confidentiality, accountability, and availability in application security. Suppose a company is engaged in the process of selling goods. In this scenario, a consumer will come to the Web site and examine the goods being offered, eventually deciding to purchase a product offering. The consumer will order the product by submitting a credit card number. Below are the security requirements for the applications.

- *Confidentiality*: The application must ensure that the credit card number is kept confidential.
- *Verification and Accountability*: The system will need to ensure that the correct goods and process are charged to the consumer. Furthermore, the Web system must validate that the correct goods are shipped within the time frame requested on the order (if one is provided).

A second example of Web security entails a company providing information on books and periodicals. The information is shared with customers who subscribe to the service.

- *Confidentiality*: In this example there is no credit card, but customer information must be kept confidential because customers need to sign on to the system.
- *Verification and Accountability*: The system needs to ensure that the correct information is returned to the customer based on the query for data. The system must also provide authentication and identification of the customer who is attempting to use the system.

Availability

Availability is at the heart of security issues for Web systems. Plain and simple: if the site is not available there is no business. Web systems that are not available begin to impact consumer and customer confidence, which eventually hurts business performance. While a failure in the other components of security mentioned above could certainly affect user confidence, none has greater impact than a Web site that is not working. Indeed, there have been a number of books and studies that suggest that user loyalty does not last long in the cyber community, especially when Web sites are not available (Reid-Smith, 2000). Therefore, availability of the Web system is deemed a component of security responsibility. The first step in ensuring availability is to understand exactly what expectations the user community has for the site's availability. Recall that the user community consists of three types of users: internal users, customers, and consumers.

The first user to discuss is the consumer, generally the user over whom we have the least control and of whom we have the least knowledge. There are two issues of availability that must be addressed with consumers:

1. Service: analysts need to know how often consumers expect the service to be available. It is easy to assume "all the time," but this may not be practical for many sites. For example, banks often have certain hours during which on-line banking is not available because the file systems are being updated. In such a case, it is the users' expectations that should receive the analyst's attention. It matters little what the organization feels is a fair downtime in service; analysts must respond to the requirements of the user base. Just having the Web site available is only one part of the system. Analysts must be aware that all of the other components will also need to be available to assist in the complete processing of the order.
2. The issue of availability is linked to order fulfillment, at least in the minds of customers. Failure to have product available can quickly erode consumer and client confidence. For example, the industry has already

seen the demise of some on-line companies that failed to fulfill orders at various times, especially Christmas. Once a company earns a reputation for not fulfilling orders, that reputation can be difficult to change.

The second user to discuss is the customer. The model for customers or business-to-business (B2B) is somewhat different than consumers. As stated previously, customers are a more "controlled" user than a consumer, in that they typically have a preexisting relationship with the business. Because of this relationship, issues of availability might be more stringent, but are also more clearly defined. In this kind of situation, the marketing group or support organization of the Web company is likely to know the customer's requirements rather than having to derive them from marketing trends. An example of special B2B customers needs occurs when a customer needs to order goods at different times throughout the day, as opposed to ordering them at fixed intervals. This type of on-demand ordering is known as "Just-in-Time," which is a standard inventory model for the manufacturing industry. Should this type of availability be required, it is crucial that the Web site not fail at any time during operation because of the unpredictability of order requests.

The third users are internal. Internal users are yet another group that depends on the Web system. The importance of this group, because they are internal and in a somewhat controlled environment, can be overlooked. However, internal users are an important constituency. Remember that internal users are those who process or "fulfill" the orders. Today, more than ever, internal users need remote access to provide the 24-hour operation that most external users demand. The access required by internal users, then, must mirror the access needed by the firm's customers and consumers. Such access is usually provided through corporate Intranets that are accessible via the Web. In this case, protecting against outside interference is critical, especially since Intranet users have access to more sensitive data and programs than typical external users.

In the end, Web systems must satisfy the user's comfort zone—a zone that becomes more demanding as competition over the Internet continues to stiffen. Furthermore, Web systems are governed by the concept of global time, meaning that the system never is out of operation and it must take into account the multiple time zones in which it operates. This concern can be especially important with respect to peak-time processing planning. Peak-time processing is required during the time in which most activity occurs in a business or in a market. So, for example, if most manufacturers process their orders at 4:00, Web systems need to handle 4:00 all over the world!

All of these issues demonstrate the significance of Web availability. Given that I define availability as a component of security, it falls into our analysis of how the analyst needs to integrate its requirements during the engineering process. It is important to recognize the severity and cost of downtime. Maiwald (2001) measures the cost of Web downtime by taking the average number of transactions over a period of time and comparing it against the revenue generated by the average transaction. However, this method may not identify the total cost because there may be customers who do not even get on the Web site as a result of bad publicity from other users. Whatever the exact cost of the system downtime is, most professionals agree that it is very high and a risky problem for the future of the business.

Web Application Security

If Web systems are to be secure, the analyst must start by establishing a method of creating application security. Because Web systems are built under the auspices of object-oriented development, software applications are often referred to as software components. These software components can reside in a number of different places on the network and provide different services as follows:

- Web Client Software
- Data Transactions
- Web Server Software

Each of these major components and their associated security responsibilities will be discussed in greater detail in this chapter with the ultimate intent to provide analysts with an approach to generating effective security architecture requirements.

Web Client Software Security

Communications security for Web applications covers the security of information that is sent between the user's computer (client) and the Web server. This information might include sensitive data such as credit card data, or confidential data that is sent in a file format. Most important, however, is the authentication of what is being sent and the ability of the applications to protect against malicious data that can hurt the system.

The advent of executable content applications that are embedded in Web pages has created many security risks. These executable components allow programs to be dynamically loaded and run on a local workstation or client computer. Executable content, which is sometimes called active content, can exist in many forms. ActiveX by Microsoft and Java applets are examples of object component programs that can be downloaded from the Internet and executed from within a Web browser. There are also scripting languages such as JavaScript and VBScript which are run-time programs that are often sent from other Web sites that allow for certain functionalities to be dynamically added during a Web browser session. Finally, many files that are traditionally considered data, such as images, can also be classified as an executable component because they are used as plug-ins. Plug-ins can easily be integrated with a Web browser to give it more functionality. Figure 14.2 reflects the components of client-side security.

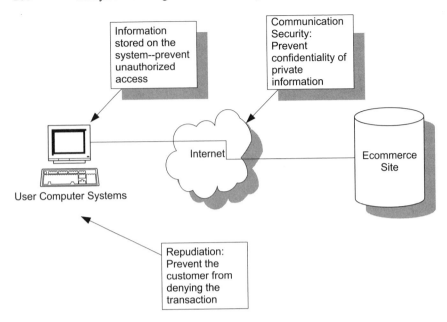

Figure 14.2 Client-side security components.

Web applications today also make use of "push" and "pull" technologies. Push technology is a way of minimizing user efforts to obtain data and applications by automatically sending it to a client from a server operation. Pull technology is somewhat opposite in that it allows users to surf the Web from their client machine and to retrieve the data application that they want to use.

The fact that the Web is open to interaction with the Internet provides both benefits and problems. The security problems with downloaded software fall into two areas: (1) authenticity of content and (2) virus security risks. Specifically, users of push and pull technology are authorizing these applications to be downloaded and written to a client local computer. Providing this function allows content that may not have been authenticated (in terms of data credibility) and opens the door for violations of security and privacy.

Because Web sessions do not by themselves retain information on prior executions, they need to contain an "agent" that holds information from past interactions. This agent is called a "cookie." Cookies are stored on the client computer and typically collect Web site usage information. This includes information about whether the user has visited a site before as well as what activities they performed while they were in the site. Unfortunately, cookies pose privacy and security problems for users. First, the collection of personal information might constitute a breach of personal privacy. Second, the residence of a cookie on the local drive can allow files to be read and written to it beyond its intended purpose. This opens the door for virus propagation.

Authentication: A Way of Establishing Trust in Software Components

Authentication provides a means of dealing with illegal intrusion or untrustworthy software. When dealing with authentication, the analyst must focus on the type of middleware component architecture being used. For example, Microsoft uses a technology called "Authenticode," which is designed to help thwart malicious code from executing inside a Windows application. This is accomplished by assigning a code that is verified by the sending application and the receiving application. This "code" is sometimes called a digital signature and represents an endorsement of the code for valid use. Thus, authentication is gained by validating the data's validity. Authenticode can provide two methods of checking ActiveX controls:

1. Verification of who signs the code; and
2. Verification of whether the code has been altered since it was signed.

These verifications are necessary because ActiveX controls have the ability to run on a workstation like any other program. Thus, a malicious ActiveX control could forge email, monitor Web page usage, and write damaging data or programs to the user's local machine. Authenticode essentially deals with ensuring that both sides of the transaction are in sync. Before a code can be assigned, each participant in the transaction (the downloading of the ActiveX control from the sender to the receiver) must apply for and receive a Software Publisher Certificate (SPC) from a particular Central Authority (CA) like VeriSign, who issues valid digital signatures. Essentially, the role of the CA is to bridge the trust gap between the end user and the software publisher.

   Once the software publisher has created a valid signature, the end user can verify the identity of the publisher and the integrity of the component when it is downloaded. This is accomplished by the browser, which detaches the signature code from the software and performs the necessary checks using Microsoft's Authenticode product. In order to accomplish this, the browser goes through a two-step process. First, it verifies that the SPC has been signed by a valid CA. Second, it uses the public keys provided with the original authentication to verify that the message was signed by the software publisher and thus verifying that it was sent from them. Figure 14.3 shows a sample SPC.

   Authenticode also determines whether the active content was altered in any way during transit so that it also offers protection against any tinkering during the transport of the data from sender to receiver.

   However, as with most software applications, analysts need to be aware of Authenticode's shortcomings. For example, Authenticode does not ensure that simply because an ActiveX control is signed it has not been maliciously tampered with. That is, the process of security is based on a "trust" model. Therefore, the user who checks signatures may get a false sense of security that the code is secure. Furthermore, since ActiveX controls can communicate across distributed Web systems, they can be manipulated during transit, without an

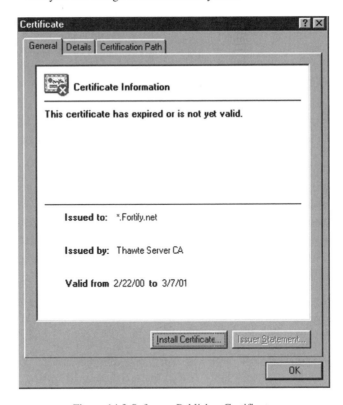

Figure 14.3 Software Publisher Certificate.

effective method of verifying the changes; the result can be trust in something that indeed is malicious. All of these situations, of course, do occur. One way of ensuring that a component is truly safe is by limiting its ability to compromise the user's privacy or violate any client security settings. So, an analyst can limit what an ActiveX component can or cannot do based on settings within the infrastructure. The important message here is that the analyst, not just the networking organization, should be very much involved with the decision.

Another default scenario is using the security options available in Windows. If the active content is enabled, a dialog box will be displayed each time an ActiveX control is downloaded. The user will have the ability to choose whether or not they will enable or authorize an ActiveX control to be stored. Some developers call this option "making security decisions on the fly." Unfortunately, this is a rather haphazard way of protecting client-side security. Users are a dangerous group to allow this type of decision-making power, and in many ways, it is an unfair way of making the user responsible instead of the system.

Another important issue that the analyst must be aware of is incompatibilities between Microsoft's ActiveX and Java, particularly as they relate to authentication handling. The essential security difference between the two is that ActiveX is based wholly on the trust of the code signer, whereas a Java applet security is based on restricting the actual behavior of the applet itself. This difference further complicates the process of establishing a consistent security policy. For this reason, many analysts prefer to use Java because of its true multi-platform compatibility; it is simply easier to create standard security policies for this reason (remember that ActiveX is supported only on Windows-based systems). Furthermore, from a programmer's perspective, Java offers true object-oriented programming, rather than those that have object extensions to a third-generation procedural language.

The security model used with Java applets is called Java Sandbox. The sandbox prevents "untrusted" Java applets from accessing sensitive system resources. It is important to note that the sandbox applies only to Web-based Java programs or Java applets, as opposed to Java applications, which have access to unrestricted program resources. Another way of separating Java versions is to focus only on Java applets for Web development. The Java "sandbox" name came from the concept of defining the area where the Java applet is allowed to "play" but not escape. This means that the functionality of the Java applet can be restricted to certain behaviors like just reading, or just writing information within a specific network environment. The Java sandbox is implemented or enforced by three technologies: the bytecode verifier, the applet class loader, and the security manager (McGraw & Felton, 1996). The three technologies must work together to restrict the privileges of any Java applet. Unfortunately, the design of the sandbox must be complete—any breaks in coding will cause the entire sandbox to malfunction. Therefore, the analyst must be careful in the design and testing of the sandbox functions. Ultimately, the selection of Java and the standards created to support its implementation is a prime directive of the analyst.

Risks Associated with Push Technology and Active Channels

This section focuses on active content that can be embedded in applications without the awareness of users. Such applications include the use of JavaScript, a run-time version of Java that downloads itself onto a client computer. This section also discusses the challenges of working with plug-ins, viewing graphic files, and executing e-mail attachments. The objective is to not only have secure Web systems protected from outside scrutiny, but also to determine what types of active content should be offered to users, both internal and external, as part of the features and functions designed into the Web application and overall architecture of the system. Remember that security issues go both ways; one from the perspective of the Web system and the other from the user's view. Analysts must always be aware of what other systems will do to check against the active contents that the Web system may wish to use.

JavaScript

JavaScript is a scripting language that can be distributed over the Web using the client/server paradigm. If JavaScript is embedded in the browser, as it is in Microsoft's Internet Explorer, the user's browser will automatically download and execute the JavaScript unless the user specifically turns the option off. JavaScript is typically used to enhance the appearance of the browser interface and Web page. JavaScript is also used to check data validity, especially data that is submitted through Web browser forms. What makes JavaScript so dangerous is that a hardware firewall cannot help once the file is downloaded for execution. Therefore, once the script is loaded, it can do damage both inside the Web system as well as to the client workstation. Obviously the safest form of action is to disable JavaScript from executing on the browser, but tha,t in effect, stops its use completely. Thus, analysts need to know that using JavaScript to deliver applications to their clients may be problematic because the client's machine may not accept it.

Plug-Ins and Graphic Files

Plug-ins are special applications that are integrated into a specific Web browser. The purpose of the plug-in is to allow the browser to support a certain type of program that will be downloaded to the client workstation. Typically, plug-ins are first downloaded and then executed so the application can embed itself into the Web browser. This usually means that once the plug-in is installed, it does not need to be reinstalled each time the browser is executed. An example of a plug-in is RealPlayer, which is a tool that supports streaming video over the Internet (see Figure 14.4). Very often if a user wants to view a streaming video file over the Web, the application will automatically scan the workstation to determine whether the plug-in software exists. If it does not, the user will be given the option to download it during the session so that a streaming file can be viewed. Regardless of whether the plug-in is pre-installed or dynamically provided, the user opens the door to potential viruses that can be embedded in the code.

One of the better-known plug-in vulnerabilities is a program called Shockwave, which is a program that allows for the downloading of movies played over the Internet. There is a flaw that allows a Shockwave file to get into the Netscape Mailer and thus invade e-mail accounts. There are no known ways of preventing this, other than of course fixing it once it occurs. The prevention of download files that could contain malicious programs within a plug-in depends highly on what type of plug-in is being used. The situation with Shockwave involves greater risk because the data is coming through a more open environment where hackers can modify files or create phony ones. On the other hand, Shockwave could be used to show a film about the company and could be well protected from an intruder, depending on how the server is secured (for

Figure 14.4 RealPlayer plug-in application.

example a firewall). Like most issues with security, the idea is to make illegal break-in so difficult that it appears impossible.

Attachments

There are a number of cases where Web systems allow attachments to be forwarded and received from users. These are often e-mail attachments because they are the easiest and cheapest way to transmit messages and files. Loading e-mail attachments becomes more dangerous to users when there are Web pages attached rather than just a file attachment. The risk then is not on the delivery, but rather against those who send attachments into the Web system. The degree of risk exposure can be correlated to the relationship with the user (this of course assumes that the user is intentionally sending a malicious e-mail attachment). If the user is known, as in an internal user or customer, then the degree of exposure in allowing upload attachments is less that if it is a consumer. While users are allowed to send responses, it is probably not wise to allow them to upload anything beyond that. Furthermore, analysts can build in scanning of uploaded software that can detect a virus; however, as we have seen, there can be embedded programs that cannot be easily detected. While dealing with attachments does not seem as serious as the other components that have been examined in this section, analysts attempting to design elaborate e-mail interfaces should be aware of the potential exposure to malicious acts.

This section covered security over the client part of the Web system. The security issues relate to both the author of the system, which entailed protecting the Web system from receiving malicious software from a client, and the spreading of problem software to users, the more relevant problem associated with Web systems. In summary, the most important issues for the analyst to understand are:

1. How internal users might obtain malicious software within the network domain.
2. How users through the Web software might return something inadvertently.
3. The challenge of what technology application technologies have to offer to users that might not be accepted through their standard configurations (like turning off JavaScript).
4. What dangers there are to providing active content because the system might become infected and thus be a carrier of viruses and other damaging software to its most valued entity, its external users.

Securing Data Transactions

This section focuses on security issues related to protecting the data transaction. The data transaction is perhaps the most important component of the Web system. Data transaction protection is implemented using various protocols such as encryption and authentication. Furthermore, there are protocols that operate only on certain types of transactions, such as payments. The issue of securing data transactions is complex, and this section will provide the types of protocols available and how analysts can choose the most appropriate data security protocol to fit the needs of the application they are designing.

Much of the data transaction concern in Web systems is focused on the need to secure payment transactions. There are two basic types of data transaction systems used for Web technology: stored account and stored value. Stored account systems are designed in the same way that electronic payment systems handle debit and credit card transactions. Stored account payment systems designed for theWeb really represent a new way of accessing banks to move funds electronically over the Internet. On the other hand, stored value systems use what is known as bearer certificates, which emulate hard cash transactions. These systems use smart cards for transferring cash between parties. Stored value systems replace cash with an electronic equivalent called "e-cash." This involves transferring a unit of money between two parties without authorization from a bank. While both systems offer the ability to facilitate the Web, the decision about which one to use is often based on the cheapest (cost per transaction) method. Figure 14.5 shows a comparison of transaction costs for electronic systems.

However, it is clear that stored value systems are much riskier because an intermediate bank is not involved in securing the transaction. Stored value

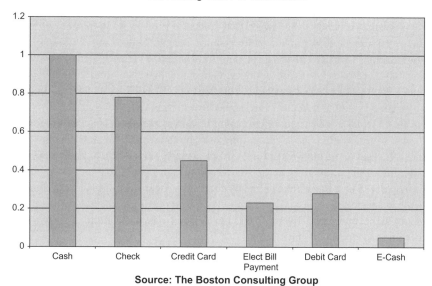

Figure 14.5 Comparison of electronic costs per transaction.

systems, as a result of this lack of security, are usually used for smaller-valued transactions such as purchasing candy from a vending machine.

Before designing payment transaction systems, the analyst must recognize which protocols can be used to secure Web-based transactions. The most popular protocol is Secure Sockets Layer (SSL). SSL does not actually handle the payment but rather provides confidentiality during the Web session and authentication to both Web servers and clients. Secure HTTP is another less widely used protocol that wraps the transaction in a secure digital envelope. Both protocols use cryptology to provide confidentiality, data integrity, and non-repudiation (no denial) of the transactions. Because the Internet is inherently an insecure channel, the processing of important data transactions that require protection should be sent via secured channels. A secured channel is one that is not open to others while a message of data is traveling from the originator or source to the destination or sink. Unfortunately, the Internet was not designed to provide this level of security. Data is sent across the Internet using a transferring protocol called TCP/IP. TCP stands for Transport Control Protocol, which runs on top of the IP or Internet Protocol. SSL is used to provide security to a TCP/IP transaction by providing end-to-end encryption of the data that is sent between the client and the server. Encryption is the process of scrambling the data using a sophisticated algorithm so that the data cannot be interpreted even if it is copied during a transmission. The originator of the message encrypts it, and the receiver decrypts the message using the same algorithm. Thus SSL is added to the protocol stack with TCP/IP to secure messages against theft while the transaction is in transit. The protocol stack with TCP/IP and SSL are shown in Figure 14.6.

The analyst needs to be aware that some form of transaction security needs to be implemented as part of Web systems design. Unlike many other system components, security software for data transaction systems is usually provided through third-party software vendors. Currently, there are three major vendors that supply transaction systems: FirstVirtual, CyberCash's Secure Internet Payment System, and Secure Electronic Transaction (SET).

FirstVirtual is based on an exchange of e-mail messages and the honesty of the customer. There is no cryptography used by the firm. Essentially, a consumer must first get an account with FirstVirtual, usually secured by a credit card. The handling of the transaction is thus bartered through FirstVirtual as an outsourced third party doing a service for the Web system. The most attractive feature of using a service like this is its simplicity, and there is no special software that needs to be purchased by the user. FirstVirtual has some built-in software to monitor any abuses of the system.

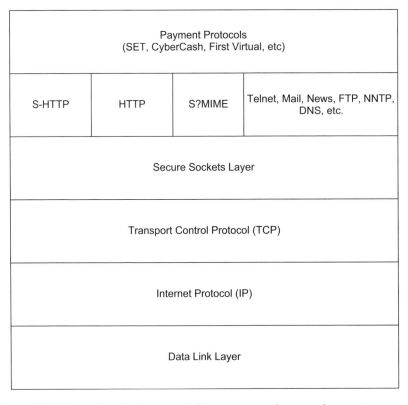

Figure 14.6 Protocol stack for secured Internet connection stored account payment systems.

CyberCash's Secure Internet Payment system does use cryptography to protect the transaction data. CyberCash provides a protocol similar to SSL to secure purchases over the Web. The system contains a back-end credit card architecture that protects confidentiality and authenticity of the user, who in many cases is a merchant. Figure 14.7 outlines the six steps in securing an Internet payment.

The steps for this type of transaction security are described below:

1. A consumer selects a product and an invoice is sent from the merchant to the consumer.
2. The consumer accepts the invoice and the browser sends the payment information encrypted with a protection key from the third-party vendor.
3. The merchant processes the transaction and forwards it to the vendor for decryption.
4. The payment is decrypted by the vendor (like CyberCash), who verifies the information through authentication procedures. The payment is brokered by the vendor with the bank.
5. The bank requests authorization from the credit card company.
6. Payment IDs are forwarded to the merchant.

It is important to note that the processing of transactions made between the bank and credit card company uses private secured networks, which also strengthens the protection of the payment. In summary, this method provides an excellent way to secure purchases of goods through Web transactions that rely on multiple

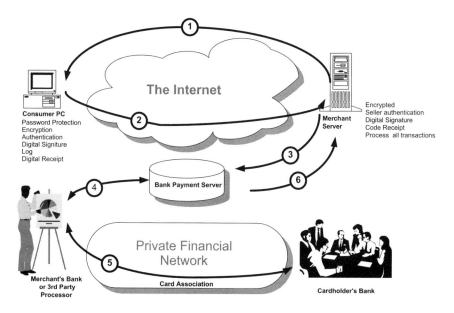

Figure 14.7 Secure Internet payment process.

parties (merchants, banks, and credit cards). It does this by ensuring that all parties get paid and that confidentiality is maintained.

Secure Electronic Transaction (SET) is an open standard that has received support from many industry credit card associations like VISA and MasterCard. SET was also developed in cooperation with GTE, IBM, Microsoft, Netscape, and Verisign. SET is not as complex as the CyberCash model; it can be implemented over the Web or via e-mail. SET does not attempt to secure the order information, only the payment information. Payment security is handled using cryptography algorithms. Figure 14.8 specifies the 10 steps in a SEC process.

The 10 steps are described below:

1. Consumer sends the request for transaction to merchant.
2. Merchant acknowledges the request.
3. Consumer digitally signs a message and the credit card is encrypted.
4. The merchant sends the purchase amount to be approved along with the credit card number.
5. The transaction is approved or rejected.
6. The merchant confirms the purchase with the consumer.

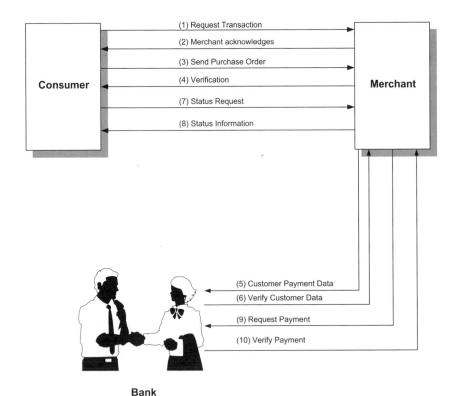

Figure 14.8 SET security process.

7. The consumer may send a status request to the merchant.
8. The merchant responds with the status information.
9. The merchant requests payment to the bank.
10. The bank sends confirmation of payment.

Stored Value Payment Systems

Stored value systems replace currency with the digital equivalent and thus have the ability to preserve the privacy of traditional cash-based transactions while taking advantage of the power of electronic systems. The major downside of the stored value model is that it requires identification of the buyer and seller, which in some instances is not what both parties want. By contrast, e-cash systems are stored in an electronic device called a hardware token. The token is used to hold a predetermined and authorized amount of money. The related bank account of the consumer is automatically debited and the token is incremented with the same value. This process allows the payment transaction to occur more in a real-time mode than in the stored account model. Although the stored value method supports online transactions, it can also be used offline if the consumer prefers. Offline transactions are more secure because they are less traceable.

The stored value model is not as secure as the stored account system. The main reason is that there is less audit trail of the transaction. This is expected since there are fewer checks and balances in the process. Furthermore, the transactions themselves are less secure because a token can be tampered with, thus changing its value in the system. Electronic cash can be represented in a hardware device or in a coin that is encrypted. In a hardware device, the prepaid amount is resident and is decreased every time there is an authorized payment. Hardware tokens are usually valid for a limited time period because they are more difficult to update. Yet another method is called "smart cards." These are similar to hardware tokens in that they contain a prepaid amount of money on a physical device; in this case a card. Figure 14.9 provides an example of an e-cash transaction using the stored value method.

Securing data transactions, especially those used for payment systems, is typically handled through third-party vendor software and systems. Web systems,

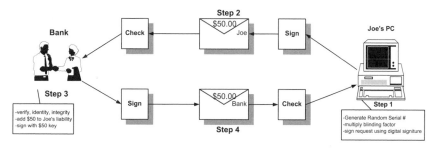

Figure 14.9 Stored value secure transaction process summary.

therefore, will need to interface with them, unless the analyst deems that it is more advantageous to design and support an internal proprietary system. Overall, it seems easier to integrate a Web system with a third-party payment security system than to create a proprietary system. If the stored value method is used, then analysts must consider how these hardware devices, cards, and software tokens will be issued and updated. These requirements will need to be part of the technical specifications provided to the development team. Obviously securing data transactions may also require that vendors be interviewed to determine which of their products and services best fit the needs of the Web system being built.

Securing the Web Server

The security issues governing the Web server are multifaceted. The security components include the Web server software, the databases, and the applications that reside on them. Thet also include a middle layer that provides communication between the tiered servers.

Web Server

The Web server software can include applications, mail, FTP (File Transfer Protocol), news, and remote login, as well as the operating system itself. Since most Web systems are server centric, meaning that most of the application software is resident on the server and downloaded to the workstation per execution, the security of the server side is integral to the ongoing dependability of the system. As can be expected, the complexity of both the server software and its configurations can be a huge area of vulnerability.

The Web server can be decomposed into three components: front-end server, back-end server, and middleware interface software. In many ways the Web server architecture has its own client/server infrastructure where there are higher-end servers that provide information to lower-end servers. The middle tier acts as a communication buffer between the back-end and front-end servers similar to the structure in a three-tier architecture. Figure 14.10 represents a more decomposed architecture of the three-tier client/server design.

From a security perspective, any one of these components that receive malicious events could result in problems with integrity and confidentiality. The best way to deal with security problems is first to understand where the system is most vulnerable. That is, once you know where the exposure is, then an "anti-exposure" solution can be designed. This section examines each decomposed component and establishes the type of security needed to maximize its dependability and confidentiality. The analyst must be involved as a driver of the process because of the amount of application and data integrity software that must be integrated into the design of the overall system. Figure 14.11 depicts the decomposed server components.

Database security involves protection against unauthorized access to sensitive data. This data could be confidential client data, such as account information

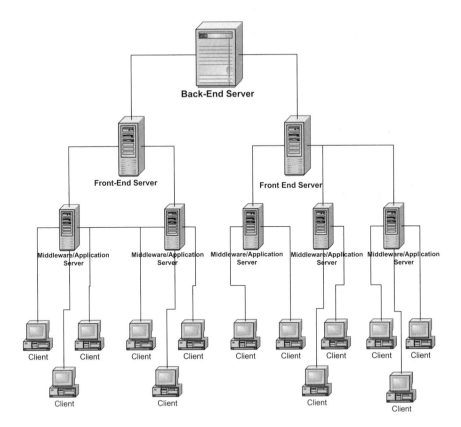

Figure 14.10 Decomposed three-tier client/server architecture.

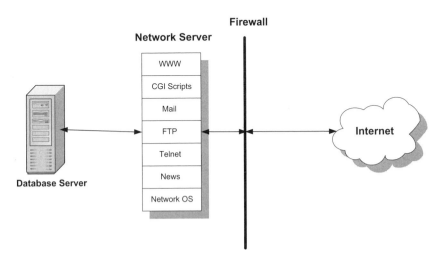

Figure 14.11 Web server components database server.

and payment history. Database security usually correlates to hardware security because most break-ins occur through hardware server penetration. However, because SQL provides the method of accessing databases from external applications, there must be security against its use. The problem with SQL is that once you can access the data it is difficult to stop the spread of any malicious acts. This means that it is more difficult to limit access once it has been granted. While it is easy to limit access to data through custom applications that require sign-on, it is much more difficult to implement against direct SQL query. It is unattractive to take away the use of direct query altogether, since this is such a powerful tool for analyzing data without the need for senior programmers. Furthermore, databases provide an unauthorized user with the ability to access data without the use of the underlying operating system. Therefore, to secure databases properly, the operating system logs and database logs should be regularly examined. For the analyst to determine how to maximize database server security, he/she must know the following information:

- The location of the database server
- How the database server communicates with the Web server
- How the database server is protected from internal users

Location of the Database Server

The physical location of the system can provide some added protection against illegal access of the data. The best location for the database server is in the organization's central network system. Since the database should never be accessed directly by external users, there is no reason that the database server should be connected directly to the Internet. It is important to clarify this point. I am not saying that the database should be accessible from the Internet, rather I am merely saying that external access should be obtainable only through authorized application programs. Thus, direct SQL query should not be allowed. In some instances, because of the level of sensitivity of the data, the server is actually placed in an even more secure location, and protected further with an internal firewall.

Communication with the Web Server

Inevitably, the database server must communicate with the application server so that transactions can be processed. In most well-secured environments, the database server will initiate the connection, but in reality it cannot always operate in this sequence. Thus, eventually the application server will need to initiate connection to the database server using SQL. In these situations, it will be necessary for the application server to store the User ID and password to gain access to the database. This ID and password will need to be embedded in a program or file on the system, which will need to be determined during the design of the system by the analyst. Unfortunately, anything stored in a computer system can be discovered by an unauthorized intruder, especially those who are aware of the architecture of the system. A solution of sorts is to limit every password to only one part of the transaction: for example, if one password allowed access but another was required for retrieval. At least this solution would make it harder to obtain a complete sequence of codes. Furthermore, the distribution of codes could also be kept in separate data files and matched using a special algorithm that would calculate the matched key sequences to complete a database transaction. While this approach sounds convincing, there are some drawbacks. First, the distribution of security levels would create the need for many IDs and passwords in the system. Users may find it difficult to remember multiple IDs and passwords. Second, the distribution of codes will inevitably begin to affect performance. Third, matching files always has the risk that indexed data will become out of sync, causing major re-indexing to occur possibly during a peak production cycle.

Another approach to reducing database exposure is to divide the functionalities between the database server and the application server. This can be accomplished by simply reducing the roles of each component, yet requiring all of them to exist for the successful completion of a database operation. This is shown in Figure 14.12.

Internal User Protection

While many systems focus on preventing illegal access by external users, they fall short of providing similar securities against internal users. The solution to this problem is rather simple, in that the same procedures should be followed for both internal and external users. Sometimes there are databases that are available only to internal employees, such as those that contain human resource benefit information. These databases should be separated from the central network and separate IDs and passwords should be required. Furthermore, as is practiced by many IT managers, passwords need to be changed on a periodic basis. Finally, the organization must have procedures to ensure that new users are signed up properly and that terminated employees are removed from access authorization.

Application Server

The application server provides the entrance for most users to the system. Indeed, the applications provide not only the functionality of the system but also the access to its data. The first component of application security is user authentication. User authentication is a way to validate users and to determine the extent of functionality that they are authorized to use in the system. Furthermore, sophisticated authentication systems can determine within an application what CRUD activities (Create transactions, Read-only existing data, Update existing data transactions, and Delete transactions) a user is authorized to perform. Further

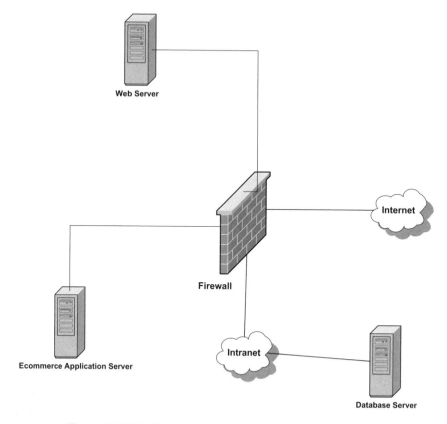

Figure 14.12 Distributed architecture for Web database operations.

security can actually be attained within an application Web page, in which only certain functions are available depending on the ID and password entered by the user.

Most companies use the following mechanisms to restrict access to Web applications:

- Client hostname and IP address security
- User and password authentication
- Digital certificates

Client Hostname and IP Address Security

This is one of the most basic forms of Web page security. It is accomplished by having the Web server restrict access to certain or all Web pages based on a specific client hostname or range of IP addresses. This process is usually straightforward because a Web request to a document residing on a host server must include the hostname of the client and its IP address. Thus, the server can use this information to verify that the request has come from an authorized requesting site. This type of security simply establishes a way of blocking access to a specific or group of Web pages. The Web server can also use the Domain Name Service (DNS) to check to see if the hostname that was sent actually agrees with the IP address sent. Figure 14.13 shows the process of hostname and IP address authentication.

User and Password Authentication

User authentication is essentially a process whereby an application verifies the validity or identification of the requestor. This is accomplished using some user identification and password—so it is a two-tiered security authentication. To set up an ID and password system, the analyst must first design a database to hold the names, IDs, and passwords of its valid users. Furthermore, there need to be additional fields that will store information about the level of the user ID. This means that a coding system must be designed so that the lookup tables can store codes that identify the specific capabilities of the requestor. The analyst must also design an application program that allows for the maintenance of all user security databases so that IDs can be added, deleted, or changed. In most database servers, the authentication file is designed using a flat-file architecture. Figure 14.14 provides the architecture flow of user authentication.

It is important to note that analysts can provide "nested" authentication tables within a Web system. This means that there are multiple tables, or ones that are more dimensional, that list all of the security levels that the user is able to perform. In Unix, this type of security is implemented with a "user profile" table that holds all of the information in one file. This file is usually formatted as a matrix or two-dimensional table. Each column refers to a specific enabling (or restricting) access capability. The user authentication design is geared toward

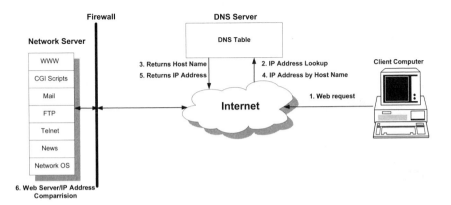

Figure 14.13 Hostname and IP address authentication.

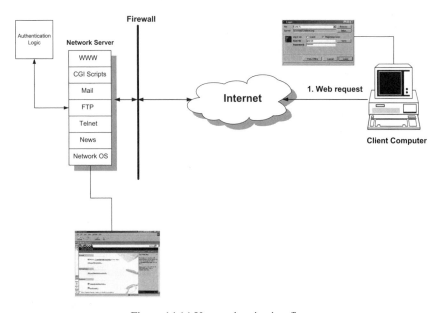

Figure 14.14 User authentication flow.

providing easier maintenance of the user's security levels. It also assumes that the security settings will be maintained by one unit rather than by many different units. For example, if a password is needed for a specific operation, it is handled by a central security operation as opposed to having each department have a separate authentication individual and system. Figure 14.15 shows a typical user profile security system.

Digital Certificates

Most of the security measures surrounding applications have been based on access control. Using access control to secure application security has a major flaw: the data holding the ID and password can be seen over the Internet—meaning that during transition they can be illegally copied. A higher level of security can be attained by using a digital certificate, which requires that both parties are involved with authenticating the transaction. This was discussed earlier in the section on SSL. Essentially, digital certificates contain the necessary

User ID	Security Level	Application A	Application B	Application C
A143	0	7	4	3
B783	1	6	3	8
R815	3	4	7	6
C777	0	1	4	4

Figure 14.15 User profile format.

ID and password in an encrypted state, so it does not matter whether the transaction is seen or copied during transit. The receiver of the digital certificate has the decrypt software to unravel the coded message.

Summary

This section provided an overview of the methods of securing the Web server. The model is complex because each component has its own security issues, while still needing to operate together to strengthen effectiveness across the Web operation. This section also identified the different types of security software available and suggested where the analyst needed to be involved in the process of determining what third-party products were necessary and how authentication should be implemented.

Web Network Security

Most of this chapter has focused on the application side of security and how the analyst needed to participate and design a Web system that could be reliable, perform, and have a high degree of integrity and confidentiality. This part of the chapter discusses the network architecture in terms of its impact on security issues. This section will outline the role the analyst and designer should play to ensure that the infrastructure is maximized to support the application design. Indeed, the system network should not be completed without the participation of software engineers.

The DMZ

The DMZ or the "demilitarized zone" is commonly understood as a portion of the network that is not completely trusted. The job of analysts should be to reduce the number of DMZs that exist in the system. DMZs often appear between network components and firewalls. DMZs are constructed to place certain systems that are accessed by external users away from those that are for internal users. Thus, the strategy is to partition the Web network to focus on security issues inside the DMZ, which is always used for external users. Internal users are behind the firewall in a much more controlled environment. Figure 14.16 depicts the layout of the DMZ with the rest of the network.

Common network components that should be in the DMZ and receive different security attention are as follows:

- *Mail*: There should be both an internal and an external mail server. The external mail server is used to receive inbound mail and to forward outbound mail. Both inbound and outbound mail eventually are handled by the internal mail server, which actually processes the mail. The external mail server then really acts as a testing repository against emails that might damage the central system.

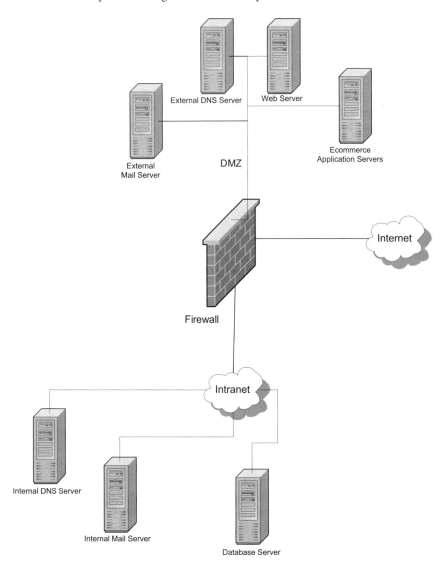

Figure 14.16 Relationship between the DMZ and the internal network.

- *Web*: The DMZ has publicly accessible Web sites. Many public Web servers offer places where external users can add content without the fear of hurting the central Web system. These types of servers can allow certain interactive chat room activities to transpire.
- *Control Systems*: These include external DNS servers, which must be accessible to queries from external users. Most DNS servers are replicated inside the firewall in the central network.

Firewalls

A firewall is a device that restricts access and validates transactions before they physically reach the central components of the Web system. Maiwald (2001) defines a firewall as "a network access control device that is designed to deny all traffic except that which is explicitly allowed" (p. 152). A firewall then is really a buffer system. For example, all database servers should contain a firewall that buffers them from unauthorized access and potential malicious acts. Firewalls should not be confused with routers, which are network devices that simply route traffic as fast as possible to a predefined destination.

There are two general types of firewalls: application layer firewalls and packet filtering firewalls. Application layer firewalls are also called proxy firewalls. These firewalls are software packages that are installed on top of the resident operating system (Windows 2000, UNIX) and act to protect the servers from problem transactions. They do so by examining all transactions and comparing them against their internal policy rules. Policy rules are enforced by proxies, which are individual rules governing each protocol rule. Therefore, one protocol has one proxy. In an application firewall design, all connections must terminate at the firewall, meaning that there are no direct connections to any back-end architecture. Figure 14.17 shows the application layer firewall connections.

Packet filtering firewalls can also be software packages that run on top of operating systems. This type of firewall, unlike application ones, can connect to many interfaces or networks. This means that many packets of data are arriving from different sources. Like the application layer, the packet system also uses proxies to validate the incoming transactions. The major difference between the two firewalls is that packet firewalls do not terminate at the firewall as they do in the application layer design. Instead, transaction packets travel directly to the destination system. As the packet arrives at the firewall, it is examined and either rejected or passed through. It is something like a customs line, where those entering the country go through a line and are either stopped or sent through into the country of arrival. Figure 14.18 reflects the packet firewall method.

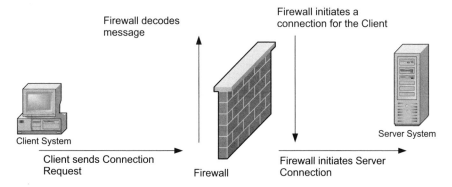

Figure 14.17 Application layer firewall configuration.

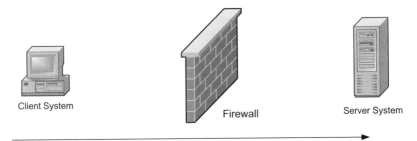

Firewall Analyzes Packets and Validates
for Direct Pasage to Server.

Client System

Firewall

Server System

Client sends Connection Request to the Server

Figure 14.18 Packet filter firewall system.

Summary

While network hardware security is somewhat outside the responsibilities of the analyst, the knowledge of how the DMZ and firewall systems operate provides important information that the analyst must be aware of. Knowing what is inside and outside the firewall is crucial for both network designers and software architects. Indeed, knowing where to place the software and how best to secure it in a complex network environment are integrated decisions that require input from both parties.

Database Security and Change Control

Database security and change control relate to the database access capabilities granted to a particular user or group of users. Limited access is always a security or control feature designed either to protect database integrity or to limit what some users are allowed to do with data.

Levels of Access

Who has the ability to access a database is an important responsibility of the analyst/designer. Access at the database level is implemented using a *privilege* that is created using special coding. A privilege is defined as the ability that a user has to execute an SQL (Structured Query Language) statement. In a database product like Oracle, a user can have two types of privileges: system and object. System privileges can be voluminous. In Oracle alone there are over 157 system-level privileges. An object privilege relates to how a user can access a particular database table or view. For example, a user must have an object privilege to access another user's database system or schema.

Object privileges are coded using commands like SELECT, INSERT, UPDATE, and DELETE, that is, each of these commands can have special rights limiting or granting a user access to the database. For example, a privilege may allow a user to select a database record for viewing, but not with access rights to delete, add, or modify a record. Such privilege rights need to be determined during analysis and conveyed to the development team.

The specifications for object privileges are no different than a program requirement but are usually conveyed through a table matrix as shown in Figure 14.19:

Roles

A role is effectively a group of privileges that is granted to run an application. An application can contain a number of roles, which in turn grant a specific group of privileges that allow more or less capabilities while running an application program. Thus, the role is a set of capabilities that can be granted to a user or group of users. For example:

1. Create Nurses role.
2. Grant all privileges required by the Nurses application to the Nurses role.
3. Grant Nurses role to all Nursing assistants or to a role named Nurses_Assistants.

The advantages of this are multiple:

1. It is easier to grant a role, rather than each privilege separately.
2. You can modify a privilege associated with an application by modifying just the privilege with that role without needing to go into each user's privileges.
3. You can easily review a user's privileges by reviewing the role.
4. You can determine which users have privileges as an application using Role level query capabilities in the data dictionary.

Privilege	User Access Ability
ALTER	Change the definition of a program
DELETE	Remove rows from a Table or View
EXECUTE	Execute a program
INDEX	Create a special Index on a database Table or View
INSERT	Insert new records
REFERENCES	Create a constraint (referential integrity) on a database Table or View
SELECT	Retrieve data for Display
UPDATE	Modify existing data

Figure 14.19 Privileges cross-referenced with user access ability.

Who Is in Charge of Database Security?

Once again, most of the security issues relating to analysis and design surround the database. For small implementations, the database administrator is usually responsible for security also. However, in larger more complex organizations with multiple integrated databases, security can be assigned to a separate role called the *Security Administrator*. The Security Administrator or whoever is responsible for database security needs to develop a security policy, which must then be abided in the analysis and design phases of software development.

The Security Administrator must focus on three aspects of security issues, which in turn become part of the analysis/design specification:

1. *Data Encryption*: Encryption applications are programs that use algorithms to change data so that it cannot be interpreted when it is traveling between applications. Most encryption occurs outside of the system because that is where such data is vulnerable. Thus, the Internet has become the most encrypted area of data that travels through cyberspace and must be protected against unauthorized access. The question becomes: who is responsible for identifying at what points data encryption is necessary? Again there are obvious points such as a terminal accessing a host over the Internet. But what of encryption between an application client and the database and the database and the application server as shown in Figure 14.20?

   While the database analyst/designer is not responsible for encryption *per se*, it is worthwhile for him/her to be familiar with three encryption alternatives:

   RC4: This uses a secret, randomly generated key unique to each session. This is an effective encryption for SQL statements, and stored procedure calls and results.

   DES: Oracle uses this encryption known as the U.S. Data Encryption Standard Algorithm (DES) using a standard encryption that is useful for environments that might require backward compatibility with earlier, less robust encryption algorithms.

   Triple-DES: Provides a high degree of message security, but with a performance penalty that may take up to three times as long to encrypt a data block than the standard DES algorithm.

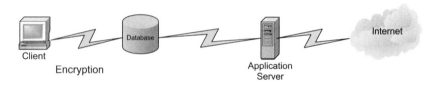

Figure 14.20 Database encryption architecture.

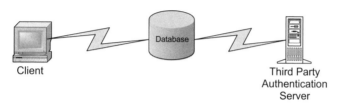

Figure 14.21 Strong authentication.

2. *Strong Authentication*: allows identification of the user. This is a critical issue to ensure confidence in network security. Passwords are the most common method of authentication. This requires a separate third-party authentication server which sends requests to the database as depicted in Figure 14.21.

   Since authentication will be integrated with the database software, the analyst needs to be engaged in the implementation and versed in the knowledge of how it relates to the design of the entire database system.

3. *Enterprise User Management:* this feature enables the storing of database users with their related administrative and security information in a central directory server. This is accomplished by having a separate database server that authenticates a user by accessing the information stored in a directory (Figure 14.22).

This configuration enables the administrator to modify information in one location and provides a more secure and lower cost solution.

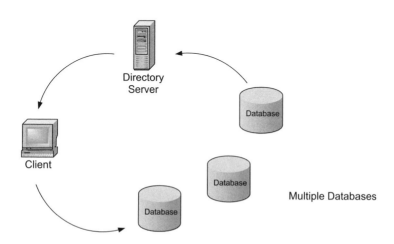

Figure 14.22 Enterprise user authentication architecture.

Version Control

Version control can be defined as a tracking and managing of changes to information. Version control has become an important database issue particularly with Internet applications and e-business operations. Internet applications often have user editable data that is stored in a database. Thus, it is an advantage to provide version control to this stored information in case of a mistake or for "audit trail" and integrity purposes. That is, audit trail is an accounting and security process of having a "trail" of changes that are made. The amount of historical changes in audit trail can vary, although for the purposes of this book I will confine the trail to the last change made—in other words, having the last change stored for historical tracking. However, audit trail and security are not the only reasons to implement version control. Version control provides an error fixing capability. For example, if a user enters a new value in a lookup table and then decides it is in error, version control can allow it to be reset back to its original value. This is similar to applications like Microsoft Word which contain an "undo" function that allows users to go back to an original setting.

Database version controls are usually by designing what is known as "shadow tables," which store the last value changed by a user (see Figure 14.23).

The use of version control obviously creates potential performance problems and space issues because of the expanded number of tables. The decision of how many historical values to store also becomes an important decision to be made by analysts, designers, and users. Most important is to understand the trade-offs to these decisions and for users and system architects to recognize the impact of such decisions.

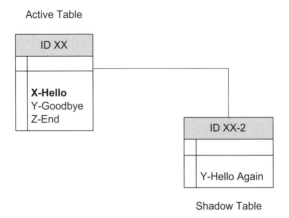

Figure 14.23 Shadow table implementation.

There are also third-party products that provide functions for version control, as well as mathematical formulas that can be used to minimize space needs when implementing shadow tables. Ultimately the best approach is to work closely with users and determine what fields require versions to address user error, and with audit firms to determine the extent of audit trails for security purposes.

15
Data Warehousing

Introduction

This chapter focuses on how to extract information from database systems. This information will be used for decision support systems (DSS) purposes and typically be presented to the user in an on-line display format or on a report. As initially discussed in Chapter 13, the concept behind DSS is that it deals with data "after the fact," meaning that the data is no longer in a production mode, but rather in a storage mode where it can be used for different forms of analytical processing. The major benefit of operating on processed data is that it cannot be changed and therefore can be accessed without concern for data integrity. Another salient issue is that because the data is not subject to change, it can be copied multiple times, allowing for some interesting performance improvements and "flattening" of the data stored in the relational database. The referential integrity that was attained in a production database does not maximize performance for the query of data for reporting purposes. The purpose of the chapter is to provide the details of creating complex warehouse systems.

In order to maximize the efficiency of accessing and analyzing data it is necessary to separate it from the production system. This is accomplished by creating copies of the data solely for decision support analysis. There are a number of different ways to do this separation. One way is data warehousing, where data is reformatted from one or more data sources and placed in a special repository for analytical processing. Another approach is to create data marts. While similar to a data warehouse, data marts are defined as more strategic in nature and more specifically organized to support the gathering of departmental data. Data warehouses can be composed of many data marts. Still another method is called data mining, in which multiple definitions of data from different systems are collected and analyzed for similarities. Data mining provides more artificial intelligence features and can perform advanced analysis against multiple data warehouses and data marts, especially when the data comes from multiple computer systems. All of these alternatives will be examined in this chapter, and its relationship to the analysis and design of ecommerce systems. In order to provide effective data warehouses, data marts, and data mining, it is necessary to understand how to obtain the data that is needed to populate these data structures.

A major component of creating effective repositories of data for DSS is how to extract the information through database query. In order to accomplish this effectively, it is important to understand the transaction processing system, since some transactions might need to be captured when they occur as opposed to after they have updated database files. Furthermore, the process of creating reports and screen displays needs to be included as part of the analyst's specification. Some reports are pre-coded, while others are generated through user-initiated query applications.

Data Warehousing Concepts Revisited

Operational databases are those that are designed to track business events in real time. In operational databases, processing data usually correlates to cost while the completion of the data's process relates to revenue. In Chapter 5, we saw that the data in operational databases is accessed at the detailed level where individual records are created, read, updated, or deleted (CRUD). Entities in the relational model are constantly updated to ensure that the integrity of the data is preserved and that no historical information on the entity's previous status is stored.

Data warehouses, on the other hand, can capture both completed events *and* their original transactions. This allows data warehouse implementations with the ability to characterize more about how the data was produced at a much more detailed and granular level than usually available in operational databases. However, it is also important to remember that data warehouses are static snapshots of historical events. As a result, they are often not in sync with an operational database, which always reflects the current aggregate picture of the data. This has both advantages and disadvantages. From an advantage point of view, a data warehouse can contain multiple copies of the same data. Each set could represent the same data at a different moment in time, or could represent different views of the same data, or any combination of all of these. Figure 15.1 depicts the relationship between a data warehouse and the operational databases in an ecommerce system.

The issue of data synchronization between the operational databases and the data warehouses is significant. The ultimate consideration when designing a data warehouse system relates to the age of the data in the warehouse and how often this data needs to be refreshed. For example, if an accounting department needs to produce a report by the 15th of every month on the previous month's activity, then the data refresh would need to occur sometime after the end of the previous month and before the 15th of the new month. On the other hand, if a daily report were needed on the previous day's activities, then an evening refresh would be required. Data refreshment requires that the data from the operational database be copied to the warehouse. Unfortunately, this may not be the end of the data refresh procedure, since the format of the data in the warehouse may be very different from that of the operational system. Thus, there is typically a need

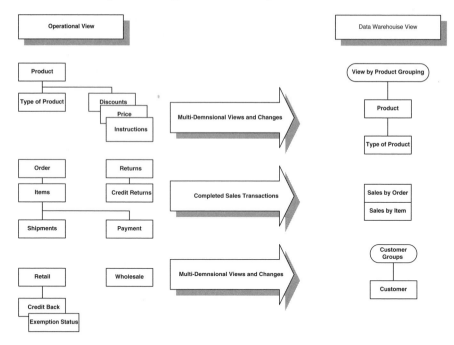

Figure 15.1 Operational databases and data warehouses.

for the data to be reformatted so it can be fed into the warehouse structure directly. Because a data warehouse might be an aggregation of the operational data, it can be necessary to perform mathematical computations on the ported data to produce derived data information. You might recall that derived data is a violation of normalization and not allowed in the operational database. Therefore, data warehouses are denormalized models of the operational systems and will typically contain data elements that were removed through third-normal form implementation.

Performance Benefits of Data Warehouses

The advantages of developing a warehouse are many. First, it allows users to analyze data without interfering with the operational systems. This is a significant benefit because of the inherent problems associated with SQL. When queries are produced against an operational database to produce reports they often require what is known as database joins. These joins create intermediate databases until the final report is produced. Furthermore, the final database of these joins is in the format of the report being requested. This means that a report from an SQL query is really a sub-schema picture of the original database. Issuing complex queries that require multiple joins can easily tie up an operational database, thus creating serious confrontations between production personnel and support organizations. Therefore, the process of performing DSS requires SQL, which in turn hinders the performance of the production system. Figure 15.2 shows an example of the quantity of dynamic tables that can be produced as a result of a simple SQL join statement.

The above example shows how an SQL PROJECT statement creates a subset schema of columns of the parent entity. Thus, the sub-schema contains the same number of records, but less columns or attributes. The SELECT statement also creates another entity, which reduces the number of rows, but contains the same number of attributes as the parent database. Finally, the join combines the results of the two sub-schemas to produce a third entity, which is in the format of the report requested by the query. This sample shows how much overhead is involved with the production of a simple report. When voluminous data is involved the time to complete the query is even more significant. Indeed, some queries have

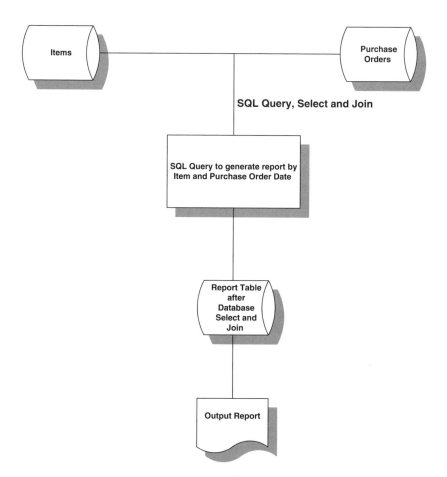

Figure 15.2 Dynamic SQL database joins.

been known to run over 24 hours! Therefore, data warehouse solutions should be the preferred method for analyzing data rather than using standard SQL directly against production databases.

Concept of Multidimensional Data

Data warehousing has often been referred to as a three-dimensional way of representing data. The three dimensions are seen as a cube of data. Each cell is viewed as a box within an array. This cube represents one data warehouse aggregation (combination) and provides a number of ways to view the data. Figure 15.3 shows a data warehouse aggregation of three viewable dimensions of information. The relational table two-dimensional; it contains rows and columns, which is synonymous with records and attributes. The corresponding multidimensional cube reflects a three-attribute dimensional view of the data. The two-dimensional part is Orders and Items, with the third dimension being Markets. Figure 15.4 reflects another third dimension, the addition of the price

Item	Market	Period	Quatity
Books	New York	Q1	1200
Books	New York	Q4	300
Books	St. Louis	Q2	568
Books	St. Louis	Q3	985
Books	Los Angeles	Q2	3500
DVDs	Los Angeles	Q1	5440
DVDs	Austin	Q4	1500

Figure 15.3 Relational table with multidimensional cubes using three aggregations.

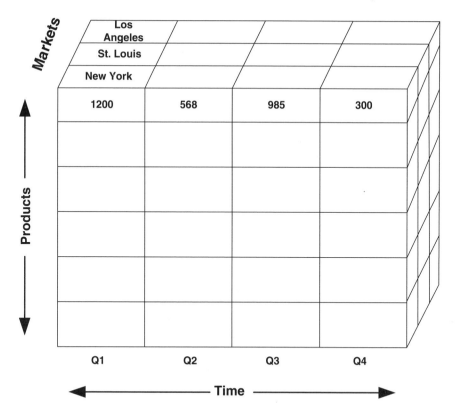

Figure 15.4 Relational table with multidimensional cubes using four aggregations.

attribute to the array. From a reporting perspective, a user could query for Orders and Items, which would only use two of the three dimensions, or ask for Orders by Item within Market. To use all the dimensions available, the user could search on Orders, by Item within Market by Price.

These examples picture the data warehouse from a logical perspective, that is, the cube does not exist physically, just conceptually. From a physical perspective, data warehouses use a standard data structure called the star schema. The star schema contains the main table in the center of the star, and each node represents another dimension of the data as shown in Figure 15.5.

The star schema in Figure 15.5 allows for queries to be performed based on an Order. In many ways it resembles an ERD in an operational database. However, most star schemas start with a multidimensioned center (concatenated primary-key), so that query time is enormously reduced because there are less joins. Figures 15.6 to 15.8 show how the number of tables dramatically reduced as the number of primary key concatenations in the center table . It is important to recognize that more key concatenations in the center table greatly reduces the types of searches that can be performed on the data, that is, the flatter the schema the less dimensions available to view the data. For example, in Figure 15.8, there

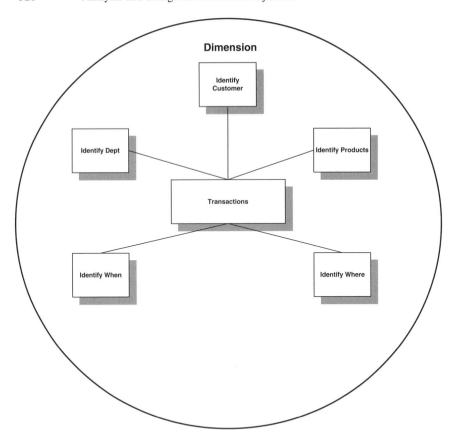

Figure 15.5 Data warehouse star schema design.

are no nodes in the star schema because there are no dimensions. Therefore, a user can only query the data warehouse to view Items within Orders, by Market and Price. It is also important to recognize that Figure 15.8 contains no validation or look-up tables, which are normally used to validate the data of certain data elements. Data validation is not required in a warehouse architecture because the data is read-only, that is, records cannot be inserted, updated, or deleted. This is significant because this structure greatly improves data access

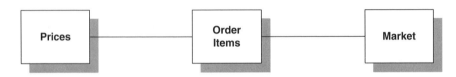

Figure 15.6 Data warehouse reduced to three tables: prices, order-items and market.

Figure 15.7 Data warehouse reduced to two tables: prices and order-items with market.

Figure 15.8 One-dimensional data warehouse.

performance. The removal of validation tables eliminates index pointers and the need for multiple joins of tables, which simply reduces overhead and increases the performance of report queries. Figures 15.6 to 15.8 also depict the number of dynamic searches that are needed to produce one report. It is also feasible to design data warehouses that contain all four types of star schemas. This could occur if there were four departments who had three different fixed views of how they wanted the data to be represented to them.

Because there can be multiple copies of data in a data warehouse environment, there is an advantage to creating more schemas that represent the data as it is needed for a specific report or analysis, as opposed to designing an elaborate star schema that allows for multiple views of the data. The reason for this position is simple: why design a data warehouse that resembles an operation database? Another way of looking at this model is to conceptualize that every data warehouse is nothing more than a view of data for a specific user view. The more alternative searches you offer the user, the less attractive the model is from a performance perspective. However, multiple warehouses require multiple conversions from the operational systems. So, the analyst must balance the design taking into consideration both performance and overhead issues.

Data Warehouse Conceptual Design

The first step in creating an ecommerce decision support system is designing the data warehouse structure. This structure or architecture provides a framework for identifying how data will be utilized within the ecommerce system. A basic data warehouse architecture is shown in Figure 15.9.

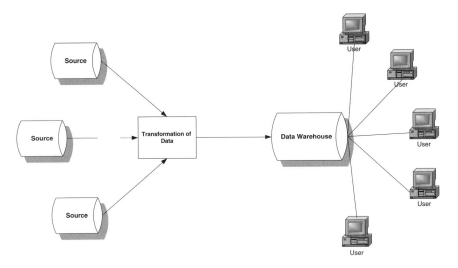

Figure 15.9 Basic data warehouse structure.

The fundamental characteristics of the basic data warehouse architecture are:

1. Data is extracted from operational databases, flat-files, and other data sources.
2. The data from all of the source systems is first integrated and transformed into another format before being loaded into the actual data warehouse.
3. The data warehouse can only be used for read-only activities for DSS.
4. Users obtain access to the data warehouse through a front-end application tool, usually supplied by the warehouse vendor.

Extracting Data from a Database Source

The data warehouse process starts with identifying the source of the data needed for the DSS. These will typically come from two places: (1) the operational databases that exist in the new ecommerce system and (2) the data files that exist in legacy systems. The most difficult part of the process is to identify the meaning of the data elements in each system so they can be transformed properly into the data warehouse. This can only be accomplished by first creating a central repository of the data—typically by using a CASE tool. Porting data into a central repository is easier when working with relational databases because they are better documented and can be reverse engineered into a CASE tool. However, legacy data is more challenging because of their lack of documentation and less conventional data formats. Notwithstanding the format of the source data, the process to define the operational data is time consuming but extremely valuable for the project to be successful. Many data warehouse products like

Sagent provide their own metadata dictionaries that can be used instead of a CASE tool. These metadata libraries store the relationships that exist among the different yet related databases in the production systems. Analysts also need to extract data from third-party products that are part of the operational system, sush as a weekly stock price file that is integrated in to the production system. In any event, most data warehouse systems can extract data from multiple databases from multiple systems.

Many operational systems can be categorized as "transaction-processing" based. This means that they are heavily geared toward capturing transactions that occur throughout the day. Typically, transaction-processing systems are those that take orders, ship them, and then record financial information. Transaction-processing systems have the following characteristics:

1. High transaction rate.
2. Constantly changing.
3. Data redundancy is avoided in order to ensure integrity.
4. Optimized indexes to ensure SQL query efficiency.
5. Two-phase commit architecture to ensure recoverability.

DSSs using data warehouses provide tremendous advantages for transaction-processing systems because they can reformat data into dimensions so that users can better understand the meaning and results of the transactions.

Staging and Formatting Extracted Data

As previously stated, a significant component of the data warehouse product is a load server that compiles the data and establishes the links among duplicate data elements. Furthermore, the load server allows for the definition of elements, especially for those attributes that have complex meanings. These attributes are called intelligent keys where portions of the attribute have special meanings. This is shown in Figure 15.10 for a Part Number data element.

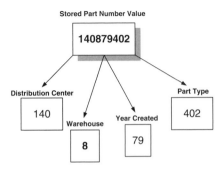

Figure 15.10 Encoded data fields.

The load server has the ability to store information about the Part Number so the warehouse can easily identify the data element's components during a query. Overall, the load server prepares the raw data, and creates a new repository of information in the format required by the data warehouse schema.

Read-Only Activities

As previously stated, the data warehouse is a read-only copy of operational data. The philosophy is that operational data and DSS data are inherently different. Specifically, DSS provides easy-to-understand formats of data so that analytical information can be created to support better tactical and strategic business decisions within the company. These analytical processes require that historical data be kept in different views, unlike the single normalized view required in operational databases. Indeed, one database format alone cannot efficiently provide for both types of functional need. Thus, at the core of all warehouse products is a read-only database that represents the primary component of information analysis.

Front-End Query Tools

In most data warehouse systems, the data access infrastructure makes up the next most important component of the DSS architecture. This data access is composed of front-end query tools and application programs that provide useful and accessible decision support information from the data warehouse. Thus, analysts need to design the warehouse schemas, query logic, and applications to create a useful data warehouse environment that operates under the auspices of the production systems. The important component of application and query support are the third-party applications that are provided with the purchase of the data warehouse. Most warehouse products, like SAS, Sagent, and Oracle, all come with sophisticated developer tool kits that allow for the generation of advanced query and application development. These add-on application products do not, however, provide the proper analysis and design process to determine what they need to do.

Alternative Types of Data Warehouse Structures

Thus far we have only looked as what can be called a "generic" data warehouse architecture. However, there are more sophisticated design considerations when formulating an ecommerce enterprise warehouse system. Figure 15.11 depicts a slightly more complex data warehouse that loads data into what are known as business areas. A business area represents a defined segment of the organization and is based on perceived business similarities. These similarities could be based

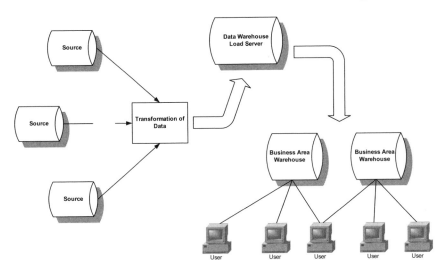

Figure 15.11 Business area data warehouses.

on where income is derived, type of clients, etc. Therefore, each business has its own view and use for a warehouse. All of these multiple warehouses are derived from one enterprise warehouse that has been ported from the integration of multiple data sources.

In Figure 15.11, data is extracted from various source systems and integrated and transformed before being loaded into an enterprise data warehouse. This data is then restructured, redesigned, and moved into separate business area warehouses, which are then used for DSS. The major benefits of using a business area architecture are to:

1. Ensure that all business areas are deriving data from a central warehouse system.
2. Create sub-warehouses that can better facilitate the needs of smaller departments.
3. Provide access to different user communities. Internal, consumers, and customers all have different business area needs and access authorization criteria.
4. Ensure that the timing of the data is consistent across all warehouses. In this way comparisons of data across the enterprise are consistent.

Another hybrid version of the business area model is to create separate area warehouses directly from the load server as shown in Figure 15.12 While this architecture does not contain a central enterprise data warehouse, it has all of the constructs that represent a true data warehouse. Obviously, the advantage is the time and space saving of creating an intermediate enterprise data warehouse. This model is advantageous when there is little need for a centralized warehouse and when there are multiple updates of the warehouse from multiple source files.

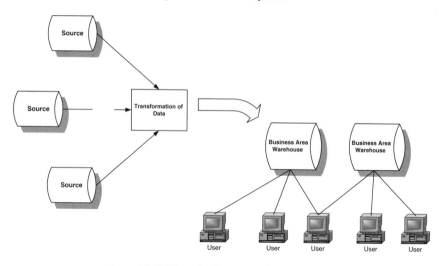

Figure 15.12 Direct business area data warehouse.

Still another intricate architecture is shown in Figure 15.13. This model creates an integrated relational database in third-normal form. The data that comes from source operational systems remains read-only; however, new data can be added to the integrated database directly from users. The purpose of these updates is to provide additional data that facilitates expanded decision support activities. Sometimes this process also helps to "clean up" bad data. Once the new data has been entered, the data is transformed into a data warehouse.

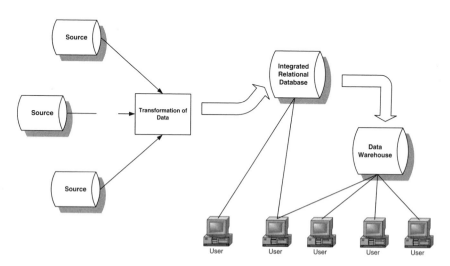

Figure 15.13 Integrated Data warehouse with new data.

A Decision Support Life Cycle

A System Development Life Cycle (SDLC) for DSS focuses on data, as opposed to processing and functionality. As a result of the elimination of many process-oriented steps, the DSS life cycle is much faster and less complex than its traditional counterpart. The main activity for the analysts is to take data from various sources and platforms and provide multiple strategic views of the data in another infrastructure.

The phases of the ecommerce DSS are:

1. Planning
2. Gathering Data Requirements and Modeling
3. Physical Database Design and Development
4. Data Mapping and Transformation
5. Data Extraction and Load
6. Automating the Data Management Process
7. Application Development and Reporting
8. Data Validation and Testing
9. Training
10. Rollout

Phase 1: Planning

The planning phase in ecommerce DSS is very similar to the project life cycle and entails the creation of a project plan and realistic time estimates. Planning, like that for any project, includes defining the project scope, plan, resources, tasks, timeliness, and deliverables. Figure 15.14 depicts the project planning components.

Furthermore, the DSS will require changes to the network infrastructure. Therefore, there will be technical infrastructure design that needs to be implemented while formulating the proper DSS environment. The technical components include capacity planning, archival strategies, data refresh/update strategies, and operations and job scheduling.

Phase 2: Gathering Data Requirements and Modeling

During this phase the analyst must understand the business needs and data requirements of the users of the system. Because ecommerce systems are comprised of internal users, customers, and consumers, the data modeling requirements for data warehouses will vary depending on the different user views. Essentially, data requirements will involve the process of identifying what elements are needed for DSS by each group of users. The assumption should be that normalized databases exist, legacy links have been made, and intermediate transaction processing systems are in place. If a central repository of all

Figure 15.14 DSS project planning steps.

data elements is in a CASE product, then identifying the components of the warehouse will be much easier and productive. Unlike regular data gathering, analysts should be looking at what users need to see in the form of screen displays and printed reports. Thus, it is the output that identifies what is needed for the data warehouse. Therefore, the analyst does not need to use process models like

DFDs to model the data warehouse, rather the specification will consist of query screens for data access, sample reports, and screen display views. The reports and screen displays need to be in prototype form so that users can validate that the information and format are correct. Another interesting aspect of data warehouse design is to determine what users might want to see in addition to what they have already identified. Basically most users will want to see the reports and screen displays that they are used to having from their existing system. However, data warehousing allows so much more, that the analysts need to consider what users might want to see given the robust power of the data warehouse query software. While this activity might seem counter to my previous position that analysts should never create requirements, I do believe that the analyst must at least reveal, usually through demonstrations, the power of the data warehouse to each user constituency. Obviously, this process may not be practical for consumers, except where the marketing department is involved with focus groups. Analysts must remember to inform users that data warehouses do not contain current data. While designing real-time data warehouses is possible, it is unlikely and difficult to implement.

What is most important, however, is not the reports and displays, but the strategy of designing the data warehouse (or data mart) architecture. Reports can usually be modified without great pain, but schema design is more complicated. This process requires that the analyst determine which type of warehouse designs to use. Remember that there can be multiple data warehouses produced from multiple sources, so the options for design are many-to-many as shown in Figure 15.15

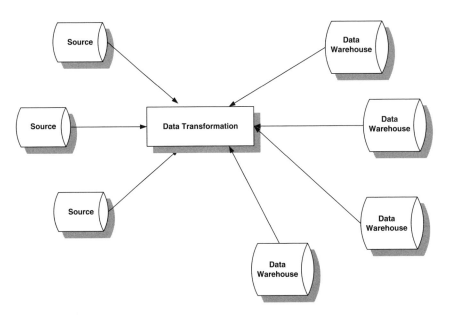

Figure 15.15 Data source and data warehouse relationships.

Notwithstanding the relationships between data sources and data warehouses, it is important to focus on the schema design, that is, what is the design of the star schema. There are essentially three approaches. The first approach suggests that the data warehouse contain a star schema that resembles the report or screen display. This design was discussed earlier in this chapter. The advantage of this approach is that data is already placed in the format required so there is little need for data manipulation. As a result, the production of the reports and displays are very efficient. Furthermore, there is little that the user needs to do other than just selecting the option to produce the report. The bad news is that the warehouse is very limited because all it can do is produce the report. The economies-of-scale for creating the report in a data warehouse form may seem like overkill, unless the process of obtaining the data in one central repository has significant time saving for the user. Figure 15.16 shows a data warehouse report schema.

The second approach is to create sophisticated star schemas that support a grouping of needs. Each schema would contain a central table that provides a data repository required by a group of users. Each node would provide the supplemental data that might be needed depending on the user group and the report subject. The benefit of this model is somewhat obvious in that it allows warehouses to serve multiple needs and provides for more DSS analysis of the data. The downsides are also obvious; users need more knowledge on how to query the data and therefore need training and an understanding of what data is available for analysis. In addition, the performance of the reports and displays will vary depending on the level of sophistication of the queries that are afforded to the end users. Figure 15.17 depicts a star schema for group user query.

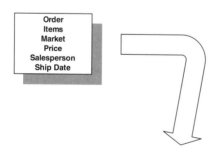

Order Analysis Report					
Order #	Item ID	Market	Price	Salesperson	Date Shipped
14387	A5567	West	120.00	Joe Smith	3/15/2001

Figure 15.16 Data warehouse report design.

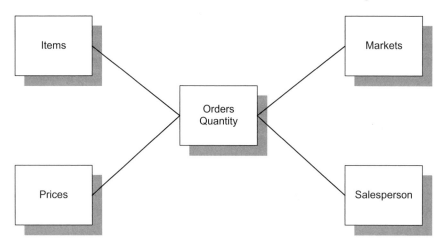

Figure 15.17 Star schema for a user group.

The third approach comes back to the earlier example of the enterprise level data warehouse. Rather than have multiple warehouses serving many users, one central complex star schema can be designed to afford the needs of an entire organization, group, or department. These types of data warehouses will contain the most nodes on the schema, and look very much like a third-normal form database. The advantage is that data is copied once per cycle to one data warehouse thus ensuring that the data all represents the same time period. The downside is that the warehouse becomes voluminous and requires significant data query manipulation in order to extract the needed information.

Another challenge in the movement of data from operations sources to data warehouses is derived elements. I previously discussed the handling of derived data as being a violation of third-normal form and a database redundancy. As a result, all derived data elements were removed from the production database. However, because data warehouses are read-only, there is no need to eliminate derived data. In fact, warehouses that contain derivations will be much more efficient for query and report production. The question to answer is how to populate derived data back into the database. If a CASE tool was used to produce the normalized operational database, then there is a good chance that derived elements might exist in the data dictionary. You might recall in an earlier chapter (Chapter 5) that many derived elements are first placed in the data dictionary and defined in a process specification. Thus, the identity of these derived data elements and their calculations can be extracted from the data dictionary. Unfortunately, such is not the case when dealing with legacy databases and flat-file systems. In these situations, the analyst must reconcile each report and screen display against the existing data dictionary to determine where derived elements exist. Furthermore, just identifying them is not enough— analysts must work with users to understand how they are derived. Once all derived elements have been discovered and defined they need to be added to the metadata dictionary usually provided with a data warehouse product.

The use of metadata (data that defines data) will be discussed later in this chapter; however, its use is important when integrating derived data elements in the data warehouse. The metadata repository will allow analysts to store the calculation formula. When the data warehouse is produced (or refreshed), a triggering operation will examine the data and calculate the derived values as set forth in the metadata repository. The process of calculating derived data elements is shown in Figure 15.18.

There may also be derived data elements that cannot be directly calculated from the supplied data sources. This means that the derived elements must be calculated outside the data warehouse domain and then imported directly into the data warehouse. This is shown in Figure 15.19.

In summary, the data gathering and modeling phase must address the following key questions:

1. What will be the number and design of the data warehouses?
2. How will data be reflected in the data warehouse model, particularly the derived data, which does not exist in the production database?
3. Is there a CASE tool that will allow for the transformation of derived data elements from a data dictionary to the data warehouse?
4. How often does data need to be refreshed?

Figure 15.20 reflects the major steps that analysts must complete in this phase.

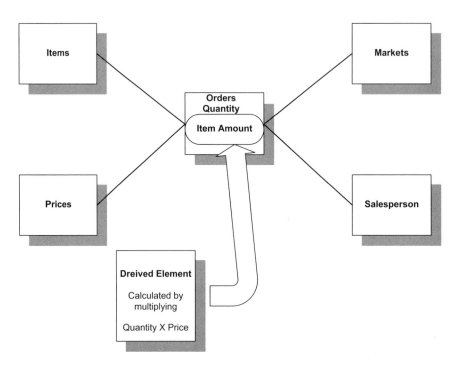

Figure 15.18 Populating derived data elements to the data warehouse.

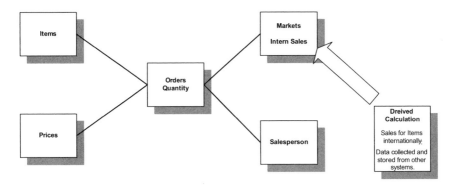

Figure 15.19 Porting derived data elements into a warehouse.

Phase 3: Physical Database Design and Construction

The physical database design entails a number of steps that enable the database to operate efficiently. There are three main components involved in the physical design process: fact tables, dimension tables, and look-up tables.

Fact tables, which are sometimes known as major tables, contain the quantitative or factual data about a business. It is, in effect, the information for which users are doing the query (Poe, 1996). Fact table information is often numerical measurements of data that contain many attributes and sometimes millions of occurrences. For example, a marketing database can contain data on various sales for the company. Dimension tables or minor tables, on the other hand, are smaller than fact tables and hold descriptive data that reflect various dimensions of the facts—like month, year, region, etc. In the previous example, dimensions of sales could be product, markets, etc. Figure 15.21 reflects the marketing data warehouse with dimension tables.

Thus, the combination of fact tables and dimension tables provides for the basis of the initial star schema. This star schema can then allow users to scan the data, and with the appropriate database constraints provide interesting analysis of the information. Look-up tables are another type of dimension table. They provide fill-in information used to describe possible values that certain fact data need. They represent entities that are similar to third-normal form validation tables. An example of a look-up table the available colors of a particular model car. Figure 15.22 shows a combined star schema physical database that combines facts, dimensions, and look-up tables.

In many ways, much of the physical database design concepts discussed in this section could be considered part of the logic data modeling phase (Phase 2). While much of this design could be done during Phase 2, there are some related decisions that require more knowledge about the physical environment, that is, the actual data warehouse environment. Furthermore, the process of

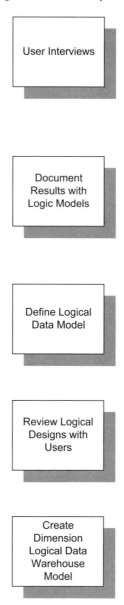

Figure 15.20 DSS data requirements and data modeling gathering.

denormalization is often accomplished during physical as opposed to logical database design. Beyond just database design, the analyst also needs to:

1. *Identify the Actual Primary and Secondary Key Structures.* Sometimes this could involve denormalized data elements.

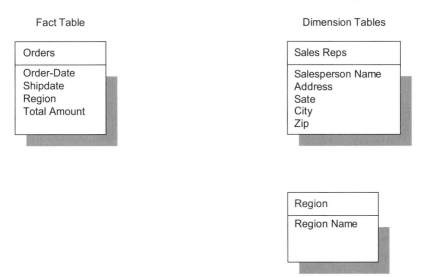

Figure 15.21 Fact and dimensional type data warehouses.

2. *Develop Aggregation Strategies.* Aggregation is the process of accumu-
    lating fact data from other transactions. This means that a derived data
    element transaction could be generated that depicts the results of many
    detailed transactions.
3. *Creating Indexing Strategies.* Indexes are separate tables that are inter-
    nally created to improve look-up performance. An index is an indirect
    address that points to where specific information exists in the database,
    without having to search every record. Figure 15.23 depicts an index
    look-up table. Any field can be indexed so that query speed to access
    that information can be dramatically increased.
4. *Develop Partition Tables.* Partitioning is the process of breaking up
    physical databases into many different storage areas. Logically, these
    multiple partitions are treated as one database, but physically are
    distributed on many different areas of a disk, or across multiple physical
    hard disks. The benefit of partitioning is purely performance. Parti-
    tioning of data maximizes performance of the data warehouse when
    particular parts of the data are needed by specific users. So, in theory,
    two users can be using the same logical data warehouse, yet be accessing
    two separate physical partitions of the same database.
5. *Performing Capacity Planning.* Analysts must determine the amount of
    storage space and processor speed that they will need in order to provide
    an efficient data warehouse environment. Analysts should not do this
    configuration alone; network architects must be involved to assist in the
    determination as to what processor types might best handle the load and
    perceived growth of the data warehouse. The key input needed from

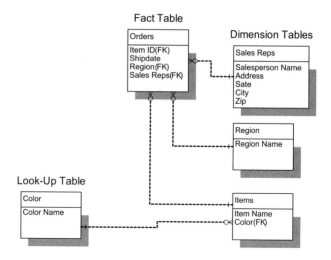

Figure 15.22 Fact, dimension, and look-up data warehouse types.

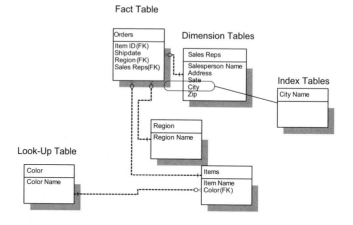

Figure 15.23 Index tables.

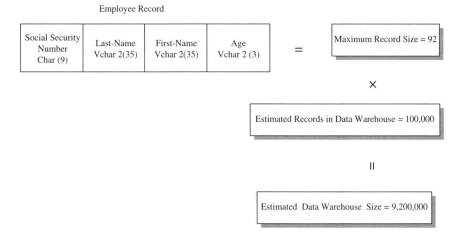

Figure 15.24 Data warehouse size calculation example.

the analyst is the number of records that will be estimated in each data warehouse. There are two components that are needed to determine space requirements. The first, which was covered in an earlier chapter, calculates the size of each data warehouse record by multiplying the total number of maximum characters in each attribute within a record. By maximum I mean the largest size for all VARCHAR2 (variable length) data elements. The result of this calculation will establish each record size. The analyst needs to then calculate the database size by multiplying this total record size by the estimated number of records in the data warehouse (see Figure 15.24).

This last step might not be that easy, but sometimes estimating maximum data warehouse sizes (i.e., the largest it could be) is the safest calculation. Furthermore, analysts must take into consideration the needs for temporary storage that are required during SQL JOINS, PROJECTS, and SELECTS of data from tables. Remember that SQL-based queries generate dynamic database tables for reporting. Thus, analysts need to consider doubling or even tripling the storage requirements of the host data warehouse. This is why partitioning can be so effective; it allows network architects to scale storage by attaching more physical hard disks. The issue of how many processors to have, the memory size, and disk access speeds needs to be determined by the proper network professionals, but heavily based on the input supplied by the analyst.

Phase 4: Data Mapping and Transformation

The data mapping and transformation phase is one where the analyst must locate the source of the data in the operational systems, do analysis to understand the types of data migrations and transformations that need to occur, and map the source data to target data warehouses. This phase ultimately determines what the source data will be, how it will be converted, and where the data will be ported. The specific steps within this phase are as follows:

1. *Defining the Data Sources*: Much of this activity can be accelerated if the analyst has loaded the data elements of each system into a central CASE tool repository. Other factors are the extent of legacy data that exists in the system, and the nature of how the data is stored. Furthermore, the amount of data redundancy and derived data elements all play a factor in the time requirements to ascertain where the data is and how it is defined.

2. *Determining File Layouts*: Once data sources have been defined, the analyst must clearly understand the file layouts of these systems and how the files interrelate with each other within a particular source repository. For example, a file that contains fact data may be linked to another table in the same system that provides validation information. Thus, the analyst needs to understand the schema of each source system. If the source is a relational database, then the best approach is to generate (if not available) an entity relational diagram (ERD). The ERD will expose the referential integrity that exists at the database level and expose those relationships that have been implemented at the application level. It might also expose data redundancies. If the system is a flat-file legacy application, then the analyst should print out the file description tables (particularly if the system is written in COBOL). The file description tables will identify all of the data elements in each file. By creating a simple template or utility program, analysts can determine where duplicate elements exist among these flat-files. This will allow the analyst to understand how the files link to one another, where there are redundancies, and how to schematically look at the system from a dimensional and relational perspective.

3. *Mapping Source Data to Target Data*: Once the source systems and schematic have been identified, the analyst needs to map or identify the source data to the data warehouse star schemas. This can be accomplished by creating a matrix that shows source elements and their attributes as well as their corresponding data warehouse data elements. Figure 15.25 shows a sample matching source-to-target matrix developed using a spreadsheet program.

4. *Develop Transformation Specifications*: The above matrix is only one component of what is called the Transformation Specification. Another name for a Transformation Specification is Conversion Document. A Conversion Document provides the requirements for a programmer to develop a utility program that prepares, moves, and transforms source data to a data-staging file. The data-staging file is an intermediate data store that is created for actual transport to the data warehouse.

Source Data Element	Attribute	Source Table	Data Warehouse Data Element	Attribute	Target Table
Company	Char(3)	Items	Company-Name	Vchar2(15)	Company
Designator	Char(15)	Items	Vendor-Style	Char(18)	PO-Item
Group-ID	Char(10)	Items	Dept-No	Char(2)	Purchase-Order
Frt-Term	Char(3)	PO	Freight-Terms	Char(1)	PO-Header
Final-Dest	Vchar2(30)	PO	Import-Whse-No	Char(4)	PO-Header
Purchase-Term	Char(4)	Contract	FOB-Terms	Char(1)	PO-Detail
Discharge-Point	Char(30)	Contract			
Arrive-By-Date	Date	Contract	Cancel-Date	Date	PO-Detail
Sup-Approval	Char(30)	Import	Whse-Message	Char(60)	Header-Mess
Coord-Item	Vchar(80)	Merchandise	Item-Message	Char(80)	PO-Detail

Figure 15.25 Source-to-target data element mapping table.

5. *Reviewing the Update Cycle*: This process establishes the refresh cycle required for each data warehouse. Refresh cycles define when a cycle begins, when it ends, and how long it runs. It is also important for the analyst to have some idea about how long a refresh cycle might take. This can be determined best by running tests on sample source files and then forecasting the total update time based on the results of the test. The determination of conversion time could be critical since the update cycle needs to complete prior to the user wanting to see the data results. Therefore, if an update cycle runs every 24 hours, then the update cycle needs to complete by the beginning of the next morning. While this might sound like plenty of time, many large-scale update cycles can take substantial time to complete. The time to complete also heavily depends on the amount of data manipulation that occurs during the conversion of data from source-to-target.

6. *Developing Strategies for Archival*: This step entails the decision of what portions of warehouse data can be archived or deleted from the DSS. Typically this becomes more of an issue when looking at transaction-based information. The decision is to determine when dated transactions, which are used to formulate results of the data, are no longer providing enough value to keep them actively stored in the live data warehouse. The reason for purging certain transaction is because of the performance degradation that it causes during warehouse queries. Sooner or later, historical transaction data needs to be removed from the active warehouse. Analysts have two options. Option one is to generate a summary transaction record that might represent a group of detailed transactions. This means that the summary transaction would provide a view of the meanings of the detailed transactions. Figure 15.26 provides an example of representing detailed transactions in a summary record. If this option is selected then the detailed transactions can be deleted or archived. The creation of summary records may also require that specific program changes be made to query applications so that a summary record can be appropriately identified from a detailed transaction. The second option is to just create a separate file of purged transactions that can be accessed using a different set of query applications. This purged

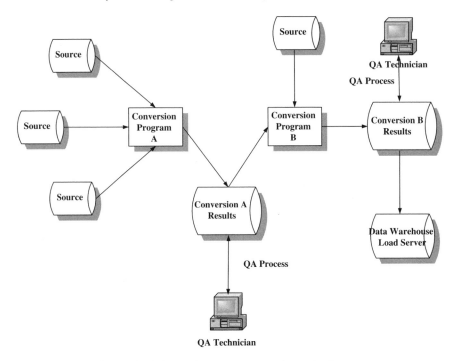

Figure 15.26 Converting source to warehouse load server.

file would typically be resident on a separate processor so that it would not conflict with normal data warehouse activities. Regardless of which option is used, the analyst needs to create specifications that identify the conditions for purging data and where the data is to be stored. Both options also require the development of specific query applications that can access purged data when needed.

7. *Review Security Requirements*: Once the data warehouse is in place, the analyst must integrate security requirements into the specification. Unlike many security issues, because data warehouses are read-only, there are no concerns about the creation of illegal or dangerous records. However, data warehouse information is still proprietary and could provide valuable information for those with malicious or illegal intentions. Thus, securing data warehouses from unauthorized use is a key component of data warehouse design. This is especially important because most access to data warehouses in ecommerce systems will occur via the Web, either from an Intranet or an Internet. So who has access to what features in a Web-based data warehouse query becomes very important in the design of the warehouse system. Much of the design issues covered in Chapter 13 are relevant in data warehouse development as well. Therefore, analysts should review the security requirements of the data warehouse using the same approach as in any other system.

8. *Capacity Plan Review*: Once the data mapping and conversion method-ologies have been completed, the analyst will have a much better perspective on the specific capacity requirements. This step simply suggests that the capacity planning and space determination is an iterative process in which the analyst and network architects will fine-tune the capacity needs as each phase in the life cycle is completed.

Phase 5: Populating a Data Warehouse

This phase involves the actual extraction, conversion, and population of the target data warehouses. This is typically accomplished with a combination of conversion and update software supplied with the data warehouse vendor's product, and with the development of specific conversion programs designed by the analyst. The steps involved with completing the population of data warehouse data are as follows:

1. *Loading and Staging the Data*: This step may involve an intermediate program that begins the process of building a repository of data where the data warehouse software will extract the information from. While many data warehouse products will allow for the loading of data directly from an operational database or file system, this is often not recom-mended. Accessing operational data is usually not a best practice for data architects.

2. *Converting and Integrating Data*: This step entails the execution of the actual conversion programs and the integration of multiple data sources. The process involves the confirmation that multiple data source migrations have been completed and the execution of one or more conversion programs (that migrate the data as per the specification) have occurred. This step should result in the formation of a warehouse load server that is ready for testing before being moved to the live data warehouse. Figure 15.26 shows the process.

3. *Testing and Load*: The Test and Load phase is the final step to creating the data warehouse. The test part of this step is to provide various reconciliation results that provide assurance that data has been converted to specification. For the most part, the testing should be consistent with audit-trail philosophies including the verification that the number of records read, written, and transferred is correct. If records are rejected for whatever reason, these should also be reported. The load portion of this step involves the actual porting of the data into the warehouse for use by users. There should also be an audit trail report specifying that the process of final load has been successful.

4. *Capacity Review*: Once again, the analyst should review the capacity needs of the system after the final data warehouses have been created, since the storage at the time of completion will represent the actual storage prior to query operations on the data.

Phase 6: Automating Data Management Procedures

While much of the work has been performed to generate the data warehouse, there is a need to create automated processes that refresh the information on a periodic basis. The periods may vary depending on the type and number of data warehouses that have been designed. Thus, once the first data extraction is completed and data warehouses are created, the analyst needs to design automated utilities that migrate new data to a preexisting data warehouse. These utilities must be automatically activated based on time and/or conditions. They must also activate the application operations that are part of the life cycle of refreshing data, namely Data Mapping, Conversion, Extraction, and Load. When subsequent or ongoing refresh is in place, data will be replaced in the load server and ultimately in the data warehouse. The procedures for verifying that this process has occurred properly also involve the creation of utility applications that report on the outcomes of each automated step, each time the refresh occurs.

There also needs to be an automatic backup and restore process should data become corrupt or damaged because of a hardware failure. There is typically a backup/restore feature available in data warehouse products, as well as from third-party vendors. Restoration procedures must be designed and tested in order to ensure that data warehouse information can be restored correctly and within the time constraints set forth by the user communities. Of course, all automated processes need to be tested, therefore, the analyst needs to design test case scenarios that will assist in the verification that data can be backed up and restored correctly.

Phase 7: Application Development and Reporting

This phase focuses on the delivery of output from the data warehouse. DSS application development is usually accomplished by using special data access tools to design and pre-build reports. Indeed, the tools selected to generate reports are critical to the success of any data warehouse. Analysts need to determine the environment to support data access and information analysis rather than just selecting a front-end software package. There are several steps that are required to understand the complexities of providing a reporting environment for users in an ecommerce environment. The first issue to address is the ways in which users can receive information from the data warehouse. There are four types of reporting as follows:

1. *Parameter-Based Ad Hoc*: This allows users to enter particular information that will act as a parameter into the report application. Parameters often consist of date information, or domain constraints like department or group. Users, while changing parameters, are not creating

new reports, but rather modifying existing reports within a pre-defined range of choices.

2. *Display Access*: This involves the display of reports on the Web or some other central place on the system. The important concept here is that reports are generated as needed but assumed to be effective in a view-only mode.

3. *Complete Ad Hoc*: The user interacts directly with the data warehouse using the query tools that support the warehouse product. Thus, users will need to be trained on how to issue queries, and how to manipulate the data in the warehouse. While this option provides the most versatility, it is also the most difficult report to use successfully. The problem is whether users can really master the query tool, be knowledgeable on how the data is stored, and can appropriately test their results. Indeed, the largest risk for users is generating reports that are not accurate.

4. *Hard Copy*: These are predefined and developed by the analyst. They typically have a fixed format and are printed and forwarded to the appropriate requester.

There are also a number of ways that users need to navigate through an ecommerce DSS. This is based on user needs, similar to my earlier definition of user categories. The three primary methods are:

1. *Executive*: Allows executives to get predefined reports quickly and on a regular basis.

2. *Structured Decision Support*: Contains predefined and ad hoc reports and outputs. Thus, structured decision support provides another level of analysis offered to the user community. This hybrid approach is usually required by middle-tier users like line managers and supervisors, where there is a clear need to generate what-if analysis in a dynamic day-to-day environment.

3. *Unstructured Decision Support*: These users have access to all types of reports, but prefer to design ad hoc reports from scratch and use them when they are needed for a particular analysis. These users are more activity-based on the information they need.

The level and categories of users vary in how they use reports. What reports are needed by users also depends heavily on whether they are internal, customers, or consumers. Typically, internal users are those who can be trained to use unstructured techniques to access data warehouse information. Figure 15.27 represents another view of how certain types of users utilize report options.

Report Access and Analysis

A data warehouse is not an automated method of getting the information you want without working to find it. Users should not be disillusioned about what a data

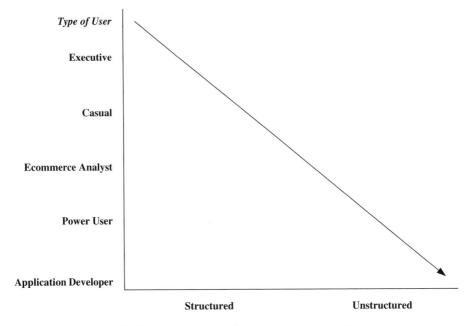

Figure 15.27 Types of users and their report access preferences.

warehouse product will afford them to do. Misunderstanding the commitment that data warehouses require, both from designers and users, is a critical factor for success (Poe, 1996). Figure 15.28 depicts the sequential steps that users should follow when using DSS and when analyzing their data.

The viewing of the reports is another important component of analysis of DSS. Users may want to specify what format they want to view the data. Thus, analysts need to provide options for users where they can select from a fixed menu of display options. While tabular and cross-tabular reports are most common, graphical output is also a common way of analyzing what reports are telling users about their data. Figure 15.29 shows various types of data warehouse report presentations.

Listed below are the most common report functions that DSS should provide to users:

1. Changing the axis: This allows users to swap rows and columns.
2. Changing sort order.
3. Adding and deleting subtotals and other information breaks.
4. Creating color reports with highlighting of certain variables.
5. Format options for fonts, styles, sizes, and colors.
6. Graphical display of information should support line graphs, dimensional and stacked bars, pie, scatter, bubble, tape, and area.
7. Ability to change graph axis labels, colors, and titles.

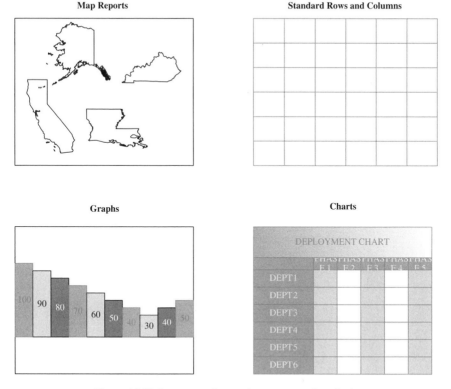

Figure 15.28 Sequence of reporting access and analysis.

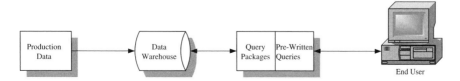

Figure 15.29 Data warehouse report design.

Data Warehouse Query Tools

There are a number of types of queries that allow for the production and viewing of the information that has been defined herein. There are four types of query tools:

1. *Report Writers*: These are third-party products that access the data warehouse directly and produce reports based on SQL type queries. Examples of third-party report writers are Crystal Reports and Cognos (see Figure 15.30).

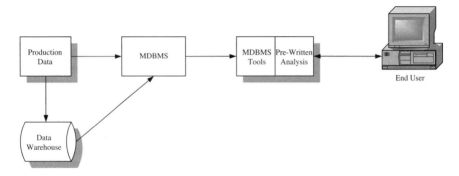

Figure 15.30 DSS report writer.

2. *Multidimensional Database Management Systems (MDBMS)*: These tools create a subset database that can be populated by both operational systems and data warehouses. These databases are usually multidimensional and are often defined as Online Analytical Processing systems (OLAP). They allow for specialized reporting of data in an aggregate form that can support advanced data mining activities (see Figure 15.30).
3. *Advanced DSS Tools*: Advanced tools are very similar to report writers except they support more advanced query capabilities and dimensional analysis. They specifically support access to multiple data warehouses from one query.
4. *Executive Information Systems (EIS)*: EIS represents a higher level of DSS. These systems contain advanced metadata facilities that can create sophisticated and predefined analysis of data. EIS also supports Artificial Intelligence activities, which are fundamental infrastructures to the support of trend analysis and decision making alternatives (see Figure 15.31).

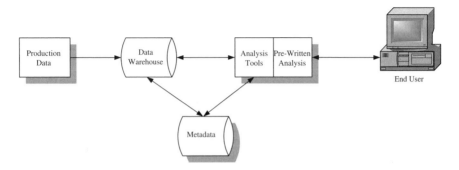

Figure 15.31 EIS architecture.

Phase 8: Data Validation and Testing

While I have mentioned that testing must occur throughout the Data Warehouse implementation, there is a need to have a central test plan strategy. Although each phase has a quality assurance process, the entire data warehouse life cycle requires integrated test scripts. These scripts establish what the expected results should be from each previous life cycle step. Sometimes this is best accomplished by having reports that provide reconciliation of what the warehouse contains. However, analysts should also suggest that users review the output reports. Users should be encouraged to hand check certain reports until they are satisfied that the system is calculating and collecting information based on their requirements. All too often we see users who just accept what the output of a report tells them!

Furthermore, analysts should plan for change—for change is inevitable with DSS ecommerce systems. Change is not only modifications to the reporting, it is the addition or changing of what data needs to be supplied to the data warehouse and in what forms. In addition, new systems are added and need to be integrated into the overall data warehouse schema. With this in mind, analysts need to design and maintain sophisticated testing systems that can be reused each time a change is made to the warehouse infrastructure or transformation process.

Phase 9: Training

While this might not be the actual responsibility of the analyst, it is important to plan for the training of users with the objective of teaching them how to work with the data warehouse. Notwithstanding that pre-designed reports do not require much data warehouse knowledge from the users, most systems will always have "super users" who want to do advanced analysis on the DSS. The training phase of the DSS life cycle includes the following considerations:

1. Understanding the scope of information in the data warehouse.
2. Training on the front-end tools and how to write queries.
3. Understanding of how to use existing reports and how to modify them.
4. Train the trainer concepts so users can eventually own the responsibility of training new employees or other users.

Phase 10: Rollout

This phase essentially involves the process of going live. It requires the actual deployment of the data warehouse into the production network environment, creating user support infrastructures including adding new users, creating the physical procedures for users to request new reports and options, providing the procedures for backup and restore, and creating a team to troubleshoot problems that inevitably occur early in the DSS rollout.

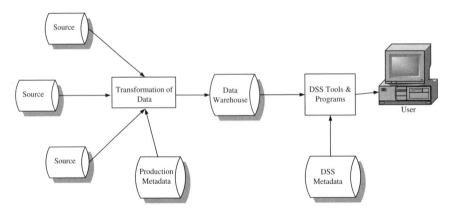

Figure 15.32 Metadata design.

Understanding Metadata

Metadata is data about data. Metadata is the fundamental component that allows data warehouse systems to provide the complex information that users require. There are two primary forms of metadata: operational and DSS. Operational metadata contains the information about where the data is in the production systems and/or in the staged database system prior to conversion. The DSS metadata establishes a catalog of the data in the data warehouse and maps this data to the query applications. Figure 15.32 depicts the metadata architecture.

Therefore, the metadata infrastructure provides the front-end users with the ability to manipulate the data without working directly with the data. That is, the user works directly with the metadata, which in turn operates on the data warehouse attributes. Thus, the metadata provides a higher level of abstraction about the data. This abstraction allows for the ease of use of operating with the database.

16
Website Design and Architecture

Introduction

This chapter focuses on the challenge of how to manage the ongoing development and maintenance of Web-based systems. In particular, this chapter targets the problem of Web systems that have dynamic content changes on a regular basis. Indeed, the Web has required businesses to become more dynamic and reactive in their thinking. Web sites that contain old images are considered slow to react to market needs. Users expect to see up-to-date information immediately. Take the New York Times Web site for example. It generates new content dynamically as stories become available (see Figure 16.1).

The problem facing many organizations is how to provide a development infrastructure that can allow users to change content without the assistance of developers, and how these systems can provide easier development for programmers and database administrators. Furthermore, there are many organizations that need to receive ecommerce content from multiple users at different locations without having to submit them to programmers for retrofitting into the existing Web screens. Indeed, static Web sites are expensive to maintain, difficult to update, and do not support the flexibility that is needed to provide competitive ecommerce on the Internet. With the average business Web site having over 8000 pages of HTML and graphical components, content management systems provide an attractive new way of building Web sites while reducing costs.

The answer to the problem is to implement what is called "content management systems." Content management systems provide an infrastructure that allows non-technical users to control their Web site commerce and communications using standardized browser interfaces, reusable template objects, and a central administrative engine that allows automated methods to update and secure an existing ecommerce Web system. Content management systems also support site administration, which allows Web administrators to control access, set design standards, edit new materials for submission to the site, and determine the procedures for information delivery.

In today's ecommerce environment it is better to generate content dynamically than to create and store static pages (Dalgleish, 2000). Dynamic content infrastructures are faster, more efficient, and easier to maintain than static architectures. Most content management systems utilize object-oriented design principles to

Figure 16.1 New York Times dynamic Web architecture.

implement ecommerce sites, which enhance reuse of Web components. Essentially Web content management systems, which utilize object management, allow organizations to:

1. Implement standards and styles through the use of template components.
2. Combine components from different sources into one or more central template frames.
3. Have control of content by a central resource.
4. Have a workflow process that allows for changes to be made to content with approval controls.
5. Contain a scheduling environment that allows certain content to become available automatically on a certain date and for a specific period of time.
6. Have multiple types of approval processes that ensure that no content is available on the Web until all requisite approvals have been met.
7. Contain multiple versions of content for Web site reuse.
8. Provide detailed audit trails and reporting that give authors a clear understanding of how long it takes to update content, and who is working on the system.
9. Implement different levels of privileges, meaning that users have different levels of security access.
10 Have users make significant content changes and modifications to the Web site without programmer interface. These users can be content writers, editors, content managers, Webmaster, and content approvers.

Dynamic Web Pages

Dynamic Web pages provide the key to creating maintainable user driven Web sites for ecommerce systems. The content itself may be reusable, e.g., company logo, and can be stored in a template or the database so that it can be reused when needed across many Web pages in the ecommerce system. While the logo itself can be stored as a file in static-based systems, any changes to the logo would require a developer to reload each occurrence of the logo in the ecommerce system. With a dynamic content management product, analysts can utilize an infrastructure that automatically loads the new content into every Web page that uses it. Thus, the content management engine resembles the reusable object component strategy. Just like object systems use a central brokering architecture such as CORBA (Common Object Request Broker Architecture) and Microsoft's .Net, the content management system provides the engine for component content for complex Web systems like ecommerce.

Dynamic Web pages in ecommerce systems do not exist until the client browser issues a request for a particular Web URL. Dynamic architecture through the content management infrastructure will build the Web page using stored components, thus always ensuring that the current content is being used (or whatever content has been identified in the content management system). Many content management systems are database-centered, as opposed to folder-centric. Folder-centric means that content is stored on a hard disk server and accessed through intelligent Windows folder systems. Database-centered content, on the other hand, stores the content in a relational/object database like Oracle 9 or Microsoft SQL Server. These database products identify and store the content as an image, and present the content to any Web page requesting it (with the appropriate authorization, of course). Many of the content management products are now using XML as a key vehicle to link stored database content with Web pages. You might recall that XML provides a versatile method of storing documents in the database and integrates its functionality with the power of the relational model. Dynamic Web pages in accordance with database-centric support can also provide powerful metadata support. This allows the data that describes an image or content group to be utilized as part of the selection criteria for relevant information. This means that the tagging of what the content represents can be extremely effective for ecommerce systems that provide various search functionalities. Suppose, for example, that a particular ecommerce Web site allowed for the searching of certain animals. The dynamic content management system, using metadata tags, could identify animals that match or closely match the searching criteria.

Content Management as a Web Site Builder

More advanced content management systems provide architectural infrastructures that allow Web pages to be generated using a template-based design system. This entails a structured approach to building a Web site for ecommerce. First, starter or "base" templates are created in the content management system so that all Web pages have a similar "look and feel" that is consistent with the firm's branding and identity. These starter templates represent a "frame" for every Web page in the system. Thus, when a new Web page is required, the first component to load is one of the base "frame" templates. Typically, there are a few different starter templates; one for the main Web page and multiple starter frames for the various sub-pages. In many ways the process of designing templates is similar to creating a consistent navigation style for the entire ecommerce system. Figure 16.2 shows a standard base frame for a Web page.

After the main frame is generated, developers, rather than generating HTML code from scratch, begin to load various templates that contain specific features and functions. In reality, the Web site builder resembles an object-based approach to building programs. Rather than rewriting code over and over, the site builder architecture allows for a component approach to Web development. While a developer is loading a template, he/she can decide on the specific content to place into the template frame. A template frame's content can be defined as "dynamic," meaning that its content can be changed dynamically. Dynamic changes can be scheduled using the content management system, or changed when deemed necessary. Therefore, every template component on every page can be "addressable," meaning that its content can be changed without directly modifying the Web page. Furthermore, the template can be changed in variable ways. For example, a template might appear in multiple locations. The content manager can change just one occurrence or can change all of them. Thus,

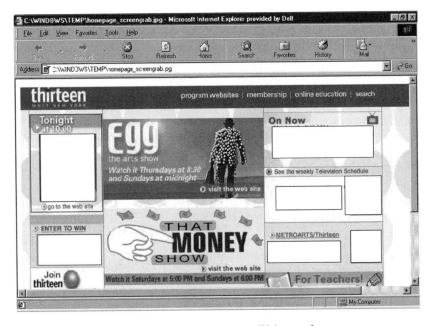

Figure 16.2 Content management Web page frame.

the content management system contains an infrastructure that can update the content and set rules on who can update it (security). Content management systems also support calendaring, which allows content to be updated automatically based on a specific time schedule. In summary, the content management site builder represents a new development environment that allows analysts to specify programming requirements using template architecture. This architecture allows programmers to build Web pages from a reservoir of standard templates. In addition, it allows authorized business personnel to update content without requiring programming assistance. Content management systems are also multitasking environments. While designers are creating HTML screens, users can be updating content. Furthermore, site builder products allow for the creation of multiple versions of a site, so ecommerce systems can actually reuse screens, or contain different screens for a specific user base. Figure 16.3 shows the component Web page templates.

   Thus, a content management infrastructure must support a site layout system that enables analysts and designers to create an overall navigation structure for a Web site. Because of the ease of use of the site builder, content can be changed by business users without requiring them to have knowledge in HTML. These

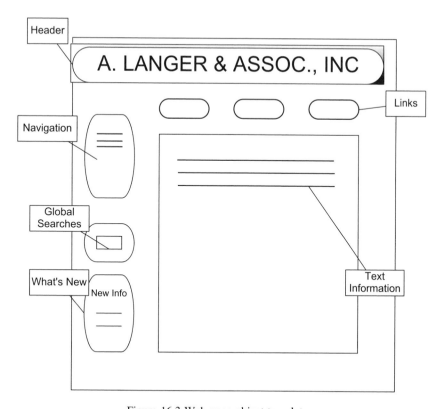

Figure 16.3 Web page object templates.

systems also uphold the business branding strategy and identity requirements. Furthermore, the site builder architecture provides security so access is controlled for only those who have been authorized to work on the Web site.

What is so unique about implementing content management is that it supports the integration of non-technical developers, that is, super users who will use the system to modify and update content without the need for a technical interface. This part of content management strategy provides a new concept in how software is developed by allowing non-technical people to update the site frequently, keeping it fresh and appealing to users.

Creating Objects

Another important component of content management is its ability to search and find relevant content when building Web sites. In other words, a complex indexing system exists that allows for content to be placed in an intelligent repository. This repository can be indexed within assigned categories. These categories are typically determined by the development team and by the users who participate in the maintenance of the Web site. Once content is stored within assigned categories it can be used to search for particular images, graphics, or text that can be incorporated in the design of any Web site.

Part of the strategy for ecommerce systems is to generate common content for reuse. This is similar to the way object-oriented systems are developed for reusable programming. That is why it is so important to know whether a content management system will be used. Once this has been determined, the design of pre-built object types can be designed and used by developers to construct the Web sites. This process does not imply that there are no modifications or custom programming required when using content management software. Indeed, developers still need to provide specific coding to handle complex ecommerce functions. However, content management does offer a structured approach to start the foundation. Content management philosophy can be compared to building homes using a pre-fabricated model. Pre-fabricated homes are those that are built off-site in a standard specification. Once built, these homes are delivered to the site, and then completed by the builder. The builder may need to add specialized features that are not included in the standard specification from the manufacturer of the home. In this example, the content template represents the pre-fabricated portion of the Web site and the developer is the builder who may need to add the specialized features required for that particular version of the pre-fabricated template.

Content Delivery

Creating content is only one part of the content management infrastructure. Another component is how content is delivered to an ecommerce system. This requires the use of various tools that allow developers to:

1. Pre-select which content is to be published on the Web site.
2. Assign publishing schedules to specific content items.
3. Pre-define rules that automate what content gets used for particular users.
4. Determine when content should be removed and replaced with updated graphics or text.
5. Determine how content is to be displayed depending on the type of browser used on the requesting client.

For example, a retail operation could display special products on sale for a period of time. The content to be display could be scheduled to appear at 9:00 in the morning and then be replaced or removed two days later. The developer or content manager could establish certain criteria in the content management system that would change the display content depending on where the user came from in the system (such as the clicks used to get to the content), the user's profile that might be stored, and the type of browser being used.

Workflow and Process Automation

Another important part of best practices for Web site design is the integration of workflow and process automation. Workflow and process automation simply provide a foundation of how content makes its way onto a Web site. Each step in the design and development of Web content needs to be mapped to its related business process. Whether this involves enforcing a production process, setting up authorization steps that are required in the development of content, or creating a method of handling incoming orders, workflow and process automation help an organization to understand how to migrate their current processes to ecommerce in an efficient and consistent manner.

In order to implement a workflow process the analyst needs to interact with business managers to define the different processes and tasks needed for their Web businesses. This could include needs for articles, pictures, videos, etc. Furthermore, business users most likely will have ecommerce needs that could include new product promotions, handling incoming user service requests, and generating special broadcast type of announcements to an entire population or group of users. The analysts will provide the framework for what each component needs to do and Web developers will program it using a content management product like SOHOnet, Interwoven, or Vinette to build the necessary templates that allow business users to modify the contents as needed. These templates are commonly referred to as workflow templates. Once the process is in place, business users can invoke the content workflow product to prepare new content for their Web site. A workflow process is designed to assign a task to a particular user, group of users, or department. Under the auspices of the security component of the content management system, users can access their workflow templates and submit new content, or change existing content. For example, suppose there is a new article that a company wants to add to the Web site, which could promote their bicycle business. The article has a photograph of the new model bicycle and an accompanying story about how a particular consumer has used the bicycle. A photographer takes a group of pictures and submits them to the marketing manager who is responsible for approving the Web content story. Simultaneously, a copywriter works on the text of the story. After the copywriter has completed the first draft of the article it is sent to a marketing manager who edits it and sends the revised copy back to the copywriter. This process is iterative until the text is ready for submission to the marketing manager responsible for approving the copy and image. After the marketing manager has approved both the photograph and the text it is forwarded to a page designer who is responsible for formatting the photo and text in a sample frame, which replicates how it will appear on the actual site. The frame is approved by the marketing manager and then deployed to the actual Web site. Figure 16.4 depicts this workflow process.

The above workflow sample shows how new content is submitted, edited, approved, and deployed onto the Web site. An automated workflow component in a content management system provides the infrastructure that allows each individual in the process to sign on, review the content, approve the content, and forward the content to the next individual in the life cycle. The above flow is just a typical example; the analyst must work with the organization to determine what the appropriate workflow process should be. Furthermore, there may be multiple workflows depending on the nature of the department or its particular business process.

E-Business Order Processing

Advanced content management products support workflow processes that involve online ordering, registration, and other real-time-based transactions systems. Such systems represent the heart of what ecommerce products are designed to do. The workflow cycle for processing ecommerce transactions is similar to the internal development cycle, yet has some unique steps. This includes designing the procedures for registration, submitting requests, and purchasing a product using an online store.

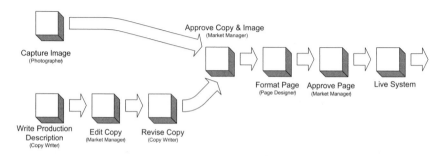

Figure 16.4 Ecommerce workflow.

Using an example of purchasing a product in an online store, a consumer would select a product or group of products for purchase. The first step validates whether the user has an account. If it is a new user, the workflow product would initiate the execution of the new registration module. If, or once, the user has an account, the order is taken using one-click ordering. The next step in the workflow is to check inventory, process the credit card, and determine the method of shipping. Once all information has been verified, including additional payment information, the consumer receives an email notification confirming the order and the shipping information. Another internal workflow process may be initiated to manage the processing of the order until it is shipped. This process would service the internal users who are responsible for ensuring that the product is shipped. Figure 16.5 shows the workflow process for an ecommerce order.

An e-business workflow component should also provide a toolbox for managing error conditions and product exceptions. These utility products allow developers to specialize the code so that the error messages and processing alternatives can be customized to fit the business model of the enterprise. The error handling of the work process software must be sophisticated enough to handle user Web browser crashes, where the product would recognize an account that did not complete its order the next time it signs onto the system.

The analyst must be the main driver to design the internal and external workflow processes. The content management software is only as good as the process that defines what it needs to do. Furthermore, the workflow processes should be defined before any selections are made on which content management product to use, since the requirements of the workflow will define what the content management product needs to offer. The workflow process is invoked

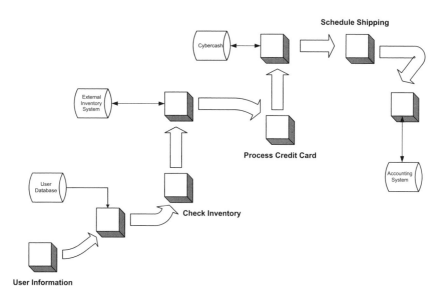

Figure 16.5 E-Commerce workflow process.

using the same business process reengineering (BPR) strategy discussed in Chapter 13. Essentially this form of BPR is focused on defining the e-service workflows and rules for processing orders and services over the Internet. The main processes that need to be considered are as follows:

1. Making service requests.
2. Ordering a product or service.
3. Providing input to online requests such as surveys and product development input.
4. Registration for service(s).
5. Updating personal information that is required by the company.
6. Request or receive emails and other push content.
7. Evaluation of products and services.
8. Provide feedback after completing a transaction.
9. Getting help online.
10. Contacting support.
11. Participating in an online forum or chat room.

Each of the above e-business activities must be designed in a workflow and mapped to the features and functions offered by a sophisticated content product. Figure 16.6 depicts a typical workflow diagram for processing an order. Workflow diagrams are very similar to process flow diagrams (PFDs).

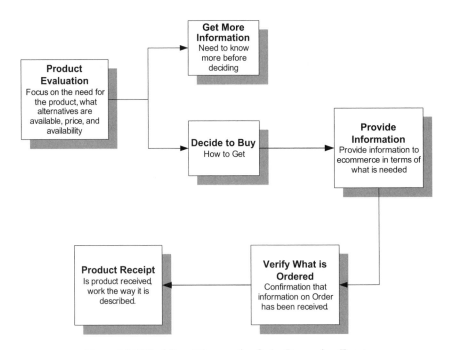

Figure 16.6 Workflow Diagram for Order Processing Event.

With respect to the entire order processing activity, common issues that need to be resolved by the analyst include:

1. What minimum information needs to be provided by a user to order product?
2. What are the specific rules that govern how each product can be ordered? This includes what constitutes an acceptable payment method, available service levels, shipping alternatives, etc.
3. What format should the user's request be provided in to facilitate processing in the workflow and content management system?
4. What product options can be identified as part of the order process and what processes require manual intervention?
5. What product selections by customers affect pricing changes in their total order, that is, what are the complexities of purchase discounts?
6. Can orders to affiliated parties be automated so that there is no requirement for manual retransmission of the user's order?

The analyst must also cover the following general areas not typically covered during process analysis. These central themes are critical for the successful integration of content and workflow products.

1. *Product Development Strategy*: Internal users need to define how new product will evolve on the ecommerce system. The concept of using templates to generate new content and applications can be a whole new culture to convey to management. Template generation is only one component of this complex commitment; it also includes service issues, transaction processing, reporting requirements, and methods to evaluate the effectiveness of the ecommerce system on an ongoing basis.
2. *Product Promotion*: The firm will want to use the ecommerce system to promote themselves. Typically this will require the use of media and other animated content. The marketing department will need to provide a perspective on how they envision promotional content to be integrated into the system. Promotional content is also temporary and needs to be integrated with the content system's calendaring component. There also need to be advanced features that ensure that the promotions are displayed to the appropriate external users.
3. *Customer and Consumer Management*: Management must determine the extent that they want external users to be able to personalize their ecommerce experience. Personalization, which will be discussed later in this chapter, involves the storage of user profiles and rule-based analysis. It also affects the overall design of the Web site.
4. *Service Improvement*: The information obtained from the use of the ecommerce system may need to be compared against other service indicators, both inside the company and across the industry. This means that the content system must have the appropriate reporting infrastructure to produce the information required. There also needs to be an understanding how that information will be compared to other

systems. The analyst does not want to implement the content system without first knowing what information is required by management on service responses.

Automated Security

Content management and workflow products should contain a sophisticated security system that automates the assignment of security levels based on the construction of the workflow roles and responsibilities. The primary security roles include system administrators, developers, analysts, business users and managers, ecommerce site members, and ecommerce site affiliates. Within each of these categories security is based on user authentication integrated with the operating system directory (such as Windows NT/2000), and user activities that govern policies particularly those that can control product access. As previously discussed, the most common security feature for the Internet is user authentication. Notwithstanding whether the security is focused on the Intranet or Internet, authentication is needed to identify users and map those users to their profiles and security policies.

Content management systems also support activity-based security control. This type of security allows business managers with the ability to define the types of activities that can be performed on a template or object. This means that when an object is produced, the developer can define whether it can be changed or deleted and how it can be displayed. Certain activity-based controls allow internal users, like a business manager, to define a set of policies for controlling how a product can be used. For example, a policy might dictate whether another user can access the image without approval from the business manager. In effect, activity-based controls can be used to store confidential information that is available only to authorized users. Furthermore, the mapping of users to activities is a very important capability of any content management product. This feature not only controls the content, but limits access to any Web page that contains that content. Thus, this feature integrates content and application security.

Database integration is yet another important component of security. Content management software should allow outside databases that contain security directories to be integrated with the activity-based control system. Having this level of integration allows companies with other application control systems to reuse them with other systems. This is typically accomplished by mapping the external database fields with the fields in the content management engine.

Personalization

Personalization is the process of keeping user profile information in the ecommerce system. User profiling allows ecommerce sites to store and track simple and complex values associated with a given user or group of users. These values can then be used to generate dynamic content when the user signs onto the system. Figure 16.7 shows the Amazon.com personalization format.

Typical user profile systems capture the name, country, email address and certain user-defined preferences, which can be used to greet the user as shown in Figure 16.7. It can also be used to display content in different languages without requiring the user to select the language they want each time they access the system. More advanced profiling can capture information over time and determine related user preferences and track past activities such as multiple shipping addresses. Content management systems provide pre-coded objects that can provide this type of functionality. Many of these products, such as Allaire, provide the end-user with links to favorite content or parts of a site thus allowing them to personalize the entire Web site configuration. This software effectively builds a special Web page for that specific user. A more advanced method is called rules-based personalization where information is created based on a more sophisticated set of stored rules for each individual or type of user. Rules can be dynamically added because the data is stored in a separate file. So, for example, if a new personalization screen was developed for buyers who spend over $500, a rule could be added to the rules file, which then would be enforced by the content system. Any user meeting this profile would automatically trigger the rule and thus see the special offering information during their browser session.

Figure 16.7 Dynamic personalization on Amazon.com.

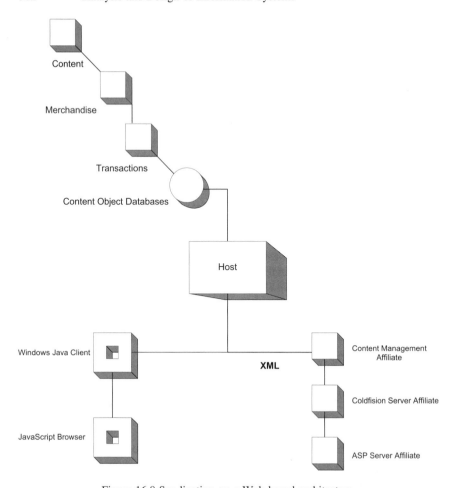

Figure 16.8 Syndication on a Web-based architecture.

While dynamic personalization offers tremendous capabilities, it also presents challenges. Content can only be as dynamic as the organization that supports it. The analyst must convey to management the overhead that is associated with supporting this type of ecommerce system. That is why having the analyst simultaneously create the corresponding workflows is so important to the setup of any content management product.

Syndication

Another important component that content systems provide for ecommerce systems is syndication services. Syndication is the function of integrating site affiliates with the ecommerce system. This means that business partners who exchange information or are part of product fulfillment can utilize all or parts of the ecommerce system. These affiliates are treated as limited Intranet users. Thus, the syndication architecture allows for site-to-site relationships to help drive the business. In today's complex business relationships, ecommerce partnerships are not unusual and integration of site features is a significant advantage. Most content systems treat site affiliates as just another group of users. However, syndication features provide a mechanism where site affiliates can link to the ecommerce system using remote site automation functions that allows the affiliate to actually use certain features of the ecommerce system. Thus, syndication allows Web systems to share and integrate specific functions as well as their corresponding databases. To attempt to automate such a system from scratch would be a very difficult challenge for developers. That is why content systems can be so attractive for the automation of these types of ecommerce activities.

Remote site automation must support multiple APIs (Application Program Interfaces) in order to provide true portability. This portability is important should other sites have different architectures. Truly open content architecture must support the following platforms and APIs:

1. Windows/Java Client
2. Javascript Browser
3. Coldfusion Server
4. Microsoft ASP Server
5. XML

Figure 16.8 shows the architecture for a syndication e-business system.

Automated Reporting

Content systems typically contain an administrative reporting function that can provide valuable information about who is accessing the ecommerce system, what Web pages users are visiting, how long users spend on the site, etc. These reports allow managers to assess the effectiveness of the ecommerce system. The infrastructure that provides this information is often implemented using a logging architecture that captures all user events, including detailed information about what screens and paths the user takes when they are on the system. Sophisticated content systems allow managers to specify what information they want to track, what level reports they need, and how often they need the information. Furthermore, content systems usually have a DSS infrastructure that allows managers to access the log database and query for information that might not be available in one of the standard reports supplied with the package. These query options support SQL-based logic and allow for export to other databases or applications.

Server Engine Technologies

There are two types of server engines that most content systems use: Macromedia's Coldfusion and Microsoft's Active Server Page (ASP). These technologies provide the internal server engines that drive the architecture for these products. The controversy over which engine best serves the needs of ecommerce systems is not clear. One significant difference between the two products, however, is that ASP can only operate on a Microsoft Windows server platform. This does not suggest that ASP cannot interface with other hardware platforms, but rather just limits the operation of the software on a Windows 2000 server. Essentially these server engines have built-in software that supports much of the functionality that has been discussed thus far in this chapter, including recording of ecommerce Web activities, integration, personalization, database interface, directory services, and email interface. These products also support various client configurations including mobile phones, Web services, hand-held devices, and of course PCs. Figure 16.9 shows the Coldfusion architecture.

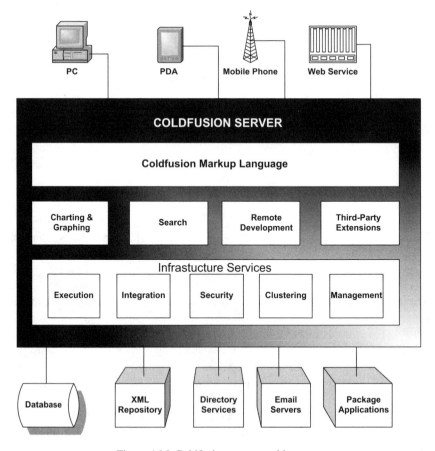

Figure 16.9 Coldfusion server architecture.

Feature	ASP	Cold Fusion	Comments
Syntax	Script-based, developer friendly, supports Visual Basic syntax	Tag-based, html author friendly. Support JavaScript style scripting as well	ASP supports multiple, extensible scripting languages. Cold Fusion tag syntax is simpler and easier to use.
Database Connectivity	Connectivity through ADO COM object-ODBC (Open Database Connectivity	Connectivity through tags-ODBC, has native drivers, OLE DB, ADO COM objects.	Cold Fusion tags are easier to use.
Data Manipulation	Direct, through ADO objects	Implicit through tag usage	ASP's recordset objects instead of tags is more flexible and powerful
Architecture	ISAPI filter	ISAPI, WSAPI, NSAPI filters and Apache	Cold Fusion runs on more servers
Extendibility	Server components can be created in any tool that produces COM objects	C++, API, or any COM objects. CORBA support	Cold Fusion can use all ASP components
Application Framework	Dynamic, using server side objects and event programming	Dynamic or static.	ASP is event based, CF is include –based.
Debugging	Error messages sent to browser upon runtime	Configurable debugging	Cold Fusion has better debugging.
Web Server Support	IIS only	Any CGI compliant Web server	Cold Fusion has an edge

Figure 16.10 Comparison of Coldfusion and ASP.

The use of content products that either use Coldfusion or ASP does create a certain level of proprietary activity in the architecture of the content system. There are differences in data manipulation, database connectivity, and syntax. Most of these proprietary features are invisible to developers and users. Figure 16.10 is a comparison between Coldfusion and ASP features.

XML Support

Most content systems have or will offer support for XML by providing conversion utilities that will automatically transfer text and graphics into the XML format. This feature allows content that has been created outside the content system to be easily imported into the content repository by simply converting it first into an XML document. This feature also allows for content objects that reside in the content system to be exported into a relational database so they can be incorporated into the entire back-end repository of data. This further supports the use of a content system as a central repository to transfer text and graphics among databases, legacy systems, and Web sites. It also allows for a better ecommerce system because information can be integrated with legacy information without replacing them.

Email and Push Technologies

Content systems have built-in engines that allow for messaging among users of the ecommerce system. This can be used to market new products and services, and obtain valuable feedback from customers and consumers. The push technology is quite sophisticated in that it allows users to be grouped into various different categories. These categories can be nested, meaning that the number of sub-categories is somewhat unlimited. Ultimately this means that the analyst must consider this interface when designing the user profile information that is captured to support Web personalization.

Another component of email and push technology is the support of chat rooms. Many content products have built-in chat room software that can allow users to share information. This may or may not be something that a business wants to do, but there are certainly operations that can benefit from users that can share information. The importance of having a chat room that is part of a content system should be obvious. The value of being able to capture certain parts of activity (this does not suggest violating any confidential conversations that might be allowed), and the sharing of this information among users could be a very powerful ecommerce feature.

Content Scheduling

I previously mentioned that most content systems provide the ability for content to be "calendarized," meaning that they can be automatically scheduled for loading and removal from the ecommerce system. While this feature is available, the analyst may need to develop a content schedule that assists business users in managing the status of their content. The content schedule is a detailed spreadsheet in which a business can monitor the progress of content development and activity across the system. In essence it represents an inventory of what content exists. The exact format of the content schedule will vary depending on the type of ecommerce system and the type of content being used. Figure 16.11

ID	Content Type	Content Owner	Source	Due Date	Status	File Name	Ecommerce Activity	Template
1.1	Text with Links	Marketing	Current Web site	9/15	In process	Xyz.doc	Marketing Sales	Main Page
1.2	Text	Production	Previous Web site		Inactive	WProd	Warehouse	
1.3	Text with Links	Shipping	Ship Request	Completed	Active	Ship.doc	Fulfillment	Orders

Figure 16.11 Content schedule example.

depicts a sample content schedule. Note that it contains active content, inactive content, and content in process.

Summary

The purpose of this chapter was to provide best practices for site architecture. The major emphasis was to implement a central content/workflow product that could help centralize many utility type functions required for all Web systems. As I have emphasized, the architecture is dependent heavily on how content is created, maintained, and stored. The following are some of the problems that analysts need to overcome to ensure that content systems are designed properly.

1. The value of spending money and time on investing in a content management facility is critical. Management does not always understand why content management systems are necessary or what they ultimately do for the firm. Good content management products can cost over $200,000.

2. Template design needs to occur early in the life cycle. If the analyst does not include template design in the interviews it may be too late to effectively implement them later. The message here is not to develop the content management templates without first understanding what the users need.

3. Content priority should be based on what the company feels is most critical, not always what customers and consumers want. This means that the analyst must be careful when gathering specifications from focus groups. Ultimately, the company must decide what they want to provide in an ecommerce system.

4. There needs to be an internal user organization to support the ownership of the content. It is important for users to understand that IT does not own the content responsibility, only the programming of it. Implementing a workflow process means establishing ownership positions for copywriting, editing, and approvals. This may require that some firms invest in skilled Web writers and a dedicated content manager to support the organization.

5. Content that needs to emanate from other departments or from third parties needs to be clarified and inherently part of the workflow process. The analyst may need to become the central person to coordinate where there are holes in the flow of content in the organization.

6. The design of search criteria on the Web must be accomplished in parallel to the design of content. Attempting to design search criteria after content has been finalized can be difficult if not impossible. This is particularly true with respect to XML documents that need to contain the proper tags so they can be categorized properly, especially when being stored in a relational database (see Chapter 8).

7. The development of the ecommerce system and the content management system require that content be defined first. Therefore, a content system should not be designed until all content analysis is completed. This means that the analyst needs to produce another document, which defines the content necessary for each Web page. Furthermore, he/she must be cognizant at all times that content can be treated as objects for reuse. The content management system becomes the equivalent repository for content object administration. The content system can store content either in a folder system or in a relational database.

8. It is important that the marketing department or the marketing effort be completed before using any content. Marketing efforts tend to be dynamic and change up until the last moment. Changing rules on how content is treated could be a setback in the development project.

9. The entire issue of content consistency is critical. This particularly addresses inconsistencies in writing and presentation. This issue further supports the need to have a centralized position that manages the writing of text, and the presentation of photos and other graphics material. The consistency of Web content becomes more difficult if the company is less centralized.

10. The legality of content must be addressed. This means that certain content needs to be reviewed and approved by a legal source. This approval should be clearly defined in the content life cycle and discussed with management so that the return of content occurs timely. Another productive approach to help legal approval is to get as much input from legal council as possible. I have found that many legal issues can be provided to users so that most of the content sent to legal has a high rate of approval. Issuing legal guidelines can be very effective.

11. It is important that the content for use by customers and consumers is user-friendly to them, not just the writers. Content writers and designers are not usually in touch with customers and consumers. Therefore they do not understand how customers and consumers think or how they make choices. Content effectiveness can be dramatically improved if writers participated in some of the JAD sessions and focus groups.

12. The turnaround of content changes is slow and not in accordance with the Web site schedules. Content writers are usually divorced from the rest of the organization, particularly the IT staff. Content writer schedules must be planned and managed as part of the Web schedule.

13. There needs to be a sophisticated system that assigns numbers or values to content. Content managers should not rely on the content management software to identify what the content means to the business. Failure to do this will result in a system where all content can be found, but few content managers know what it represents. This is particularly important when tracking multiple versions of the same content.

14. Web content needs to be reviewed after it is populated on the Web site and before it is published. This means that the analyst should have a

system that allows content to be viewed on a staged system prior to being rolled in a live environment. This can get complicated when using an automated update scheduling system, since the updates go directly to the production system. There are two solutions to this dilemma. First, the updates could be initially rolled to a staged system, reviewed, and then moved to the production server. While this adds another step, it is a safe way to go. It also requires that there is always someone available to approve the content. Second, the updates can be done directly to the production system, but must be reviewed immediately. This requires that updates are made in the morning or at night, and that there are support personnel available at those times.

15. Prototypes must be shown to users with their content included. To demonstrate a prototype without content has no real value.

16. There is a need for audit trail of how customer and consumer requests get resolved and recorded in the e-business system. I have seen too many designs that do not walk through the process of user resolution and end up with unhappy external users who have unresolved issues.

17. All departmental interfaces must be clarified as they relate to fulfilling a user request. If this is not done, orders that require manual intervention will get lost.

18. The process of Web branding and identity must be simplified. Web sites typically cannot get finalized unless the image of the business is clear and simple.

19. There needs to be a constant communication between marketing activities and Web design activities. Too often market personnel are working on campaigns that have not been discussed with ecommerce support staff. New marketing content tends to get thrown at Webmasters without enough prior notice and planning.

20. Product rules must be clear, especially in terms of how they are purchased, their price, and shipping criteria.

17
Concepts of ISO 9000

Developing a System of Procedures

Perhaps one of the most significant challenges in analysis today is its role in the software life cycle. There has been much criticism of the lack of discipline applied to software development projects and personnel in general, and we continue to be an industry that has a poor reputation for delivering quality products on schedule. Although many organizations have procedures, few really follow them and fewer still have any means of measuring the quality and productivity of software development. A system of procedures should first be developed prior to implementing a life cycle that can ensure its adherence to the procedure. These procedures also need to be measured on an ongoing basis. This book restricts its focus to the set of procedures that should be employed in the analysis and design functions.

The process of developing measurable procedures in an organization must start with the people who will be part of its implementation. Standard procedures should not be created by upper management, as the steps will be viewed as a control mechanism as opposed to a quality implementation. How then do we get the implementors to create the standards? When examining this question, one must look at other professions and see how they implement their standards. The first main difference between computer professionals and members of many other professions is they lack a governing standards board like the American Medical Association (AMA) or the American Institute of Certified Public Accountants (AICPA). Unfortunately, as mentioned in previous chapters, it seems unlikely that any such governing board will exist in the near future. Looking more closely at this issue, however, we need to examine the ultimate value of a governing board. What standards boards really accomplish is to build the moral and professional responsibilities of their trade. Accountants, attorneys and doctors look upon themselves as professionals who have such responsibilities. This is not to imply that governing boards can resolve every problem, but at least they can help. With or without the existence of a standards board, analysts within an organization must develop the belief that they belong to a profession. Once this identification occurs, analysts can create the procedures necessary to ensure the quality of their own profession. Currently, few analysts view themselves as part of a profession.

If analysts can create this level of self-actualization, then the group can begin the process of developing quality procedures that can be measured for future improvement. The standard procedures should be governed by the group itself and the processes integrated into the software life cycle of the organization. In fact, analysts should encourage other departments to follow the same procedures for implementing their respective quality procedures.

Although not typically required, many firms employ ISO 9000 as a formal vehicle to implement the development of measurable procedures. ISO 9000 stands for the International Organization for Standardization, an organization formed in 1947 and based in Geneva. As of this writing, 91 member countries are associated with it. ISO 9000 was founded to establish international quality assurance standards focused on processes rather than on products.

Why ISO 9000?

ISO 9000 offers a method of establishing agreed-upon quality levels through standard procedures in the production of goods and services. Many international companies require that their vendors be ISO 9000 compliant through the certification process. Certification requires an audit by an independent firm that specializes in ISO 9000 compliance. The certification is good for three years. Apart from the issue of certification, the benefits of ISO 9000 lie in its basis for building a quality program through employee empowerment. It also achieves and sustains specific quality levels and provides consistency in its application. ISO 9000 has a number of subcomponents. ISO 9001, 9002, and 9003 codify the software development process. In particular, 9001 affects the role of the analyst by requiring standards for design specifications and defines 20 different categories of systems. Essentially, ISO 9000 requires three basic things:

1. Say what you do.
2. Do what you say.
3. Prove it.

This means that the analyst needs to completely document what should occur during the requirements process to ensure quality. After these procedures are documented, the analyst needs to start implementing them based on the standards developed and agreed upon by the organization. The process must be self-documenting; that is, it must contain various control points that can prove at any time that a quality step in the process was not only completed but done within the quality standard established by the organization. It is important to recognize that ISO 9000 does not establish what the standard should be but rather that the organization can comply with whatever standards it chooses to employ. This freedom is what makes ISO 9000 so attractive. Even if the organization does not opt to go through with the audit, it can still establish an honorable quality infrastructure that:

- creates an environment of professional involvement, commitment and accountability,
- allows for professional freedom to document the realities of the process itself within reasonable quality measurements,
- pushes down the responsibilities of quality to the implementor as opposed to the executive,
- identifies where the analyst fits in the scope of the software life cycle,
- locates existing procedural flaws,
- eliminates duplication of efforts,
- closes the gap between required procedures and actual practices,
- complements the other quality programs that might exist,
- requires that the individuals participating in the process be qualified within their defined job descriptions.

How to Incorporate ISO 9000 into Existing Software Life Cycles

The question now is how to incorporate an ISO 9000-type process for the analyst function and incorporate it into the existing software life cycle. Listed below are the essential 9 steps to follow:

1. Create and document all the quality procedures for the analyst.
2. Follow these processes throughout the organization and see how they enter and leave the analyst function.
3. Maintain records which support the procedures.
4. Ensure that all professionals understand and endorse the quality policy.
5. Verify that there are no missing processes.
6. Changes or modifications to the procedures must be systematically reviewed and controlled.
7. Have control over all documentation within the process.
8. Ensure that analysts are trained and that records are kept about their training.
9. Ensure that constant review is carried out by the organization or through third party audits.

In order for ISO 9000 guidelines to be implemented, it is recommended that the analyst initially provide a *work-flow diagram* of the quality process (see Figure 17.1).

Figure 17.1 reflects some of the steps an analyst must perform in a quality process. Note that certain steps reflect that there is an actual form that needs to be completed in order to confirm the step's completion. Figure 17.2 illustrates document AN0010; Figure 17.3 shows AN0050; and Figure 17.4 displays AN0160.

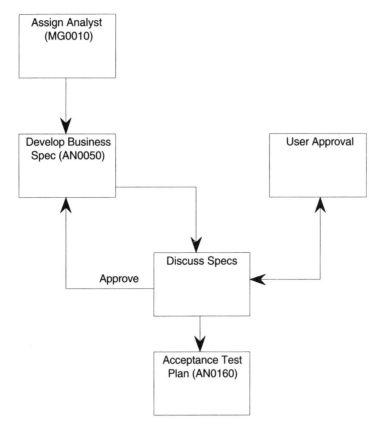

Figure 17.1 A sample work-flow diagram.

These forms confirm the activities in the quality work-flow process outlined by the analyst. At any time during the life cycle, an event can be confirmed by looking at the completed form.

In order to comply with the documentation standards, each form should contain an instruction sheet, as shown in Figure 17.5. This sheet will ensure that users have the appropriate instructions. Confirmation documents can be implemented in different ways. Obviously if forms are processed manually, the documentation will contain the actual storage of working papers by project. Such working papers are typically filed in a documentation storage room similar to a library where the original contents are secure and controlled. Access to the documentation is allowed, but must be authorized and recorded. Sometimes forms are put together using a word-processing package such as Microsoft Word. The blank forms are stored on a central library so that master documents can be accessed by the analyst via a network. Once the forms are completed, they can be stored in a project directory. The most sophisticated method of implementing ISO 9000 is to use a Lotus Notes electronic filing system. Here, forms are filled

Project Status Report

Period Ending: / / :

Date:	**Project:** **Date Delivered To Users:**	**Analyst:**

Previous Objectives:

Objective	Previous Target Date	Act Completion Date or Status

New Project Objectives:

Objective	Target Date Start	Target Date Complete

Financial Performance:	Budget	Actual	% Remaining

\AN0010 Rev. 3/21/94

Figure 17.2 ISO 9000 Project Status Report.

out and passed to the appropriate individuals automatically. The confirmation documents then become an inherent part of the original work flow. In any event, these types of forms implementation affect only automation, not the concept of ISO 9000 as a whole.

Interfacing IT Personnel

We mentioned earlier that ISO 9000 requires qualified personnel. This means that the organization must provide detailed information about the skill set requirements for each job function. Most organizations typically have job descriptions

Figure 17.3 ISO 9000 Analysis Acknowledgment form.

that are not very detailed and tend to be vague with respect to the specific requirements of the job. In addition, job descriptions rarely provide information that can be used to measure true performance. Questions such as "How many lines of code should a programmer generate per day?" cannot be measured effectively. There is also a question about whether lines of code should be the basis of measurement at all. A solution to this dilemma is to create a *job description matrix*, which provides the specific details of each job responsibility along with the necessary measurement criteria for performance (see Figure 17.6).

Figure 17.4 Quality Assurance Test Plan (AN0160).

Name: **Confirmation/Service Acknowledgment**	**Date Issued: 3/8/94**
Form Instructions	**Supersedes:**
	Revision: 1.00

The purpose of this form is to track the status of various services such as Requirements Definition, Conceptual Detail Design, Development, System Tested Enhancements, and User Accepted Enhancements.

The appropriate project # must be attached. The type of form must be checked for each type of Confirmation.

\an0050i Rev 3/8/94

Figure 17.5 An ISO 9000 form instruction page.

The document in Figure 17.6 is a matrix of responsibilities for an analyst. Note that the analyst has a number of efficiency requirements within the managing engagements (projects) responsibility. Efficiency here means that the analyst must perform the task at a certain indicated level to be considered productive at that task. To a degree, efficiency typically establishes the time constraints to deliver the task. Measurement defines the method used to determine whether the efficiency was met. Reports are simply the vehicle through which the analyst proves that the task was completed and on what basis.

The job description matrix represents a subset of the entire job description that focuses strictly on the procedural and process aspects of the individual's position. It not only satisfies ISO 9000, but represents a healthier way of measuring

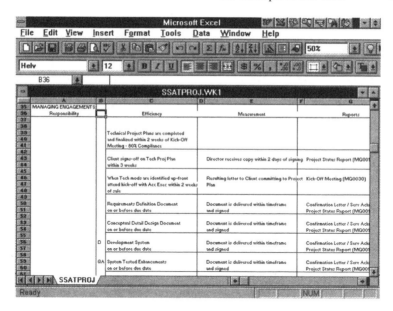

Figure 17.6 Job description matrix.

individual performance in an IT environment. Most individuals should know their exact performance at any time during the review period. Furthermore, the matrix is an easy tool to use for updating new or changed performance tasks.

Committing to ISO 9000

We have outlined the sequential steps to implement an ISO 9000 organization. Unfortunately, the outline does not ensure success, and often just following the suggested steps leads to another software life cycle that nobody really adheres to. In order to be successful, a more strategic commitment must be made. Let's outline these guidelines for the analyst functions:

- A team of analysts should meet to form the governing body that will establish the procedures to follow to reach an ISO 9000 level (this does not necessarily require that certification be accomplished).
- The ISO 9000 team should develop a budget of the milestones to be reached and the time commitments that are required. It is advisable that the budget be forecasted like a project, probably using a Gantt chart to develop the milestones and time-frames.
- The ISO 9000 team should then communicate their objectives to the remaining analysts in the organization and coordinate a review session so that the entire organization can understand the benefits, constraints and scope of the activity. It is also an opportunity to allow everyone

to voice their opinions about how to complete the project. Therefore, the meeting should result in the final schedule for completing the ISO 9000 objective.

- The ISO 9000 team should inform the other IT groups of its objectives, although analysts should be careful not to provoke a political confrontation with other parts of the IT staff. The communication should be limited to helping other departments understand how these analyst quality standards will interface with the entire software life cycle.

- The work flows for the analyst tasks must be completed in accordance with the schedule such that everyone can agree to the confirmation steps necessary to validate each task. It is important that the ISO 9000 processes allow for a percentage of success. This means that not every process must be successful 100 % of the time, but rather can be acceptable within some fault tolerance level. For example, suppose that the analyst must have a follow-up meeting with the users within 48 hours after a previous step has been completed. It may not be realistic to meet this goal every time such a meeting is necessary. After all, the analyst cannot always force users to attend meetings in a timely way. Therefore, the ISO 9000 step may view this task as successful if it occurs within the 48 hours 80 % of the time, that is, within a 20 % fault tolerance.

- All task steps must have verification. This will require that standard forms be developed to confirm completion. While we have shown samples of these forms earlier, the ISO 9000 team should beware of producing an unwieldy process involving too many forms. Many software life cycles have suffered the consequences of establishing too many checkpoints. Remember, ISO 9000 is a professional's standard and should cater to the needs of well-trained professionals. Therefore, the ISO 9000 team should review the initial confirmation forms and begin the process of combining them into a smaller subset. That is, the final forms should be designed to be as generic as possible by confirming multiple tasks.

- There should be meetings held with the analysis group that focus on the alternatives for automating the confirmation forms as outlined earlier in this chapter. It is advisable that this topic be confirmed by the group since their full cooperation is needed for the success of the program.

- Allow time for changing the procedures and the forms. Your first effort will not be the final one; therefore, the ISO 9000 team must plan to meet and review the changes necessary to make it work. Analysts should be aware that the opportunity for change always exists as long as it conforms to the essential objectives of ISO 9000.

- The ISO 9000 project should be at least a one-year plan, from inception of the schedule to actual fulfillment of the processes. In fact, an organization must demonstrate ISO 9000 for at least 18 months prior to being eligible for certification.

- The ISO 9000 group needs to be prepared and authorized to make changes to the job description of the analyst. This may require the submission of requests and authorizations to the executive management team or the human resources department. It is important not to overlook this step since an inability to change the organization structure could hinder the success of the ISO 9000 implementation.

As we can see from the above steps, establishing an ISO 9000 group is a significant commitment. However, its benefits can include a professional organization that controls its own quality standards. These standards can be changed on an ongoing basis to ensure compliance with the business objectives and requirements of the enterprise. Certification, while not the focus of our discussion, is clearly another level to achieve. Most companies that pursue certification do so for marketing advantage or are required to obtain it by their customers. Implementing ISO 9000 should not require that the entire company conform at once; in fact it is almost an advantage to implement it in a phased approach, department by department. The potential benefits of ISO 9000 concepts may fill the void in many of the IT organizations which lack clearly defined quality standards.

Problems and Exercises

1. Explain why ISO 9000 represents a system of procedures.
2. What are the three fundamental things that ISO 9000 tries to establish?
3. What are the overall benefits of ISO 9000?
4. How is ISO 9000 incorporated into the life cycle?
5. Why are work flows the most critical aspect of developing the ISO 9000 model?
6. Why are forms used in ISO 9000?
7. How are personnel affected by ISO 9000?
8. What is a job description matrix?
9. What steps are necessary for an organization to adopt ISO 9000?
10. Does ISO 9000 need to be implemented in all areas of the business? Explain.

Appendix A
Case Study: The Rainforest Book Company Problem

The following four events are services provided by the Rainforest Book Company:

Event I

A customer wishes to set up an account to purchase books. The Sales Department at the Rainforest Book Company receives the request and sends out a blank Account Request form. The form has space for the following information:

    Customer Name
    Customer Address
    Customer Phone Number
    Customer Fax Number
    Credit Card Information (if applicable)
    Credit Card Number
    Type of Credit Card
    Expiration Date
    Cardholder's Name
    ZIP or postal code of the billing address for this card

The customer sends back a completed Account Request form. The "for office use only" section is filled out by the Sales Group. This information includes the processor's identification, the date the account is opened, and a customer account number that is assigned. The customer account file is updated, and the Account Request form is filed. The Account Processing Department receives notification of the new account and sends the customer a confirmation letter. This letter notifies the customer of their customer account number. This number can be used to expedite the ordering process.

Event II

A customer makes a book inquiry. The customer can request a book by giving any of the following information: (book title and book author) or ISBN number.

The Sales Department first verifies that the customer has a valid account. If the book is found based upon the information that was given, the customer receives the following information about the book:

Title of the book
Author of the book
Paperback/Hardcover
Price
Date Published
Availability
Reviews

If the book is not available in stock, all of the above information is returned and an out-of-stock notice is sent specifying the approximate date the book will be in stock. If the book is no longer in print and has been discontinued, an out-of-print notice is sent to the customer. This out-of-print notice includes a list of Used Book Stores in the customer's country.

Event III

A customer decides to purchase books, places the order for the books, and requests a book order form from the Sales Department. A blank book order form is forwarded to the customer. The customer account number and the date the order is being placed is entered. The following information is included in the book order:

Customer Account Number
Date Order is placed
Title of the Book
Author
Paperback or Hardcover
ISBN, if available

In addition, the customer indicates the shipping option by entering the following information:

Standard Shipping or
Second Day Air or
Next Day Air

Placed orders are sent to the warehouse, and the customer account file is updated. The warehouse issues an order confirmation when the books are shipped. The invoice is generated and then sent to the customer. The customer then sends the invoice slip and a payment or authorizes the use of a credit card on file to the Accounting Department. The Accounting Department processes the payment and updates the customer account.

Event IV

The Sales Department generates a monthly sales report and forwards it to Management.

Assignment

1. Create DFDs for the four events.
2. Decompose the four top-level DFDs into their respective functional primitives.
3. Create the data dictionary entries for all the named data flows found in the child diagrams from (2). The entries in the resulting data dictionary should be reported in alphabetical order.
4. Write process specifications for all of the functional primitives from (2).

Case Study created by Cynthia Hernandez.

Appendix B
Case Study: The CGT Rental Service Problem

The following five events represent the services provided by the the CGT rental agency:

I. Events

1. Potential renters call CGT and ask them if apartments are available for either beachfront or mountainside views. All callers have their information recorded and stored in an information folder. The most important information for CGT to obtain is the caller's maximum monthly rent limit.
2. CGT examines their database and searches for potential matches on the properties requested.
3. People call the agency to inform them that they have an apartment for rent. The agency only deals with rentals for beach fronts and mountain sides. All other calls are forwarded to their sister organization that handles other requests.
4. Fifteen days before rent is due, CGT sends renters their monthly invoices.
5. Sixty days before the lease is up, CGT sends out a notice for renewal to the renter.

II. High Level Data Elements

The following data elements should be broken down to their elementary level and added, if necessary.

Renter Name
Renter Address
Renter Phone Number
Maximum Monthly Rent
Rental Property
Rental Monthly Rent
Rental Number Bedrooms

Rental Dates
Rental Owner Information
Rental Number of Blocks from Beach
Rental Beach Side
Rental Mountain Range
Rental Mountain Ski Area
Rental Mountain Lake Site

III. Assignment

1. Draw the Data Flow Diagrams (DFD) at the Functional Primitive level.
2. From the DFD perform Logical Data Modeling and show 1st, 2nd and 3rd Normal Forms.
3. Draw the final ERD.
4. Produce a CRUD diagram.
5. What does the CRUD diagram show us?

Appendix C
Case Study: The Collection Agency Problem

I. Background

Statement of Purpose

The purpose of the ABC organization is to process customer payments on credit cards. ABC processes these payments for banks and other financial institutions. Currently, the operation is done manually, and you have been called in as a consultant to do the analysis for an automated system.

The Event List

During your analysis, you have met with departments and determined that there are essentially 8 events as follows:

Event 1

Mary gets a delivery of mail every morning from a messenger who picks up the mail at the local Post Office. Mary starts her day by opening and processing the mail. There are, however, a number of types of information contained in an envelope:

1. A check with a payment form
2. Cash only
3. Check only
4. Cash with a payment form
5. Payment form only

Note: All of the above can sometimes be accompanied with correspondence from the customer.

The information on the payment form is necessary to process the payment. The payment form is shown on Attachment I.

Mary fills in the "FOR OFFICE USE ONLY" portion and sends the Payment Form and cash/check to Joe, the Bookkeeper. Correspondence is forwarded to the Support Dept (including forms with no payment).

Payments made without a form are sent to Janet in the Research Department.

ATTACHMENT I
PAYMENT FORM

DATE INVOICED: _/_/_   PERIOD COVERED: _/_/_ TO_/_/_

ACCOUNT NO.:_____(30/NUMERIC)

NAME:_____(30/ALPHANUMERIC)

ADDRESS:_____(30/ALPHANUMERIC)

_____(30/ALPHANUMERIC)

STATE:____(SELF-DEFINING) CITY:_____(15/ALPHANUMERIC)

ZIPCODE:_____(9/NUMERIC)

____ADDRESS CORRECTION (Y/BLANK)

===

(A)   (B)   (C)

PREVIOUS   BAL:$____.__   NEW   PURCH:$____.__

PAYMENTS:$____.__

OUTSTANDING BALANCE:$_____.___(A+B-C)

MINIMUM PAYMENT DUE:$_____.___

PAST AMOUNT DUE: $_____.___

PAYMENT DUE THIS PERIOD: $_____.___

AMOUNT ENCLOSED: $_____.___

===

FOR OFFICE USE ONLY

OPERATOR CODE:____(4/NUMERIC)

DATE RECEIVED: _/_/_   AMOUNT PAID:$_____.___

CORRESPONDENCE:____(Y/N)   CASH:____(Y/N)

Event 2

Janet receives payments from Mary and begins a process of looking up the information that the customer has provided. This can typically include Name, Address, etc. If the customer account number is located, Janet fills out a blank Payment Form to substitute for the original and forwards the form and the check to Joe, the Bookkeeper. If the account number is not found, a substitute Payment Form is still developed with whatever information is available. These payments are also forwarded to Joe in bookkeeping.

Event 3

The Support Department receives the correspondence from Mary. The correspondence requires written response. Correspondence falls into 4 categories:

1. An error in the outstanding balance or address of a customer. This will require support to fill out a balance correction form (Attachment II). This Form is forwarded to the Correction Dept.
2. A complaint about service. The complaint is researched and a written response is sent to the customer. A monthly summary report of customers with complaints is also forwarded to the department manager.
3. A client default request, stating that the customer cannot pay due to a hardship. The Technician will send the customer a request for default form (Attachment III).
4. A request for default form (3) is received for processing. These are sent to the Correction Department.

Event 4

Joe, the bookkeeper receives payments. Payments are posted to the account master ledger. A deposit slip is prepared for identified account payments. Unknown account payments are deposited into a separate bank account called "Unapplied Payments." The payment forms are filed by account number. A daily report of payments by customer (including unapplied payments) is produced.

Event 5

The Correction Department receives balance correction forms or requests for default notices; the appropriate adjustments are made to the account master ledger. The forms are filed by type and account number. A daily and monthly report of adjustments is produced.

ATTACHMENT II
BALANCE CORRECTION FORM

DATE:_/_/_

SUPPORT TECHNICIAN:_____(30/ALPHANUMERIC)

ACCOUNT NO.:_____(30/NUMERIC)

___ADDRESS CORRECTION (Y/BLANK)

NAME:_____(30/ALPHANUMERIC)

ADDRESS:_____(30/ALPHANUMERIC)

_____(30/ALPHANUMERIC)

STATE:___(SELF-DEFINING) CITY:_____(15/ALPHANUMERIC)

ZIPCODE:_____(9/NUMERIC)

==
CURRENT BALANCE:$_____.___ (A)

ADJUSTMENT AMT:$_____.___ (B)

NEW BALANCE:$_____.___ (A+/−B)

==
AUTHORIZATION CODE:_____(10/NUMERIC)

SUPERVISOR NO:_____(8/NUMERIC)

SIGNATURE:_____

Event 6

The department manager receives the monthly complaint report. After analyzing the information, a summary report is produced by Complaint Type (e.g., unhappy with service, credit card problem, and wrong outstanding balance) and the department manager issues a report to management. A quarterly client survey questionnaire on service is sent to customers. This report includes statistics on client satisfaction which resulted from the previous questionnaire.

ATTACHMENT III
REQUEST FOR DEFAULT

DATE:__/__/__

SUPPORT   TECHNICIAN: _____(30/ALPHANU-
MERIC)

ACCOUNT NO.:_____(30/NUMERIC)

NAME:_____(30/ALPHANUMERIC)

ADDRESS:_____(30/ALPHANUMERIC)

_____(30/ALPHANUMERIC)

STATE:____(SELF-DEFINING) CITY:_____(15/ALPHANUMERIC)

ZIPCODE:_____(9/NUMERIC)

==
REASON FOR DEFAULT
(CHECK ONE)

1.   ____ DEATH (ATTACH DEATH CERTIFICATE) NO PAYMENT
      REQUIRED
2.   ____ BANKRUPTCY (ATTACH LEGAL DOCUMENT) 180 DAY
      TERMS
3.   ____ REQUEST FOR NEW PAYMENT TERMS 60 OR 90 DAY
      TERMS

==
FOR OFFICE USE ONLY

OPERATOR CODE:____(4/NUMERIC)

DATE RECEIVED:__/__/__ ACTION CODE:___(1/2/3)

Event 7

Joe, the bookkeeper, receives bounced checks from the bank. He fills out a
balance correction form and forwards it to the Correction Department such that
the outstanding balance can be corrected. Joe sends a bounced check letter to the
customer requesting another check plus a $15.00 penalty (this is now included
as part of the outstanding balance). Checks are never re-deposited.

Event 8

Joe, the bookkeeper, issues a weekly update report on the balance of each account where there was a transaction during that week.

II. Assignment

1. Based on the above statement of purpose and event list, develop preliminary data flow diagrams (DFDs) on a separate sheet for each event.
2. Level each DFD to at least three levels. Functional primitives must be accompanied by a process specification (using psuedocode).
3. Develop the ERD in 3rd normal form.
4. Develop the data dictionary entries from the DFDs, ERDs, process specifications or other data elements. Your data dictionary should be in alphabetical order and reduced to the elementary data element level.
5. Create a CRUD diagram.
6. Map the DFD, ERDs and CRUD to an object diagram.

Appendix D
Case Study: The Mobile Telephone Company Problem

A Global System for Mobile communications (GSM) cellular telephone company provides wireless telephone equipment and services for customers. GSM telephones are packaged for sale in the form of a "pre-sale-distribution-kit" at the company's product assembly center. Each kit consists primarily of a Telephone Handset and a SIM card. (A "Subscriber Identity Module" is a credit card-like device that is inserted into digital cellular phones and identifies each customer to the telephone system.) The telephone handset manufacturer assigns each and every handset a unique International Mobile-communications Equipment Identifier (IMEI) number.

An individual may own more than one SIM, but must own at least one SIM to be considered a Customer. A customer may own more than one telephone handset; however, handset ownership is not a requisite. The SIM is interchangeable among the various handset models sold by the company. (In practice, nearly all customers own at least one telephone handset. Following the initial sale, some customers chose to "upgrade" their handset to a smaller, lighter, more functional model.)

In the back office, the company maintains an inventory of available, yet unassigned, telephone numbers. To make the technological leap from wired-telephone-number to wireless-telephone-number, each conventional Telephone Number is assigned to a Mobil Identification Number (MIN). Each unique MIN will ultimately be associated with a specific customer's SIM card when a new account is activated. A unique International Mobile SIM Identifier (IMSI) number identifies each SIM.

For billing purposes, the company maintains a record of each Call Delivery Notification (CDN) event. The unique identifier for the CDN is a concatenation of the CDN_id + IMSI.

Assignment

Using the crow's-foot notation method, prepare an Entity Relation Diagram (ERD) based on the following business case. Provide only the primary key(s) (PK) and foreign key pointers (FK) for each entity, as needed. Do not include other attributes.
Case Study created by Greg Vimont.

Appendix E
Case Study: Northwest General Practitioner's Office

The following represents information obtained during an interview with the Northwest General Practitioner's office:

Potential patients contact the Northwest General Practitioner's office to make appointments to see a General Practitioner. All patient information is stored in a patient medical history folder.

The patient must provide the following information:

Name
Social Security Number
Address
Home Telephone Number
Work or Mobile Telephone Number
Insurance Provider Name
Insurance Provider ID
Name of Primary Insurance Holder
Reason for Visit
Medical History
Family Medical History
List of Allergies

The office examines the patient medical history file and tries to make an appointment for the patient to see the General Practitioner the patient has specified as his/her "preferred" doctor. If the patient's preference is not available at the time the patient requests for the appointment, then the office provides the patient with a list of practitioners who are available at that time.

Additionally, practitioners join the Northwest General Practitioner's office every day. Their information is stored in a practitioner's information folder.

A new practitioner must provide the following information:

Name
Social Security Number
Address
Home Telephone Number
Work or Mobile Telephone Number
Specialty (or list of specialties), if applicable
Hospital Affiliations, if applicable

Seven days before patients are due to come in for their appointments, the office begins to send reminder notices to them. There are three reminder notices sent. The first is sent seven days beforehand, the second is sent three days beforehand, and the third reminder takes place one day beforehand, via an automated phone call.

For those patients who are billed for services, a notice is mailed to them 30 days before payment is due.

Assignment:

- Draw one data flow diagram depicting the logical equivalent for the above business process description.
- Level the diagram to its functional primitives.
- To the best of your ability, provide the data elements you will need for your data entities. **NOTE:** Pay particular attention to the patient medical history file, the physician information file, any file that keeps track of appointments, and, for extra credit, the invoice file.
- Create an entity relational diagram depicting the relationship between your tables. **NOTE:** You should end up with at least eight entities, if not more.

Case Study created by Melanie Caffrey

Appendix F
Case Study: University Student Enrollment Database

The following enrollment form has been obtained from Southeast University's Computer Science program:

Student Enrollment Form

Last Name: _____
First Name: _____
Social Security Number: _____
Address Line 1: _____
Address Line 2: _____
City: _____
State: _____
Zip Code _____

Course #	**Section #**	**Course Cost**
_____	_____	_____
_____	_____	_____
_____	_____	_____
_____	_____	_____

Total Amount Due: _____

The students are choosing their courses from the following Course List:

Course #	Course Name	Section #	Section Time	Course Cost
QC2500	Intro to Programming	1	9:00 A.M.	800.00
		2	10:30 A.M.	800.00
		3	3:15 P.M.	800.00
		4	6:00 P.M.	800.00
QC2625	Intro to Analysis	1	11:00 P.M.	910.00
		2	4:00 P.M.	910.00
		3	5:30 P.M.	910.00
QC2790	Intro to Web Design	1	12:45 P.M.	725.00
		2	2:30 P.M.	725.00
		3	6:00 P.M.	725.00

Assignment: Using the above form, create a normalized ERD. Make sure you are in 3rd normal form.

HINT: You should end up with at least four entities, possibly five.

Case Study created by Melanie Caffrey

Glossary

Abstract object An object that is not at the lowest level in a class. Abstract objects are not executed directly.

Acceptance test plans Set of tests that, if passed will establish that the software can be used in production.

Alternate key An attribute that uniquely identifies a row of occurrence in an entity. An alternate key cannot be the primary key.

Application server The middle tier of the three-tier client/server architecture. The application server contains common programs that are available to frontend workstation computers.

Attribute A component of an entity or object. An attribute may or may not be an elementary data element.

Back-end server The top level of a tiered architecture. This tier usually houses databases that are required to support applications.

Border Also known as a "frame," defines the boundary of a window view.

Business process reengineering (BPR) A method to redesign existing applications.

Business specification A document that reflects the overall requirements of a process or system written in a prose format. The focus of the business specification is to provide the user with enough information so they can authorize the development of the technical requirements.

Cascading Multiple iterations of subtypes. A subtype entity within a subtype. A subtype that cascades is also a supertype to its cascading subtypes.

CASE (Computer-Aided Software Engineering) Products used to automate and implement modeling tools and data repositories.

Case A format for developing application logic in a process specification.

Character-based screens Support only keyboard-driven data entry. Icons and graphical symbols facilitated through the use of a mouse are not supported (or required).

Class A group of objects that have similar attributes and methods and typically have been put together to perform specific tasks.

Client An application that requests services from applications.

Cohesion The measurement of an application's self-dependence.

Concrete object The lowest-level object in a class.

Control bar Represents an array of choices and commands that need to be viewed in an accessible area of the screen and are maintained in the display area. Examples include button bars, color or pattern palettes, toolbars, rulers, and ribbons.

Coupling The measurement of an application's dependency on another application.

Crow's foot A method of showing the relationship of association between two entities.

CRUD diagram An association matrix that matches the types of data access between entities and processes. CRUD represents *c*reate, *r*ead, *u*pdate, and *d*elete.

Data dictionary (DD) A dictionary that defines data. A component of the data repository.

Data flow Component of a data flow diagram that represents data entering or leaving a process, external, or data store.

Data flow diagram (DFD) A tool that shows how data enter and leave a process. A data flow diagram has four possible components: data flow, data store, external, and process.

Data replication The process that copies data from one file to another, ensuring that all copies are synchronized with each other.

Data repository A robust data dictionary that contains information relating to data element behavior.

Data store Component of a data flow diagram that represents data that can be accessed from a particular area or file. A data store is sometimes call "data-arrest."

Data synchronization The process of ensuring that copies of the same data are equivalent.

Data warehousing A de-normalized database created to focus on decision support activities. Data warehouses hold historical information and cannot be used to update data.

Dynamic line library (DLL) An area that stores the active version of an object. Object classes are formed from DLLs at execution time.

Elementary data element A functionally decomposed data element.

Encapsulation Attributes of an object that can be accessed only through the object's methods.

Entity An object of interest about which data can be collected. Entities can consume a number of attributes.

Entity relational diagram (ERD) A diagram that depicts the relationships among the stored data.

Executive sponsor An individual at an executive level who has responsibility for a business area. The executive sponsor is a defined role in JAD sessions.

External Component of a data flow diagram that represents a provider or user of data that is not part of the system. Externals are therefore boundaries of the system.

Facilitator An impartial individual responsible for controlling the flow of JAD sessions.

Firewall A network component, usually in the form of a server, that provides access security to the network. Security is accomplished by the firewall's ability to validate data packets that attempt to enter the network.

Front-end client Workstations that function within a client/server architecture. Workstations are typically microcomputers running an operating system; however, a client can also be a dumb terminal.

Functional decomposition The process for finding the most basic parts of a system.

Functional overview A subset view of a specification. The subset usually covers a particular function of the system.

Functional primitive A functionally decomposed data flow diagram.

Gantt chart A tool that depicts progress of tasks against time. The chart was developed by Henry L. Gantt in 1917.

Graphical user interface (GUI) A screen interface that adopts the use of icons and symbols to represent functions that a user can implement.

HTTP (hypertext transfer protocol) A standard format for publishing information in a hypertext format known as HTML.

Inheritance The process by which child objects effectively retain all of the capabilities of their parents. Inheritance is implemented using an inverted tree structure.

Instantiation Independent executions of the same class.

Internet A cooperative message-forwarding system that links computer networks all over the world.[32]

Internet/Intranet development Application that operates within a browser product such as Netscape or Internet Explorer.

Intranet A network confined to a single organization or unit.[33]

ISO 9000 International Organization for Standardization, quality standard 9000.

Job description matrix The portion of an individual's job description that focuses strictly on the procedural and process aspects of the individual's position.

Joint application development (JAD) A method of developing the requirements for a system by focusing on group sessions. The sessions are typically under the direction of a facilitator.

Key An attribute of an entry or database that uniquely identifies a row, occurrence, or record.

---

[32] Douglas Downing, Michael Covington, and Melody Mauldin Covington, *Dictionary of Computer and Internet Terms*, 6th ed., Barron's Educational Series, Inc., p. 239.
[33] Douglas Downing, Michael Covington, and Melody Mauldin Covington, *Dictionary of Computer and Internet Terms*, 6th ed., Barron's Educational Series, Inc., p. 242.

Key business rules Business rules of key attributes that are enforced at the database level (as opposed to the application level).

Legacy system An existing automated system.

Leveling Functional decomposition of a data flow diagram. Each decomposition is called a "level."

LINUX Derivative UNIX operating system. Linux was developed by Linus Torvalds and was created as a free operating system.

Local area network Separate computers interacting together. A server or peer connection establishes a gateway of communication among each computer or node.

Logic data modeling (LDM) A set of procedures that examines an entity to ensure that its component attributes should reside in that entity, rather than being stored in another or new entity.

Logical equivalent An abstraction of the translation from physical requirements to software.

Long division An abstraction of the relationship of arithmetic formulas to functional decomposition.

Menu bar Is used to organize and provide access to actions that are listed horizontally across the top of the screen and below the title bar.

Metadata Data about the data being sent or received in a client/server network.

Method A process specification that invokes services in an object.

Microsoft exchange Microsoft's e-mail system, which operates under the Windows 95/98/NT and 2000 environments.

Middleware Middle tier of the three-tiered client/server architecture. Middleware contains the necessary APIs, protocols, metadata, gateways, and object messaging necessary to provide communications across client/server networks.

MIME (Multipurpose Internet mail extension) An e-mail protocol used to send messages across the Internet.

Mutual exclusivity Used specifically in relation to supertype/subtype entities. Subtypes that are mutually exclusive cannot coexist with the same supertype entity.

Network workstation Desktop computer connected to a LAN or WAN.

Normalization The elimination of redundancies from an entity.

Object A cohesive whole made up of two essential components: data and processes. The data are often referred to as attributes and processes as services.

Open systems Standards in applications software that allow such software to run across multiple operating system environments.

Persistence An object that continues to operate after the class or operation that invoked it has finished.

Polymorphism Dynamic change in the behavior of an object based on its execution circumstance.

Pre-post conditions A format for developing application logic in a process specification.

Primary key A key attribute that will be used to identify connections to a particular entity. Normalization requires that every entity contain a primary key. Primary keys can be formed by the concatenation of many attributes.

Process A function in a data flow diagram in which data are transformed from one form to another.

Process flow diagram (PFD) A tool that depicts process flow in relation to sequence and time.

Process specification A document that contains all of the algorithms and information necessary to develop the logic of a process. Process specifications can be comprised of the business and programming requirement documents. Pro-cess specifictions are sometimes called "minispecs."

Program or technical specification A technical algorithm of the requirements of a process or system.

Prototype A sample of a system that does not actually fully operate. Most software prototypes are visual depictions of screens and reports. Prototypes can vary in capability, with some prototypes having limited functional interfaces.

Pseudocode A generic or structured English representation of how real programming code must execute. Pseudocode is used in the development of process specifications.

Rapid application development (RAD) A method of application development that combines the analysis and design steps through the use of prototypes and CASE tools.

Reverse engineering The process of analyzing existing applications and database code to create high-level representations of the code.

Reusable object An object that can be a component of different classes.

Robust Software that operates intuitively and can handle unexpected events.

Schema generation CASE interface that allows a logical database to be generated into a specific physical database product.

Scribe A person who is designated in a JAD session to record minutes and decisions made by the group. In certain situations, scribes can also be responsible for data modeling.

Scroll bars Appear when all displayed information cannot be presented within the current window boundaries. The vertical scroll bar at the right of a window controls the up-and-down scrolling, while the horizontal scroll bar controls right-to-left movement.

Server An application that provides information to a requesting application.

Size grip Is a handle in a window that permits the window to be resized. The resizing is accomplished by dragging the grip and moving the window to the desired size. The grip is located in the lower right corner of the window. It is identified by three angled parallel lines.

Spiral life cycle Life cycle that focuses on the development of cohesive objects and classes. The spiral life cycle reflects a much larger allocation of time spent on design than the waterfall approach does.

Split box/Split bar Is a window that is split into two or more pieces, or panes. Split boxes can be manipulated using the split bar, which is located above the vertical scroll bar.

State transition diagram (STD) A modeling tool that depicts time-dependent and event-driven behavior.

Status bar Also known as a "message bar," provides information to the user about the state or status of the information or object inside the window.

Stored procedures Application code activated at the database level.

Structured query language (SQL) Query language and data element construct originated by IBM Corporation. SQL data descriptions are de facto standards in most relational database products.

Supertype/subtype A relational database entity construct where rows of data are divided into multiple separate entities or components. Each component or subtype is stored as a separate entity with a one-to-one relationship with its parent or supertype.

System menu button This button is located at the left corner of the title bar and is also called the "control menu" or the "window menu." This button is used as an aid to keyboard users and lists options for manipulating the window. This includes commands such as *Restore, Minimize, Maximize,* and *Close.*

Tier A level of processing in a client/server architecture. The most common client/server network environment is the three-tier model, which consists of a back-end tier, a middle or application server tier, and a client or front-end tier.

Title bar Is the top line of the window and explains the purpose or name of the window's function.

Title bar icon This icon is located in the left corner of the title bar and is used to retrieve a pull-down menu of commands that apply to the object in the window.

Triggers Stored procedures that are activated at the database level.

UNIX Operating system developed by Bell Labs in 1969, a subsidiary of AT&T. The operating system is written in the C language.

User category The conceptual view of the user from the analyst's perspective. There are three types of user categories: (1) Executive, (2) Department Head or Line Manager, and (3) Functional.

User interface The relationship with end users that facilitates the process of gathering and defining logical requirements.

User level The tier of computer project experience of the user. There are three levels: (1) Knowledgeable, (2) Amateur, and (3) Novice.

Waterfall system development life cycle A life cycle that is based on phased dependent steps to complete the implementation of a system. Each step is dependent on the completion of the previous step.

Web (World Wide Web) Loosely organized set of computer sites that publish information that anyone can read via the Internet mainly using HTTP (Hypertext Transfer Protocol).

Wide area network (WAN) A group of LANs that are connected through a gateway.

Window sizing buttons These buttons are located on the right corner of the title bar and are used to manipulate the size of the active window.

Work area The portion of the screen inside the borders of the window where the user performs tasks.

WYSIWYG (What you see is what you get) A concept that requires that what a program displays on the screen represents exactly how it will appear if printed or otherwise displayed.

References

Barker, R. and C. Longman (1992) *Case Method: Function and Process Modeling.* Berkshire, UK: Oracle Corporation.

Baudoin, Claude and Glenn Hollowell (1996) *Realizing the Object-Oriented Lifecycle.* Upper Saddle River, NJ: Prentice Hall.

Berson, Alex (1996). *Client/Server Architecture.* New York: McGraw-Hill, Inc.

Booch, Grady (1996). *Object Solutions.* Menlo Park, CA: Addison-Wesley.

Brodie, Michael L. and Michael Stonebreaker (1995). *Migrating Legacy Systems: Gateways Interfaces and the Incremental Approach.* San Francisco, CA: Morgan Kaufmann Publishers, Inc.

Brooks, Frederick Jr. (1995). *The Mythical Man-Month.* New York: Addison-Wesley.

Burd, Stephen D. (1998). *Systems Architecture,* 2nd ed. Cambridge, Massachusetts: ITP, Inc.

Conger, S. H. and R. O. Mason (1998) *Planning and Designing Effective Web Sites.* Cambridge, MA: Course Technology.

Connell, John and Linda Shafer (1995). *Object-Oriented Rapid Prototyping.* Englewood Cliffs, NJ: Prentice-Hall.

Date, C.J. (2000). *An Introduction to Database Systems* 7th ed. New York: Addison-Wesley.

Dalgleish, J. (2000) *Customer-Effective Web Sites.* Upper Saddle River, NJ: Prentice-Hall.

DeMarco, Tom (1979) *Structured Analysis and System Specification.* Englewood Cliffs, NJ: Prentice-Hall.

Deutsch, Michael and Ronald Willis (1998). *Software Quality Engineering: A Total Technical and Management Approach.* Englewood Cliffs, NJ: Prentice-Hall.

Dewire, Dawna Travis (1993). *Client/Server Computing.* New York: McGraw-Hill, Inc.

Downing, Douglas, Michael Covington, and Melody Mauldin Covington (1998). *Dictionary of Computer and Internet Terms,* 6th ed. Hauppauge, NY: Barron's Educational Series, Inc.

Fleming, J. (1998) *Web Navigation: Designing the User Experience.* Sebastopol, CA: O'Reilly & Associates, Inc.

Fleming, Candace and Barbara von Halle (1998). *Handbook of Relational Database Design.* Menlo Park, CA: Addison-Wesley.

Fournier, Roger (1991). *Practical Guide to Structured System Development and Maintenance.* Englewood Cliffs, NJ: Prentice Hall.

Gale, Thornton and James Eldred (1996). *Getting Results with the Object-Oriented Enterprise Model.* New York: SIGS Books.

Harold, E. R. & W. S. Means (2001) *XML in a Nutshell: A Desktop Quick Reference.* Sebastopol, CA: O'Reilly & Associates, Inc.

Hipperson, Roger (1992). *Practical Systems Analysis: A Guide for Users, Managers and Analysts.* Englewood Cliffs, NJ: Prentice-Hall.

Jacobson, Ivar, Maria Ericsson, and Agneta Jacobson (1995). *The Object Advantage.* New York: ACM Press.

Kalakota, R., and Andrew B. Whinston (1997). *Electronic Commerce: A Manager's Guide.* New York: Addison-Wesley.

Kerr, James and Richard Hunter (1994). *Inside RAD.* New York: McGraw-Hill, Inc.

Langer, A.M. (2005). *Information Technology & Organizational Learning.* New York: Routledge.

Lorenz, Mark (1993). *Object-Oriented Software Development: A Practical Guide.* Englewood Cliffs, NJ: Prentice-Hall.

Maiwald, E. (2001) *Network Security.* Berkeley, CA: Osborne/McGraw-Hill.

Martin, James and Carma McClure (1988). *Structured Techniques: The Basis for CASE.* Englewood Cliffs, NJ: Prentice-Hall.

Martin, James and James Odell (1995). *Object-Oriented Methods: A Foundation.* Englewood Cliffs, NJ: Prentice-Hall.

Mattison, Bob (1996). *Data Warehousing: Strategies, Technologies and Techniques.* New York: McGraw-Hill, Inc.

McGraw, G. & E. Felton (1996) *Java Security: Hostile Applets, Holes, and Antidotes.* New York: John Wiley & Sons, Inc.

Montgomery, Stephen (1991). *AD/Cycle: IBM's Framework for Application Development and CASE.* New York: Multiscience Press, Inc.

Microsoft Press (1994). *Computer Dictionary: The Comprehensive Standard for Business, School, Library, and Home*. Redmond, WA: Microsoft Corporation.

Muller, Pierre-Alain (1997). *Instant UML*. Birmingham, U.K.: Wrox Press.

Orfali, Robert, Dan Harkey, and Jeri Edwards (1994). *Essential Client/Server Survival Guide*. New York: John Wiley & Sons, Inc.

Perry, William (1991). *Quality Assurance for Information Systems: Methods, Tools, and Techniques*. Wellesley, MA: QED Information Sciences, Inc.

Pfleeger, Shari L. (1998). *Software Engineering: Theory and Practice*. Upper Saddle River, NJ: Prentice Hall.

Poe, V. (1996). *Building a Data Warehouse for Decision Support*. Upper Saddle River, NJ: Prentice-Hall.

Powell, T. A. (2000). *Web Design: The Complete Reference*. Berkeley, CA: Osborne/McGraw-Hill.

Purba, Sanjiv, David Sawh, and Bharat Shah (1995). *How to Manage a Successful Software Project: Methodologies, Techniques, Tools*. New York: John Wiley & Sons, Inc.

Rothstein, Michael, Burt Rosner, Michael Senatore, and Dave Mulligan (1993). *Structured Analysis & Design for the CASE User*. Englewood Cliffs, NJ: Prentice-Hall.

Rumbaugh, James, Michael Blaha, William Premerlani, Frederick Eddy, and William Lorensen (1991). *Object-Oriented Modelling and Design*. Englewood Cliffs, NJ: Prentice-Hall.

Rumbaugh, James, Ivar Jacobson, and Grady Booch (1999). *The Unified Modeling Language Reference Model*. New York: Addison Wesley, Inc.

Rummler, Geary and Alan Brache (1990). *Improving Performance: How to Manage the White Space on the Organization Chart*. San Francisco, CA: Jossey-Bass, Inc.

Shlaer, Sally and Stephen Mellor (1992). *Object Lifecycles: Modeling the World in States*. Englewood Cliffs, NJ: Prentice-Hall.

Simon, Alan R., and Tom Wheeler (1995). *Open Client/Server Computing and Middleware*. Chestnut Hill, Massachusetts: AP Professional.

Smith, E. R. (2000) *e-Loyalty: How to Keep Customers Coming Back to Your Website*. New York: HarperCollins Publishers, Inc.

Sommerville, I., and Pete Sawyer (1998). *Requirements Engineering: A Practical Guide*. New York: John Wiley & Sons.

Sullo, Gary (1994). *Object Engineering: Designing Large-Scale Object-Oriented Systems.* New York: John Wiley & Sons, Inc.

Ullman, Jeffrey D., and Jennifer Widom (1997). *A First Course in Database Systems.* Upper Saddle River, NJ: Prentice-Hall.

Whitten, Jeffrey, Lonnie Bentley, and Victor Barlow (1994). *Systems Analysis and Design Methods.* Burr Ridge, IL: Richard D. Irwin, Inc.

Whitten, Neal (1995). *Managing Software Development Projects.* New York: John Wiley & Sons, Inc.

Wood, Jane and Denise Silver (1995). *Joint Application Development.* New York: John Wiley & Sons, Inc.

Yourdon, Edward (1989). *Object-Oriented Systems Design: An Integrated Approach.* Englewood Cliffs, NJ: Prentice-Hall.

Yourdon, Edward, Katharine Whitehead, Jim Thomann, Karen Oppel, and Peter Neverman (1995). *Mainstream Objects: An Analysis and Design Approach for Business.* Englewood Cliffs, NJ: Prentice-Hall.

Bibliography –Additions

Barker, R. and C. Longman (1992) *Case Method: Function and Process Modeling.* Berkshire, UK: Oracle Corporation.

Conger, S. H. and R. O. Mason (1998) *Planning and Designing Effective Web Sites.* Cambridge, MA: Course Technology.

Dalgleish, J. (2000) *Customer-Effective Web Sites.* Upper Saddle River, NJ: Prentice-Hall.

Fleming, J. (1998) *Web Navigation: Designing the User Experience.* Sebastopol, CA: O'Reilly & Associates, Inc.

Gulutzan, P and Pelzer, T (1999). SQL 3 Complete, Really (New York: R & D Books).

Grudin, J The Case Against User Interface Consistency, Comm. ACM, 32(10), 1992 pp. 1164–1173.

Harold, E. R. & W. S. Means (2001) *XML in a Nutshell: A Desktop Quick Reference.* Sebastopol, CA: O'Reilly & Associates, Inc.

Langer, A.M. (2005). *Information Technology & Organizational Learning.* New York: Routledge.

McGraw, G. & E. Felton (1996) *Java Security: Hostile Applets, Holes, and Antidotes.* New York: John Wiley & Sons, Inc.

Maiwald, E. (2001) *Network Security.* Berkeley, CA: Osborne/McGraw-Hill.

Mullins, C.S. (2006). DB2 Developer's guide (5th ed) (Indianapolis, In: SAMS).

Poe, V. (1996). *Building a Data Warehouse for Decision Support.* Upper Saddle River, NJ: Prentice-Hall.

Powell, T. A. (2000). *Web Design: The Complete Reference.* Berkeley, CA: Osborne/McGraw-Hill.

Reed-Smith, E. (2000). *e-Loyalty: How to Keep Customers Coming Back to Your Website.* (New York: HarperCollins Publishers, Inc.).

Smith, E. R. (2000) *e-Loyalty: How to Keep Customers Coming Back to Your Website.* New York: HarperCollins Publishers, Inc.

Spencer, P (1999), XML Design and Implementation. (Birmingham, UK: Wrox Press Ltd).

Index

Printed in the United States of America.